The Documentary Tradition

The Documentary Tradition

From Nanook to Woodstock

Selected, arranged and introduced by

Lewis Jacobs

Hopkinson and Blake, Publishers, New York

For my mother

Preface

It is almost half a century since the word "documentary" was first used by John Grierson to describe a type of factual film innovated by Robert Flaherty. Since then a massive body of documentaries of many diverse kinds has been made in all parts of the world.

Indeed, documentary has now reached so high a level of accomplishment, style, and assurance, and its influence on other types of movies has become so marked, that a stocktaking of achievements, major talents, and critical ideas has become essential.

This book represents the first attempt to survey the development of documentary—from the beginnings to the present. Its central aim is to define the convention that came to be called "documentary"; to trace its growth and its major exponents; to provide analyses and interpretations of the classic and transitional achievements; to indicate the varied trends, movements, and schools that have made this genre one of the most representative forms of social and artistic expression, and finally to offer an insight into the present state of documentary's rich and living tradition.

The work, however, is not meant to be a history in the usual sense of the word. It is rather a selection of contemporary source materials, a first step toward a necessary synthesis for a history of the documentary idiom, with particular emphasis on the American contributions. Nor does it aim at completeness. It would be impossible in a single book to do justice to such a task.

Many of the essays and reviews chosen for this collection are by filmmakers. The other contributors come from many backgrounds, directly and indirectly related to the documentary medium: criticism, history, screenwriting, editing, sociology, theater, teaching, and television. Collectively their writings convey an enormous range of ideas and observations and open up a world of insights into the complex nature and goals of the documentary idiom and its art.

The arrangement of the book is chronological. It follows an evolutionary course with five main divisions, each dealing with a single decade, beginning in the 1920s and ending in 1970. Filmmakers are arranged arbitrarily within the specific era that shaped their vision and influenced the form of their work. To consider a filmmaker or a picture solely in the framework of a particular decade may at first seem a distortion of the value of the work or the director.

However, my concern was not with the development of any film-maker, but rather with the achievements of directors in the fullness of their stature, and with the changing character of the documentary genre in response to the times. It seems to me that such an arrangement provides an overview which sets the wide range of selections in a more meaningful relationship one with the other, and fixes themes, doctrines, personalities, and pictures within the context of their times.

Certain omissions should be explained. I have not included those documentaries commonly classified as industrials, educationals, art and architecture, training films, and other types of sponsored films primarily aimed at instructing, improving public relations, or increasing sales. I have selected only those films which seem to me to best illuminate the artistic and social concerns of their times and which had the most influence in advancing the genre. These include films made for television.

In assembling this collection, I drew almost entirely on material which appeared in newspapers and magazines. Much of it was scattered and difficult to find. Some pieces originated in fugitive, obscure journals, and little magazines long out of print. A few came from privately published pamphlets and from program notes no longer available. Some material, covering subjects for which I could find no existing source, was written especially for this book. Many of the contributors as well as pictures and directors they have written about, are entirely unknown to the present generation of students and filmmakers.

It is hoped this anthology will testify to the tremendous vitality of the documentary heritage, further the spirit which informs its purpose, and deepen the commitment of those who endeavor to meet its creative challenge.

In preparing this book, I am deeply indebted to Harold J. Salemson for his perspicacious editorial assistance and advice, and to Jay Chapman for his help in research.

As in all my works, my wife helped considerably by providing constructive criticism and encouragement.

LEWIS JACOBS

New York City

Contents

INTRODUCTION

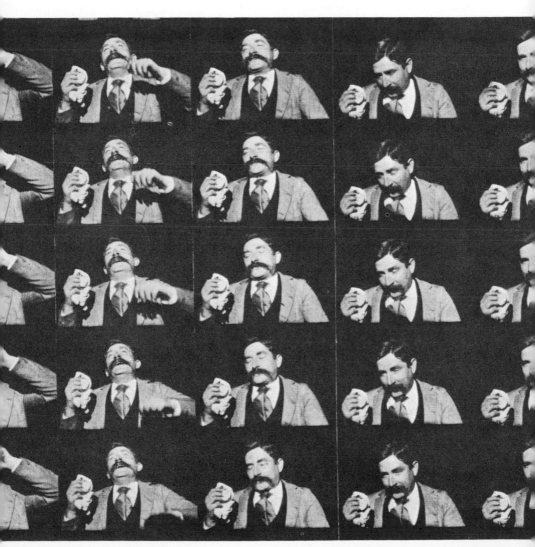

Record of a Sneeze (1894), directed by W. K. L. Dickson

Precursors and Prototypes (1894–1922)
by Lewis Jacobs

What has come to be called "documentary" developed slowly over a period of almost thirty years, from 1894 to 1922, emerging finally as an original model distinct from all other types of motion pictures. The documentary film came to be identifiable as a special kind of picture with a clear social purpose, dealing with real people and real events, as opposed to staged scenes of imaginary characters and fictional stories of the studio-made pictures.

The earliest hint of the character of documentary was evident in the very first motion pictures projected on a screen, W. K. L. Dickson's *Record of a Sneeze* (1894) and the Lumière Brothers' *Workers Emerging from a Factory* (1894). These movies revealed a new medium that could perceive and represent reality with greater fidelity than any medium known theretofore. Although they lasted only a minute or so, these first motion pictures recorded real events with an accuracy and heightened actuality that made them seem "objects of magical wonder . . . marvelously true to life." Vested with this kind of significance, these early records of human beings and the circumstances of their involvement can be said to represent the first films of fact and the very genesis of the documentary idea.

From 1895 until about 1900, movies continued to seek their material directly from life. Nothing was too slight to photograph so long as it moved: people strolling in the streets, trees swaying in the wind, trains speeding, horses jumping. "Caught without pre-arrangement and consequently most natural," they continued to "evoke awe and admiration for their faithfulness to true-life action."

As they extended in length to two or three minutes, the movies continued to be free of any subjective purpose. Their subjects were selected by chance, expressing no idea or feeling, their character that of a straight-on snapshot, their frame of reference limited. Extremely popular, these factual "living pictures" were then further lengthened to five minutes. The range of content broadened, as indicated by these titles: *Easter Parade, New York in a Blizzard, Arrival of the Paris Express, The Henley Regatta in England, Czar Nicholas in His Summer Palace, The Spanish Coronation,* and *The Kaiser Reviews His Troops.* The film of fact was now advancing from random observation to selective aspects of reality, vividly acquainting moviegoers with national and international figures and events. The subjects were no longer limited to interesting bits of movement and action; the purpose now was to inform.

In 1903 there was a a major breakthrough in film technique and it sent movies into a new direction. The invention of editing— representing a kind of technological quantum jump—endowed the movies with great new capabilities for controlling and manipulating the flow of time, the speed of events, and screen continuity or order. Editing propelled movies to a radical change in screen subject matter. Motion pictures, until then almost exclusively devoted to the film-of-fact's objective recording of unmanipulated actuality, now were suddenly opened up to the rearrangement and reconstruction of reality for narrative and dramatic purposes. It now became possible to alter the measures and dimensions of the real world by staging and arranging events for the camera which later could be edited into a specific order or continuity to fill a fictional screen story.

The fictional story film brought dramatic excitement to the screen, and gave rise to the enormously popular "nickelodeon era" (1904–1910). The film of fact, which had dominated the screen for the first eight years of motion pictures, was quickly and almost entirely abandoned by the commercial manufacturers of movies. This kind of picture was left to itinerant cameramen, globe-trotters, big-game hunters, scientists, explorers, and other nonprofessional moviemakers, who for a variety of reasons, including the zeal of scholarship and the instinct of journalism gave the film of fact new scope and topicality and even new graphic vitality. As a newspaper of the day reported, they brought "the world of invention, the world of imagination and the world of nature to the very door of the people." Their films fell into these broad categories: popular and research studies (*The Empire of the Ants*, 1905); distant and exotic places (*Life in a Burma Teak Forest*, 1906); sport and nature films (*The Ascent of Wetterhorn*, 1907); travel and scenic views (*Amongst the Natives of Borneo*, 1908); picturesque and unusual occupations (*Cigar Pickers in Paris*, 1909); topical personalities (*The Funeral of King Edward VII*, 1910), and the fight and wrestling films (*Jeffries-Johnson Match* and *Gotch-Zbyszko Match*, 1910)

These films exhibited a common quality. They isolated and defined actuality with a sense of participation that marked a transition from a straight record toward a more personal expression on the part of the filmmakers. There was a growing interest in probing into the social environment.

The decade that followed, 1910–1920, was a time of feverish activity in commercial motion pictures. There were momentous changes in every facet of production, distribution, and exhibition, the rise of intense competition, and the emergence of an aggressive entrepreneurship with interlocking organizations all aiming at a mass audience and international markets.

A major development during this period was the enlargement of the story film from one reel to two, then to four, and finally to six and more reels, lasting an hour and more. These films—known as "features," to distinguish them from "shorts"—became firmly established as the pictures of the future. Soon, large and elegant theaters were built specifically for the showing of motion pictures, and with this new respectability the movie audience—which had been composed almost entirely of working class people—suddenly was swelled by the great middle class.

Under such stimulus and growth, the nonfiction film also gained some new measure of importance. An increase in length from half a reel to one, two, and three reels helped enhance its prestige. A style of screen journalism that had some of the character of magazine articles developed. Cameras focused on the issues of war and peace, political strife among nations, problems of street life in the large cities, the growing interest in the polar regions, and manners and customs in strange and distant lands.

A vivid sense of place and the recognition of the importance of milieu was demonstrated in such factual films as *Lisbon Before* and *After the Revolution* (1910), *Captain Scott's Expedition to the South Pole* (1911), *Votes for Women* (1912), *Old Women of the Streets of New York* (1913), *Thirty Leagues Under the Sea* (1914), *Lady MacKenzie in Africa* (1915), *Battle of the Somme* (1916), and *The Western Front* (1919).

Reality was not treated as background, but was the very subject of these films. This concentration on milieu signaled a new point in the factual film's efforts to achieve a synthesis of the real environment and the forces that move through a culture—almost a precondition of the documentary form.

Another major attribute of documentary came into existence during this period. Since the inception of the movies topical events had been filmed and exhibited at random intervals. These news pictures consisted in the main of parades, auto races, horse races, political inaugurations, coronations, and state funerals. Now, along with the feature story-film, the idea of presenting a continuous motion-picture news service to theaters—the newsreel—was initiated. It involved the addition to the program of a weekly shorter attraction, motion pictures of ten to fifteen minutes in length that "recorded and presented news events in theaters on a regular basis."

The newsreel began in 1910 with Charles Pathé, a Frenchman whose company organized a branch in the United States called Pathé News. Photographers in major cities throughout the world filmed headline news—railway disasters, social upheavals, marine catastrophes, earthquakes, floods, airplane accidents, and sporting events. These films were distributed on a regular schedule. They were so well received that within two years, encouraged by the extraordinary expansion of the movie industry, four additional companies entered the newsreel field: Hearst, Universal, Paramount, and finally, Fox.

The competition of the "Big Five" for weekly filmed news presentations brought the film of fact into a broader concern with world issues than ever before. During this period newsreels were a worthy rival of the newspapers. Typical of their wide ranging coverage of the news were these events: *The Lord Mayor of London Opens a Hospital* (1910), *The Chicago Stockyards Fire* (1911), *The Great Riots at Budapest* (1912), *Balkan War Scenes* (1912), *The Derby* (1913), *The Austrian Tragedy* (1914), *Bombardment at Przemysl* (1915), *Sinn Fein Rebels* (1916), *Suffragettes Riot at White House* (1918), and *Kidwelly Poison Trial* (1920).

At first newsreels confined themselves to an objective reporting of hard news and human interest news. They presented the facts without bias or special viewpoint. But as they grew in influence and acquired a special province of their own in the film world, newsreels began to treat such controversial subjects as war, politics, and labor in such a way as to affect public opinion. This constituted a major new extension of the nonfiction film simply by demonstrating that visual news material could be so manipulated as to serve an ideological point of view.

The documentary form was again advanced in 1921 by the appearance of a picture that was totally different from all its predecessors in its use of factual material. The film was conceived and made outside of the movie industry by two Americans—a painter, Charles Sheeler, and a still photographer, Paul Strand. It was called *Mannahatta,* after a poem by Walt Whitman. One reel in length, *Mannahatta* was an abstract filmic portrait of New York City, expressing the city's power and beauty, movement and excitement through a discerning and selective camera eye. Carefully composed angle shots, foreshortened viewpoints, patterns of mass and line; the contrast of sunlight and shadow defining pyramidlike office buildings stretching upward into space; ant-like crowds inching through deep, narrow canyons; silvery smoke rising in plumes to drift across filter-dimmed skies; a ferryboat scudding out of a dazzling bay into a darkened pier; a sudden swarm of commuters radiating into sun-drenched streets in a climax of flowing movement and myriad rhythms.

A kind of camera poem, *Mannahatta* made no reference to actual people, places, or events. Instead of reportage pure and simple, the picture tried to realize its subject in terms of the potentialities of the medium by manipulating factual material to express the feel of a city through abstract design.

Its spirit and insight reflected the 1920s' "new philosophy" of freedom in the arts. In complete contrast to any factual film that preceded it, *Mannahatta*'s contribution lay in its aesthetic vision, a commitment to a plastic order that governed the selection and arrangement of its images. The aim was not to mirror nature, but to break down reality and reorganize it into a rhythmic composition. This emphasis on the formal values of the motion picture was an innovation for the times, and introduced the film of fact to a new aspect—art.

Mannahatta was seen by only a few people in the United States and had little immediate effect. But in Paris, where it was shown in a Dadaist program that included music by Erik Satie and poems by Guillaume Apollinaire, it received an ovation. A few years later its influence was to become apparent in a series of European documentaries, particularly René Clair's study of *The Eiffel Tower* (1927), Walter Ruttmann's *Berlin* (1927), Georges Lacombe's *La Zone* (1927), and Joris Ivens's *The Bridge* (1927) and *Rain* (1929).

In 1922 the first feature-length film of fact appeared. This picture was to have greater consequences than any previous non-fiction film. Robert Flaherty, an American explorer for mineral deposits in the Hudson Bay territory of Canada, had spent several years in the wastes of the Canadian North prospecting the region with the help of Eskimos. On one of these expeditions, he took along an Eyemo movie camera (after a three-week course in the rudiments of motion-picture photography) and recorded thousands of feet of Eskimo life. While editing the footage he accidentally dropped a cigarette on the negative and it went up in flames. However, he was able to show a "work print" to some friends at the Explorers Club and at the American Geographical Society. They were not too enthusiastic. "Amateur that I was," he later recalled, "I was not sorry. It was a bad film. I had learned to explore, but had not learned to reveal."

Several years later he returned to the Hudson Bay territory, this time for the express purpose of making a motion picture. The idea was to take "a typical Eskimo family and make a biography of their lives throughout one year."

He went well prepared. He had obtained $50,000 in financial backing from Revillon Frères, fur merchants who operated trading posts in Canada, in exchange for a credit line on the picture. He took along the best equipment he could get for his purpose: two Akeley motion picture cameras, a gasoline generator to provide lighting, a developing and printing outfit so he could process his own film, and a projector to enable him to see "rushes" as he went along. He was virtually a one-man studio and filmmaker combined (but he trained some of the Eskimos to be technical assistants). After a year of shooting, he returned to New York, where he spent the next six months editing the film, and finally it was completed.

The picture was *Nanook of the North* (1922), a landmark in

film history. It can be said to be the classic progenitor of the documentary idiom and certainly the most influential in that form. The
story was simply of the Eskimo's struggle for food and shelter. "His
life is a constant fight against starvation," said Flaherty. "Nothing
grows; he must depend entirely on what he can kill; and all of this
against the most terrifying of tyrants—the bitter climate of the
North."

Nanook, its protagonist, copes with blizzards and blinding snow-
storms. He constantly endangers his life hunting walrus and seal
to provide food and clothing for his family. He works frantically
to complete an igloo, assisted by his wife and children who ardu-
ously haul up barrels of water to ice the snow walls. The scenes are
full of minute observation, with no false gestures, no artificiality.
The Eskimos play themselves, but they do not act. Even in the
scene at night, when the family prepares for sleep in the freezing
air of the igloo, undressing under their fur coverings and snuggling
against each other for warmth and the movements of love—even
here everything seems genuine, true.

The drama of *Nanook* was not imposed, but derived from the
material itself, arranged into a loose narrative to express what the
filmmaker had learned and experienced from living with his subject and what he wanted the viewer to know and feel about these
people and and their way of life.

Nanook marked the advent of a type of film new to the world.
Its use of environmental details and skilled continuity broke with
the purely descriptive; it swept away the notion that what the
camera recorded was the total reality. Flaherty proved there was
another reality which the eye alone could not perceive, but which
the heart and mind could discern—what his wife was to call "that
high moment of seeing, that flash of penetration into the heart of
the matter."

Nanook appeared at a time when tawdry Hollywood movies,
like the tabloids and the confession and sex magazines of the day,
were booming. *Male and Female, Forbidden Fruit, Foolish Wives,
Flaming Youth*—these were the typical titles of the "Jazz Age."

In sharp contrast to these studio-produced fabrications, *Nanook*'s vision was fresh and uplifting. But no major company would
touch it for distribution.

It finally opened in Paris, where it was a striking success with
the public and critics. Then the film was shown in Berlin and

London, and the success was repeated, attracting the attention of many writers on the arts who until then had been indifferent to movies. The critical acclaim abroad persuaded the American companies to reconsider its exhibition here. When at last it was shown in the United States it evoked further praise and led Paramount Pictures to commission Flaherty to make "another *Nanook*" in the South Seas.

The singular treatment of reality in *Nanook* was the fullest expression up to that time of the film of fact. It brought the nonfiction film to a new level of achievement. Discovering the essential drama within the material itself became the method which created the prototype of documentary film and established its tradition.

Nanook swept across the world. In Russia, Flaherty's vision was expanded and applied to the dramatization of collectivism. In England, the stunning freshness of *Nanook* inspired John Grierson, a social scientist, to become a movie critic and filmmaker and to institute a full-blown documentary movement "to make drama from the ordinary" based on a credo that was "social not aesthetic." In Germany and France, Flaherty's distinctive use of the camera as a penetrating eye was adopted and refined.

In the next years, the documentary idea caught on so strongly —in this country and abroad—that it became a cult term. In Europe, as in the United States, the medium underwent further development and expansion, and soon it was being utilized prominently for humanistic and artistic expression, for commercial purposes, for educational aims, and for the advancement of ideological goals. As it achieved greater social vitality and aesthetic sensibility it became an essential element of the film tradition.

L.J.

(Top) *Admiral Dewey Landing at Gibraltar* (1897)
(Bottom) *New York Fire Brigade* (1897)

PART ONE / 1922–1930

Nanook of the North (1922), directed by Robert J. Flaherty

The Feel of a New Genre
by Lewis Jacobs

Documentary's essence lies in the dramatization of actual material.
PAUL ROTHA

The 1920s were an age of betrayed idealism, disillusionment, and cynical materialism—but also a period of high creativity in the arts. Radical experimentation appeared in literature, painting, music, and theater. Some of the inventiveness overflowed into the motion pictures. Movies from France, Germany, and Russia reached for new heights of screen expression.

The impact of this creative vitality made it easier to recognize the unique vision of *Nanook*. Within a short time its innovative spirit, its affirmation of a theme that evolved naturally from the interaction of man and his environment became the model for the creative drives and innovative skills of other nonfiction filmmakers.

Merian C. Cooper and Ernest Schoedsack, two independent cameramen-journalists, in imitation of Robert Flaherty left modern society to find their subject and theme in the primitive life of man in central Persia. Their picture, *Grass* (1925), documented the semi-annual trek of tens of thousands of Bakhtiari tribesmen in search of grazing fields for their cattle. The popular success of this adventure sent the team to the jungles of Siam for a second picture, *Chang* (1927), which dramatized a family's endless fight against the advancing jungle and marauding animals.

In that same romantic spirit Robert Flaherty himself went to the South Seas, to carry out Paramount Pictures' injunction to make "another Nanook . . . with South Sea equivalents of hunting seals, walruses, and bears." But instead, the director's sense of truth and his reverence for real life made *Moana* (1926) a lyrical study of the loveliness of the Polynesian islands and the dignified grace of Samoan life.

At the same time that these American documentalists were filming reality in a style often associated with what would be called "naturalism" in literature, there appeared in Europe a second stylistic trend which took a dramatically opposing approach. The members of this group, following the lead of the avant-garde painters of the day, turned away from the traditional conventions of naturalism to document reality in an abstract manner reminiscent of *Mannahatta*. They did away with the story or narrative line within a particular environment and amplified the formal qualities inherent within the medium of film itself. Rather than document far-off places with a sociological or anthropological interest, they remained at home, candidly to snatch fragments of raw and unposed life from the most ordinary circumstances and incorporate the experience into a context of rhythmic patterns structured "symphonically."

The main drive of what might be called these "art-for-art's-sake" documentalists was to capture some of the essence of city life. Among the outstanding pictures were Alberto Cavalcanti's lyrical cross-section of Paris, *Rien que les heures* (1926), Walter Ruttmann's contrasting portrait of a day in Berlin, *Berlin, The Symphony of a Great City* (1927), Dziga Vertov's celebration of Soviet urban life, *The Man With the Movie Camera* (1928), and Joris Ivens's two cinepoem studies in Holland, *The Bridge* (1927) and *Rain* (1929).

Toward the close of the decade a third decisive trend appeared. Its creative aim was derived from that of the city documentalists, to which was now added a moral fervor issuing from political ideology. The initial consequence of this working credo in England was *Drifters* (1929), a fresh and intimate study of the herring industry, and in Russia *Turksib* (1929), a dynamic account of the building of the trans-Siberian railroad.

Drifters, made by John Grierson, was the result of the British government's interest in using the arts as a means of publicity and public relations. Its success was to make it possible for Grierson to develop a unit of young filmmakers who, in the next decade, would use documentary to dramatize the activities of British workingmen for public education and to advance specific community ideas for social betterment.

Turksib's socio-political message was stronger and more specific than that of *Drifters*. It presented a panorama of Soviet energy and power, eloquently realizing Lenin's exhortation to use the movie as a medium of propaganda to consolidate the gains of Soviet society.

By 1930, the documentary film had become an acknowledged category and had achieved a secure, if as yet small, niche in the world of film. Its first decade of life had turned out to be quite fertile. It had produced a group of distinguished films and filmmakers, acquired a select but growing audience, and gained a confidence in its own powers that was to become more pronounced in the years ahead with the selection of increasingly meaningful subject matter and the intensification of its art.

Robert Flaherty's *Nanook of the North*

by Robert Sherwood

*Mr. Sherwood, playwright, historian, and Presidential
speechwriter, also was one of the first important
American film critics. This selection is from a book he
edited, "The Best Moving Pictures of 1922-23."*

There have been many fine travel pictures, many gorgeous "scenics," but there has been only one that deserves to be called great. That one is *Nanook of the North.* It stands alone, literally in a class by itself. Indeed, no list of the best pictures, of this year or of all the years in the brief history of the movies, could be considered complete without it.

The potential value of the movies as an educational medium is frequently stressed by men of prominence and triteness; and as a result, the word "educational" in connection with a motion picture has become almost synonymous with dullness, dryness, and boredom.

The screen is no blackboard, and the prime test of every film that is projected on its surface is that it shall be interesting to the spectator. It may be teeming with genuine instructive value, it may contain what is generally called a "message," but if it fails to hold the audience's attention, the value and the message will be lost.

Robert J. Flaherty realized this when he produced *Nanook of the North*. He wanted to make a picture of Eskimo life (and, to the average mind, there is no character that is colder or less enthralling than an Eskimo), and he wanted to record the tremendous vitality, the relentless force of the Arctic. He knew that there was good material here, but he also knew that this material would be worthless unless he presented it in an interesting way. He appreciated the fact that mere photographs of Eskimos in their various daily activities would be hopelessly dull if he treated his subject as instruction instead of as drama.

The backbone of every motion picture is the continuity—and by this I do not mean the plot. *Nanook of the North* had no plot whatsoever, and struggled along very well without it, but it did have continuity. The arrangement of scenes was sound and logical and consistent.

Mr. Flaherty selected one character, Nanook himself, to serve as the protagonist of his drama. Nanook was the center of all the action, and upon him was the camera focused. In this way Mr. Flaherty achieved the personal touch. Another producer, attempting to do the same thing, would have been content to photograph "A Native Spearing Fish" or "Another Native Building His Igloo." Moreover, he would have kept himself in the foreground, as is the way of all travelogue rollers. Mr. Flaherty made Nanook his hero— and a fine, stalwart hero he was.

Nanook of the North, however, was not all Nanook. There was a co-star in the title role, and that was the North. The North was the villain of the piece, the dread force against which Nanook and his kind must continually battle. So Mr. Flaherty showed us Nanook, fighting sturdily to obtain food, and warmth, and shelter, and he showed us the North hitting back with its gales, its blizzards, and its terrible, bitter cold.

Here was drama, rendered far more vital than any trumped-up drama could ever be by the fact that it was all real. Nanook was no playboy, enacting a part which would be forgotten as soon as the greasepaint had been rubbed off; he was himself an Eskimo, struggling to survive. The North was no mechanical affair of wind machines and paper snow; it was the North, cruel and incredibly strong.

The production of this remarkable picture was no light task. Mr. Flaherty had to spend years with the Eskimos so that he could learn to understand them. Otherwise, he could not have made a faithful reflection of their emotions, their philosophy, and their endless privations. He had to select from among them those who were best qualified to tell the story of their race. He had to do his photography, his developing, and his printing under terribly adverse conditions. He had no studio, no artificial lights, and only the crudest of laboratories.

The motion picture [as we know it] represents the combined talents of hundreds, sometimes thousands, of different people. But *Nanook of the North* is the notable exception to that rule; it was essentially a one-man job.

Of the difficulties which confronted him in producing *Nanook of the North,* Mr. Flaherty writes as follows:

"The film *Nanook of the North* is a by-product—if I may use the term—of a long series of explorations in the north which I carried on in behalf of Sir William Mackenzie from 1910 to 1916. Much of the exploration was done with Eskimos. I have been on long journeys for months at a time with only two or three Eskimos as my companions. This experience gave me an insight into their lives and a deep regard for them.

"In 1913 I went north with a large outfit—an exploring ship with lumber and material for a wintering base and food for eight men for two years. A motion picture outfit was incorporated. I hoped that the results from it might help defray some of the costs of what were now beginning to be expensive explorations. I had no preliminary motion picture experience, other than some two weeks with a motion picture camera demonstrator just before leaving. We wintered in Baffin Land on this expedition, which was of a year and four months' duration, and during those intervals while I was not seriously engaged in exploratory work, a film was compiled of some of the Eskimos who lived with us. Naturally the results were indifferent. But as I was undertaking another expedition in another part of the north I secured more negative and chemicals, with the idea of building up this first film.

"On this expedition I wintered on the Belcher Islands, which I had re-discovered and explored. Again, between explorations as it were, I continued with the film work and added to the first film very materially. After a lot of hardship, which involved the loss of a launch and the wrecking of our cruising boat, we secured a remarkable film on a small island ninety miles out at sea, of walrus-hunting. This picture particularly, and some interesting stuff of native life, together with the scenes showing the dismasting of the Laddie, our exploring ship, which owing to our condition was broken up and used for fuel, formed the nucleus of what I hoped would be a good picture. After wintering a year on the islands, the Laddie's skipper, a Moose Factory half-breed, and myself, finally got out to civilization along with my notes, maps, and the above-mentioned film.

"I had just completed editing the film in Toronto when, through gross carelessness of my own, the negative caught fire, and I was minus all (some thirty thousand feet of film). The editing print, however, was not burned, and this was shown to some private groups several times—just long enough, in fact, to enable me to realize that it was no good. I knew then that the reason I had missed out was that the whole thing was episodic. But I did see that if I were to take a single character and make him typify the Eskimos as I had known them so long and well, the results would be well worth while. To make a long story short, that is what happened. I went north again, this time solely to make a film. I took with me not only motion picture cameras, negative, and developing outfit, but apparatus for producing electric light so that I could print and project my results as they were being made; thus I could correct the faults and re-take wherever necessary, and more particularly still, my character and his family who lived with me through the year could understand and appreciate what I was doing.

"Though Nanook and his crowd were at first highly amused at the idea of the white man wanting to take pictures of themselves, the most common objects in all the world, as soon as I got my projection apparatus going and showed them some of the first results, they were completely won over. As luck would have it, the first picture that was made was the walrus hunt, which many of the younger generation had never seen. I shall never forget the night it was first projected, on a white cotton sheet in my wintering hut. The audience—men, women, babes, and children, squatted on the floor—completely forgot that what was unfolding before them on the sheet was a picture. They yelled, screamed, and shouted their advice where the four stalwarts were shown in the walrus tug of war. In the language of the trade, that first picture was a knockout. From that time on they were with me to a man. Indeed, they vied with one another to be cast in the angerooka's big aggie (picture)."

After Mr. Flaherty had completed the picture, and had brought it to New York, he encountered a new set of problems: he ran into the movie distributors. He learned that the Eskimos were remarkably tractable as compared with these important gentlemen who are empowered to decide what the public shall see and what it shall not see. He had been backed on this Arctic expedition by Revillon Frères, the furriers, but Revillon Frères could not sell his picture for him.

He took *Nanook of the North* to five different distributing corporations, all of which turned him down flat. They told him that the public is not interested in Eskimos; the public wants to see people in dress suits. Finally, he effected a deal with Pathé, and *Nanook of the North* was timorously submitted to the exhibitors. One of them, Samuel Rothafel of the Capitol Theatre in New York, decided to give it a try, although he was frankly dubious about its possibilities as a box-office attraction. The week that *Nanook of the North* played at the Capitol Theatre, it did $43,000 worth of business.

It was instantly hailed by every critic in New York, and the public (which wants to see people in dress suits) responded nobly. *Nanook of the North* has since proved to be a substantial if not a sensational box-office success.

One of the distributing companies, the Famous Players-Lasky, which elected to throw *Nanook of the North* back into the cold from whence it came, has made amends in an honorable and emphatic way. Jesse L. Lasky has sent Mr. Flaherty to Samoa to make a Polynesian *Nanook*. Moreover, he has made no restrictions as to money, time, or quality—so that we may expect, eventually, to see the first real representation of the glamorous South Sea Isles on the screen.

There was a tragic sequel to *Nanook of the North* which did not appear in the film itself. Some time after Mr. Flaherty departed from the Arctic with his negatives and his prints, the gallant Nanook died of starvation. The villainous North finally won in its mortal combat, and Nanook became the first hero in movie history who has gone down to ultimate defeat. But his soul goes marching on. His shadowy form still flickers across the screen, to prove to distributors and other shortsighted persons that Eskimos are human beings, after all.

Another View of *Nanook*
by Ricciotto Canudo

One of the earliest theoreticians of film, Ricciotto Canudo
included this reappraisal of Nanook *in his book, "L'Usine aux*
images" ("The Picture Factory"), published in Paris in 1927.
It was translated from the French by Harold J. Salemson.

The prodigious *Nanook of the North,* made merely as an advertising
film for a French fur company, with its human struggle against the
elements, haunts our minds as profoundly as does the misery of
Aeschylus' Atridae. Here, "reportage" and "documentary" have
ventured so far into space and into reality that a true tragedy has
spontaneously taken shape within the magic of celluloid. And the
Everyday Tragedy of polar man spreads out into the emotions of
the entire world, more moving, more "direct" than all the most
pathetic plot complications that the poets have ever imagined.

This tragedy in which, from the beginning to end, the protagonists remain the Elements pitted against Man with his Needs, is,
quite simply stated, a picture of the eternal struggle of the Human
Being. Nanook's family, for a time, I repeat, captures as much of
our sympathetic emotions as does the family of the Atridae. The
lens has replaced the poet's mind. The miracle of emotion has been
accompanied by the very magic of the immensity of truth.

The subtitle [given in France] to this incomparable film, *The
Man of Primitive Times,* is a phony. It is the only phony detail in
the whole film. Primitive man did not remain attached to his icefloe
with that solid determination characteristic of the man of the soil
attached to the roots of his trees. Primitive man followed the path
of heat, of the very flame of life, and, fleeing the glacial regions,
took refuge ever closer to the warm zones of the globe. From
geological times until our own, animal life has observed the con-
temporaneous stages of the cooling of the globe and the descent of
life toward the Equator, so that fossils that are today found in the
frozen North have their living counterparts in the warmer regions
of the earth.

But let us not nitpick over a subtitle. It is totally unnecessary,
anyway. Nanook is not primitive man, any more than he is polar
man. He is Man, in all his truth. His tragedy, in its absolute simplicity, is that of Man, under any climate, despite all the possible

complications of that many-shaped, changing outer dress known as civilization. In the desert of snow, he resists the implacably hostile mobile and immobile elements, the engulfing storms and the deadly paralysis of the cold. He follows the imperious needs of existence and, in order to live, kills the few animals nature has thrown into his desolate world: walrus and seal. Here is the ingenious, energetic, powerful hunter, whose every gesture seems part of a sacred ritual: the ritual of life through death. The harpoon, in his hands, is a strange instrument, indeed, one with which he spears and reels in his prey. The half-starved chorus of dogs is always close behind. And when, after one of the most exciting long struggles with the captured animal, who fights back with every ounce of his dying strength, Nanook finally succeeds in prying him from his frozen lair, the beast is cut up and the pieces are tossed hot and raw into the mouths of the humans, women and children, and into the maws of the dogs, the act of the hunt is over. Man has once again won out.

Immediately after this, comes the act of struggle against the elements. The white blinding storm is raging. Human muscles are a poor weak thing against it! Man's courage alone comes into play here, his courage animated by intelligence. And man attempts to outsmart the elements cutting up blocks of ice, building his circular igloo, without any corners that might allow the blizzard a hold. That is his abode. A square of transparent ice becomes his window open on to the vision of nature. Man closes himself into his sphere of ice, rounds his life out in it, surrounded by the deadly desert, like an animal crawling into his shell in order to hold out.

Next to the man, are the women, the naked children, the puppies, all huddled together, warming themselves on each other's blood, while outside the grown dogs, so beautiful, passively allow themselves, since they have no other possible course, to be covered by the heavy sheet of white-lighted death.

The tragedy comes to its end. Nanook, the man, the center of this small knot of life, head of this tiny troop of beings who refuse to die, does not even think of the possibility of leading them all away from there. He knows of the existence of other people, whom he periodically meets at the closest trading-post, when he goes there, in his sealskin boat, to deposit his foxskins in exchange for a few tools and some fats. But fate made him master here, in this huge and solitary whiteness, in which his children, like him, are destined to live and die.

Grass and Chang
by Richard Griffith

These notes on Grass *(1925) and* Chang *(1927) were written for the bulletin of the Museum of Modern Art Film Library (New York) in 1941. Mr. Griffith was curator of the library and author of several books on film.*

Merian C. Cooper and Ernest Beaumont Schoedsack have probably given more pleasure to the armchair traveler than any other producer of films except Robert J. Flaherty. Although Cooper and Schoedsack probably admired and imitated the technique of *Nanook of the North,* their approach to filmmaking differed radically from that of Flaherty, who was an explorer filming the life of peoples he knew; Cooper and Schoedsack were adventurers attracted by the *unknown.* The friendship of the two men, and their eventual partnership in filmmaking, was founded on a mutual interest in the strange, the dangerous, and the unvisited which was kindled during World War I. Schoedsack was originally a cameraman for Mack Sennett who made a reputation during the war for camera records of infantry action under heavy shell fire. In 1919, he went to Poland with the Red Cross Photographic Department and there struck up an acquaintance with Cooper, recently a captain of aviation in France and at that moment a lieutenant-colonel in the Russo-Polish War. When peace finally came to Europe, the two separated and went their gypsying ways, until Cooper, armed with funds and an idea, summoned Schoedsack to meet him in Turkey. The funds were privately supplied: the idea had to do with the making of a film in Turkish Kurdistan; the result was *Grass.*

When *Grass* was made, most travel films dispensed with any structure more complex than chronological continuity and the roughly consistent following-out of a preordained route, usually shown in the first shot as an animated map. *Grass* is at first equally conventional: a change in plans made it necessary to film the tribes of central Persia rather than those of Kurdistan but, though the picture does not really begin until Persia is reached, the directors display nearly as much interest in photographing events along the route through Turkey (with their fellow-traveler, Mrs. Harrison, as a sort of star) as in the more important material which follows. But the dramatic impact of that material would not be denied. When 50,000 Bakhtiari tribesmen float and swim their flocks across a treacherous river or toil over a twelve-thousand-foot mountain range, the film suddenly enlarges to epic scale. Though the camerawork lacks Flaherty's skillful and penetrating analysis, though the construction seems abrupt and episodic today, *Grass* embodies the drama of conflict between man and nature, the suspense which derives from the spectacle of thousands of people driving through terrific obstacles toward an apparently inaccessible goal. Romantically seeking faraway thrills, Cooper and Schoedsack had actually produced a dramatic document of the pastoral stage of man's struggle to live.

Though most of the drama lay inherent in the material rather than in the treatment, Cooper and Schoedsack were rightly acclaimed for an achievement which, considered in terms of courage and endurance, is almost incredible. *Grass* was bought for distribution by Paramount, and geographers and ethnologists rushed into print to spread its fame. The picture was a great *succès d'estime,* something of a popular success, too—and inevitably it sent the producers to Hollywood seeking finance for a new film of far places.

It was Jesse L. Lasky (whose foresight had sent Flaherty to Samoa) who gave Cooper and Schoedsack their next chance to make the wilderness speak with its own voice. This time the directors were determined to produce consciously the dramatic conflict between man and nature which *Grass* had captured accidentally. After some deliberation they chose [for] their next *mise-en-scène* the Siamese jungle, where tigers yearly kill one out of three of the adult population. *Chang,* as it emerged from their cameras, centered wholly around the struggle of one small family with the hostile animals of the surrounding jungle. The picture has been divested of every other interest; there are none of the usual corroborative incidentals, no interpolated scenes of village life to bolster up "authenticity." But if Siamese social life seems distant from the camera in *Chang,* the wild animals are uncomfortably close. Even with telescopic lenses and automatic cameras, Schoedsack had to risk life and limb a dozen times to secure these extraordinary shots of charging tigers, pouncing leopards, elephants on the rampage.

Cooper and Schoedsack called their film "a melodrama with man, the jungle, and wild animals as its cast," and it was this narrative interest and intimacy which gave it greater appeal than the more sober travel films like Marc Allégret's and André Gide's *Voyage au Congo* or Léon Poirier's *La Croisière noire* (both 1926). This charming family and their animal friends and enemies were irresistible; audiences felt they were actually in the jungle. *Chang* became the most successful of all travel films.

It was hard to follow up such a triumph. Cooper and Schoedsack traveled to the Sudan to shoot background material for *The Four Feathers* (1929), but Paramount finished the film as a part-talkie and it was no better than most of its hybrid kind. *Rango* (1931) was fresher and more authentic, but it followed the pattern of Frank Buck's and Martin Johnson's wild-animal thrillers. After that, Cooper and Schoedsack settled down separately in Hollywood to make films. None of their more recent productions, not even the amusingly horrendous *King Kong* (1933), has achieved the distinction of *Grass* and *Chang*. But it is hard to begrudge the adventurers their abandonment of the strenuous life. For another World War has arrived to put a period to the era of their adventuring, and to reveal that civilization holds conflicts more savage than any of those they so patiently and courageously filmed in the secret places of the earth.

Flaherty's Poetic *Moana*
by John Grierson

*The anonymous reviewer for The New York Sun of February 8,
1926, who signed this "The Moviegoer," was John Grierson. Here for
the first time he gave currency to the term "documentary" in English.*

The golden beauty of primitive beings, of a South Sea Island that
is an earthly paradise, is caught and imprisoned in Robert J.
Flaherty's *Moana* which is being shown at the Rialto this week. The
film is unquestionably a great one, a poetic record of Polynesian
tribal life, its ease and beauty and its salvation through a painful
rite. *Moana* deserves to rank with those few works of the screen
that have a right to last, to live. It could only have been produced
by a man with an artistic conscience and an intense poetic feeling
which, in this case, finds an outlet through nature worship.

Of course, *Moana* being a visual account of events in the daily
life of a Polynesian youth and his family, has documentary value.
But that, I believe, is secondary to its value as a soft breath from
a sunlit island washed by a marvelous sea as warm as the balmy air.
Moana is first of all beautiful as nature is beautiful. It is beautiful
for the reason that the movements of the youth Moana and the
other Polynesians are beautiful, and for the reason that trees and
spraying surf, soft billowy clouds and distant horizons are beautiful.

And, therefore, I think *Moana* achieves greatness primarily
through its poetic feeling for natural elements. It should be placed
on the idyllic shelf that includes all those poems which sing of the
loveliness of sea and land and air—and of man when he is a part
of beautiful surroundings, a figment of nature, an innocent primitive
rather than a so-called intelligent being cooped up in the mire of
so-called intelligent civilizations.

Surely the writer was not the only member of the crowd that
jammed the Rialto to the bursting point yesterday afternoon who,
as *Moana* shed its mellow, soft overtones, grew impatient with the
grime of modern civilization and longed for a South Sea island on
the leafy shores of which to fritter away a life in what "civilized"
people would consider childish pursuits.

Moana, which was photographed over a period of some twenty
months, reveals a far greater mastery of cinema technique than
Mr. Flaherty's previous photoplay, *Nanook of the North.* In the

first place, it follows a better natural outline—that of Moana's daily pursuits, which culminate in the tattooing episode, and, in the second, its camera angles, its composition, the design of almost every scene, are superb. The new panchromatic film used gives tonal values, lights and shadings that have not been equaled.

The film traces pictorially the capture of a wild boar by the youth Moana and his family, the capture of a giant turtle, surf ridings, the preparation of a native meal (made fascinating by clever cinema technique), and finally winds into the already talked of tattooing episode. Here, as a tribal dance proceeds, a fantastic design is pricked by a needle onto Moana's glossy epidermis. It is a period of intense pain for him, but as the sweat pours off his face he bravely bears it, for, as the subtitle has it, "the deepest wisdom of his race has decreed that manhood shall be won through pain."

Possibly I should become pedantic about this symbolizing of the attainment of manhood. Perhaps I should draw diagrams in an effort to prove that it is simply another tribal manifestation of the coming of age? It is not necessary, for the episode is in itself a dramatic, truthful thing. And if we regard the tattooing as a cruel procedure to which the Polynesians subject their young men—before they may take their place beside manhood—then let us reflect that perhaps it summons a bravery that is healthful for the race.

The film time and again induces a philosophic attitude on the part of the spectator. It is real, that is why. The people, these easy, natural, childlike primitives are enjoying themselves or suffering as the case may be before the camera. Moana, whom we begin to like during the first reel, is really tortured and it affects us as no acting could. Moana's life is dramatic in its primitive simplicity, its innocent pleasure, and its equally innocent pain.

Lacking in the film is the pictorial transcription of the sex life of these people. It is barely referred to. Its absence mars its completeness.

The most beautiful scenes that Mr. Flaherty conjures up are (1) Moana's little brother in the act of climbing a tall bending tree flung across a clear sky; (2) the vista showing the natives returning after the boar hunt; (3) Moana dancing the Siva; (4) all the surf and underwater scenes, and (5) the tribal dance.

I should not, perhaps, say that any group of scenes is any more beautiful than any other; for all are beautiful—and true.

Moana is lovely beyond compare.

Stark Love and *Moana*

from Movie Makers

*This unsigned review in the magazine Movie Makers
appeared in November 1928.*

This reviewer recently saw two of the well-known racial films on the same program, *Stark Love* [1927] and *Moana* [1925]. Both are products of Paramount and both were made by directors of independence and good taste. Karl Brown's *Stark Love* is less epical than Robert Flaherty's *Moana* but it catches the essence of a people just as successfully.

These are both films that have been widely exhibited but they are films which, if you have missed them and get a chance to see them, you should not omit. Chiefly they are interesting because they present graphically the daily life of out-of-the-way minorities. Secondly they are natural pictures with a minimum of posed and directed action. They are photographically excellent and both show indications of cinematography, which is not carried to the extent to which we have become accustomed in later films.

Flaherty had a clearer concept than Brown of what he wanted as a compelling motif for his offering. He shows us a Polynesian people, giving us their daily life in an almost unselective filming until he wishes to record their outstanding performance, which is the stern test they require before a youth is admitted to manhood. We see these islanders gay, laughing, casual, and uncompelled by any force beyond the desires for food, activity, and compensating rest and sleep. Next we are shown the tribal ordeal of tattooing and we see that the entire population is stirred by it. The film then recedes to a peaceful close. Here, the drama is impersonal and epic.

Brown was more interested in securing a tale of specific human beings under dramatic pressure and he tells a worthwhile tale adequately and honestly. Unfortunately for the fullest success of *Stark Love* the milieu is so unfamiliar that the audience shares a continually divided interest between characters and setting. The director could have handled his theme as Flaherty did *Moana* and have kept the drama impersonal. Treating it personally, as he did, it is impossible to build up enough audience knowledge of the background —so strange are the mountain people of Tennessee to the modern

American—to make it possible for the beholders to fix their chief attention on the actors in the story. There are so many fascinating bits of local color, so many incidental characters over which we should like to pause for reflection that we feel rushed away from our enjoyment of the unusual when we are asked to follow the very honest and sincere tale of the chief characters. On the whole, Flaherty's method is sounder, although it lacks box-office value. Both he and Brown have contributed to the small number of racial and geographical film epics, such as *Grass* and *Chang*. These films are not entirely ethnological documents like the Smithsonian *Pygmies* or Haeseler's Berber study, neither are they comfortable dramas. They have a distinct place in the film world and it is hoped that the supply will increase rather than diminish.

Symposium on Soviet Documentary:
S. Tretyakov, V. Shklovsky, E. Shub, and O. Brik

*The following is an excerpt from a symposium held by the Soviet
journal New Lef in 1927. It was translated by Elizabeth
Henderson as part of a doctoral dissertation. The symposium
participants were Sergey Tretyakov, playwright and poet; Victor
Shklovsky, screenwriter and theoretician of film art; Esther Shub,
one of the earliest women directors, and Osip Brik, screenwriter
and critic. (Throughout the discussion the word "material" is
used to indicate the objects, people, and scenery filmed. It does not
mean either the scenario or the technical equipment.)*

SERGEY TRETYAKOV:

The basic problem in the cinema today is the argument over fiction
and nonfiction films. Here we must do a scientific analysis in order
to clarify the basis of the distinction and the juxtaposition. Perhaps the very juxtaposition of "fiction" to "nonfiction" is simply
an unsuccessful formulation. There have been attempts to ascertain
the degree of the fictional element at various stages of film production. The fictional element—arbitrariness—can come from the
director, the scenario writer, or the actor, and this arbitrariness
determines the degree of fiction in a given film.

I have never held that Lef necessarily must concentrate only
on newsreels. I consider this somewhat onesided. It has always
seemed perfectly justified to me that there are both of these names
on the cover of Lef—Eisenstein and Vertov. These are men working
for the same purpose, but with two different methods. With Eisenstein the agitational impulse predominates, while the material
shown takes an auxiliary position. With Vertov the informational
impulse predominates and the material itself is most important.

Vertov's work can hardly be called pure newsreel. Pure newsreel is the montage of facts selected only for their currency and their
social significance. But when a fact is taken as a brick for a construction of another sort, the pure newsreel disappears. It is all a
matter of montage.

Whether a film is fictional or nonfictional is, in my opinion, a
question of the greater or lesser falsification of the material that is
being filmed. There is an arbitrary element in any film. The "treatment" of the material already shows the side chosen by the director.

Take for example the film, *The Great Road*. It is a fiction film, but there is only one person performing—Esther Shub. Her arbitrariness is artistic, her selection of material is purely aesthetic, directed towards attaining a particular emotional charge in the audience by means of the manipulation of montage attractions. But Shub is dealing with highly cultured material because it is minimally falsified.

Not so stupid is the remark of one viewer, who, after seeing Shub's film, *The Fall of the Romanov Dynasty,* said sympathizingly: "It's a shame that there are empty spots—they should have staged them and put them in where needed." The genuineness of the material was not important to this person, but he valued the charge which the film gave him, and in the name of this charge demanded that the empty spots be plugged with artificial material.

We still place our emphasis on the attraction, on the effect which the film produces on the viewer. There are various kinds of material. The material of an erotic film will act on any viewer, no matter how uncultured he may be. But, if a film contains purely historical material, the cultural knowledge of the audience is still insufficient. It's not hard to sexualize an audience with kisses and nudity on the screen. . . .

But we are interested in arousing emotions, in stimulating people by means of the most cultured, the least falsified material of current reality. We have not done this fully yet.

People say now that it was difficult to assemble the film, *The Great Road,* because people ten years ago did not know what to photograph. Let's say we win our battle for the newsreel, can you be sure that in ten years people will be any happier when they get our film archives?

I think that to distinguish fiction from nonfiction (the terminology is arbitrary), we must keep in mind that there is a gradation in the falsification of the elements of which the film is made. I define falsification as the arbitrary distortion, the displacement of genuine elements. We find this distortion, first of all, in the material (what to photograph?—the selection of what we need from the whole mass of things before us); secondly, the distortion of the material by the placement of the camera and the selection of lighting; and, thirdly, by the director's montage.

According to the degree of distortion, film material falls into three basic groups. The first—"raw" material; the second—staged; and the third—fictional. Raw material is caught at the scene of the crime. This is Vertov's "life caught unawares." The distortion is minimal.

Nevertheless there are gradations of distortion even in raw material. You can photograph a person so that he does not suspect that you are photographing him. I told Shub that it might be possible to plant cameras in the walls along the streets so that they could photograph the people who pass by. These would be typical shots with no arbitrary element in the camera placement.

But when a cameraman shoots it is always individual. Well and good, if the cameraman works from some fixed premise—such as typical lighting, its selection motivated by the sharpness of the shot, or some relation between groups calculated in advance, etc. It is time for us to conduct a struggle against the arbitrary way cameramen place their cameras.

Why do they dance around an object? They say—this way we can show a thing from all sides. But just try to figure out which point is necessary to show a thing fully and which is chosen for an arbitrarily aesthetic kind of all-encompassing admiration.

Consequently, the first group—raw material—is the most objective. The second level—rawness slightly impaired—is when the observed lens influences the behavior of the people being photographed. The person sees you turning the handle and starts moving in some unnatural way. He distorts himself, presents himself as an image, and not as you would have liked to see him. The third level is when we shoot raw material but manipulate the lighting. Let's say we are photographing a Svanetian family in its natural surroundings in an absolutely dark room, in a cave, but we rearrange and change the lighting.

I call the second group of material staged. . . . This applies to work with non-actors. A person is taken as material: his material qualities, habits, and automatic movements correspond with the figure which is needed on the screen.

That is the way Eisenstein works. He selects people who have the appropriate face, manner, and walk. Of course, here, too, there is an unquestionable emphasis on acting, but less than with an actor. The actor's "arbitrariness" is replaced here by the accuracy of the correctly found reflex in action.

The task of nonfiction filmmakers is to catch raw material unawares. For us it is important to establish the limit which is practically workable and dictated by today's social demand, the limit to which we will go in our concrete work today. Therefore, as our maximum program, we say: Give us "cinema-eye," "life caught unawares," etc.

But since we want to arouse emotions, we work with the method of montage of attractions. We must have a free hand to affect the audience. Thus we also will have to use another kind of material, we will have to defend staged material, that is, to work with Eisenstein's methods.

Now two words about depersonalized material. In a newsreel it is important to know that on the screen a particular person is shown, in a particular place, at a particular time, doing a particular thing. If this specificity of the shot disappears, then the thing becomes generalized and we look on it as typical, depersonalized.

Thus it seems to me that the demarcation between "fiction" and "nonfiction," which appears to be so clear, is actually only relative. The real question of "fiction" and "nonfiction" is the question of the preference of fact to invention, of current events to the past. Our blows must fall with particular force on those who take material that is not too bad in itself and cook it up as exotica, sentiment, and opera.

VICTOR SHKLOVSKY:

The fact is that sometimes you find extraordinarily useless intelligent people and extraordinarily useful mistakes. When I talk with newsreel-makers, I know that it is fairly simple to defeat them. But the mistakes which they make are extraordinarily useful artistically and cinematographically.

These are the mistakes which lead to invention.

I, of course, consider the division of cinema into fiction and nonfiction as elementary. . . .

You say that the fiction film means Kuleshov and Eisenstein, and the nonfiction film Shub and Dziga Vertov. They all sat together in the same crowd—and Shub learned montage on fiction films while the fiction-film director learned assemblage on the newsreel.

It's very difficult to resolve according to the laws of physics: should there be a motionless point with the cameraman running around the performing actor, or should the actor run around the nonfiction cameraman.

Here from the very beginning is the problem of placement—which involves an element of fiction.

The best part of Shub's film is the Dybenko sequence. He does not know how to behave in front of a camera; first he smiles, then he puts on a heroic expression. And this playing with the filmmaker is a perfectly brilliant part of this magnificent film.

Speaking of nonfiction and fiction films, let me tell you, I've seen how responsible leaders are filmed. You can sign them right up for the actors' union. As soon as the camera starts to roll, they are already moving into the frame and they stop and stand and chat with one another.

Therefore this distinction is incorrect because it sets up a rule in general.

What Shub is doing and Dziga Vertov is getting ready to do has a huge number of analogies in literature. . . . We should not exaggerate the fictional side of art. The fact of fiction is established, but art periodically undergoes a re-emphasis on raw material.

And the mistaken newsreel-makers were right about this and they are right now when they promote raw material. The priority of material is the result. For today. . . .

Lef's task is broader than the problem of the fiction and non-fiction film. Our problem is the priority of raw material.

It is curious that recently the Artists' Union sent us a sample writer's contract, where, among other things, there is one very curious item. They determined how many hours are necessary to write a scenario.

And they decided: 75 hours, paid by the hour.

And Karl Marx has written that anything can be translated into hours, except literary work.

He wrote that book a long time ago, but, of course, it was based on statistical material.

But the Artists' Union does not even think of that.

Let us examine their formula for gathering material. They have the totally wild notion that first of all there is a story, and then this story is filled out with material. Our conception is that a person first of all researches the material, and then poses the question of how to give form to the material.

Besides, material can be presented with or without a story. Storyless films still have a plot.

We are talking about complicated things, but when we get to the studio we should take a grammar book along.

I have worked in the following organizations: Sovkino, then VUFKU, and now Mezhrabpom, and I have not seen an encyclopedia in any one of these organizations.

We send off expeditions to Svanetia [Caucasus], to photograph the Orenburg steppe and we don't know what awaits us there. There was that wonderful occasion when people traveled 900 miles into Siberia and there they found another "Moscow River."

What am I proposing practically? First of all, instead of dividing films into newsreels and fiction films, let's have story and nonstory films. . . .

Saltykov-Shchedrin said that only family affairs can be included within the framework of the family novel. We are going through the Soviet "Empire style," Restoration forms, that is our great misfortune. . . . And everywhere without fail they want to get in a love story.

The same thing happens with the scenario of *Stenka Razin*. He was on the Don, in Moscow, in Astrakhan, in Persia, and back in Moscow, and I'm supposed to drag a woman along with him wherever he goes. It's so stupid and unnecessary.

Let's take our cinema—a worse administration than we have could not be invented. Absolutely no culture. It's the worst administration in the world. . . . Then there's the illiteracy of the directors; there are no actors, or else only bad ones.

And the result—a good cinema.

A curious thing happens. The Soviet cinema is held together by Party instructions. And the Party Central Repertory Committee of Soviet Cinema is its most cultured organization. That is, an educational film, fulfilling the Central Repertory Committee's instructions, would be a Lef film.

ESTHER SHUB:

The whole problem is what we must film now. As soon as that is clear to us, then the terminology won't matter—fiction or nonfiction. The important thing is that we are Lef.

We believe that in our epoch we can only film newsreels and

thus preserve our epoch for future generations—only that. This means that we want to film the present day, today's people, today's events. Whether Rykov or Lenin performs well in front of the camera and whether that is a fictional element does not bother us at all. For us the important thing is that a camera has photographed Lenin and Dybenko, even if they don't know how to show themselves in front of a camera, because that moment best characterizes them.

And why does Dybenko come across to you without any abstraction? Because it is he himself, and not a man playing the part of Dybenko. And it does not bother us that there is a trace of performance here.

Therefore we insist that you not kill the term "nonfiction cinematography." Let's talk about nonfiction cinematography. Let there even be fictional elements in it. But what is the difference when you watch a wonderful fiction film made three years ago? You cannot stand to look at it—it becomes simply indigestible. But when you see a nonfiction film, you watch it, and it comes across and it is interesting because it is a piece of genuine life which is now in the past.

What makes you think that we don't want to make emotionally effective films? It's all in the material, in the question of what material we want to work with.

Do we negate the element of skill? We do not. We are convinced that with great skill it will be possible to make a film out of nonfictional material which will beat any fiction film. Everything depends on the approach and the method of work. That's what we must talk about.

OSIP BRIK:

It seems to me that we are letting a whole series of very crude mistakes slip by. First of all, beginning with the infamous distortion of material. How long have we been talking about the possibility of communicating facts with conventional signs? Cinematic material, by the single fact that it is two-dimensional, distorts. Shub has stated correctly that the problem is what to film, and not what distorts more or less. Everything distorts equally. . . . To maintain that we in Lef stand for filming only what is true is incorrect. If we were told to show Nikolai I as he really was, and some people say that he was not all that bad, we would not do it. The question is what do we consider essential to show in the cinema? And we say: First of all we want to achieve in the cinema the same thing as in all our literary work, that is, to train people to value facts, documents, and not to value an artistic invention inspired by these documents. . . .

But besides this there is other work. The question is not clear: Should we take the stand that we will give only documents, or should we create an intermediate film form, that is, using the same material, create a broader form? I'm not clear on this. . . .

In order to film a newsreel, it is necessary not only to know cinematography, but to be a highly cultured political person. Even a White Guard can film some story about a tsarist official, but only a politically educated person, a person with a very precise knowledge of the goal of what he wants to film can film the Soviet Caucasus. Therefore, when we say that the reflection of reality must be filmed, this does not mean to set the camera up on the street and go away, but to reflect reality from a definite point of view.

SERGEY TRETYAKOV:

Today we have tossed around the bases for the classification of fiction and nonfiction. I believe that the material determines this difference. But there is yet another division—into educational films and entertainment films. This is a division according to the function a film fulfills. . . .

There are intellectualizing films (instructional, documentary, scientific), after which the viewer leaves better educated, and emotionalizing films, after which the viewer is more aroused, his mood is heightened.

Here too we must sharpen our position—where we stand.

The newsreel and the nonfiction film are not fetishes for us. As soon as the newsreel, in its turn, becomes an aesthetic device, we should shout danger. And that danger exists, and already some fiction films are not above masquerading as nonfiction.

Laying bare the device, throwing open the "kitchen" of film-"creation"—that is Lef's first obligation.

Two Aspects of the City: Cavalcanti and Ruttmann
by Jay Chapman

*Mr. Chapman is a doctoral candidate in the Department of
Cinema Studies at New York University. This is a selection
from his monograph "The Problem of the City Films."*

What is the city? This is a question posed and answered many
times over in print, in thought, in discussion. It is also answered
in film. And the answers here are as varied as they are under other
circumstances. The basis of their validity—the personal viewpoint
of their creators, as influenced by their specific subject and
experience.

One element of the city is its inhabitants, and a most striking
distinction can be made in this respect by contrasting the attitude
of Cavalcanti in *Rien que les heures* with that of Ruttmann in
Berlin. Clearly, the people in *Rien que les heures* are of paramount
importance. The city is its people; the people (different kinds and
classes) are what make up the fabric of the city. In fact, one could
almost go so far as to say that *Rien que les heures* is concerned only
with people and with nothing else. Even the shots of the empty
streets are noteworthy for their lack of people, rather than for any
quality in and of themselves. If the city is the people, then these
shots only serve to emphasize the loneliness and emptiness of the
city without people. Yet, a number of these shots of the streets
during the very early morning are not totally devoid of anyone of
interest, as is the case in *Berlin*. For, it is at this point that the
viewer is introduced to one of the two main "characters" in the film
—the prostitute.

And here we come to the crucial difference between *Rien que
les heures* and *Berlin* in terms of their respective filmmakers' attitudes toward the people of the city. Generally speaking, Cavalcanti
is more immediately concerned with people as individuals, while
Ruttmann is more concerned with people as a mass. The people in
Berlin are anonymous beings; we don't know who or what they are;
they are merely anonymous elements of which the masses are composed. In *Rien que les heures* the people are specific individuals
who also serve as symbols for specific types of people. One method
used by Cavalcanti which enabled his two main "characters" to
become individuals was to have their individual "stories" run

through various parts of the film. For example, the prostitute "character" appears in the beginning, middle, and end of the film. The thread of narrative continuity which such a device provides does not occur in *Berlin*. With respect to this, the differences of style and ultimately of attitude between the two directors can be most effectively distinguished by contrasting the treatment of the most tragic point in each film—the death of the woman newspaper seller in *Rien que les heures* and the suicide of the woman in *Berlin*. The death of the woman newspaper seller in *Rien que les heures* is "felt" by the viewer much more than the suicide of the woman in *Berlin* specifically because the newspaper seller is more of an individual with whom the viewer is acquainted, due to the fact that her particular situation is developed over a longer period of time and appears in various parts of the film. We see her getting her newspapers, with the fortune teller, running and selling newspapers in the streets, fighting with and finally being killed by the man. This thread of continuity, which is characteristic of the "development" of the two main "characters" in the film, and which runs throughout the film rather than being concentrated in just one sequence played from beginning to end uninterrupted by any other action, stands in direct opposition to the style of *Berlin*, where the suicide of the woman is just one brief incident showing the climactic action, totally unrelated to and uninterrupted by anything else. The viewer doesn't have any idea who the suicide victim is or why she found herself forced to take her life. She is only an abstract symbol—not an individual.

These climactic moments in both films are interesting from another point of view with respect to the same problem of the individual versus the mass. The death in *Rien que les heures* is shown to take place without any other people present than the two directly concerned participants (except for the prostitute as a lookout), whereas Ruttmann shows a mass of people around the spot where the suicide falls to her death. The feeling for the individual as opposed to the mass is evoked by Cavalcanti through his use of individual situations as opposed to mass situations. We seldom see any kind of masses or shots of a great many people anywhere in *Rien que les heures*. Cavalcanti has made his film with a very small cast, and he concentrates on his few actors, for the most part ignoring the masses which presumably surround them. On the other hand, even when Ruttmann relates little personal incidents (e.g., the vendors, the two men in a fight on the street, the prostitute and her customer), the participants are always surrounded by quite a number of people. They are never alone together on the screen, the incidents are never developed from anything nor do they develop into anything, and the events exist only momentarily in time. The people involved are not allowed to become individuals—they remain merely a part of the mass. When speaking about quantities of people, solely in terms of volume, an interesting comparison can be made between the lunch sequences of the two films. In *Rien que les heures* we are shown exactly two people eating lunch—a poor man sitting on a curb and a wealthy man eating in a restaurant. In *Berlin,* however, we see several different classes of people eating different types of lunch in many different ways—each represented by a number of people.

Turning to what is commonly referred to as the "pace" of the city, there is quite a jump from the relatively slow pace in *Rien que les heures* (except, of course, for the amusement ride sequence and the very end of the film) to the pace in *Berlin.* From the fantastically edited initial sequence of the train speeding toward Berlin, the viewer is made acutely aware of the fact that he is in an entirely different world. The vibrant pulse of the city, along with a certain sense of a "life" of the city itself, is felt here as it had not been felt in Cavalcanti's film. The strict rhythmic style of editing indicates that Berlin doesn't wait or pause for anything, and that the rhythm of the city, of which the activities of the masses function as a part, is the very essence of the city itself. What is normally thought of as the quick pace of city life plays a relatively small role in *Rien que les heures,* but increases in importance in *Berlin,* although here it is really a concern more with the rhythm of that pace than its relative speed.

An interesting comparison between *Rien que les heures* and *Berlin* can also be made with respect to the social consciousness of the filmmakers. Cavalcanti, through his concentration on the poorer classes of people in the city, and use of the technique of showing their living conditions juxtaposed with those of the wealthier classes (e.g., the contrast between the poor man eating in the street and the wealthy one eating steak in the restaurant), turns *Rien que les heures* into a rather blunt personal statement which compares the mode of life of the wealthy and poorer classes, and which is obviously quite sympathetic toward the latter. In contrast to this style of reportage, there is the generally much more matter-of-fact, less insistent style of *Berlin*. To begin with, Ruttmann covers a much wider range of social strata than Cavalcanti (everything from the top to the bottom, not just the top and the bottom). And there is relatively little overt social comment about the various classes. In the few instances when it does come to statement by juxtaposition, we are led to infer the social comment from the combination of visuals rather than being insistently banged over the head with it, as is the case in *Rien que les heures*. Understatement or indirect statement is the key, and there is no omnipresent distinction between strictly class differences. For example, in the sequence of inter-cutting between a mass of people walking in the street and a herd of moving cattle, the people are neither wealthy nor poor—they are merely an undifferentiated mass of people of the city. Ruttmann shows some of the differences in the classes, but this is most defi-nitely a minor theme. *Berlin* indicates rather matter-of-factly that these differences exist, but the overall general tone of the film implies that we should accept these differences. (Diametrically opposed to this, of course, is Cavalcanti's overtly sympathetic atti-tude toward the poor and, via the bluntness of his statement, his insistence on a change.)

Another aspect of these films which should be taken into considera-tion is the relative "coldness" of each work. *Rien que les heures* has the advantage of two characters as "individuals" and the sympa-thetic involvement of both filmmaker and viewer to counteract any coldly rational social commentary. But, when we come to *Berlin,* we come to a problem. The strictly formal editing structure of the film, preoccupied with its own immaculately disciplined, highly ordered rhythmic pattern, to the exclusion of everything else, makes for a cold, impersonal, mechanically calculated work which exhibits no real feeling for anything—not the people, as in *Rien que les heures;* not even the machine or mechanical processes, as in some avant-garde films of the same decade. The sense of pleasure one gets from viewing *Berlin* derives from an absorption with the rhythm of the editing, and any sense of "warmth" achieved emanates from within the viewer, rather than from the screen.

What it is, of course, that makes Cavalcanti's and Ruttmann's attitudes, opinions, and approaches clear to the viewer is the style in which their respective films are executed. Ultimately it is the style of the film and the style alone which enables the viewer to "feel" the city the same way the filmmaker does.

Rien que les heures, arising, as it does, from the French avant-garde film tradition of the 1920s, is executed, as a whole, in a comparatively slowly-paced style of editing, punctuated occasionally by a rather dazzling display of visual virtuosity. At these moments we realize that it is actually a rather virtuoso piece of "filmmaking," characterized by a sense of "play" with the camera and assorted visual effects. It repeatedly, although only momentarily, astounds and amazes with its *joie de cinématographie.* Two examples of this are the amusement ride sequence with the distortions of swish pans and multiple exposures and rapid movement of camera in several directions, and the superimposed collage-montage at the very end of the film as we travel through the busily-trafficked streets of the city. However, when Cavalcanti deals with the subject matter proper —the people—he is the perfect model of level-headed good sense and intelligence. His concern and feeling for the people as individuals is made clear and is effectively instilled in the viewer by means of really rather simple devices. Basically, we seldom see any shots of masses of people because the camera concentrates mainly on individuals alone or in combinations of only two or three. *Rien que les heures* is a series of individual situations, not mass situations. Furthermore, once the main "characters" are singled out for observation, these "characters" continue to appear throughout the film in continuing situations which are extended in time. In other words, the prostitute and the newspaper seller are allowed to become individuals whom the viewer can feel compassion for.

Just about everything which has been said about the people as individuals in *Rien que les heures* is reversed in the mass situations with no development in time and the fleeting, momentary appearance of unknown personages in *Berlin.* But the people, even as a mass, aren't all that important in Ruttmann's film. Neither, really, is the pace, although it is quicker in many parts and as a whole than it was in *Rien que les heures,* mainly because of the increased pace of the editing and action, as well as the fact that in *Berlin* you are dealing with the movement of masses of people rather than mainly with individuals. For Ruttmann, the essence of the city is its rhythm, and nothing else. This is felt most deeply by the viewer through the exquisitely controlled rhythm of the editing, as well as the ebb and flow of visual rhythms within individual shots and sequences, which is miraculously sustained for most of the film. (The only time Ruttmann loses control is in the final night-life section, where the tightness of the editing exhibited in the previous sections tends just to fall apart. As compared with the rest of the film, this section is too loose in terms of composition, visual rhythms, and editing. It may be superior in surface visual excitement, but it is inferior in the formal qualities of order and precision characteristic of the rest of the film.) With rhythm, in editing and in everything else, being the most important, overriding element in the film, and with Ruttmann's concern with all aspects of how the city operates within this pattern, there is apt to be little aggressive social comment. The strict rhythmic style of *Berlin* makes the film a matter-of-fact depiction of a day in the life of a city.

It is obvious by now how each film, through its unique style, becomes a personal statement. As can only be expected, each filmmaker likes or finds beautiful in the city that thing which he has chosen to concentrate on in his film. Cavalcanti feels closest to the people of the city, while Ruttmann somewhat abstractly stands back in admiration of the rhythm of the city.

Rien que les heures is a homage to the lower-class people of the city.

Berlin is a formal exercise, a reflection of the rhythm of the city.

Cross-Section Films
by Siegfried Kracauer

*This chapter is taken from the author's impressive
study of German films, "From Caligari to Hitler"
(Princeton University Press, 1947).*

Berlin inaugurated the vogue of cross-section, or "montage," films.
They could be produced at low cost; and they offered a gratifying
opportunity of showing much and revealing nothing. Several films
of that kind utilized stock material. One of them summarized the
career of Henny Porten (1928); a second, similarly produced by
Ufa, extracted love episodes from old movies (*Rund um die Liebe,*
1929); a third was the *Kulturfilm, Die Wunder der Welt (Miracles
of the Universe,* 1929), a patchwork of various explorer films.

Of greater interest were two cross-section films which, after the
manner of *Berlin,* reported actual life through an assemblage of
documentary shots. In *Markt am Wittenbergplatz (Street Markets
in Berlin,* 1929), Wilfried Basse used the stop-motion camera to
condense the lengthy procedure of erecting tents and stands to a few
seconds. It was neat and unpretentious pictorial reportage, a pleasing succession of such characteristic details as bargaining housewives, stout market women, glittering grapes, flower displays,
horses, lazy onlookers, and scattered debris. The whole amounted
to a pointless statement on colorful surface phenomena. Its inherent
neutrality is corroborated by Basse's indifference to the change of
political atmosphere under Hitler. In 1934, as if nothing had
happened, he released *Deutschland von Gestern und Heute* (Germany Yesterday and Today), a cross-section film of German cultural life which also refused "to penetrate beneath the skin."

Shortly after this market film, another more important bit of
reportage appeared: *Menschen am Sonntag* (People on Sunday).
Eugen Shuftan, Robert Siodmak, Edgar Ullmer, Billy Wilder, Fred
Zinnemann, and Moritz Seeler collaborated in the production of
this late silent film. Its success may have been due to the convincing
way it pictured a province of life rarely noticed until then. A sales-
girl, a traveling salesman, an extra, and a chauffeur are the film's
main characters. On Sunday, they leave their dreary homes for one
of the lakes near Berlin, and there are seen bathing, cooking, lying

about on the beach, making futile contacts with each other and
people like them. This is about all. But it is significant inasmuch
as all the characters involved are lesser employees. At that time,
the white-collar workers had turned into a political factor. They
were wooed by the Nazis as well as the Social Democrats, and the
whole domestic situation depended upon whether they would cling
to their middle-class prejudices or acknowledge their common interests with the working class.

People on Sunday is one of the first films to draw attention to
the plight of the "little man." In one sequence, a beach photographer
is busy taking pictures which then appear within the film itself.
They are inserted in such a way that it is as if the individuals photographed suddenly became motionless in the middle of an action. As
long as they move they are just average individuals; having come
to a standstill, they appear to be ludicrous products of mere chance.
While the stills in Dovzhenko's films serve to disclose the significance
of some face or inanimate object, these snapshots seem designed
to demonstrate how little substance is left to lower middle-class
people. Along with shots of deserted Berlin streets and houses, they
corroborate what has been said above of the spiritual vacuum in
which the mass of employees actually lived. However, this is the
sole revelation to be elicited from a film which on the whole proves
as noncommittal as the other cross-section films. Kraszna-Krausz
states of it: "Melancholic observation. Not less, not more." And
Béla Balázs points out the "fanaticism for facts" animating *People
on Sunday* and its like, and then comes to the conclusion: "They
bury their meaning in an abundance of facts."

Turksib: Building a Railroad
by K. J. Coldicutt

These program notes, reprinted from the April 1933
bulletin of the Realist Film Association in Melbourne,
Australia, were written for the screening there of
the film written and directed by Victor Turin in 1928-29.

Turksib deals with one of the great achievements of the first Soviet Five Year Plan, the building of the Turkestan-Siberia railway to link the cotton fields of Turkestan with the granaries of Siberia. The film was released while the railway was still in construction, one of the purposes of its production being to speed the drive for completion of the project by 1930. . . .

The film opens with a sequence showing the potentialities of Turkestan as a cotton-growing land. The whole Soviet Union needs the cotton of Turkestan, but its production is limited. The people of Turkestan must eat, so good cotton land and scarce water supplies are given over to grain crops.

The remainder of the film is divided into five parts, oddly described as "acts" in Grierson's English version.

PART I emphasizes the problems of water supplies. It can be resolved into three sequences:

(a) In the parched fields of Turkestan men are hoeing and tending the irrigation channels. Cracked mud lies in the ditches; men sweat in the hot sun. Without water their work is in vain—there is nothing to do but wait. The workers in the fields, a panting dog, a baby, a calf, the machines in the cotton mill—all are waiting for water.

(b) But in the snow-capped peaks the snow is melting under the hot sun. The water flow increases in a gradual crescendo until there is a mighty torrent to supply the thirsty fields. As the stream enters the dry irrigation channels the workers spring to life and work frantically to control its flow. Hoes dig, water splashes and whirls, the cotton machines spin, in a frenzied rhythm. But there is only enough water for grain. The cotton must still thirst.

(c) It is necessary to bring grain to Turkestan; then the land will be freed for cotton—cotton for all Russia!

PART II also falls into three sequences:

(a) The economy of Turkestan is still primitive. Timber is

scarce and fuel is sold by the pound. In addition to cotton growing, sheep, goats, and cattle are reared. Transport is by camels and mules.

(b) The desert land is fascinating and terrifying. The sands are silent and still until the wind stirs from the northeast. In a mounting tempo the movement increases until a camel train is caught and engulfed in whirling sand by the dreaded simoon.

(c) Suddenly the scene is transferred to the north—to Siberia. Horse-drawn sleds in the snow contrast sharply with the camels we have seen plodding through hot sand. In Siberia there are vast supplies of timber and grain, but for Turkestan the way is closed. It is necessary to break through.

Part III tells of the work of surveying the route. There are again three sequences:

(a) The surveyors, "the advance guard of the new civilization," blaze the trail by plane, motor truck, horse, and foot.

(b) In the huts of a nomad village, the people are asleep in the heat of midday. Dogs give warning of the approach of strangers. The children are first to investigate, but others emerge from the huts as a truckload of surveyors arrive. Doubt and suspicion give way to smiles and handshakes as gifts of food and drink are thrust upon the newcomers. There is momentary panic amongst the children and dogs when the motor-horn is sounded, then the survey party is off again, with an escort of tribespeople running behind.

(c) Back to headquarters in Alma-Ata, draughtsmen are at work on charts and plans. On a map of Turkestan, rivers, lakes, and desert areas appear, and a probing line representing the railroad seeks a way from north to south past or through all obstacles. 900 miles of steel will weld Turkestan to Siberia.

Part IV shows plans becoming reality. Again we find three sequences:

(a) Railway trucks or camels carry rails and sleepers to the base of operations. Under the hot sun, men work with pick, shovel, and machine, thrusting out mile after mile of track.

(b) The way is barred by a huge rocky outcrop. While men and work-animals rest, and a steam shovel waits hungrily for its prey, the rocks are drilled to receive charges of explosive. Finally the obstruction is shattered and men and machines move in to the attack.

(c) Nomad tribesmen strike their tents and make their way

from the furthest corners to see the new wonders. Somewhere along the track a group of nomads, mounted on camels, donkeys, ponies, and steers, cluster around a giant locomotive. They panic when it blows off steam, then when it moves off there is a glorious chase. But they have to admit defeat. A camel left at a curve in the track bows its head in acknowledgment.

PART V recapitulates what has gone before and leads up to a pulsating climax exhorting the completion of the railroad by 1930. The desert simoon and Siberian blizzard are defied, explosions rend the earth, sleepers are dumped, rails laid, rivets driven. With the coming of the railroad civilization breaks through. Education is brought to the previously illiterate desert people; new methods of irrigation and farming are introduced together with the new machines. The old herds are built up with new stock. A great future of increasing plenty for Turkestan and the U.S.S.R. is the spur which impels every worker on the railroad to help complete the immense project by 1930.

. . . [Director] Turin's achievement in *Turksib* is his organization of material. The great footage, covering a tremendous variety of subjects and ranging over a wide geographical area, could have become, in less skillful hands, a travelogue that would have left its audience exhausted before half its length had run.

Turin's scenario and editing, however, have given the material a classical form and a rhythm that make it analogous to a symphony. After the introduction, *Turksib* is divided into five parts or movements. Each part deals with a separate and clearly defined aspect of the subject, but throughout the film there are recurring themes which help to intensify the total effect, at the same time providing strong continuity links. Each of the first four parts is divided clearly into three sequences, which are developed in such a way that the tempo rises gradually to a climax. The last part is a sustained whole, and is largely recapitulation, leading up to a rhetorical conclusion. It can be compared with the finale of a symphony.

Throughout the film, the control of tempo is amazingly exact, two outstanding sequences being the coming of water and the desert sandstorm.

Turksib contains hundreds of shots which repay study from the point of view of composition within the frame, but the shots are never held on the screen so that we become aware of their beauty in isolation; they are there only to fulfill their part dynamically in the integrated whole; the eye is assailed by a rain of emphatic images. The shots are bold and immediately comprehensible; significant detail is strongly emphasized; centralized or powerful diagonal patterns constantly recur.

Camera movement is never resorted to (as in so many films) to conceal inability to analyze and select the material. In *Turksib* the camera moves, as a rule, only to concentrate attention on moving subjects.

The main transition devices used are the cut and the fade. There are very few examples of dissolves or wipes, which in many films are used to dazzle the audience and conceal the director's lack of ideas. There are some dissolves which are used for a definite purpose, e.g., from an expanse of water to fields of cotton.

Grierson's contribution to the film—the English subtitling—has been over-praised. The English subtitles are self-consciously literary in tone, and usually redundant—they interrupt the flow of pictorial images and rarely contribute any facts or emotional overtones which are not already evoked by the images. On the credit side (if we grant that the subtitles are justified at all) it can be admitted that the titles are used in a cinematic way. Sentences and phrases are split into fragments and distributed so that they correspond with the tempo of the editing. The size of the lettering has also been used as a creative factor; the words assume the required character of menace, excitement, or exhortation.

Grierson, who became somewhat inflated by success in recent years, has criticized this film which gave him so much of his initial impetus. *Turksib,* he says, "gave every impression of building a railway, but the approach was again too detached to appreciate just how precisely or humanly it was built." To which it must be said that *Turksib* was never intended as an instructional film to show "how precisely" a railway is built. Its purpose was to drive home the importance of the railway for the peoples of Turkestan and Siberia (and, through the sectors of the first Five Year Plan which depended on its completion, its importance for the whole of the Soviet Union).

Two Vertov Films
by Oswell Blakeston

This account of the work of Dziga Vertov appeared in the August 1929 issue of Close Up, the Swiss-published English-language film magazine. Mr. Blakeston, a former filmmaker, now devotes his time to painting and writing novels.

Dziga Vertov's *The Man With the Movie Camera.* In Paris. Can we see it? Naturally. And would you like to see *The Eleventh Year?*

Thus we were received by Mr. Carlovitch, who looks after Russian films in Paris, and we want to thank him specially for his great courtesy and kindness.

The Eleventh Year opens with shots from an airplane; rocks and sea drifting by. Mines. Three lines of movement; men and trucks on a road, a bridge, and under an archway. This is so careful there must have been a reason for taking us up in the air. Ah! we are going under the ground. Humping up into the skyline a hillock, belted with machine band of workers carrying lanterns and picks. We are going under the ground. The flapping mouth of a coal scoop swings by us. We had to go up into the air to realize what it means to go under the ground. Above the black and white smoke from the furnaces a giant miner hammering; time that is passing but not time that is lost. These men are working for their own ideal (whether we agree with it or not), working for a land of new codes. There is something fine and beautiful, caught chronographically in the sweat-gleaming arm of a stoker; indeed these machines do not ask for our opinion.

The screen is split horizontally into two long-shots; one moves away, the other is static. It is magnificently done. Men walking home; away from the mines but the ideals in their homes. They are building an electric station for their state. The black and white smoke is building. (Women and children in the hay fields are building by releasing men for the more skilled work.) There are no obstacles to the willing; rocks are blasted to black and white smoke; smoke that builds.

Waters of the river rise to augment the electricity; rise by means of constructed dams. The town is seen under water; the one unifying idea. Windmill is seen under water. The village that has set out with one purpose; any village of the new order.

It is surprising how long we can watch, how long we can watch the women making hay and the electrician climbing a telegraph pole with knives clamped to his boots. Perhaps we are already taking a personal interest in the village?

Then we see the factory chimneys through the corn, in case we forget the linking-up. Factory chimneys are themselves a cornfield, with black and white ripples of smoke.

A ballet of telegraph wire (you remember the still?) suggesting the work inside the factory.

We must not forget, either, the activity under the ground. Pit ponies are as sturdy as the heavy rafters in the roof. Change of camera angle makes the rafters wrench with the ponies, drawing the eye to the quiet workers as the beasts draw the leads. And the lifts go up, to emphasize the men who stay below.

We leave them with a man with a drill, it brings vitality and truth to the abstract arrangements of the avant-garde.

Women at the pit-heads lustily wheel away the trucks.

A subtitle says, "The flag of Lenin." Courageous workers hidden in masks. So the flag of Lenin is a bright shower of sparks. No silk to drape across Utopia of ease and content; something searing, dangerous and alive.

Watching over the workers, the sentinel.

Wake of a boat, taken romantically from sea level. Sailors. A head and rifle against the cylinder curve of a waterfall. *One picture one turn* shot of the sky gives shredded clouds.

A subtitle says, "The flag of Lenin." Light from the home and the clubs. The flag is always light, light to kindle or to welcome; never silk.

We build with golden light. That is the message of the picture. Streaked fingers of light sweeping over the factory floor. Bars of red-hot metal, and coiled metal shavings doing things one finds in the work of Bruguière.

Men marching up skyline, up the hillock; and smoke from the factory chimneys balancing the corner of the composition. Where there is no smoke the tripod is tilted to give balance.

It is grand propaganda. We are quite impartial but only a stone could remain unmoved. The machinery and men working in harmony for something which they believe to be better. "Towards socialism," says a title. The art of the director does the rest. Final, clashing chords of a symphony. There it is, like it or not.

*   *   *

The Man With the Movie Camera is lighter than *The Eleventh Year*. M. Kaufman is again the operator and Swilowa again helps with the cutting.

Berlin and *Rien que les heures!* Forget all that. To begin with here is a Russian typewriter. Russian customs and habits, that alone puts it apart. Then there is a freedom from the usual smirkiness. The birth of a child is shown without the coyness of *Nature and Love*. Birth and death are being contrasted; the face of the mother is cross cut with linen face of the corpse; the mother's twitching lips and nostrils, the calmness of death. It is brought out that death is terrible and birth a conquest. It would be a joy to any new woman, not a shock.

Forget the other documents, for Vertov has the idea of making you conscious of the camera. The lens racks out and in, the scene comes into focus; the lens racks out and in and the eye of the cameraman is in the lens. The eye of the camera, the eye of the cameraman, and the eye of the camera recording it all.

We were reminded of a scene in *The Postmaster,* where the daughter is dressing for a party in front of an oval mirror which the cameraman frames in the black circle of an iris: another mirror, the mirror of the screen.

An accidental effect; Vertov's are minutely devised. He stops the film at a certain point to show a photograph of the film, cutting to a joining girl at work on the first copy. Rolls of the scenes we have just seen glint from the neat shelves. A woman driving along the streets, petrified to a single frame in the film strip of the woman driving along the streets. Long shot from the roof of a house; a camera pans down into the picture. A cameraman climbs a girder. We see him taking a picture, we see the picture he has taken. We are frightened for the safety of the unseen cameraman. Astral projection of self!

The film is different! A doll in a shop window; so, so threadbare. Vertov catches shadows from a tree outside which put breath into the china throat. Shutters, and views through the slats; so, so threadbare. Vertov crosscuts with a young lady blinking sleepy-dust eyes; eyes open and shut in a twinkling, slats twinkle.

Vertov's first reel is devoted to people entering a cinema; to the projectionist threading up his apparatus; to seats in the cinema being occupied, one by one, by invisible patrons.

A girl asleep. There is a ring on her finger. Wind stirs in an empty café. The café where she gained the ring? She sleeps. Children sleep. Down-and-outs sleep. The town sleeps. They all have a right to sleep.

The cameraman sets out for the day. He stretches himself across a railway line. There is a thrill as the train swoops down. The woman still sleeps.

The streets are washed, the girl washes. A relaxation for the cameraman. Not for long. He rides on a fire engine. He finds an attractive fountain. Because we are constantly reminded of the camera we cannot complain of the contrived; for instance, of the way in which the fountain is turned on a moment after it is discovered by the eye of the camera.

As in *The Eleventh Year* there is a good deal of footage devoted to factories, light-splashed tunnels of miners, and great chimneys blowing smoke rings.

We come back to the morning streets. Hand of policeman, hand on motor horn, in lightning cuts; mixed first, with the lens of a camera, then with a gigantic eye.

Finally, we watch the audience, watching the screen on which are scenes we saw being taken by a cameraman who we knew was being taken by Vertov's Debrie. The *montage* is stupendous and leaves most of the accredited masterpieces in some vague category with the Asquith person. The propaganda, without the stern beauty of *The Eleventh Year,* is a little too stormy, the contrasts between the wealthy woman enjoying a manicure and the manual worker being obvious and tiresome.

The work of Vertov is no longer legendary. We have seen it, others have seen it. Everybody must fight till they do see it!

The Man With the Movie Camera
by Dai Vaughan

*This selection, which appeared in Films and Filming (London),
in November 1960, is the latter part of an article which began
by placing Dziga Vertov in his historical context and proceeded
into a discussion of his Kino-Pravda newsreels and the way in
which the demands of newsreel in a revolutionary situation led
to the formulation of a new theory of cinema reality. Mr. Vaughan
is a film editor specializing in television documentary in England.*

Dziga Vertov's progress in evolving a newsreel technique appropriate to the times was punctuated by a number of manifestos in which he outlined his theoretical position. These manifestos—which, with commendable zeal, demanded the complete annihilation of the fiction-cinema—served mainly to propound the principle of the Kino-Eye.

The point, briefly, was this. The cine-camera is endowed with all the potentialities of human sight—and more. It can peep with unblinking gaze into every corner of life, observing, selecting, and capturing the myriad details of appearance and transaction which constitute the reality of our epoch. The camera should therefore be used to record not the simulated emotions of paid actors in locales created by the plasterer and set-decorator, but the authentic and unrehearsed behavior of real people in the streets and houses in which we live. All artifice should be eliminated, except in the unavoidable process of editing. And this process should be used to create, from the elements of unvarnished reality, an edifice of fact which would face us with the world, its joys and its sorrows, and hence with our own responsibilities toward and within it.

Dziga Vertov wrote lyrically of "the possibility to render the ordinarily invisible visible to all" and said, looking back upon the movement in 1935, "Kino-Eye was able to show on the screen the emotions of a man during a parachute jump—the changing expressions on his face: resolution, excitement, the joy of triumph." He believed—perhaps surprisingly for an uncompromising film enthusiast—that his methods had spread beyond the realm of Cinema, and claimed an indirect influence upon the style of such writers as Dos Passos.

Having glanced at the historical background to Dziga Vertov's work, and at the style and the theories which emerged from it, let us take a look at *The Man With the Movie Camera* where, as we shall see, these theories are taken to their logical conclusion.

The Man With the Movie Camera has no plot. It begins with an empty movie theatre, the lights going on, the seats coming down, the projectionist adjusting his carbons, the machine jerking into motion, the orchestra striking up. . . . When the film proper eventually starts it is with long, lingering shots of the city at daybreak: machines stand idle; streets are empty; leaves rustle in the morning breeze. A girl sleeps. Here we are introduced to many of the elements which will recur throughout the film—the girl will wake, the streets fill with traffic, the machines start busily spinning and packing, and the leaves rustle again at evening. Then the cameraman appears, carrying his tripod over his shoulder. He crosses the hall, passes through the swing door into the street, and climbs into the back of an open car which drives off. The city begins to stir.

At a leisurely pace we watch the city through its day, seeing the trams glide solemnly out of their garage, seeing the miner hewing coal, seeing the factory girls laughing over their work—and all this interspersed with shots of the cameraman cranking away in the most uncomfortable situations. We return to the hall from which he has set out. Feet pass across it. And dogs. In due course, work stops; and everyone goes for a drink, for chess, or for a dip at the beach. Sports competitions are shot in graceful slow motion, occasionally stopping altogether and leaving the participants in midair. The cameraman ambles into the sea, still carrying his camera.

When it is all over, we cut back to the theatre. The camera and tripod assemble themselves on the screen, take a bow, and walk off. There follows a wild finale in which the various leitmotifs of the film are reintroduced, sent haywire, and happily alternated with shots of the audience watching them. It ends—if you can call it ending—with the lens of the camera and an eye superimposed upon it.

The most discouraging thing about this film, when one calls to mind *Kino-Pravda,* is that it doesn't seem to *care* very much about the people it shows us, or about what they are doing. This is not to say that, like Ruttmann's *Berlin,* it treats human beings as moving parts in a mechanical toy. Indeed, it has a winsome humor and a slack sort of poetry which make it—to say the least—engaging. Nevertheless, there is little of the sympathetic human observation which we noted in *Trial of the Social Revolutionaries,* and the cutting, for all its abandon, doesn't seem to carry much real force. Why should this be? Perhaps because the film is not really *about* anything.

But this, one's first impression, is untrue: for the film is in fact— as its closing shot suggests—about the kino-eye. It is not only an application of the theory, but at the same time an attempt to prove it. Thus we are shown the cameraman setting up in the most exacting circumstances: climbing by iron rungs up a tall factory chimney; walking along the girders of a bridge; and being hoisted by crane above a surging torrent. The camera can go anywhere. (He fits a telephoto lens.) And see anything. At one point an eye, in big close-up, swivels round in one direction and another; and this is intercut with quick, uncomprehending pans back and forth. The iris closes over the lens, and the screen blacks out. To make a film to prove the potentialities of filmmaking—rather than to exploit them—may have an air of circularity. This is only the start.

"Life caught unawares"—that was one of the slogans; but there is a limit to what you can catch unawares with a cumbersome cine-camera. Dziga Vertov had claimed for the camera a mobility greater than that of the human eye. But in fact its mobility is more restricted. This means that many an apparently spontaneous episode, even of the simplest nature, has really to be staged if the full variety of everyday living is to be presented on the screen. Vertov's answer to this denial of his principles is to show us not only the scene itself, but also a shot of the cameraman shooting it. Thus strict filmic honesty is preserved.

This formula for honesty does not apply only when physical circumstances make an unrehearsed shot difficult to obtain. A man hewing coal or working at a bench may appear to behave quite naturally; but in reality he is aware that he is being photographed: and so we, the audience, must be made aware of it as well. This, of course, can go on indefinitely. And in *The Man With the Movie Camera* it does. A tracking shot follows a motorcyclist; then we have a long shot of the motorcyclist being followed by the cameraman who is on another motorcycle; then we see the same scene being projected in the theatre, and we cut to reaction shots of the audience. Alternatively the scene we are watching comes to a halt, and we see the editor examining this section of the film; she runs it through her fingers, rewinds it, and puts it away. On a rack hang trims from shots we have seen: we cut in close; the thing starts moving, and we are back in the action.

Persistently we are shown the mechanics of what we are seeing. The shadow and reflection of the camera appear in the picture; and a woman smiles at the cameraman, miming his cranking action. Slow and fast motion and various split-screen effects are used not only—or even mainly—for dramatic purposes, but to remind us that what is before us is merely an image, and that true reality lay in the subject of the shot. *The Man With the Movie Camera* is, in fact, a study in film truth on an almost philosophical level (the levity of its treatment—the fact that it is argued in the mode of fun—does not disqualify this judgment). This film does deliberately what most others try hard to avoid: it destroys its own illusions. It refuses to allow us to accept the screen as a plane of reference for reality, and instead seeks to dissolve all such planes of reference successively, as soon as they are formed, in the hope that reality will "emerge" from the process, not as a creature of screen illusion but as a liberated spirit.

Perhaps one might claim an affinity in this film's technique with the way in which cubism, discarding the naturalistic conception of the painting as a little segment of world existing in illusory perspective behind the proscenium of a frame, created a new sense of spatial objectivity through the clash of openly artificial elements. But the comparison is a false one. For the truth of the matter is that film is not, in the same sense as painting, a visual art—an art which makes its effect through its rendering of the visual essence of things. The photographic image as an equivalent for the real is a "given" element in film; and so is the means for creation of screen space (which is *already* close to cubist space in that it is built up from a juxtaposition of aspects). Film art lies in selection—selection of shots, and of emphasis (composition, light-and-shade, movement) within the shots. Film reality is not to be revealed, mystically, by drawing attention to the artificiality of all "equivalents," or by the shattering and reassembling of planes of reference. It is itself synthetic.

We can now see why *The Man With the Movie Camera* exhibits less enthusiasm, less attention to human detail, and less concern for promoting attitudes than *Kino-Pravda;* for enthusiasm, even if it betrays itself only in dynamic cutting style, must be enthusiasm *for* something (and hence *against* something else)—and this implies a choice of images on grounds of moral content or of their significance in relation to something outside themselves. Organization of subject matter on such a basis was evidently against the spirit —if not the letter—of Dziga Vertov's theory. To eliminate artifice meant, in this last resort, not to avoid frolicsome camera tricks, but to jettison the criterion of significance in favor of that of reality pure. In taking this step Vertov—in this film at any rate—broke with the very source of his inspiration and his technique; and the technique consequently died on him.

The Man With the Movie Camera is an "actuality," in the old sense—a picture of reality reinforced by a gimmick. (In the beginnings of cinema the gimmick was a legitimate one—the mere movement of leaves, of breakers, of steam from a locomotive; later the function was delegated to tints and dyes.) The film says nothing about what it shows, and confines itself within limits which were forced upon the primitive filmmakers by the inadequacy of their resources. In struggling to show the true relevance of events in a time of chaos, Dziga Vertov had developed a relatively sophisticated technique. But he became obsessed with a desire for visual impartiality—a desire to preserve intact the realness of his subjects. In trying to be impartial he managed only to be undiscriminating. And in chasing the chimera of absolute reality on the aesthetic plane he neglected that involvement in events which, from the social and hence the human point of view, makes reality real.

Nor is this the only drawback: for actuality, when pursued single-mindedly in a mature cinema, can soon prove itself the enemy of realism. It is sometimes tempting to define documentary (in contradistinction, say, to neorealism) as a style of filmmaking in which "it doesn't matter if they look at the camera"—i.e., to define it by an element of actuality inadmissible in other sorts of film. But this will not bear examination. There are many scenes of intimate feeling or behavior, by no means outside the accustomed province of documentary, where a glance at the camera would be disquieting or even ruinous. (One might instance the girl getting up and washing in Dziga Vertov's own film.) We are not now concerned with the physical problems of shooting such material impromptu, and with the consequent need for rehearsal—though scenes of emotion or intimacy usually are difficult to obtain unless, as in On the Bowery, the participants are blind drunk. What matters is that such things would not normally be happening *at all* in the accidental presence of cameramen and technicians; and merely to flaunt the presence of the camera gives no clue as to how people might have behaved had the camera not been there. The people involved must therefore be genuinely unaware of the camera, or they must act. In either case they must not look at us from the screen. And if there are *some* circumstances where this must not occur, then the definition of documentary by actuality collapses. To insist upon it would be to impose insane limits upon the filmmaker.

The silliest part about it is that many things in *The Man With the Movie Camera*—*especially* the scenes showing the cameraman shooting other scenes—must have been set up with a good deal of care and forethought. (We ought to have been shown the rehearsals.) But this film, mainly by virtue of its failings, performs a valuable function. It enables us—indeed, invites us—to speculate on the nature of screen truth; and it provides a happy and palatable indication of a direction in which cinema cannot hope to proceed. Events *must* be contrived for the camera; and to make the audience aware of the contrivance is to fall into the absurdity of an endless regression. We are therefore at liberty to contrive things as much as we like. (We know, for example, that Jennings would rehearse a man countless times in an action which was already part of his everyday routine.) Once we have accepted that there is no purely technical criterion for realism—no gimmick of presentation which can guarantee authenticity—then we are forced to recognize that we must rely upon the integrity of the artist for its creation and upon the judgment of the viewer for its proof.

What, then, is our final comment on *The Man With the Movie Camera?* What, apart from its enlightening lunacies, are its claims to recognition? It is a silent film running for six reels without a single title. It doesn't hurry, and it doesn't shout. If you are new to old films you may be delighted by it. If you are mature enough to sneer, you may be bored. For those interested in the Soviet Union it has considerable value as a period-piece—not profoundly revealing, but at least unashamed. And it has many quietly memorable images of the sort which hang around in the mind for a long time, until we start wondering where they came from. But perhaps the most important point is that this is the only major work accessible to us of one of the greatest pioneers of the cinema.

Author's note (written August 10, 1970): This article—along with one on the prehistory of documentary and one on Flaherty—was as far as I ever got with a plan for a series of articles which could later be amplified into book form as a history of the documentary idea. So it is gratifying to think that, after all this time, it may serve something like the purpose for which it was originally intended.

By some mischance I still have a copy of this article, and find myself concurring with most of what it says. Had I written it today, I should no doubt have drawn attention to the fact that many of the scenes in *The Man With the Movie Camera* have an extraordinarily up-to-date quality, notably where the hand-held camera is moving around in the thick of the action. Only when 16mm synch equipment became as lightweight as the old 200-foot-loading 35mm mute camera did this sort of visual involvement again become possible, at which point all the same problems—practical, aesthetic, and philosophical—re-emerged to be thrashed out again by the theorists of *cinéma-vérité* (which is synonymous with *Kino-Pravda*).

The discussion about the permissibility of looking at the camera has less force after 10 years of television documentary than it seemed to have in 1960. The presence of the camera in intimate situations is now taken more for granted—not necessarily by the people being filmed, but by the audience. A glance at the camera is therefore an element which, like the use of the zoom lens, has ceased to affront our sense of the reality of what we are seeing.

Dai Vaughan

The Making of *Rain*

by Joris Ivens

In this selection, which appeared in "The Camera and I" (International Publishers, 1969), the famed Dutch documentary director describes the genesis of one of his earliest films.

The idea—let's make a film about the damn rain—came quite naturally.

Although this idea arose almost as a joke, when I returned to Amsterdam I talked it over with Mannus Franken, who sketched an outline. We discussed and revised the outline many times, until it became a film for both of us. Unfortunately, Mannus Franken lived in Paris, so the shooting in Amsterdam was done by me alone. Franken, however, came to Amsterdam for a short time to assist in the editing.

In making such a film of atmosphere, I found that you couldn't stick to the script and that the script should not get too detailed. In this case, the rain itself dictated its own literature and guided the camera into secret wet paths we had never dreamed of when we outlined the film. It was an unexpectedly difficult subject to tackle. Many artistic problems were actually technical problems, and vice versa. Film experience in photographing rain was extremely limited, because a normal cameraman stops filming when it begins to rain. When *Rain* was finished, and shown in Paris, the French critics called it a *ciné-poem,* and its structure is actually more that of a poem than the prose of *The Bridge.* Its object is to show the changing face of a city, Amsterdam, during a shower.

The film opens with clear sunshine on houses, canals, and people in the streets. A slight wind rises, and the first drops of rain splash into the canals. The shower comes down harder, and the people hasten about their business under the protection of capes and umbrellas. The shower ends. The last drops fall, and the city's life returns to normal. The only continuity in *Rain* is the beginning, progress, and end of this shower. There are neither titles nor dialogue. Its effects were intended as purely visual. The actors are the rain, the raindrops, wet people, dark clouds, glistening reflections moving over wet asphalt, and so forth. The diffused light on the dark houses along the black canals produced an effect that I never expected. And the whole film gives the spectator a very personal and subjective vision. As in the lines of Verlaine:

> *Il pleure dans mon coeur*
> *Comme il pleut sur la ville.*

At that time I lived with and for the rain. I tried to imagine how everything I saw would look in the rain—and on the screen. It was part game, part obsession, part action. I had decided upon the several places in the city I wanted to film and I organized a system of rain watchers, friends who would telephone me from certain sections of town when the rain effects I wanted appeared. I never moved without my camera—it was with me in the office, laboratory, street, train. I lived with it, and when I slept it was on my bedside table so that if it was raining when I woke I could film the studio window over my bed. Some of the best shots of raindrops along the slanted studio windows were actually taken from my bed when I woke up. All the new problems in this film sharpened my observation and also forced me to relax the rigid and over-analytical method of filming that I had used in *The Bridge*.

With the swiftly shifting rhythm and light of the rain, sometimes changing within a few seconds, my filming had to be defter and more spontaneous. For example, on the big central square of Amsterdam I saw three little girls under a cape, and the skipping movements of their legs had the rhythm of raindrops. There had been a time when I thought that such good things could be shot tomorrow as well as today; but you soon learn that this is never true. I filmed those girls without a second's hesitation. They would probably never again walk at that hour on the square, or when they did it wouldn't be raining, and if it was raining they wouldn't have a cape, or skip in just that way, or it would be too dark—or something. So you film it immediately. With these dozens of interrelated factors you get the feeling of shooting—now or never. . . .

It took me about four months to get the footage I needed for *Rain*. To achieve the effect of the beginning of the shower as you now see it in the film, I had to photograph at least ten beginnings and out of these ten make the one *film* beginning. The rain itself was a moody actress who had to be humored and who refused anything but a natural make-up. I found that none of the new color-corrective film emulsions on the market were suitable for my rain problems. The old extra-rapid Agfa film with no color correction at all, and used without a filter, gave the best results. All lenses were used with a fully opened diaphragm, because most of the work was done with a minimum of light.

It's remarkable how easy it is to forget the most basic elements of your subject and how important those basic elements are to your work. In *Rain* I had to remind myself constantly that rain is wet—so you must keep the screen dripping with wetness—make the audience feel damp and not just dampness. When they think they can't get any wetter, *double* the wetness, show the raindrops falling in the water of the canal—make it super-wet. I was so happy when I noticed at one of the first screenings of the finished film that the audience looked around for their raincoats and were surprised to find the weather dry and clear when they came out of the theater.

To give the rain its fullest, richest quality I had to make sure that the sunlight that began and ended the film showed its typical differences. You have to catch the distinction between sunlight before rain and sunlight after rain; the distinction between the rich, strong enveloping sunlight before the rain and the strange, dreamy yellow light afterwards. I know that this sounds oversubtle, but it is important, and you have to be aware of it and remember to catch these subtleties with your camera.

In addition to careful photography, these nuances in light quality can be emphasized in movement. For example, I heightened the sharp quality of the sunlight that precedes the rain by keenly defined movements of light and shadow. The sharp, dark shadow of a footbridge rips across the wide deck of a boat passing swiftly underneath. This movement is cut off by immediate contact with a close-up of another boat moving in an opposite diagonal across the entire screen. As the rain begins I added to the changes in light, a change in these movements emphasizing the leisurely movement of barges, wet puffs of smoke, and waving reflections in the water. When cutting these shots, I was careful to avoid abrupt contrasts, letting them build up leisurely on the screen.

Another interesting thing I learned about the values of shots and movements was their relation to humor. In editing, I guided the eyes of the audience to the right of the screen by a close shot of water gushing out of a drainpipe, following this immediately by a shot of a dripping wet dog running along. My intention was merely to pick up the movement and rhythm in the pipe shot with the shot of the dog, and my simple movement continuity always got a laugh. If I had been a more skillful editor at that time, I would have made a more conscious use of such an effect, but I was still learning. I was still too preoccupied with movement and rhythm to be sufficiently aware of the special film capacities for communicating the humorous movement around us.

However, *Rain* did teach me a great deal about film emotion— much more than the emotional story of the *Breakers*. In editing *The Bridge* I had discovered the sad effect achieved by the rhythmic repetition of slow, heavy movements. In *Rain* I consciously used heavy, dark drops dripping in big, pear-shaped forms at long intervals across the glass of the studio window, to produce the melancholy feeling of a rainy day. The opposite effect of happiness or gaiety in a spring shower could be produced by many bright, small, round drops pounding against many surfaces in a variety of shots.

To strengthen the continuity of *Rain* I used the repetition of a second visual motif—birds flying in the sunlight, and then, as the rain starts, a flock moving against the gray sky (continuing a rhythm indicated in the previous shot by leaves rustling in the wind). During the storm I showed one or two birds flying restlessly about. After the rain has stopped there is a shot of some birds sitting quietly on the wet railing of a bridge.

I shot the whole film with my old Kinamo and an American De Vry hand camera. My assistant was a young Chinese sailor, Chang Fai, whom I had met as a waiter in a Chinese restaurant on the Zeedyk. Chang Fai had jumped a large Indies liner in order to stay in Holland and learn a profession before going back to Asia. His main job as my assistant was to hold an umbrella over my camera.

Grierson's *Drifters*

by Harry Alan Potamkin

This selection appeared in the October 1930 issue of Close Up, the Swiss-published magazine. The author was one of the most highly regarded American film critics of the 1920s and '30s.

The failure to recognize the method of montage as an integral process is the explanation of the sad attempts to sovietize films outside of the U.S.S.R. I have had the opportunity of seeing Grierson's *Drifters* at last; and it is the immediate provocation for my statement.

The zeal of the British, and Mr. Grierson himself, have been unfair to *Drifters*. The film does not deserve the anticipation the English comments have caused. As a first job of a young man, it is commendable. As an example of cinematic art, it is far from meritorious. Grierson has said he derived the *energies* of his film from the U.S.A. cinema, the *intimacies* from that of the U.S.S.R. If these could be joined together, the result would be hybrid. Why did Mr. Grierson not seek his energies also in the Soviet *kino?* Montage is an expression of the energies as well as of the intimacies. That is to say, montage is the progression and the intensive unit. Moreover, I suspect that Grierson has defined energies as muscular impact. The American film is a film of muscular impact. It cannot be said to contain anything so plural as energies, for the energies— the creative expressive energies—of the U.S.A. are suppressed. The energies of a film are the energies of a land.

Grierson, it must be said to his credit, sought to revitalize the documentation with a structural intention. Yet he did not bring to his desire for intimacies the scrutiny—the over-tonal interplay— which such a revitalization demands. Where are the people in his film? He is more engrossed with the independent graces of fish in the water—well-done details in themselves, but no part of the human process which the film was to be. The picture, therefore, is indeterminate; it is not the straight document such as *Business in Great Waters,* which satisfies its own demands; it is no revitalized revelation of human activity.

Nor does the film achieve the simplest of processes: that of accumulative muscular impact. It does not compel response to the fishers, to the sea. The filming of the nets as they are thrown over-board is good—catching them "on the go," but this too remains an independent grace, because it is not integrated in an ascending structure. This was a film intended to show labor. If Mr. Grierson thought to extend it to inferences beyond the facts of toil, to the total economy of exploitation, his attempts at inter-reference be-tween sea and market, fisher and broker, were certainly too in-adequate. The intention of labor is not fulfilled.

Moana (1926), directed by Robert J. Flaherty

Rien que les heures (1926),
directed by Alberto Cavalcanti

Berlin: The Symphony of a Great City (1927),
directed by Walter Ruttmann

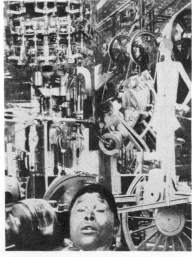

The Man With the Movie Camera (1928), directed by Dziga Vertov

Turksib (1929),
directed by
Victor Turin

Drifters (1929),
directed by
John Grierson

A Selection of Documentaries of the Period

Berlin: The Symphony of a Great City, Walter Ruttmann (1927)

The Bridge, Joris Ivens (1927)

Chang, Merian C. Cooper and Ernest B. Schoedsack (1927)

La Croisière noire, Léon Poirier (1926)

Drifters, John Grierson (1929)

The Eiffel Tower, René Clair (1927)

Finis Terrae, Jean Epstein (1928)

Grass, Merian C. Cooper and Ernest B. Schoedsack (1925)

H₂O, Ralph Steiner (1929)

The Man With the Movie Camera, Dziga Vertov (1928)

Mannahatta, Charles Sheeler and Paul Strand (1921)

Mechanics of the Brain, V. I. Pudovkin (1926)

Melody of the World, Walter Ruttmann (1926)

Moana, Robert J. Flaherty (1926)

Nanook of the North, Robert J. Flaherty (1922)

People on Sunday, Robert Siodmak (1929)

Rain, Joris Ivens (1929)

Rien que les heures, Alberto Cavalcanti (1926)

Turksib, Victor Turin (1929)

The Twenty-Four-Dollar Island, Robert J. Flaherty (1925)

Voyage au Congo, Marc Allégret and André Gide (1926)

La Zone, Georges Lacombe (1927)

PART TWO / 1930–1940

The Four Hundred Million (1939), directed by Joris Ivens

From Innovation to Involvement
by Lewis Jacobs

The basic force behind it [documentary] was social not aesthetic. It was a desire to make drama from the ordinary . . .
JOHN GRIERSON

The 1930s began with a great depression and ended with a world war. It was a period, first, of severe domestic upheaval; later, of a rallying to national unity. In the turbulence of the early thirties the documentary film began to be used with frequency—and with telling effect—as a means of political persuasion, and by the time the decade came to a close it had been developed into a major medium of propaganda.

The documentary as an instrument for propagating social and political views got its biggest initial boost in Britain, where earnest young filmmakers, under the aegis of John Grierson, turned out pictures aimed at exposing injustices inflicted on working men. Many films made by this group attracted worldwide attention. *Contact* (1932–3), *The New Generation* (1932), *Telephone Workers* (1933), *Aero Engine* (1933), *Granton Trawler* (1934), *Shipyard* (1934–5), *Housing Problems* (1935), *Song of Ceylon* (1935), *Coal Face* (1936), *Night Mail* (1936), *We Live in Two Worlds* (1937), and *North Sea* (1939) won international prestige as powerful documents for social betterment. Many of the group's directors, including Edgar Anstey, Alberto Cavalcanti, Arthur Elton, Stuart Legg, Paul Rotha, Harry Watt, and Basil Wright, achieved distinction for their artistry and their humanity.

On the continent, notably in Soviet Russia and Nazi Germany, where government sponsorship decreed a documentary philosophy aimed at national glorification, documentaries that were brilliant in technique emerged. In Russia, Vertov's film, *Enthusiasm* (1930), was a virtuoso performance in praise of the successful creation of the Don Basin industrial area. The picture dramatized the love relationship between Soviet workers and their machines in fulfilling the great objective of the First Five Year Plan. *Three Songs About Lenin* (1933–4), by the same director, lyrically celebrated the memory of the Father of the Revolution in heroic style, telling the story of Lenin's life through the songs of peasants and long lines of freezing mourners at his funeral in snow-covered Moscow.

German documentary in the pre-war period of the Third Reich was concerned exclusively with what Kracauer called the effort "to suppress the faculty of understanding which might have undermined the basis of the whole (Nazi) system." *Triumph of the Will* (1936), a film by Hitler's favorite director, Leni Riefenstahl, recorded the Nazi Party's Nuremberg convention, a gigantic and elaborately organized extravaganza deliberately staged "in concert with the preparations for the camera work." The rigor and discipline of pictorial composition and the imposing authority of formal arrangement were used with remarkable force to communicate the power of the Nazi mystique and to exalt its fuehrer, Adolph Hitler. *Olympia* (1938), also by Riefenstahl, was intended to document the Olympic Games held in Berlin in 1936 in such a way as to advance the notion of Aryan superiority, but this objective was defeated—despite an imaginative filmic rendering that elevated the event to a significance beyond mere time and place—when the black American athlete, Jesse Owens, turned out to be the hero of the Games.

In contrast to Europe, where government sponsorship was very much in evidence, American documentary filmmakers depended on their own resources, or the occasional support of progressive groups, unions, and educational foundations. U.S. government agencies were slow to recognize the effectiveness of the medium.

As in England, the dominant filmmakers in the U.S. in the early thirties were supporters of the political left and the product of these filmmakers poured out in a crusade of pamphleteering documentaries aimed at spreading social and political enlightenment. Especially effective was an informal group of New York City filmmakers known as the Film and Photo League. In addition to short guerrilla newsreels concerned with strikes, evictions, hunger marches, and unemployment, it made a number of longer pictures. Two were notable: *Taxi* (1934), which dealt with the cab drivers' strike and the benefits of militant unionism, and *Sheriff* (1934), which showed the inhumanity of evicting people from their homes.

Nykino (New York Kino) was a more formal offspring of the Film and Photo League. Its purpose was to study and advance the documentary form. During its researches it produced *The World Today* (1936), a film consisting of two episodes: evictions in a community housing project, and the atrocities of the Black Legion (a white vigilante organization) in mid-western America. The picture combined documentary shooting, archives material, and staged re-creations of news events. It was not unlike the then recently established *March of Time* in its concept of screen journalism, but its intention was to counteract the latter's conservative viewpoint with a more progressive interpretation.

Nykino led to the formation of Frontier Films, "a non-profit organization devoted to the production of realistic films of American life." Starting in the mid-thirties, Frontier Films, which borrowed the best of European technique, attracted a great deal of attention with a number of documentaries of power and importance. *The Wave* (1934–5) dramatized the birth of militantism among oppressed fishermen along the Gulf of Vera Cruz. *Heart of Spain* (1937) concerned itself with American medical aid for the Spanish Loyalists. *China Strikes Back* (1937) documented the role of the Eighth Route Army in helping to unite Chinese resistance against the Japanese invaders. *People of Cumberland* (1937) presented the struggle of the Cumberland mountaineers to build a union and fight serfdom. *Return to Life* (1938) revealed the problems of the rehabilitation of wounded Spanish Loyalist soldiers.

During these years a number of independent documentary filmmakers vividly reported the growing crisis in Europe. Joris Ivens, with Ernest Hemingway, made *Spanish Earth* (1937) behind the Loyalist lines in the Spanish Civil War. Herbert Kline and Alexander Hammid, in *Crisis* (1938), documented the disintegration of Czechoslovakia after the Munich Pact. The same team covered the Nazi invasion of Poland and the beginning of World War II in *Lights Out in Europe* (1939). Joris Ivens's *The Four Hundred Million* (1938) depicted the Chinese fight against the Japanese invasion of 1937. Julien Bryan's *Siege* (1939–40) captured the human story behind the fall of Poland.

A film that might have become one of the most significant documentaries of the age, *Que viva Mexico!*, was never completed. What happened was this: In 1930 the great Russian director, Sergei M. Eisenstein, was invited to come to the United States to work for Paramount Pictures. Two years later, after his remarkable scripts for *An American Tragedy* and *Sutter's Gold* had been rejected, he got independent financing—with funds raised by Upton Sinclair—to make a documentary picture in Mexico. He had been at work for more than a year when his backers decided to drop the project. They recalled the director and took the photographed but unedited material away from him. Later, after he had returned to Russia, they released a condensed version, cut by a Hollywood editor, with the title *Thunder Over Mexico* (1934). A cry of protest went up in America and Europe, led by the film magazine Experimental Cinema and followed by other serious film journals, film students, critics, and intellectuals. The protestors insisted that Eisenstein be allowed to assemble the film himself, according to his original concept of its montage, but the clamor was to no avail.

Next to the disaster of Eisenstein's Mexican film, the documentary event of the period was Pare Lorentz's production of two films for the U.S. Resettlement Administration, *The Plow That Broke the Plains* (1936) and *The River* (1937). Other governments had been active in the production of documentary films, as we have noted, but until Pare Lorentz, until then known only as a movie critic, made his films for the Resettlement Administration, the U.S. government had shown little interest in producing films for the general public. *The Plow That Broke the Plains,* a dramatic report on efforts to alleviate the conditions of farmers in the "dust bowl" of Oklahoma, was acclaimed everywhere as an important record of social reform and a triumph of lyric documentary. Lorentz's second film, *The River,* was a panoramic history of the Mississippi Basin, showing the effects of soil erosion on land "twice impoverished . . . first by the Civil War, later by the greed of lumber mills," and the improvements made by the Tennessee Valley Authority's program of soil conservation and flood control.

The River was clearly the freshest and most lyrical expression of American documentary to date. With poetry and music woven with hard editorial content into an organic rhythmic structure, his film was hailed as an "epic rooted in American history, American geography, and American politics." Seen by millions of people in more than 5,000 theaters, *The River* at last made the word "documentary" a part of the vocabulary of the nation.

The period was also distinguished by a challenging film called *The City* (1939). Produced by the American Institute of Planners, from a treatment by Lorentz and a scenario by Henwar Rodakiewicz, and directed by Willard Van Dyke and Ralph Steiner, the film traced the development of our modern cities, showing how they had been neglected, and ending with a plea for planning cities of human feeling.

The City's relevance to the realities of contemporary experience was reflected in one of the most urgent issues of the times: the need to formulate a design for living in an environment grown more and more destructive of humanity.

The City summed up graphically the decade's longing for a better life.

Jean Vigo's *A propos de Nice*

by Boris Kaufman

*This selection, based on an article written by the film's cameraman
for the magazine Cine Club of February 1949, is included in an
index of the work of Jean Vigo compiled by Joseph and
Harry Feldman and published by the British Film Institute.*

A documentary about the French Riviera. It has been described as
"one of the most unconventional documentaries ever made—with
a bitterness and irony comparable to Von Stroheim's, the camera
explores this center of middle-class decadence, the monstrous
hotels with their armies of servants, the baroque casinos, the
amorous elderly women with their ruthless gigolos, the stinking
alleys and grimy *bistros* filled with tramps, ponces, fences: a scath-
ing contrast of the idle poor and the idle rich" (George Morrison in
Sequence 6).

The film, unfortunately, has been unavailable for years, and was
never publicly shown in the United States or Great Britain. It was
three months in the making. . . . *Point de vue documenté* was the
phrase used by Vigo to describe his first film.

On June 14, 1930, *A propos de Nice* was shown at the Vieux
Colombier, to a special audience composed of the *Groupement des
Spectateurs d'avant-garde*. Vigo gave an introductory talk, called
Vers un cinéma social, in which he paid tribute to the work of Luis
Buñuel and outlined some of his own ideas:

"I would like to talk about a more defined form of social cinema,
something to which I am closest: the social documentary—or, more
precisely, *point de vue documenté.*

"In this area of endeavor, I affirm, the camera is King—or at
least President of the Republic.

"I don't know whether the result will be a work of art, but I
am sure it will be cinema. Cinema, in the sense that no other art,
no science, can take its place.

"The maker of social documentaries is a man thin enough to
squeeze through a Rumanian keyhole and shoot Prince Carol
getting up in his nightshirt—assuming that were a spectacle worthy
of interest. He is a fellow small enough to squat under the chair of
the croupier—the Great God of the casino at Monte Carlo—and
that, as you may well imagine, is no easy thing.

"Social documentary is distinct from the ordinary short film and the weekly newsreel in that its creator will establish his own point of view: he will dot his own i's.

"If it doesn't involve an artist, it at least involves a man. . . . Conscious behavior cannot be tolerated, character must be surprised by the camera if the whole 'documentary' value of this kind of cinema is to be achieved.

"We shall achieve our end if we can reveal the hidden reason for a gesture, if we can extract from an ordinary person his interior beauty—or a caricature of him—quite by chance, if we can reveal his complete inner spirit through his purely external manifestations.

"*A propos de Nice* is only a rough draft. . . . In this film, the description of a whole town begging from sheer laziness, we are spectators at the trial of a particular world. After indicating this life and atmosphere of Nice—and, alas, elsewhere—the film proceeds to a generalized impression of gross pleasures, to different signs of a grotesque existence, of flesh and of death. These are the last twitchings of a society that neglects its own responsibilities to the point of giving you nausea and making you an accomplice in a revolutionary solution."

He seemed both to love and to hate the town in which, for reasons of health, he and his wife had been obliged to live for two years.

Nice was getting ready for the Carnival. . . . The focal point was the Promenade des Anglais, center of action (or inaction) for the internationally lazy.

The method was to take by surprise facts, actions, attitudes, expressions, and to stop shooting as soon as the subject became conscious of being photographed.

Le point de vue documenté.

Old Nice, its narrow streets, washing hung between the houses, the baroque Italian cemetery. Pleasures. Regattas. Warships at anchor. Hotels. Arrival of tourists. . . . Factories. An old woman. The young girl changing her dress in the middle of the Promenade (trick shot) and finally appearing nude. A burial service. . . . Crocodiles. Sun. The female ostrich. The Carnival, the Battle of Flowers, the gradually slackening dances.

Above all this absurd gaiety, the ominous vistas of chimneys.

All this may look a little naïve now, but we were sincere. We rejected out of hand anything that was picturesque without significance, any facile contrasts. The story had to be understood without commentary or subtitles. We shot the film relying on the evocation of ideas by purely visual means. Which is why, in the cutting, we were able to juxtapose the Promenade des Anglais with the Nice cemetery, where marble figures (baroque style) had the same ridiculous features as the human beings on the Promenade.

Working with Vigo—his unfailing taste, his integrity, his depth and his lightness, his nonconformism, the absence of any kind of routine—took me into a kind of filmmaker's paradise. It was ideal!

Editor's note: The film *A propos de Nice* recently became available in the United States.

The Making of *Que viva Mexico!*
by Morris Helprin

*This selection from Experimental Cinema, No. 4, 1934, is an
account of the making of Eisenstein's famed Mexican film which,
as a result of a falling-out with its backer, Upton Sinclair,
was never completed in the form its director intended.*

"Que viva Mexico!"

It is the first film made in the Western hemisphere to assume the
mantle of maturity. The furthest step yet from the idiocies of corn-
fed Hollywood. It turns its tail up at the banal; thumbs its nose at
the benign. It is pictorial rhetoric of such vital force that it thunders
and roars. Yet it contains every aspect of the popular cinema.

"Que viva Mexico!"

That day at Los Remedios, when we walked over the hills in
search of a suitable location, served as an indication of Eisenstein's
preciseness, his exciting demands that his subject be even in quality.
All Mexico around us was "beautiful enough to swoon in." Here
was no prettiness of the postcardy cinema, none of your oak-
paneled pictures that need but sprinklings of chemical brilliants
to turn them into revolting chromos. The top of a mountain and an
ancient aqueduct jutting at a seven-thousand-foot height into a
stilled canopy of swan-white clouds. You could set your camera
down at almost any spot and grind. And have a beautiful scenic.

But the Russian, followed hastily by Tisse, his cameraman;
Aragon, a young Mexican intellectual who serves as a guide, interpreter, and go-between, a camera boy, and myself, trailed by five
peons who were the day's actors at a peso each, led a frantic chase
to find *the* spot. Following which were at least a dozen of *the* spots.

Eisenstein was introduced to Mexico by his Mexican friend,
the film-student, Agustin Aragon Leiva, whose forebears took root
400 years ago and whose love for his country is as intense as
Eisenstein's love for the cinema. Through this young Mexican and
other friends of the Russian, Mexico was thrown practically into
Eisenstein's lap. There is hardly anything in the country not at his
disposal.

Toiling in the sun from early in the morning through the noon
that is characteristically Mexican with its burning heat, until the

landscape began to cool, we dragged Christ from the church to lie, pathetically unaware of Eisenstein, staring at the blue bowl that is Heaven, while a machine recorded its image on revolving celluloid. Poor Father who art not in Eisenstein's heaven, hallowed by thy name now, for who knows how you will be used eventually in this record of living Mexico!

A fine Christ the largest statue was. Brought from Spain with blood painted beautifully down his sides and a slot, like openings into which one inserts nickels, carefully chiseled in the thinnish chest. And the beard, fine pictorially, stylized into a Grecian combing with decorative loops. The whole, sprinkled with the dusts of decades that have filtered beneath the crevices of the glass covering, lay on purple silk in the open courtyard, while the populace of Los Remedios gathered in appropriate awe—awe and reverence in spite of the boy who ordinarily pulled the bell ropes in the steeple, but who now insisted on passing wind against a nearby tombstone and who mingled his derisive laughter with the reverberations of his gaseous intestine.

And the padre, inducing a member of his flock to shed a pearly tear on the statue as the camera ground on. And the two little girls who sold votive candles who were recruited for the scene but who fled at the last minute, showing up later on the roof, beshawled and still timid before this Frankenstein monster.

"Perhaps," says the padre, "we could have some enlarged pictures of this for the members of my parish?"

And Eisenstein assenting a too-ready "yes."

No food for us during the day's work except a bottle of warm beer that was as quickly spat out at the flies.

No rest while Eisenstein sees light in the skies. After eleven months of it he is as active in his picturemaking as during the first days. What significance fatigue, when this will be the first film made on the American continent worth preserving for its sociological import? What are the dangers of jungle, mountain, or sea, when you coincidentally explore human nature?

How can men like Carleton Beals, Stuart Chase, and the like, live and travel in a country for months, years, without sensing what the Russian grasped in so short a while? How can writers who have lived decades in Mexico publish learned and boring works on the country without so much as nodding in the direction of certain Mexican fundamentals? Chase regurgitates a literary catalogue that tells about an isolated community, hardly representative of Mexico, which, because its bandstand is like a bandstand of another township, is labelled the "Middletown" of Mexico. He wonders naïvely about silk stockings, radios, and autos. Beals's connection with Mexican officialdom would never permit an undistorted view of conditions as they exist.

Yet Eisenstein walks in and senses the basic force that motivates Mexican life and that will eventually be the prompting means of securing freedom. He has recognized the part that woman plays in the social and economic life of the country and around this has constructed his film.

As an admirer of the work of Rivera, the Diego Rivera who is now accepting fabulous sums for painting frescoes in America, his cinematic work was first influenced by that painter's representations. The fiesta, the flowers, the color, and the action were of prime importance in the early stages of filmization, but one wonders, after hearing of the change, whether or not Eisenstein's film will not more closely resemble the lower-keyed work of Orozco whose sympathies are more clearly defined, less prettified with paint, and hardly sentimental journeys in line.

Eisenstein, the newcomer, the enthusiast, has tried to make the most of a beauty and a glory that are rarely matched elsewhere on the face of the globe. As his work progressed his story developed and he made the discovery that served as a thread upon which he has hung his episodes.

This discovery, namely, Eisenstein's recognition of the importance of woman's position in that country as in no other in the world, converted his film from a dimensionalized fresco to the presentation of a sociological problem as old itself as Mexico and as important as its breath of life. In reality, woman makes no appearance in the film except in a few secluded instances. But her influence is as subtle as the Indian's overconquest and swallowing-up of his Spanish conqueror.

The peon is ruled by his wife, the soldier goes to war but refuses to fight unless his wife is with him. There particularly is woman important, for sometimes she is the advanced guard, going forward to prepare a town for the force's comfort, sometimes, when there is fighting, bringing up the rear with consolation and ministering presence.

Mexico City politicians are frequently judged by their mistresses. It is common practice there to have both wife and mistress, one with a complete knowledge of the other.

In Tehuantepec the woman is absolute, not only ruling, but doing the heavy work as well, while the husband dozes at home, happy for the first time to be unleashed from the fetters of responsibility.

With the female's importance in mind and the physical beauty of the country to consider on the other hand, a beauty bewildering in its variety, ranging from tropical to frigid country, Eisenstein had to combine elements into a whole that would appeal in subject matter as well as pictorial beauty. Eisenstein's secret is his universality—his appeal to the man in the street as well as the man of letters.

He therefore divided his picture into five irregular parts. The fifth and last episode will also serve as an epilogue. There is a prologue as well. All this will be included in a single film of 9 or 10 reels.

The first part he may call *Tehuantepec: Paradise*. It is here, a tropical province of cocoanut palms, verdant fields, and easy living, that woman is absolute. She tills the fields, barters in the marketplace, and rules the home. Her husband is a procreative force and no more.

The matchless carriage of the Tehuantepec woman, together with her beauty of form, due to the heavy objects she has carried on her head for generations, is a pictorial poem in itself. A supple body with strong conical breasts and a straightness of limb ascribed only to the ancients. Such characters pervade the reels.

The second episode is *Maguey*. In it Eisenstein has stressed man's supremacy, but indicated his reliance upon his female counterpart. The entire sequence occurs on a farm which in virility of landscape is in complete contrast with that of the preceding chapter. Here a phallic symbolism is engaged to emphasize the complete *masculinity* of the terrain. He accents the stem of the maguey, the upright stripes of the peon's zarape (the shawl-overcoat-blanket of the native), the unmistakable masculine strength of the land where a living is wrested by force only.

With the maguey plant, which sometimes rises to ten-foot heights, as a thematic runner, his drama is enacted against a background of twin volcanoes. The cruel charros, attired in their silverbangled vests, swinging henaquén lassoes, ride their prancing mounts over the head of the boy who has been planted alive, chin deep, on a flat-topped mound.

The third part may be called *Romance,* the lull before the storm. In this part Eisenstein's satirical thrusts will penetrate and punctuate a pretty affair about a bullfighter and his love for another man's wife. It is the interlude in preparation for the ensuing drama which is a turgid, seething account of revolution—all revolution—not alone of Mexico, but extending through the ages in which man has arisen from his stocks to brandish the torch. It is laid in Mexico, but its import is much more universal.

And following this is a promise of a perfect Mexico—one without strife, want, incipient bloodshed. This is a sort of liqueur. You take it or leave it. You can always ignore the dessert.

Whether purposely or not, Eisenstein has so completely covered Mexico that it will be difficult for another picture-director to enter the country and make a scene without repeating. The locales are so varied as to permit any form of life and existence and, taking full advantage, the Russian runs the gamut. Mexico harbors romance and glamour, and cruelty and privation. There are tropics, mountains, deserts, jungles. The director has traversed it from one section to another. All this is in the picture, pieced together, as only Eisenstein can do it.

This man with two others, one of whom grinds a simple camera, has completely thrown off the fetters of the Hollywood system of picturemaking, and has exploited Mexico thoroughly in a manner never done before, having been aided on all sides because this time the exploitation is all to Mexico's advantage.

Comparative working costs are interesting to note. The day's work at Los Remedios cost but very few dollars. His equipment consisted of a 400-foot-load French-made camera, two gilded reflectors, and five actors, each earning one peso (38 cents at the current rate). Transportation cost a few more pesos. Add to this the incidental developing, printing, and negative costs, together with the cutting and final duplication, and the sum total is surprisingly small. Naturally, there are days when hundreds of persons will be engaged for scenes and the costs soar accordingly, but for the most part the expenses are negligible.

In Hollywood the same business would have entailed transportation for the stars and directors, two or three cameras, artificial illumination, if necessary, overhead at the studio that covers a multitude of such sins as publicity, props, advertising, costumes, etc., etc. Somebody's system is basically at fault.

Eisenstein says that the cinema is the representative art of today as painting was of yesterday. He has already buried painting. He explains the growth in attendance at art exhibits as a result of publicity and additional newspapers devoting more space to them, and not as a manifestation of a naturally stimulated life. He says he knows how to do nothing but work at motion pictures.

But he forgets for the moment the monastic seclusion into which he retires on occasion to work on his volume of aesthetics, which will devote a sufficient amount of space to the heretofore sorrowfully neglected cinema.

He also forgets his interest in mathematics (that day as Los Remedios when he had to wait ten minutes for something, he drew out of his pocket a paperbacked Russian volume on higher mathematics and in a moment was lost in its intricacies, while perched in the cabin of a truck). He forgets the papers he writes tirelessly for every advanced journal on the cinema, mostly free. The cinema may be his profession, but his high, broad forehead sees beyond its technical limitations into a meaning that may exploit or advance life, the living, the helpless. Directing a scene, turning a crank, cutting a film, he considers but the cog in a huge wheel that is beginning to turn with tremendous speed.

Eisenstein may return to the Soviet Union next month (March) with his comrades, Alexandrov and Tisse, to film a document in celebration of the fifteenth anniversary of the Bolshevik Revolution.

Que viva Mexico! may or may not stir an eddy of interest. Because of the flooded book marts that sag with volumes on tourist Mexico, there is a tremendous curiosity about the country. Even now everyone there is planning for the influx of Americans tired of the transatlantic crossing. Because of a universal undercurrent of unrest, the message of the film may stir a reaction. Because of its pictorial beauty it will be something to look at. Because of its mature outlook it will merit serious consideration. Who knows what it may do for Mexico?

Eisenstein's Film on Mexico
by Agustin Aragon Leiva

*This selection also is taken from Experimental Cinema, No. 4,
1934, which identified the author as a special assistant to
Eisenstein on the controversial film. This interpretation of the
film, the publication noted, was "authorized by Eisenstein."*

Subject of the Film

Projecting the concrete into the abstract, a greater generalization: the subject of the film had to be a selection of the fundamental elements of the Mexican drama.

Therefore, it deals:

with all our historical and prehistorical periods,

with our main geographical sections that have remarkably conditioned collective life,

and with all influences that are foreign.

So, the subject of the film is

the whole Mexico. Past, present, and future.

As ages in Mexico are not in a vertical sequence, but in a horizontal development, spread out like an unusual fan.

Time of the Action

Being ideal, the construction, considered as a whole time, is dissolved in a combination of epochs. But on quite a few occasions it becomes definite.

Structure of the Film

Like a symphony, in which different movements are unified in spirit and form through the expression of the same IDEA of a superior order.

Technique

The cinematographic melodies have their own counterpoint and every one requires a different harmonization.

In this fashion there are as many rhythms, graphic compositions, and photographies, and, finally, montages, as there are parts in the film.

Conflicts

Spontaneity, or nature in itself—

Man with nature

Man with man

and the emphasis of the conflict between the two principal geographical sections of the country—the tropics and the highlands, where air is subtle as the breath of a blithe spirit and life is hard.

Each one producing different cultures, habits, types, problems, and struggles.

But both of them the same in the final result produced by revolution, through which the Mexican people has striven to build up its collective unity—and still is striving.

Conclusion

The film is a poem of a sociological character. Rather an interpretative essay on Mexican evolution.

By its deep significance and form, I consider it a new type of *genre* in cinematography, with no antecedents, and achieving perfection at once. Also a film very difficult to surpass and even to imitate.

The Elements Described

Eisenstein uses about three thousand different elements:

all distinctive and important types of Indians,

Meztizos,

Spaniards,

Europeanized and Americanized Mexicans,

genuine *costumes* and multifarious combinations of them with background, illuminations and faces . . .

architecture—primitive, Mayan, Aztec, Toltec, etc.

colonial Spanish at the periods corresponding to three hundred years . . .

all tropical landscapes on both coasts, so combined as to look just like a tropic splendid beyond literary description and never seen on the screen before:

the desert, the sacred snow-peaked mountains,

woods, rivers and the two oceans,

animals of every kind, especially monkeys,

the plants that symbolize human struggle. So, he uses:

palmtrees of about twenty types,

the Maguey plant in the most plastic variety,

the Henaquén plant,

the virile cactus (organs)

every one correlated to the group-drama it conditions:

bullfights

ritual dances
chiefs
skeletons, the very counterpoint of the play when combined
with:
toys.
Besides this:
predominance of women, or matriarchate;
the dominion of men,
confusion.
And an infinite variety of combinations of the above-listed
elements.

In this way Eisenstein has practically stolen from the Mexican nation all her secrets, dreams, and feelings accumulated during
five thousand years.

But all this looks very monumental. The interesting fact to be
noticed lies in the choice of materials. Eisenstein has selected only
the genuine, the pure, the refined, the generical, because he has a
wonderful taste. So he rejects the exotic, which has been the passion
of all tourists and superficial writers who have visited Mexico in the
last hundred years.

Eisenstein has proven to be the greatest bandit of our beauty!

He deserves capital punishment. We should burn him at the
stake!

If we don't do it, we should at least leave him to the rage of the
legion of his imitators and followers who are going to find out that
he sucked up everything and left nothing to their craving for the
exotic.

Some Details

He shows actual primitive life as a paradise, and this can be
verified by anyone at Tehuantepec, for instance.

And just after this delightful impression he shows the contrast
of the hard life of the high plateaus, so near to the skies, where
beauty endures, but there is no abundance and pain dominates.

We are sad, tragedy beats our emotion; we are suffering. Then,
just like in Beethoven's symphonies, the *scherzo* comes.

There is joy, and external over-adorned beauty,
gayety, fiesta, celebrations, love.
We are happy, we feel adoration toward the magnificence
of life.

Then . . . humor . . . irony . . . sarcasm . . . and we get back to reality. . . .

Tragedy stills . . .

Revolution is on the wheel . . .

Here, the Greek conception of the theatrical—but the chorus are desert steppes, calcinated mountains, the sound of machineguns. We get to despair.

Finale . . . The suffering of men upon Earth is not without an aim or a positive result. We return to happiness, an ideal happiness, that we wish for and that maybe we shall never see. But it exists. The Mexican revolution has to lead Mexicans to a place where they can rest in peace, working and fighting for the new order.

We see that in this film Eisenstein displays every kind of emotion: the religious, the mystic, the solemn, the dramatic and the melodramatic, the frivolous, the tragic, the humorous and the ironical, the sarcastic. But all is shaped in lyrical molds. The sensual appeal of his film is astonishingly great.

Philosophy

We must use this mysterious word to designate the profound significances that involve some parts of the film.

Eisenstein looks for collective expression and we cannot find these in contemporary art. Primitive mentality, primitive life call our attention to the collective expressions. Because, in the corresponding art, every trace, each detail, conveys a transcendental collective meaning. Subjective art, or so-called "art," imitates this achievement only in external appearances. But nothing is left for the fetishistic significance that is transmissible and understandable for everybody.

Eisenstein has realized this in a startling way, and we must look through his whole picture for this inner significance. I think that only a few will get it. Because symbolism of this kind is not detectable at first sight. For instance, there is a sharp connection between the thing portrayed in the maguey episode and the shape of this plant. Both relate to the predominance of men in the corresponding society group. And the whole composition follows the indications of this shape.

This is why Eisenstein sometimes looks to me as if he were thousands of years old!

And

I think that Eisenstein has brought bad luck to my country. We Mexicans are going to live eternally ashamed of our sins against ourselves. We had not realized how great and profound is our tradition, our life, our beauty. We were looking for cheap importations of the exotic. Despite the fact that we had a legion of heroes of our own discovery. But they were Mexicans and got immersed in the whole panorama and at the same time sank into oblivion. Now Eisenstein has signaled a road, but we feel too poor, feeble, and discouraged to follow his steps. For many years the Mexican land shall be dominated by intellectual sterility. Probably we'll wake up when the film of Eisenstein shall be only a memory of the past.

For he has practically stolen all the beauty of our country!

Mexico City, November 7, 1931

The Revolutionary Film — Next Step
by Leo T. Hurwitz

This selection appeared in New Theatre magazine (New York), for May 1934. The author, a film and television producer-director, is now chairman of the Graduate Program of Film and Television at New York University.

The film movement in America has for some time been faced with the problem of what film forms are its true concern. The Film and Photo Leagues have up to now produced mainly newsreels. They are necessary because of the rigid censorship and the malicious distortion that the capitalist film companies use in their treatment of events relative to labor and labor's struggles. These newsreels serve an agitational and revelational function to arouse the working class, and as a corrective for the lies of the capitalist agencies. A strike, demonstration, or hunger march is shown with the full brutalities of the police, with the full heroism and militancy of the workers, without the distractive mocking comment of the bourgeois announcer.

Because newsreels are fractional, atomic, and incomplete, the revolutionary movement has required a more synoptic form to present a fuller picture of the conditions and struggles of the working class. And so the synthetic documentary film has become an important form for film workers in the revolutionary movement— a form which allows for more inclusive and implicative comment on our class world than the discursive newsreel. For this great and rich medium the bourgeois filmers have had little use, since they cannot face the truths that the documentary camera can report. Their lies are better served by a more closely supervised camera in a shadowed studio under the kind sun of California. Aside from a few reels on sports, some shorts of believe-it-or-nots, and the half-truth-half-lies of industrial and "educational" films, Hollywood has ignored the vast possibilities of the synthetic film document.

Another factor, besides its great effectiveness, has determined the preoccupation of the radical moviemakers with the documentary film. At this time, with the radicalized working class as small as it is, it is almost impossible for economic and technical reasons to undertake the vast task of producing and distributing revolutionary dramatic films, which, in some ways, are capable of going beyond the document (as the synthetic document transcends the newsreel) in width of scope, synoptic approach, and ability to recreate events and emotions not revealable to the camera in the document.

The problems of documentary montage are very different from that of the dramatic film. The former may be called *external* montage, the creative comparison, contrast, and opposition of shots, externally related to each other, to produce an effect not contained in any of the shots—or, as Samuel Brody has well described it, "reality recorded on film strips and built up into wholes embodying our revolutionary interpretation of events." For this type of cutting, *The Man With the Movie Camera* is the textbook of technical possibilities. The dramatic film presents the problem of what may be called *internal* montage, which is essentially a recreative analysis and reconstruction of an internally related visual event in terms of shots of film, to reveal best the meaning of the event. The documentary film embodies the reporting on film of actual events and the creative addition of these bits of cinematographed reality to render an interpretation of that reality. The dramatic film involves in its cinematography the interpretive breaking-up of the recreated reality, and, in its montage, the synthesis of these analyzed elements to recreate the event on film from a given point of view.

Any acted sequence in an ordinary film will serve as an illustration of internal montage—any direct succession of acts to render a dramatic event. An example of external montage may be taken from a recent newsreel compilation by the New York Film and Photo League. The newsreel shots are sure: President Roosevelt signing a state paper and looking up at the camera with his inimitable self-satisfied smile, and a shot of fleet maneuvers—two shots taken in widely separated times and places and not essentially (but *externally*) related to each other. By virtue of splicing the shot of the warships just after Roosevelt signs the paper, and following the threatening ships of war with the rest of the first shot (Roosevelt looks up and smiles), a new meaning not contained in either shot, but a product of their new relation on film, is achieved—the meaning of the huge war preparation program of the demagogic Roosevelt government.

External and internal montage, as described here, are by no means mutually exclusive. Both may be used, and in fact have been used frequently to complement each other—sometimes with emphasis on the document, as in *Ten Days That Shook the World,* sometimes with the emphasis on the recreated drama, as in *The End of Saint Petersburg.*

A mixed form of the synthetic document and the dramatic is the next proper concern of the revolutionary film movement: to widen the scope of the document, to add to the document the recreated events necessary to it but resistant to the documentary camera eye —a synthetic documentary film which allows for material which recreates and fortifies the actuality recorded in the document, and makes it clearer and more powerful.

Movies About Us

by Robert Gessner

This selection first appeared in New Theatre magazine in June 1935. Prof. Gessner was the author of "The Moving Image."

Every time I come out of a movie, when I hit the hard pavement and the overhead lights and the street jam, I say, "Well, that's just about what you expected, wasn't it?" And despite the reality of the taxi brakes and monoxide I'd turn around and go back in the next time. That is, I used to. But I haven't gone back since *Black Fury*.

Well, then, if the movies Hollywood offers us continue to slobber vulgarities based on decadent philistine tastes and ideas, or drip sentimentalities designed to cool the heated brow of a socially-ill body politic, or romantic song-and-dances drawing curtains across the slow, plodding breadline, or now brazenly express the ideals of fascism—if all these continue month after month for years now, what are we going to do if we want movies about *us?*

First of all, who are we? We are labor in America. We are the mass of American people who are fed up with the National Run Around. And there's plenty more like us, getting more truth-conscious every day. And for us the cinema is not only a cultural habit, more than any other entertainment, but it is a *revolutionary necessity*. Lenin once told Lunacharsky that he should "bear in mind that of all the arts the cinema is the most important for us."

Who, then, is going to make our films? The answer is obvious— if we can no longer expect Hollywood to make films of reality, films of labor, then we must make them for ourselves.

Immediately, a hundred questions arise: how, where, with what? These inquiries need not floor us this time. The answer is: It's been done. The baby's been growing nicely all this time, thank you—in fact, too quietly. Not enough people know, have heard, and are assisting. It is a shame that more people have not come to an understanding and appreciation of the work of the Film and Photo League. Fortunately, the recent premiere of the League's latest production gives me an opportunity to review the achievements of the revolutionary film to date.

Taxi is the first feature film in America about *us* and produced by *us*. Although it is the first enacted movie by the Film and Photo

League, it will perhaps be on record as time goes on as their worst. From the point of view of production, it is disappointing: the photography is erratic and amateurish; the direction is almost entirely absent and the editing is weak, the titles misplaced and poorly worded. The scenario, if any, is so much in the background that you feel the cameraman is doing the writing while shooting. All this is obvious. But these faults are *not* the important features of this film. They are redeemable faults, which can be easily corrected by experienced and competent creators. The importance of *Taxi* is that it shows *what can be done*. Because of the material it deals with —the struggles of the taxi-drivers—the film is interesting. The raw meat of social reality is preferable diet to the creampuffs of Hollywood. This we know. We have the material for production. What is needed is the immediate production of good films.

The Film and Photo League has done pioneering work in its production of shorts. It has proven a technical proficiency in editing newsreels and shooting short stuff around New York. *America Today,* for example, is a fine example of revolutionary montage. From commercial newsreels the story of America today has been graphically told. The section on Roosevelt is perfect: showing the President signing a bill—then a shot of the Fleet at maneuvers firing off broadsides—then Roosevelt blotting his signature and looking up at the camera and giving the ol' campaign smile. The Ambridge massacre sequence is also in *America Today*. I'd like to know why this short hasn't been more widely shown, especially to workers' clubs throughout the country. And the workers will wonder too, when they've seen it, why it's been in a vault. The commercial distributors took the Ambridge shots off the screen when they saw it, believing such true "propaganda" too hot to handle. Has it been too cold for us?

In *World in Review* Hitler salutes and the Hitlerites march. Here also is a perfect montage of Mussolini speaking, where his oratory (silent) is interspersed with the cheers of the crowd: the demagogue jerking the puppet strings. *World in Review* likewise deserves a wider distribution.

United Front is a documented short on the recent Madison Square demonstration against fascist legislation. The indoor shots are as good as any of its type I've seen. The same can be said for the documentary job just finished on the I.W.O. congress, also in

Madison Square. The direction and editing of Edward Kern in *United Front* is excellent. This short should do much, when distributed through the American League Against War and Fascism, to gain new recruits in the fight.

East Side, West Side is a hodge-podge of interesting shots, attempting to contrast the life in New York on the opposite sides of Fifth Avenue. This is a swell idea, and should be taken up more seriously and done probably as a feature. The shots, for instance, of models in expensive show-windows and the revolving doors and the fainting Prometheus of Rockefeller Center are both humorous and pathetic alongside of West Side breadlines and evictions.

Marine is the best creative short yet done by the League. It was directed by Edward Kern and shot by Leo Seltzer. The short is an attempt to portray the struggles of longshoremen, and is done by shooting their life from the moment they awake at dawn, sleeping out on the docks of New York. The photography of this early sequence is artistically excellent. The actors are the workers themselves, many of them not knowing they were being shot, and the result has been better than most Hollywood casting. *Marine* is weak, however, on scenario. This is the general weakness of all the creative productions of the League. The acting of *Taxi* is the best part of the film, because the taxi-drivers themselves did their stuff together with professionals from the Theatre Union—but the scenario was the weakest factor, as it was in *East Side, West Side*.

We have the actors—the American working class is our casting list—and we have some trained producers. A few of us have done time in the jails of Hollywood. What is needed is coordinated action for production—and money. These problems can best be solved by reorganizing and enlarging the League until it becomes for the workers in the field of cinema what the New Theatre League already is in the theatre. Then we can have full-length movies with sound which will be, as a weapon *against* war and fascism and *for* the workers, "the most important for us."

Filming Real People
by Robert Flaherty

This account of his work by the "dean of American documentarians" appeared in Movie Makers, December 1934.

The question that I am most frequently asked after a screening of *Man of Aran* is, "Where was your camera during those sea scenes?" or, "How could you get those steady near shots of the small boats when they were being battered by gigantic waves?" The answer should, of course, be obvious to anyone who has used long-focus lenses. Yet it seldom fails to elicit surprise, and I, in turn, am surprised to find that lenses of focal length greater than six inches are so little used in motion-picture photography, despite the fact that still-portrait photographers have found them valuable for years.

It was in the South Seas while I was making *Moana* that I first became aware of the peculiar virtues of the long-focus lens. Of course, the chief function of the telephoto is obvious—one can photograph objects at a great distance. Without the telephoto lens, most wild-animal photography would be impossible. I had used the telephoto lens on my first picture, *Nanook of the North*, notably in the animal episodes, such as the walrus hunt. In the South Seas, however, it was in filming intimate scenes, and particularly in making portraits, that I learned the true value of long-focus lenses. I began using them to take close-ups, in order to obviate self-consciousness on the part of my subjects. The Samoans, I found, acted much more naturally with the camera thirty or forty feet away than when I was cranking right under their noses—and in this I am sure the Samoans are no different from other folk.

But the elimination of self-consciousness was not the only good thing that came from the experiment. The shots, when projected on the screen, showed a quality I had never been able to achieve with lenses of wider angle. The figures had a roundness, a stereoscopic quality that gave to the picture a startling reality and beauty. Almost all of *Moana* was shot with lenses of six-inches focal length and upward. Shots of the Samoan boy in the top of a tall cocoanut tree became intimate close-ups with my twelve-inch lens set up on the ground seventy-five feet below.

In middle-distance outdoor photography, too, I learned the superiority of long-focus lenses. In photographing a Samoan dance in a grove of breadfruit trees, instead of using a two-inch lens from a position close to the dancers, I went some distance back and used a long-focus lens. There was no doubting the result. The figures were alive and real, the shadows softer, and the breadfruit trees seemed like living things rather than a flat background.

Cameramen in motion picture studios rarely use a lens of more than four-inch focal length. This, I have found, is because the large, elaborate studio camera will not support the added size and weight of the longer-focus lenses without resultant "whip" or "weave" when the picture is projected.

While making a short film of New York City in 1927, I made further use of long-focus lenses. This was not a film of human beings, but of the skyscrapers which they had created, completely dwarfing humanity itself. I think I made shots from the top of every skyscraper in Manhattan, looking down into the canyons of streets with their antlike human life. I shot New York buildings from the East River bridges, from the ferries, and from the Jersey shore looking up the peaks of Manhattan. The effects obtained with my long-focus lenses amazed me. I remember shooting from the roof of the Telephone Building across to the Jersey shore with an eight-inch lens and, even at that distance, obtaining a stereoscopic effect that seemed magical. It was like drawing a veil from the beyond, revealing life scarcely visible to the naked eye.

When shooting a scene I always look at it through several different lenses, and frequently I shoot a subject with different lenses from the same position. This saves time and the bother of moving to new setups. There is usually one shot that is right. The greater the focal length of the lens, the smaller the field, and, as a consequence, with the longer telephoto, the photographer is easily able to eliminate unnecessary details and to give his picture the emphasis he wants. This is important because good photography, like good writing, is largely a matter of emphasis.

Three years ago, I found the motion picture camera I had long been looking for. It was a little spring-driven model, simpler in operation than any other camera I had ever seen, and not much heavier to carry around than a portable typewriter. These to me are vitally important considerations: for example, many of the shots in *Man of Aran* would have been lost in the time it takes to set up a studio camera. In shooting the big seas, I would place the equipment as near the water's edge as possible; then, when the seas would come crashing in, I would have to pick up the camera, tripod and all, run back and set it up in a safer spot. Particularly was this true in the scene in which the islanders are overwhelmed by the sea while rescuing their net—a bit of unforeseen drama which nearly cost the islanders their lives.

But more important even than its portability is the steadiness of this little camera. I had with me on the Aran Islands a very complete lens equipment—wide-angle, two-inch, three-inch, four-inch, six-inch, nine-inch, and eleven-inch lenses, and an enormous seventeen-inch telephoto, twice as long as the camera itself. Even in the shots made with this seventeen-inch lens, there was no "weave" on the screen; the image was rock steady. If there is any other camera in the world that will give the same result with such a long-focus lens, I have yet to hear of it.

Some of the best seascapes in *Man of Aran* were shot with this seventeen-inch lens, notably the shot almost at the end of the picture, in which a wild Atlantic surge strikes the base of a towering cliff, slowly climbs to the top, curls over, and sweeps across the land. The cliff is three hundred feet high, and the camera was two miles away.

An objection often raised against the use of telephoto lenses is that the quality of the photography suffers, that telephoto pictures are dull and flat in tone. This objection is not altogether justified, and filters aid greatly in improving such shots. There are scenes in *Man of Aran,* made with my seventeen-inch telephoto lens, the quality of which I defy anyone to distinguish from that of a shot made with, say, a four-inch lens.

In brief, I owe almost everything to long-focus lenses. Here are some of the shots in *Man of Aran* which would have been impossible without them: The seascapes. The shark scenes. These scenes were shot mostly from the deck of a trawler, at distances of from a hundred yards to half a mile, often in a rough sea.

The scenes of the canoe coming in during the storm. The camera was on shore, a quarter of a mile to half a mile from the canoe.

I should add that the still portraits of the Aran Islanders, made by my wife, were mostly done with a six-inch lens on a miniature camera. When longer lenses are made for small still cameras, I shall be among the first to use them.

Three Songs About Lenin
by Marie Seton

*This review of the Dziga Vertov film appeared in the Winter 1934
issue of Film Art (London). Miss Seton, a filmmaker, is the author
of a biography of Eisenstein and a book on the work of Satyajit Ray.*

Almost every superlative adjective has already been used in admiration of this film. Most of the adjectives were unnecessary, for any picture pertaining to Lenin must be intensely moving—the impression of his influence is upon the creative endeavor of a hundred and seventy million people of a hundred-and-fifty-something nationalities living on a sixth part of the earth. Since it is impossible to sum up the total force directed into motion by Lenin, it is unreasonable to expect any movie director at the present time to have so profound an understanding of the movement of which Lenin was the articulate voice as to be able to create for it complete expressive form in a medium of art still in its infancy. *Three Songs About Lenin* is nowhere near as great a picture as some people have declared it to be. It is a sincere construction of a historical document rather than a great work of film art. The formal skeleton upon which Vertov has reconstructed a mass of documentary materials, shot by him over a period of seventeen years for a hundred and fifty different pictures, are three songs written by unknown poets of Central Asia. The songs are utterly, almost incredibly personal in their feelings toward Lenin; he is as great a reality to the writers as their fathers or brothers.

The first song is the Song of Love.

The material is straightforward document, cut without any of the earlier experiments characteristic of Vertov's earlier montage.

The second song is the apex of the film—the lying-in-state of Lenin.

The third song—the thoughts of Lenin translated into rapid action—is little more than super-newsreel, a vital and interesting review of social and industrial development—in fact, Stalinism. A certain falsity, not of content but of form, enters toward the end with the introduction of the studio shots of various speakers recounting the progress of their work; they are theatrical in their presentation and they break the rhythm of what is best described as an epic documentary impregnated with an objective lyricism.

Basil Wright's *Song of Ceylon*
by Marie Seton

*This review appeared originally in the Autumn 1935
issue of Film Art (London).*

Basil Wright's *Song of Ceylon* has been received with indifference
not because it is a "documentary," but because it presents an unfamiliar subject in a style contrary to all the popular "isms."
Though *Song of Ceylon* explores half a dozen new ways of using
sound and commentary and constructing sequences, no distributor
would take it, while many critics condemned it as dull. The reason
for their adjective is that here is a contemplative film which demands
a receptive rather than dogmatic mood. It asks the spectator to
discard his respect for tramcars, wireless, allure of pseudo-religions
of the Theosophical and Buchman-Coughlin class, and to watch
a very old religion drawing the common daily task within the pre-
cepts of Buddha.

Though Buddha is the central theme, this is not a religious film
in our Western sense. Basil Wright has understood that in Asia
religious thought does not commence at the temple door; it is an
atmosphere affecting material as well as spiritual things. Though
Song of Ceylon is a travelogue designed to "sell more tea," it is [as]
remote from the usual "Magic Carpet" trip to foreign climes as the
travels of Marco Polo are from a Baedeker handbook. The "Magic
Carpet" series makes capital by cataloguing racial peculiarities in
snappy commentary calculated to appeal to the pun-minded. Supposedly "exotic" races are sent round the world to compete in
oddity with the Lobster-Clawed Man and the Ugliest Woman in the
World. But, if asked for his history, the Lobster-Clawed Man tells
an interesting but not sensational tale, and ends by saying that if
the Labour Exchange would let him, he would rather be a worker
than an exhibit. He is then more normal, psychologically, than the
average film star. Likewise, the customs which appear so freakish
in the usual travelogue probably express experience and traditions
common to mankind.

Mr. Wright has discarded the sensational. He has selected scenes
from native life and arranged them in a pattern and with a rhythm
which suggest the inner as well as outer life in Ceylon. Each episode

has been chosen in relation to the idea that the life of Ceylon is given cohesion through the belief in Buddha. Because the reasons for Wright's choice are not always obvious, the film has been called plotless and about nothing.

The structure of the film is musical. It is divided into four movements. Part One, "The Buddha," is directly concerned with Buddhism. The commentary, an account of Ceylon written in 1860 by Robert Knox, and spoken by Lionel Wendt of Ceylon in a voice as meditative as it is beautiful, says that in course of time Buddha appeared on earth and his worship absorbed the older Devil cult. A pilgrimage of men, women, and children observe the glory of Buddha, who, it is said, left this world and passed into Nirvana from the island's highest mountain, Adam's Peak, which bears the imprint of his foot. In Part Two, "The Virgin Island," the daily life is shown. Each man laboring for himself but reluctant to hire himself out to another. The fishermen fling out their nets with movements as rhythmic as music, the wandering priests beg their rice. In the villages, small boys learn the primary steps of the dance which in manhood they will perform in memory of Buddha. Part Three, "The Voices of Commerce." Despite the invasion of Europeans, the traditional ways of agriculture continue. It is the commentary of Part Three which imposes the staccato voice of business upon the island's tropical life. Different voices give the account of stocks and shares, orders and invoices, prices and business letters.

In the fourth and last movement, "The Apparel of a God," the film returns to the traditional and personal aspects of Buddhism. A solitary native comes through the jungle and across the plain to make his small sacrifice of rice to the reclining Buddha at Gal-Vihara. Centuries of tradition have contributed to that single act of devotion, deeply moving in its simplicity. Tradition in ritual form comes in the final and most impressive sequence, the dance in honor of Buddha. Holy lore says that the dancer's robes, the Vess, were designed by God two thousand years ago. Each ornament is symbolical of the thirty-two signs of Buddha. The dance grows ever more ecstatic until it approaches the climax and is interlocked with rapid shots of the Buddhas seen in the first part; each expresses a different state of meditation. The soundtrack accompanying these cut-in shots appears to be the most extraordinary twanging of instruments, and it perfectly conveys a sense of approaching ecstasy. This ingenious effect was obtained with six gongs in the G.P.O.

Unit's London studio. The first was held toward the microphone with the hollow side outward. As soon as it was struck, the microphone at the other end of the studio was swung forward so that the vibrations were picked up; the track was then run backward. The dance melts into the opening shots of the jungle with its mysterious tropical vegetation. . . .

Song of Ceylon is not a perfect film, there are times when the sequences fail to follow one another with that inevitableness which makes for perfect continuity, but it is a very important attempt at creating a picture of an entirely strange life, from the native rather than foreign point of view, and to express the tempo of that life in the texture of the film itself.

De Rochemont's *The March of Time*
by Robert T. Elson

*This selection is from Mr. Elson's book, "Time Inc.,
The Intimate History of a Publishing Enterprise, 1923-1941"
(Atheneum, New York, 1968).*

On February 1, 1935, at the Capitol Theatre on Broadway, then the flagship of the mighty Loew chain, and at other theaters across the country, there was shown the first release of a new series of short subjects, *The March of Time*. Time Inc. had entered the business of making motion pictures in an attempt to make the cinema an instrument of more effective journalism. In terms of the millions who would see this and subsequent releases, *The March of Time* was the most ambitious publication Time Inc. had yet undertaken. As in the case of *The March of Time* on the air, the company was venturing an experiment in mass communication which departed radically from the rationale of the magazines with their carefully selected audiences.

The first release of *The March of Time* was the culmination of eight months' experimental work. By coincidence, just as Luce had decided to disband the Martin Experimental Department, Louis de Rochemont, director of short subjects for Fox Movietone News, was calling on Roy Larsen to propose translating the *March of Time* radio program into motion pictures. This project became the major new undertaking of Time Inc. in 1934 and 1935.

De Rochemont's was not an original idea. A few months after the first *March of Time* broadcast Larsen had learned that two Hollywood agents were trying to sell the idea to the studios, and he had written his friend Paul Hollister of B.B.D.&O.: "As this is an idea which Fred Smith and I have had ever since we started the radio re-enactments, no one can have any copyright . . . and if you know anyone who wants to make some money and have a damn interesting job, here it is." Shortly after Luce's friend David O. Selznick [then vice-president of RKO-Pathé] suggested that Time Inc. look into the newsreel business. Larsen replied: "Harry and I are agreed that before we even consider it, we must be sure that there is a lot of money to be made in it," adding that if they entered the field "we would of course try to change the technique." All this was in 1931. No more was done about the project until de Rochemont sought the meeting with Larsen.

De Rochemont was a man of imagination who from early boyhood had been deeply involved in newsreels; he had made his own crude camera from designs in Popular Mechanics and sold footage taken with it to his hometown movie theater in Chelsea, Massachusetts, where it was shown under the title, *See Yourself as Others See You*. As a free-lance newsreel cameraman he scored his first news beat when officers re-enacted for him the arrest of a suspect in the attempted bombing of the international railroad bridge at Vanceboro, Maine, in 1915. When the U.S. entered World War I, de Rochemont enlisted in the Navy and was commissioned; remaining in the service after the Armistice, he was attached to U.S. headquarters in Istanbul, where as officer-cameraman he shot newsreel-type footage for recruitment films. In 1923 he resigned from the Navy to enter the newsreel business, though he continued to make Navy films on contract. His work involved worldwide travel, in the course of which he scored a notable exclusive with his pictures of Indian rioting following the arrest of Gandhi, films which he had to smuggle past the British censor. On his own initiative he financed and produced a documentary, edited from newsreel archives, called *The Cry of the World,* which won critical acclaim but was not commercially successful. While at Fox Movietone News he produced a series of travelogues, "The Magic Carpet of Movietone," and another series, "The March of the Years," foreshadowing in format *The March of Time*. These films, centered on great news stories of other years, were largely based on archival material combined with brief reenacted scenes. De Rochemont felt the technique could successfully be adapted to *The March of Time,* and this is what he proposed to Larsen. Previous proposals for making *The March of Time* in motion pictures had been based on the assumption that the episodes would have to be wholly re-enacted, at prohibitive cost. De Rochemont proposed instead that current newsreel footage be linked with archival material, reducing re-enactment to a minimum.

Larsen was immediately enthusiastic and avid to get started. Luckily, de Rochemont had arrived at just the right moment. Luce, well disposed to some new venture, gave Larsen the go-ahead to experiment. With no other assurances whatever, de Rochemont quit his job with Movietone, setting up an arrangement with his former employer for the use of footage from its library and rental of a projection room and working quarters in the Movietone offices at 54th Street and Tenth Avenue. In June 1934, he and Larsen began work with a staff of six—film cutters, a negative matcher, a writer, and an office boy. Luce did not meet de Rochemont until some time later.

De Rochemont and Larsen had no small ambition; their objective was to revolutionize the newsreel and give it a new journalistic purpose. The newsreel business was at a low ebb, one reason why de Rochemont wanted to leave Movietone. But it had not always been in such sad shape. The motion-picture camera had entered journalism almost with its invention. Since before the turn of the century, it had been recording history—President McKinley's inauguration, Admiral Dewey at Manila Bay, Queen Victoria's funeral. There were cameramen following the Balkan wars and in the trenches on both sides during World War I; immediately afterward worldwide organizations for covering news had been developed. The silent cameramen risked their lives and fought one another for exclusives, and the cinema archives are richer for their initiative.

The film companies which controlled the newsreels were not run by men with journalistic aspirations; their interest was in profits to be made from the feature films, and the expenditure on newsreels seemed to them unnecessary and excessive. There was little or no profit in the newsreels because they were sold as part of a package, a sideline to the features which kept customers coming to the box-office. Moreover, the editing of most newsreels was wretched. They were little more than moving snapshots of disasters or sporting events interspersed with such trivia as bathing-beauty contests and lunatic fashions. With the addition of sound in 1928, a new dimension was added to the camera's coverage, but with it a new item of expense. The sound cameras were costly and heavy, and with them the cameraman lost his oldtime mobility. There was more pressure to economize. Neither initiative nor creativity was encouraged, and any venture into controversial ground was positively discouraged. The producers and the exhibitors alike were spineless when confronted with any protest by politicians, local censors, or patriotic groups. In 1934 Adolf Hitler was scarcely seen in any newsreel, and never in any context that might be considered unfavorable. Yet the public liked newsreels and expected exhibitors to provide one as part of every program. A phenomenon of the 1930s was the opening of theaters devoted solely to newsreels and other short subjects.

Larsen and de Rochemont aimed at producing each week a short film dealing with contemporary subjects that might be found in any issue of Time and Fortune. They did not, however, obligate themselves, as did the radio program, to draw the material directly from a current issue. What they wanted to do on the screen was what Time did in print—tell a story with a background and insight and in a coherent form. They first aimed at an overall length of ten minutes—the average running time of the current newsreels—divided into five episodes of two minutes each, the whole a blend of news clips, re-enactment, and dialogue, linked, as on the radio, by the vibrant voice of Westbrook Van Voorhis. One episode from the first of two short experimental reels illustrates the technique.

The subject chosen was the three-way naval-arms race among the U. S., Britain, and Japan; it was introduced by pictures of Admiral Heihachiro Togo, just deceased, and as these flashed on the screen "The Voice of *Time*" reminded viewers that Admiral Togo was "honored and revered . . . for his victory at Tsushima—the kind of victory for which nations and navies build and spend and strive and dream for generations—the kind of victory for which Japan has built her present navy."

The film then cut to the British fleet steaming back from spring maneuvers, and the episode concluded with shots of Franklin D. Roosevelt at a recent grand review of the U.S. fleet. As the camera panned over the assembled ships the narration came to its climax: ". . . U.S. citizens have new assurance that in their navy they have a mighty fighting machine, trained, equipped, prepared to protect every foot of America's ten thousand miles of coastline."

The March of Time combined newsreel, documentary, and a dramatic presentation in a new form of compelling journalism. In an age of electronics when television can intrude scenes of actual battle into the cocktail hour, the method of *The March of Time* is no longer acceptable as journalism. Yet TV, the modern film documentary, the new school of *cinéma-vérité* owe much to its pioneering methods. The much-praised Italian movie *The Battle of Algiers* is a superior recent example of what *The March of Time* achieved in a more limited way—the re-enactment of an event so effectively that it simulates reality itself. A. William Bluem, a student of the documentary, wrote [in "The Documentary in American Television," Hastings House, New York, 1965] that *The March of Time* "stretched the limits of journalism by implicitly arguing that the picture as well as the word was, after all, only symbolic of reality. What mattered was not whether pictorial journalism displayed the facts, but whether, within the conscience of the reporter, it faithfully reflected the facts." Luce put it somewhat more succinctly: *The March of Time,* he said must be "fakery in allegiance to the truth." The producers did not in every case use actual films of an event or person even when available; they often used re-enactment by preference if this served better to clarify or dramatize the narrative. The viewer could not in most cases—nor did the producers intend him to—distinguish re-enactment from reality. But every sequence was anchored in fact. However, as *The March of Time* matured and its resources expanded, the producers relied less and less on re-enactment and more and more on their own documentary films.

The achievement of *The March of Time* was not so much its technique as its introduction into cinema of subjects of current controversy and significance. In its first year it tackled such subjects as the re-arming of Germany, the Nazi persecutions and the emigration of the German Jews to Palestine, the struggle between Church and State in Mexico. On the domestic scene it focused on such current and worrisome phenomena as Huey Long's Share-the-Wealth, Father Coughlin's Social Justice movement, and Dr. Townsend's Townsendites. It did a documentary on TVA, then big news, touched on the Nye investigation of the munitions industry and [on] the debate over the Neutrality Act. It also prided itself on some exclusives: the first motion pictures of Sir Basil Zaharoff, the legendary "merchant of death," and of Anatole ("Papa") Deibler, the official French executioner.

In maintaining "allegiance to the truth," the *March of Time* cameramen had remarkable success in persuading public figures and just ordinary people to become participants. Making the sequence in the first release in which Fred Perkins re-enacted his struggle with the NRA, the producers discovered that real people are often better at portraying themselves than any actor. The producers were soon stage-directing Cabinet members, Senators, politicians, labor leaders, and hundreds of individuals to perform more effectively than any Hollywood extras. Colonel François de La Rocque mustered thousands of his fascistic Croix de Feu supporters to a torchlight rally in Chartres for *The March of Time*'s cameras;

Father Coughlin posed for *The March of Time,* which re-enacted the extinguishing of a fiery cross that had once burned on his rectory lawn; Huey Long cooperated in a sequence which turned out to be a devastating satire; Wendell Willkie, counsel for Commonwealth & Southern Corporation, appeared as one of the principals in the TVA episode; General Douglas MacArthur assigned U.S. Army units to cooperate with a *March of Time* film unit and appeared in the same release. In the beginning, hired camera crews were used. Soon *The March of Time*'s own cameramen were on special assignment in the Far East, in Europe, in Latin America, and on location across the U.S.

After seeing the test reels, Creighton Peet, a movie critic on the old New York Post, had warned the producers that they would be getting into trouble because "what people see in films is twenty times more powerful than what they read in print. This is the real basis of all censorship complaints. The movies have power . . . . no other means of conveying ideas begins to touch the films. . . . In this reel you have dynamite. If it builds up a following, it can, in time, become a terrific force in the land. The only question is whether the timid movie people will stick with you; they are yellow-bellies from the word go."

His prophecy of trouble proved correct. *The March of Time* was in hot water from the beginning. Ordinarily, newsreels were exempted from censorship by the then omnipresent municipal and state censors; *The March of Time* was not always granted the same right. The Province of Ontario Censor Board turned down the second release, which contained episodes on Hitler and the Hauptmann trial. In Ohio and Illinois, censors rejected a sequence on the Nazi persecution of the Jews as "gruesome" and provocative. In Britain the censors snipped out pictures of Father Divine on grounds of blasphemy (he claimed to be God). Huey Long disappeared from an issue shown in New Orleans theaters. Pictures of the Dominican Republic dictator, President Trujillo, brought a diplomatic protest. (Secretary of State Cordell Hull reminded the Dominicans of the freedom of the press, but Radio City Music Hall dropped the film. The New York Times commented: "You could probably count off the patrons of the Music Hall from the Dominican Republic on a book of matches, but that's the way they are over there.") The National Legion of Decency was outraged by scenes showing Lady Godiva's Ride, the feature of the Texas Centennial celebration at

Dallas. The Hearst newspapers attacked *The March of Time* because of pictures taken in the Soviet Union, which they declared to be overt Communist propaganda. [The sequence on the Soviet Union was purchased from Julien Bryan, an independent cameraman who had Soviet cooperation. Extremely naïve, the film showed crammed food shelves in Soviet stores and described consumer goods as plentiful at a time when there were notorious shortages of everything in Russia.] But from Lord Beaverbrook in Britain came a note of commendation: "It is bound to become an influence exercising great power over the minds of men."

The March of Time, like Time, tried to indicate "which side it believes to have the stronger position." Implicit in a film of Gerald L. K. Smith, as in the one on Huey Long, was a vein of heavy satire. The pictures on the Jewish emigration to Palestine were sympathetic and therefore, by contrast with the scenes of persecution in Germany, a condemnation of the Nazis. But, like Time and Fortune at that period, the series did not consistently follow a specific editorial policy. This irritated some critics; George Dangerfield wrote in the New Republic "I wish (the editors) would say—outright, beyond question—that somebody was right or wrong." Soon the criticism would change; *The March of Time* would be accused of following a definite and internationalist line.

A year after its founding *The March of Time* was playing in more than 5,000 theaters in the U.S. and 709 in Great Britain, and its international monthly audience was estimated at 15,000,000. An elaborate illustrated book was published by Time Inc. to celebrate *The March of Time*'s anniversary, referring to the film as the company's "third major publication": ". . . not a product of ink-on-paper to be distributed to individuals through the mails . . . a product of acid-on-celluloid . . . distributed from the screens of cinemansions to big and little crowds. *The March of Time* had, therefore, to earn its right to existence under rules quite different from those which ordinarily govern the practice of journalism. That right . . . has now been earned—a franchise granted by the owners and managers of thousands of theatres to serve the demands of a large public.

". . . *The March of Time* is now established in the world. . . . It is a chapter in the history of pictorial journalism. . . ."

In support of these claims were impressive testimonials from the men who then were leaders in Hollywood—Darryl F. Zanuck,

Walter Wanger, Irving Thalberg, and David O. Selznick. Selznick was quoted: "I feel the inauguration of *The March of Time*—with its courage and its novelty—will prove to have been the most significant motion picture development since the invention of sound." A year later, on his nomination, *The March of Time* received a Special Award Oscar from the Academy of Motion Picture Arts and Sciences for "having revolutionized one of the most important branches of the industry, the newsreel."

English Documentary Films
by Evelyn Gerstein

*This selection is reprinted from New Theatre magazine
(New York), January 1936. The author was one of the first
important American film critics.*

Documentary films, without a footnote to explain them, are apt
to be confused with the staid American ritual, the newsreel: child
life on parade, the fleet parading the Pacific, and Rockefeller parading the dime, the smile, and the homily.

The name suggests an arid compilation of data. But the document, whether it is scientific miniature, geography in a single reel,
or notes on the life of a coal miner, is the realistic core from which
the film of the future must grow.

The phrase itself is bare and unevocative. Yet, in the hands of a
director like Dziga Vertov and in his film, *Three Songs About Lenin,*
collected statements of fact become threnody and paean through the
imaginative conversion of the artist.

There are three kinds of documentary films: the simple statement
of fact, impartial, external; the films with editorial bias, implied
or stated; and the films, very few, that attain conviction beyond their
partisanship. Ruttmann's silent film, *Berlin, Symphony of a City,*
belongs in the first group; *The March of Time* and Alexander
Korda's imminent *Conquest of the Air,* the film that is taxing the
zest and the budgets of London Films and the British Air Ministry,
are in the second category; Dziga Vertov's films are in the third.

The Russian document derives from the news chronica, those
brief, inter-Russian dispatches that are shown between feature films
in a separate room in the film theaters; the American documentary
film originated with Robert Flaherty.

At a time when the Hollywood movie never stirred from the
studios, when the *Hunchback of Notre Dame,* Lon Chaney, and the
gargoyles represented models of cinema fidelity to literature, Robert
Flaherty went north for Revillon Frères and made *Nanook of the
North,* a plotless film about Eskimo life. Like each of his later films,
Nanook was half camera record, half poetic thesis on the beauty of
isolation and primitive living. His films are notably barren of the
drama latent in social contrasts.

Flaherty has made *Moana, The Twenty-Four-Dollar Island,* or New York as a still life between rivers, and *Man of Aran.* He is now in India filming *Kim. Man of Aran* is all sea, kelp, and fishing; it has neither wakes, nor dirges, nor people in their homes. It is no longer a document of reality but a photographed song of the surf. Flaherty has gone off the thin edge of the document into the sea.

But, in Flaherty's wake in England today, there is a school of younger film directors led by John Grierson, the film critic, who once touted Flaherty as the creator of cinema and leader in the escape out of the studio impasse. Today, Grierson has rejected Flaherty as an exotic, and established a unit for the production of realistic documentaries. His sponsor is the British General Post Office.

The list of the G.P.O. films is formidable; but the films themselves are seldom electric. Grierson says that it is not the individual directors, the separate films, that are significant, but the bulk of output; the list of the box-offices they have forced; the Rotary clubs that will book their films; the film library of three-hundred-odd films that they have to lease; and the permanence of their future endowment.

The English documentary film began when Grierson left New York for London to make films for the Empire Marketing Board. In 1933 Grierson acquired the title and post of Film Officer of the General Post Office, with the disposal of cameras, scripts, and salaries to whomever he chose.

Today, in offices off Soho Square, with a self-sustained national campaign to insure them an audience in Wales, Edinburgh, or Manchester, or wherever a film society, workers' film club, or Rotary has risen to cheer them, the General Post Office unit lists eight directors, two apprentices, and two staff composers.

W. H. Auden, one of the two apprentices, will help in the filming of *Air Mail to Australia,* or "the decay of materialism," as Grierson puts it. In addition, certain film-struck amateurs, musicians, artists have joined the band. Directors include Basil Wright, who made *Song of Ceylon,* that lyrical film of the tea industry, sunken temples, and Buddhas; Elton, the director of the slum-clearance film for the Gas Company; Stuart Legg, who made the British Broadcasting tract; Mary Field, who did *This Was England* for British Instructional Films; Marion Grierson, Taylor, Watt, and Austen. Paul Rotha is working for the British Instructional Film unit.

Among their films are: *Night Mail, S.O.S., The Calendar of the Year, Derby, The Summer Post Card Industry, The Christmas Post Office, Stamps, Post Office Engineers, Negroes, Gas,* and a comedy, *Thrift,* directed by Cavalcanti, as well as an original color cartoon painted directly on the film strip by the Australian Len Lye.

These films, though ostensibly advertising media for the Post Office unit, are not too obviously tagged except at the close. They are sent out to some four or five million people a year, with road-shows of six months apiece, a thing possible only is a country where a town of the capacity of Newcastle-on-Tyne boasts a film society of about eight hundred members, and the Young Farmers' Club of York has monthly bulletins of recommended films.

The English documentarians have been their own publicists. "The secret of our growth," says Grierson, "is the public instruction we pretended. The documentary film might have been a greater commercial success in a sentimental and popular journalism and might have gone the way of Flaherty into exotic places, but it discarded him, got down to themes and materials under its own nose, with a clearer social theory than the French and Germans and a closer observation of work and workers than the Russians."

These English films are sober, accurate chronicles of work in progress of the British islands, in vistas that reproduce well in stills for the film magazines. But, all ballyhoo to the contrary, they are basically government tracts, intended to applaud the progress of the Crown.

Song of Ceylon is not always clear in its symbolic references. [Cavalcanti's] *Coal Face,* however, is a tour de force, a vigorous experiment in sound with a score composed by Water Leigh in oratorio form, with solos and chorus integrated contrapuntally with the film. Paul Rotha's *Shipyard* details the building of the Orient liner Orion in Barrow-on-Furness. The film was made for British Instructional, an offshoot of Gaumont British. It is full of magnificent close-ups of machinery and heads; its cutting is thoughtful and vigorous; the score is an ingenious commentary on the film. Yet the film as a whole is meticulous and arid.

Mary Field's *This Was England,* with its thatchers, mole catchers, flint nabbers, and two-handed sowers, each recounting his trade and his prowess in the soft accents of Suffolk speech, is closer to earth and the folk. As such, it is vivid and animate.

Progress is the dull cavalcade of mechanical invention from the death of Kind Edward to a radio in every car; and *Citizens of the Future* is significant as the first of a group of children's films. Korda's Jubilee film that Winston Churchill wrote to order, *The King and the Man in the Street,* has been discarded, they say, for "lack of time."

As in France, the English amateur has become the film professional. The English documentarians have talked films into the dark corners of England, Scotland, and Wales; they publish their own magazines and proffer their own lecturers with or without their films. They have acquired audiences, cameras, and sponsors.

In retrospect, their films are more alert as physical commentary than drama. Their documents merely state and illumine; they explore the medium with highly formalized and studied photography and the avidity of the English for details. They posit a social inquiry and resolve it superficially by concluding that slum clearance has been ended by the Gas Company and the abuses of the coal pits blotted out with electricity for all. The Empire takes care of its own.

Joris Ivens's *Borinage* is a document, too. He made it during the Belgian mine strike, with a camera hidden under his coat. The miners sheltered him in their yards, and the film was shipped out of the city each night for developing. *Borinage* is not handsomely photographed, but in the swift, brief mounting scenes of the strike there is a drama of revolutionary truth.

The English films, by contrast, are static and a little naïve in their pretensions. Yet, despite their inability to search deeper into the realities that underlie the surface, the English documentarians, led by Grierson and Rotha, have demonstrated how far a consistent point of view and determination may go in the battle against the commercialized fantasies and wish-fulfillment exercises of Hollywood and Elstree.

Marco Polo, Modern Style
by Herman G. Weinberg

This appraisal of the French film La Croisière jaune *(The Yellow Cruise), directed by Léon Poirier and André Sauvage, appeared as a program note in the 55th Street Playhouse Review (New York), for November 17, 1936. Mr. Weinberg is the author of "Josef von Sternberg," "The Lubitsch Touch," "Saint Cinema."*

Knowledge is cumulative, hence some fifty or more centuries of civilization can be said to have gone into the preparation of the Citroën-Haardt-Audouin-Dubreuil Expedition across Central Asia. That knowledge is power was also proved in the splendid lesson in valor vouchsafed us by the members of this expedition, who drew upon their wisdom and courage to see a heartbreakingly difficult journey to its victorious finish.

There have been men as courageous before this. Marco Polo, traversed pretty much the same route six hundred years ago. In Haardt, leader of the expedition, and Audouin-Dubreuil, his associate, was the same lust for adventure and distant horizons mixed with a dash of economic penetration that characterized the Venetian nobleman, Polo. Both came back with fabulous tales of the East— Marco Polo laden with silks and spices, rare jewels, and fantastic tales of strange lands which none knew existed: Haardt (who did not come back, who broke and died under the terrific strain of the expedition) left as his heritage a tale as fantastic as the most incredible stories of Marco Polo—a film, *The Yellow Cruise*. Whereas Marco Polo was not believed, Haardt most certainly is. For in his beautiful, moving, and tragic film is imprisoned for posterity the log of his journey and the strange things he saw on it. The Chinese have a proverb: "A picture is worth a thousand words." Poor Marco Polo may have had to burst his spleen to convince his compatriots that he wasn't lying. Haardt, even if he is not with us, is believed through the eloquence of his pictures, which speak more profoundly than anything we can say about them in awe, in admiration, or in breathless astonishment.

Not only did Haardt show us pictures to substantiate the stories once considered incredible by Marco Polo's listeners—he let us hear the sounds of the great Orient, through the magic of the photoelectric cell. He has blown the breath of life into his images by recording the calls and cries, the kaleidoscopic tumult of their daily lives. Murmurs of strange tongues, snatches of even stranger songs and folk-melodies, groans and screeches, whistles and clanking, dull rumbling of carts and animal cries, chantings of the Koran, the wail of Chinese infants, the song of a Mongolian princess, the skirl of a Highland pibroch at Khyber Pass, the street noises of the bazaars, the machinegun fire across the barren wastes of Sinkiang during a rebellion, the shells falling in Shanghai during the Japanese invasion, the scurry in the streets, the grateful blast of trumpets at the French Legation in Hanoi, effusions, smiles, handclasps, congratulations—they merge, swell, and sway like a great wave breaking over the strand, they become a veritable babel, a cacophonic symphony . . . they are the very stuff and pattern of life.

Truth is indeed stranger than fiction. "And nothing," said the newspaper Gringoire, in Paris, of *The Yellow Cruise,* "is so beautiful as the truth." Is it because of its straightforwardness, its almost aloof presentation of the most incredible things, that the film reaches such heights of poignancy?

An Event: *The Wave*
by Sidney Meyers

The film Redes *discussed in this selection from New Theatre (New York), November 1936, was eventually released in the United States as* The Wave. *The author directed* The Quiet One *and many other films.*

The emergence of the film *Redes* (Nets) from the welter of world film production is an event of incommensurable importance. Not only is *Redes* the first full-length film made in America on a working-class theme, embodying the aspirations of the great masses of men, but it is moreover extraordinarily beautiful and moving as few films in our experience have been.

We saw *Redes* in the usual tiny, bare projection room, in its original Spanish, a language unfamiliar to us. Nevertheless, in spite of these handicaps and the unfavorable advance reports of acquaintances who had previewed the film on the coast, our wonder at what was unfolding before us increased from moment to moment. The old thrill one gets when present at the "beginning" of things was there, but more than that was the joy that *Redes* should have risen so high above the tyranny of circumstance that usually dooms "beginnings" to mediocrity.

Redes was produced in Mexico. The project, under the supervision of Paul Strand, was initiated by Carlos Chavez, the Mexican composer and conductor, when he was chief of the Department of Fine Arts in the Secretariat of Education in 1933. Full credits for the production follow: Production (save for synchronization of the sound): Paul Strand; story: Paul Strand, assisted by Velasquez Chavez; screen treatment: Henwar Rodakiewicz; direction: Fred Zinnemann, assisted by Gomez Muriel; photography: Paul Strand; edited by Gunther von Fritsch; music by Sylvestre Revueltas; stills by Ned Scott.

The setting of *Redes* is Alvarado, a fishing village on the Gulf of Vera Cruz.

There, in the midst of strangulating poverty, the fishermen make an heroic pilgrimage from abject, suicidal resignation to conscious full-statured protest against their lot. As the film opens, we see a village exhausted by inanition and poverty. There has been no catch for months. Miro, one of the fishermen, has lost a child because he has been unable to afford medical attention. The child is buried. Miro, himself, takes a spade from the hands of the gravedigger and throws earth on the coffin in a last self-imposed agony. He speaks for the first time in the film to say, "It isn't right—it isn't just for a man's child to die because he has no money to cure it." Miro is led away by his companions. After an interval of time, fishermen rush into the village telling that a school of fish has entered their waters. Then follows the fish hunt, frenzied yet grave, surely among the greatest single sequences in the history of films. The men take their catch to a nearby city. The local dealer, a wealthy padrone, gives them a meager handful of pesos in return. The men stand overwhelmed with shame and misery. But Miro, already embittered by the death of his child, is aroused to action. He calls a meeting at which some of the men decide not to sell unless they receive higher prices. But not all of them are persuaded. A group under the leadership of Miro's friend, Miguel, hold that action against the dealer can only lead to further disaster. They attempt to scab. There is a struggle. A politician, Juan Garcia Sanchez, hating Miro for his influence over the men, and currying the favor of the padrone, takes advantage of the tumult and shoots Miro, wounding him fatally. At the sound of the shot the battle ends. Miro's followers take him to his home. The others are confounded by the events and slowly perceive the folly of their dissension and the consequences of their cowardice. They return to Miro to find him dead. Miguel, through the death of Miro, has quickly come to realize the need for unity. He speaks the funeral oration over the body of his dead friend. Miro is placed on a boat on a stretcher of oars. The fishermen row back toward the city. Other crews gather; two boats become many. As the film ends, we see a phalanx of ships which suggest the power of the waves as they rise higher and higher, rushing in to break on the shore.

Here we have a story of utmost simplicity, told directly with almost a complete absence of symbolic digression.

I tried to think of the people who had made *Redes,* and chiefly of Paul Strand, who had conceived and guided it to completion. I thought of Paul Strand's still photographs, perhaps the most beautiful created in our time. It seemed strange. How could a man who had spent most of his life arresting the fugitive nobility of real things, whose photographs arouse such elusive ideas and feelings in the onlooker, how could this man give voice so completely and unerringly to the forthright statements of *Redes?* And the answer came—there was no essential difference between the stills and the film. From his earliest works, like the blind woman in Stieglitz's magazine, Camera Work, to *Redes,* Strand has spoken of one thing predominantly—the dignity of human life and of the things man has made that reflect his image. But, in addition, *Redes* was under the necessity of pointing to those relationships that stand in the way of man's rightful assumption of a desirable and dignified life. Hence the difference in approach. But the substance is the same.

Strand moved toward this simplicity with conscious deliberation. In the course of a statement prepared for the Secretariat of Education of Mexico, he declared: "We assume that these pictures are not being made for subtle and sophisticated people or even very sensitive minds accustomed to follow the intricacies of esthetic nuance. On the contrary, we assume that these films are being made for a great majority of rather simple people to whom elementary facts should be presented in a direct and unequivocal way; a way that might even bore more complicated sensibilities, though we believe otherwise. We feel that almost a certain crudeness of statement is necessary to achieve the purposes of these films." Yet, despite this foreknowledge, there is in *Redes* not the slightest trace of condescension or the quaint archaism that results from the self-conscious turning of a sophisticate to simpler modes. This we can only attribute to Strand's complete belief in what he was saying. The dialogue of the film, for example, strikes the ear with the true ring of authenticity.

In the weighing scene:

MIRO: We sure got a haul this time.

FOGONERO: If it keeps up this way I'll hitch up with Elena.

ANTONIO: Which is more a fool, a man or a fish?

YI-YI: Who knows? You're asking me?

MIGUEL: Any man who lets a woman hook him—

FOGONERO: How well yours caught you.

Or later:

MIGUEL: There's no use griping—the sharks always eat the robalo.

MIRO: Yes—but don't forget—we are not fish.

But, after the vigor of much of the dialogue has been noted, one must always return to the visual expressiveness of the film. In a conversation with Mr. Strand some time ago, he conveyed his surprise that so few films were visually beautiful, particularly since the film was a visual medium. He pointed out that even so majestic a work as Dovzhenko's *Frontier* was photographically indifferent; that seldom did the photography begin to approach the heights of Dovzhenko's conception. *Redes* makes it easy for one to agree with him about *Frontier*.

In thinking over Redes, two films inevitably come to mind— Flaherty's *Man of Aran* and Eisenstein's unfortunate *Thunder Over Mexico*. This, not only because both films possess great photographic beauty, but because Strand has admitted the influence of Flaherty and the Russian school. As early as 1933, however, Strand pointed out certain shortcomings in Flaherty's aesthetic. Talking of *Nanook of the North* and *Moana,* he said: ". . . It was necessary for Flaherty more or less to reconstruct the past, since all these people are already undergoing changes from the contacts of so-called Western civilization. And, unless Flaherty widens the scope of his work, this dramatic theme of elemental struggle for survival would seem to be a limited one." In other words, the true enemies of man were the man-made social and economic relationships. These were the things you had to struggle against. Undoubtedly, Flaherty, by taking himself off to the Arctic, the South Sea Islands, or the Island of Aran, was, in his way, expressing dissatisfaction with modern life. But in so doing he was utilizing symbols that no longer obtain today, symbols that men couldn't believe in. As a consequence, *Man of Aran* was merely *picturesque*.

In *Redes,* Strand turned his back on the purely picturesque. To quote further from his letter to the Secretariat of Education: ". . . In a world in which human exploitation is so general, it seems to me a further exploitation of people, however picturesque, different, and interesting to us they may appear, merely to make use of them as *material*." True, Mr. Strand was himself, as he admitted, in a not altogether impregnable position, but he was confident of defending himself. "As to the criticism that the people will know and always accept the injustice of their lot, this one does not know. It is well to remember that new generations are being born and that children may have other feelings and ideas from those of their parents." As in the phrase of André Malraux, the artist "has created an illusion of conquest for the reader."

Thunder Over Mexico, mutilated in America by blind and unknowing hands, is certainly not to be thought of as the work of Eisenstein. Therefore is it only possible photographically to compare *Thunder Over Mexico* with *Redes*. On that score Strand is more human, simpler, closer to the people than Eisenstein's photographer Tisse. Perhaps the gigantic scale on which *Thunder Over Mexico* was conceived militated against complete success. Thesis and antithesis run through every frame. Not only did Tisse have to show the Mexicans as they are today, but he also had to point out that they came of an ancient race of great cultural achievements, a race brought to a point just short of annihilation by imperialist oppression.

Whether *Redes* will or can be followed by films of a similar nature is open to question. In times like these, with great numbers of men blind to their true interests, perhaps a more oblique introduction of progressive thought is necessary in films—the greater use of melodramas like *The General Died at Dawn* and *Fury*, social comedies like *Mr. Deeds Goes to Town*. Yet it is difficult to believe that so complete an affirmation of man's faith as *Redes,* so rich an intimation of a more desirable world will fail to move audiences wherever it is shown.

Pare Lorentz's *The River*
by Gilbert Seldes

Mr. Seldes, one of the pioneers among critics of the "lively arts,"
wrote this review for the January 1938 issue of Scribner's.

Without benefit of Hollywood, Pare Lorentz has created in *The River* one of the splendors of the American film. He has done it in a field more cultivated by the Europeans than ourselves, that is, the documentary film. He has taken as his theme the Mississippi River and its tributaries, the physical aspect of the great valley, its cities and its industries, the people who live in it, the crimes they have committed against "the richest free gift that was ever spread out before civilized man," the hopes for a decent life which that valley, in spite of human folly, still offers to humanity. That was the material with which he worked and over it has played so much intelligence and so much imagination that in about half the span of the usual feature picture he has managed to get everything in.

I repeat that this is a documentary film—a film of fact and not of fiction; and I would say that Mr. Lorentz has omitted only one fact, the one presented by Mark Twain's "Life on the Mississippi," the fact, in brief, of romance. I should also say I do not know how he could have brought it in. Possibly because it had to be omitted, there rises from *The River,* as it is shown, a sense of nobility. You follow the picture with complete absorption; from the moment the Mississippi and its tributaries appear in a diagram on the screen like a veritable genealogical tree of the United States of America, you feel yourself in the presence of a powerful drama. Before the picture is halfway over, you feel a rare emotion, a kind of elation in the presence of actual grandeur.

The picture was made for the Farm Security Administration of the Department of Agriculture, and half a dozen other branches of government gave their assistance. It stands, therefore, totally out of the line of commercial films, and this may have some effect on its distribution. (The reluctance of exhibitors hindered the showing of Mr. Lorentz's earlier documentary film, *The Plow That Broke the Plains.*) I have so often advised readers to protest against the films they do see, that I now feel free to urge them with all the vehemence and authority I may possess to demand the showing of this picture at their local movie houses. Incidentally, nothing more useful to the entire industry can be accomplished than to force exhibitors to go outside their commercial contracts to show this picture.

The Mississippi Valley was not only a great gift to America; it was, and is, a treasure house for the movies, and they have passed it by. Not only were producers uninterested in the river as theme, they even neglected the river as background, as theme song, except in the most trivial ways. They might have done with it what Emil Ludwig did with "The Nile"; they might, at least, have placed a dozen historical romances upon its currents. What has happened illustrates a law of society, which is that when individuals do not do the necessary work, the government will step in and do it, giving rise to loud expostulations about the extension of centralized power. In this case, the Federal Government has not only done something eminently worth doing, but—on past performances—has done it better than private enterprise, so lamentably unenterprising, could possibly have done it.

Mr. Lorentz starts you near the headwaters of the great river and, while you are watching the streams flow together, you become aware of geography and history, of farms and mines and cotton plantations, and presently of the Civil War and forests cut down and men working on dikes and the river beginning to swell; and then the atmospheric pressure of the picture is changed, and the brooks and rivulets are no longer flowing together to make a river, but are destroying the land through which they course, and erosion has begun and floods are coming; you see gullies like cuts through the earth, and scenes of desolation, and you feel that generations have lived since the earlier pictures which seemed so rich and fruitful. And so, without your knowing it, you arrive at the Tennessee Valley—and if this is propaganda, make the most of it, because it is masterly. It is as if the pictures which Mr. Lorentz took arranged themselves in such an order that they supplied their own argument, not as if an argument conceived in advance dictated the order of the pictures.

The sense of something important going on is the essence of a good picture, and *The River* has it to the highest degree. Inspired by it, Mr. Lorentz provided a text crammed with fact and uplifted by an unusual lyric quality which shows up in all their triviality the "narrations" of most nonfiction films. It is a little too cadenced in spots, but in the main the rhythm of the speech goes naturally with the rhythm of the picture; there is a list of names which makes you think of Homer's catalogue of the ships or of Scott Fitzgerald's guests at the house of the great Gatsby. It makes pure poetry out of its syllables: "Down the Yellowstone, the Milk, the White, and the Cheyenne; the Cannonball, the Musselshell, the James, and the Sioux; down the Miami, the Wabash, the Licking, and the Green, the Cumberland, the Kentucky, and the Tennessee." And so on, with the Judith, the Osage, the Platte, the Skunk, the Salt, and all the rest. The vegetation, the species of trees, the industries, and the routes of trade ("New Orleans to Baton Rouge; Baton Rouge to Natchez . . ." and so on) use the same device, and the names take on reality and gain glamour at the same time.

When the words had been written, Mr. Lorentz gave them to be spoken by Thomas Chalmers, an actor, but not a professional recorder of the narrative, and Mr. Chalmers is perfect. He does not press his points too far; the frightful oiliness and knowingness of the usual movie voice is gone; the prose is spoken rhythmically, but as if a stressed rhythm were natural. A change in tempo or in emphasis, when names are given a second time, gives a cue to the changed emotion of the picture; the voice always has dignity and warmth.

I cannot report fully on the musical score by Virgil Thomson; I was too absorbed by the picture and the prose; I know that at times I felt the music and the sound effects were essential elements. (The six blasts of the whistle which mean a rising river was one of the best.) They were never out of place. But to know the musical score well, I should have to see the picture a second time.

Mr. Lorentz has said that he tried to compose the elements of *The River* (film, voice, music) as Walt Disney composes his pictures. The narration was recorded without watching the picture; the music likewise; then Mr. Lorentz put them together, getting the proper level and volume for the two soundtracks. The total result is magnificent.

The City Goes to the Fair
by Archer Winsten

*This review appeared in the New York Post on June 23, 1939,
on the opening of the film at the New York World's Fair.*

People who have never cared for documentary pictures, even when they were as impressive, eloquent, and meaningful as *The Plow That Broke the Plains* or *The River,* will have to revise their opinions when they see *The City,* that extraordinary documentary arguing for city planning. It will be shown several times daily at the little Theatre of the Science and Education Building at the World's Fair.

If there were nothing else worth seeing at the fair, this picture would justify the trip and all the exhaustion.

The City shows what *One Third of a Nation* could have been in the movies and was not. It contains more thrillingly genuine shots of life in New York City than all the feature pictures ever made, and this in merely one section out of the five. It is filled with tragedy, beauty, magnificence, ugliness, and sheer cinematic genius. It will be a revelation and an education to the public. For the benefit of Hollywood, one could hope it would be the same to the West Coast treadmill athletes.

One lesson should be emphasized: the enormous effectiveness of actors who don't act or, as in this picture, amateurs. This seems very hard to learn. It must be learned over and over again. The living theatre is constantly sending its stage-trained folk into motion pictures, a different medium, though many have trouble believing it. *The City* is a rich demonstration of things that can be accomplished on the screen with images and music and commentary. These unique effects cannot be even approximated in any other way.

The film is divided into five parts. A foreword begins, "Year by year our cities grow more complex and less fit for living. The age of rebuilding is here. We must remold our old cities and build new communities better suited to our needs. . . ."

Thus the American Institute of Planners, who decided to make this propaganda film. It is a fair enough statement, one which could have led to a dull little treatise—but didn't.

PART 1. "In the Beginning"—New England.

Out of the life that was New England years ago, the camera

picks out things like a boy on a wagon looking at the sky, a barrel of apples, a white spire of a church sticking up from a fold in the Connecticut hills, a town meeting with an old man speaking while his wife's hand plucks at his sleeve, a blacksmith's shop. The man walking beside the blacksmith has overalls which have been worn long and hard. An old cemetary, the flat tombstones; and death is a ripe seed falling into the earth, ready for rebirth. This part is a New England idyll, beautiful and quiet, like something that Sarah Orne Jewett might have written, translated into screen imagery.

PART 2: The Industrial City—"City of Smoke."

The camera riots among the mighty stacks, turrets, girders, long and hard. An old cemetery, the flat tombstones; and death and belching smokes of a steel town. It angles up at the steel skeleton of giant basic industry. Those shots are infernally magnificent, like the valley of a thousand smokes, like the ground floor of a Hell where business is great. Then it turns to houses where workmen live. Identical rows of boxes dim in smoke, dirty children playing on railroad tracks, streets of mud, leaning shacks, outhouses everywhere, water coming from a hand-pump, men washing in bowls, not at faucets. The commentator remarks, "Smoke makes prosperity, they tell you here, even if you choke on it." He says, "There's prisons where a guy for doing wrong can get a better place to live than we can give our children." These shots of a steel town are footnotes for a feature that cries to be made. They are beautiful and terrifying.

PART 3: The Metropolis—"Men into Steel."

Never has a camera been so cannily directed into catching the mood and appearance of the big city. The tempo is wonderfully repeated in mechanism (the eight pieces of toast which repeatedly hop up, and the automatic pancake turner), in the cutting of the film, and in the music. People cross streets, stop, start, stop, are caught between cars. Traffic congeals, fire sirens scream, and an amazingly comic, anonymous little man steps out from the curb, is motioned back by the cop, goes back to his curb. Satire sinks its teeth into our city life in what is a small masterpiece of camera observation. The commentator remarks. "Cities, where people count the seconds and lose the days. . . ."

PART 4: The Highway—"The Endless City."

The insanity of the Sunday highway jam is treated in a manner that makes you wonder why people do it. They're all here: the flat tire, packed car, crying children, the horn that won't stop blowing, the ugly highways, the automatic stops and goes, the small wreck and the big wreck. You can almost feel the heat and strain of it out on the shadeless, white cement strip of highway. It's funny, and it's crazy.

PART 5: "The Green City."

This is the happy ending. It is what the city planners want: homes with grass around them, trees a little way off, factories that look like the Modern Museum of Art, schools that look the same (glass bricks so the sun shines through), kids on bicycles, lakes, men playing baseball (wholesome, like Y.M.C.A. secretaries), throwing one of their number in the lake, flowerbeds, libraries, happy faces of children, clean kitchens with modern conveniences, women who play bridge while washing-machines complete the labors that used to break backs.

Like many happy endings, this section has the dreamy aspect of wishful thinking. But since it utilizes scenes of such realities as Radburn, N.J., where children cannot get run over by automobiles, and Greenbelt, Md., a model community, the dream is not too remote. That it is couched in terms of grass, earth, sky, books, and baseball, making a nature-lover and intellectual's paradise, doesn't rule out the many other desires. They might also have added the ways and means, what it would cost to set up everyone in a "Green City."

At any rate, the first four sections of *The City*, the parts which show a country and the city life it grew into, constitute one of the most brilliant jobs of filmmaking ever accomplished.

If all documentaries could be like this one, there would be no reason why they shouldn't run for two hours, instead of this forty-four minutes, and delight millions of people. A new horizon has come into clear sight.

The names of those who worked on the picture make its quality less surprising. Ralph H. Steiner *(Plow That Broke . . .* cameraman) and Willard Van Dyke *(The River* cameraman) directed and photographed the picture. Oscar Serlin underwent the headaches of supervising production. Henwar Rodakiewicz, who worked on *The Wave,* wrote this scenario. Lewis Mumford wrote the narrative and Morris Carnovsky spoke it. Pare Lorentz furnished the original outline. Aaron Copland did the musical score, his first for pictures.

No one should do himself the injury of missing *The City.*

Les Maisons de la misère
by Paul Strand

This review of a distinguished Belgian 30-minute featurette was written by Mr. Strand, the American filmmaker, for the November 1939 issue of Films.

Lately I have been privileged to see one of the most moving documentary films that I have seen in a long time. This film, *Les Maisons de la misère,* was directed by Henri Storck and photographed by Eli Lotar and John Ferno.

A single seeing of this picture does not permit final judgments nor detailed analyses. The impact of the work, however, is so strong that the following impressions received at one seeing still endure.

Les Maisons de la misère is a film about housing in Belgium. More than two-and-a-half of its three reels is the most devastating picturization of a slum that I have ever seen documented. Nothing in British or American films dealing with similar material approximates the understanding and sensibility which those who made this film brought to the task. For they have dramatized not only the horrors of slum filth, all the inhuman living conditions of a steel town street, but they have also revealed the people living there with a profound sense of their dignity and worth. We come very close to these people as the texture of their lives is woven from moments which the camera discovers: the hurry call for the midwife and the funeral of the new-born child; the eviction of a family as the neighbors watch from their windows, unable to help. These and other visits into the houses of this one street which take the audience into the intimate lives of these slum-dwellers never allow us to be disinterested spectators.

To this end, photography and sound have been used richly and sensitively. The instrument of commentary is not used in this film. Dialogue, music, and natural sound carry the meaning and build the dramatic texture. Both exteriors and interiors are the real houses of the real street. The people are the people of the street, except in the case of some of those who have lines to speak. They were professional actors, I am told, taken from the companies of local people's theaters. They are all examples of superb casting, because there is absolutely no separation between the actors and the non-actors.

The use of the camera is extremely interesting, being used over and over again as a discovering agent, ferreting out the truth of a scene. It wanders over walls, gropes among poverty's odds and ends, to find the human being who inhabits these quarters, perhaps a whole family asleep amid the cramped disorder of a single room.

On first viewing, the conclusion of the film is not clear, but the great body of it is one of the finest dramatizations of human need I have seen. It is to be hoped that this film will reach American audiences by means of English titles. What it says and the richness of its speech is as true for America as it is for Belgium.

Some New American Documentaries:
In Defense of Liberty
by John H. Winge

*This British overview of documentary production in the United
States appeared in Sight and Sound (London), Spring 1939.*

"Democracy depends upon the easy and prompt dissemination of
ideas and opinions. The motion picture is potentially one of the
greatest weapons for the safeguarding of democracy. But if it is
hobbled and haltered—if it cannot speak truthfully and freely
where great issues are involved—then it can be a weapon turned
against democracy. Democracies, unwisely fearing the power
of the medium, have not allowed it to speak for democratic
principles, whereas the totalitarian States have used it to the nth
degree to spread their doctrines. What we who believe in our
democracy would like to do is to make films that would counteract
these totalitarian ideologies, and make ours more effective by using
the truth that is on our side. I do not call this propaganda. I call
this a necessary patriotic service.

"We have a large group of able, talented people in the industry
today who are eager to take their full share of these new responsibilities. They are bitterly criticized by the old order, by the tradi-
tionalists, by people in high places who, unlike the public, are afraid
of ideas. This group is attacked by various publications and outside
elements, simply for being good citizens as well as artists, directors,
producers, technicians. I think no single fact is more promising for
the future of the motion picture than the emergence of these first-
class citizens who are no longer vagrant, strolling players, but free-
men in a democracy, conscious of their social duties—and anyone
who snipes at them for taking their citizenship seriously invades the
basic rights of the American individual in a viciously un-American
way."

As you have already guessed—it was indeed an American who
spoke these remarkable sentences. But not a temperamental after-
dinner-speaker, who likes to indulge in commonplaces, no outsider
who puts his nose in another's business, but a very well known and
successful producer, acknowledged even by Hollywood: Walter
F. Wanger. He really dared to say these frank words very publicly

a short time ago and, as we have learned, he nevertheless is still allowed to mingle with the distinguished people of Hollywood and to receive their salutations as before.

The age of miracles is not past. Of course, Hollywood still produces its charming stupidities and fights chastely against the temptations of the box-office, aided by the courageous knight Will Hays. But the Sleeping Beauty of the Coast has begun to have nightmares. Coincidental with the "normal" activities of the studios Mr. Wanger made this troubling speech and about the same time even the respected brothers Warner rubbed their eyes and saw the light. They realized the necessity of producing profitless shorts to aid the democracy. But these two are still not enough and an anonymous group decides to produce features behind the secret gates of Hollywood.

The Warners have already released a couple of shorts dealing with events in American history and the revolutionary ideas of Washington and Lincoln. They also announce a series of shorts with similar themes.

Just before the last elections in California a certain Motion Picture Democratic Committee produced a remarkably good picture called *California Speaks*. It was backed by members of the Democratic Party, and this frank and open declaration of the needs of California was a big success. Some of the members of this Committee afterwards founded a Film Guild with the avowed intention of producing anti-fascist pictures. There are some well-known Hollywood people who are sponsoring this enterprise, but at the same time they are afraid to have it known. Their bosses are unable to sell their films to the totalitarian States, but they hesitate nevertheless to offend them. They would prefer to follow venerable principles like "Do not offend anybody, perhaps he could again become your customer some day." Therefore their employees—actors, writers, producers—remain quiet publicly, but act secretly.

Therefore you will not be surprised that only a few names can be officially linked with the activities of the Film Guild. The president is the photographer Floyd Crosby, who was on the staff of Pare Lorentz's *The River*. The secretary is the moviewriter James Gow, while the company also includes director Herbert Biberman and film editor Slavko Vorkapich, montage expert with Metro-Goldwyn-Mayer. They all work mainly nights and weekends. Why? Because during the day they are busy with their official duties and it is only afterwards they do what they really like. They are now preparing the script for their new film, *School for Barbarians,* based on the book by Erika Mann.

As you know, Hollywood is the capital of the picture business, but even in the United States itself there are other places where movies are made. I mean the modest city of New York, where the studios on Long Island are used every day in what may be called a boom. Because some democratically minded people living in New York City had the idea of using the film to put over democratic propaganda.

The Mexican government, filled with enthusiasm by the gorgeous stills taken by Mr. Paul Strand of New York in 1935, ordered him to produce a film dealing with the strike of the much exploited Mexican fishermen. The picture was *The Wave,* a much discussed, beautifully photographed documentary, in which the fishermen themselves were featured.

Even at that time there was a small group of young aspirants around Mr. Strand, from the Film and Photo League, all amateurs, and all particularly interested in the problem of making better and truer films.

First they discussed films only aesthetically, but during the election of 1936 they discovered that the great excitement of the country about the problems surrounding Franklin Delano Roosevelt was to be seen everywhere except in the charming dreams from the Hollywood factories. Thus they were awakened to reality. They realized in 1936 the necessity to use the films as an instrument for democracy and progress. And now Strand and Leo Hurwitz had the opportunity to do the photography of *The Plow That Broke the Plains,* first progressive documentary film produced by the American government.

The small group around Mr. Strand, consisting of young writers, photographers, and even poets, used its leisure time for making its first picture, *The World Today.* The rather pathetic title, apparently inspired by *The March of Time,* headed a picture of two reels, the first about the evictions of Sunnyside. Half a year before there had been a lot of trouble with evictions of residents of a New York settlement called Sunnyside, and this rather sensational affair was remade by the group. Most of the parts were played by the real heroes of the affair, the inhabitants of the settlement.

Afterwards they hired little-known actors and made a second

short (with the eviction-story as a story, *Black Legion*) and previewed it together with *The Wave* and *World Today* before an audience of artists and people interested in progressive films. It was a tremendous success and they dared then to invite the visitors to help so that they could found a special group to produce progressive films. The exalted visitors understood and in 1937 Strand's group founded Frontier Films, aided by people like Bishop Francis J. McConnell, the writers Paul de Kruif, Dudley Nichols, Clifford Odets, Dorothy Parker, Irwin Shaw, Donald Ogden Stewart, William Allen White, the composers Carlos Chavez and Aaron Copland, the artists Melvyn Douglas and Lewis Milestone.

Eager to make pictures about the reality of American life, their first picture was, paradoxically, *Heart of Spain*. The former editor of New Theatre, Mr. Herbert Kline, and Mr. Geza Karpathi had returned from Spain with lots of interesting picture material for the North American Committee to Aid Spanish Democracy. Creating a new scenario and adding to this material the best newsreel clips on the Spanish War, Paul Strand and Leo Hurwitz edited this footage into a moving documentary film. Thus they produced *Heart of Spain* with a commentary written by David Wolff and Herbert Kline, and for seven weeks the audience of the Playhouse on New York City's 55th Street enjoyed the close-ups of transfusions of blood to badly wounded Spanish warriors.

Heart of Spain was already running in numerous cinemas, in clubs and trade unions on 16mm films, when in 1938 the new film company handled the material Harry Dunham had brought home from China, mostly photographs taken in districts never seen before by white men. Mr. Dunham was sponsored by interested Chinese and American people and so Frontier Films was able to edit a very topical picture, *China Strikes Back,* an even bigger success than the Spanish beginning. Forty-five theaters in New York City played it and the audience devoured the heavy stuff which did not pretend to be a fairystory despite the fact that the commentary was sometimes a genuine poem by Mr. Wolff.

Now partly aided by a regular distributing company, Garrison Films, in 1938 Frontier Films was able to make the first real American picture, *People of the Cumberland,* which started as a bitter document of the miserable life of the people in that section of the country and became a rather sweet one of the favorable influence of the newly founded Highlander Folk School. You could see for the first time in a picture the folkdances of the Cumberland, truly American scenes, encouraged and managed by the very active school. This interesting and often remarkable film had the advantage of a commentary by the famous writer Erskine Caldwell, author of "Tobacco Road."

After this vivid picture the company returned to the business of editing. A French director Henri Cartier[-Bresson], having brought material from fighting Spain, Frontier Films was again ordered by the Committee to Aid Spain to produce the English version and commentary of *Return to Life*. Favored by the reception of *Heart of Spain,* the new Spanish picture also got enthusiastic approbation from the United States, nearly as much as *People of the Cumberland,* which succeeded especially because of its realistic theme.

1939 brought an order to do a picture for the Transportation Building of the New York World's Fair, a purely commercial vehicle about the means of transportation, consisting of newsreels and original shots to be performed on a giant map.

But more interesting is the newest picture about certain strange incidents gathered in documents by the famous Civil Liberties Committee, which is headed by Robert La Follette, Jr., and Elbert D. Thomas. This first feature of seven or eight reels, made by Frontier Films, will deal with some notorious violations of civil liberties in the United States of America which happened recently and were recorded by the Committee. Both La Follette and Thomas helped the young people of Frontier Films to gather materials and the original heroes of the events. But, of course, the "villains" would not like to repeat their crimes before a camera, therefore only the heroes are the same as in the real events and the less reputable parts are taken by actors. The background remains realistic. In contrast to customary Hollywood usage, the foreword will read, "Everything herein is related to real people and real events."

The picture is nearly completed. To finish it they need only means and it is the old tragedy of people with common sense being hardly able to raise money. What Frontier Films has done on this picture so far presages an unusual, daring, and courageous film.

Leni Riefenstahl's *Olympia*
by Parker Tyler

This retrospective appraisal is taken from Mr. Tyler's book,
"Classics of the Foreign Film" (Citadel, New York, 1962).
Mr. Tyler's most recent book is "Underground Film."

Here is unrolled a paean to the human body in action, to athletics as a modern ideal, an obsession with the out-of-doors. Conceived by Nazi officials as a propaganda film to be made from the Olympic Games held at Berlin in 1936, it was issued in several versions suitable for export to participating nations whose winners were respectively featured. As Nazi propaganda, the film harmonized with the exceptional passion of German scholars for Classical culture. Enlisting the finest photographic skill in Germany, it had the further asset of supervision by the talented Leni Riefenstahl, an actress turned director-editor. *Olympia* survives as one of the grandest documentaries in the world film archives and it undoubtedly is the most impressive film ever to deal with field sports. Regarded aside from its political function, it provides a fascinating study of its innate content: whole-souled, harmless physical competition.

Reel-washed of its Nazi motivation, it can even rate as a sincere tribute to the Greek ideal as still perpetuated in the Olympic Games. Fräulein Riefenstahl tried systematically to make her film as "classical" as possible. It opens solemnly with multiply exposed views of the temple colonnades, and shifts fluently to a torch being lit by a runner at Olympia in Greece, following the torch as it is handed from runner to runner, till the last one, in long, easy strides, enters the huge, decorated Berlin stadium. Considering that any existing version is apt to have haphazard editing, these Games emerge as an exciting, dramatic, and even lyric expression of the beauties of physical being in the flush of competition among champions. The diving contest, in thrilling montage, is treated as a poem of human flight, while the high jump, filmed glamorously at twilight, is a marvel in slow-motion. Innumerable cameramen, as well as many editors, are responsible for an Homerically scaled collective piece of filmmaking.

One can discern national traits in the performances as well as the looks of the athletes. The American Negro, Jesse Owens, is a portrait in swift, highlighted black and deep force. Glenn Morris, American winner of the Decathlon, seems to bring kinetic life to the ancient statue of the Discus Thrower. The obstacle race for equestrian Army officers shows each national entrant at the same hazardous jump. An incredible tension is built up as, time after time, each national entrant is announced, and we witness his and his mount's effort to exalt their country's honor. The German officer who wins, clearing the jump successfully with perfect aplomb, forces us to gasp, while the Italian officer's spread-eagled fall from his mount wrings a howl from every throat. The climactic Marathon, won by a Japanese, is accorded the elaborateness due its high prestige; now the camera becomes the very eye of Mercury, hovering over and encouraging the winner, even seeming to touch his head and ankles, making it clear why, in winning an Olympic event, each athlete becomes the heroism of a nation incarnate. Nazified Germany, in having to grant athletic supremacy to the United States in the 1936 Games, could mark up one supreme conquest of its own: the bylines on this film.

The Triumph of the Will
by William K. Everson

This study is reprinted from Infinity (New York), September 1964. The author teaches film history at the New York University Graduate School of Cinema and has written several books, including "The Bad Guys" and "A Pictorial History of the Western."

One of the greatest documentaries of them all, certainly one of the most pictorially eloquent, and one that still influences documentary-makers today [. . .] is Leni Riefenstahl's paean of praise to the Nazi party, *The Triumph of the Will.* Long kept out of circulation because of its allegedly inflammatory nature, the film has in recent years been made available for wholesale pillaging (without credit to the source) by contemporary documentary producers, and has even been getting into occasional specialized art-house bookings. When the enterprising New Yorker Theatre ran the full version (in excess of two hours) a year or two back, the lines around the block were so enormous that another showing was set up for the small hours of the morning! So this discussion is not of a purely academic nature, because the chances are that—with a little effort—you *will* be able to see it.

Earlier I called it one of the greatest documentaries of all. I'll go further on a limb and call it one of the greatest *films* of all time. Whether it is strictly a documentary is a case of splitting hairs. It was a filmed record of a public event, the Nazi rallies at Nuremberg. But that event was deliberately pre-planned and staged so that a movie could be made from it. Fantastic groupings of massed troops and banners, intricate miles of camera tracks, cameras mounted at specific points to get just the right close-ups at just the right time, camera trucks given every freedom—these are advantages seldom enjoyed by the average documentary producer, and never on the same scale as here, with the result that *Triumph of the Will* has all the gloss and production polish of the biggest Hollywood super-special. The film was made in 1934 as a propaganda film first, and a documentary second, to "hard-sell" the German public on Nazism—which was far from being a complete *fait accompli* at that time. Purely and simply as a propaganda job, it is superb, completely lacking the aggressively heavy-handed technique of the Soviet propagandists who spent less time espousing their own way of life than they did attacking all other systems. Triumph of the Will, using inspiring and heroic images throughout, backed by a stirring Wagnerian score, concentrating on flawlessly handsome or beautiful German faces, stressing work, health, and progress, makes it easy to understand how the German people came to be so completely under the hypnotic spell of Nazism. If all their propaganda was as effective as this, the unquestioning acceptance of Nazism is no mystery at all. Even in retrospect, and fully aware of the horrors and degradations that followed, the film still retains its hypnotic impact. Fortunately, the filmic record *is* complete. If all that remained on celluloid of the Nazi regime was this work, future generations might well wonder what all the ill-feeling was about! Hitler was such a showman in his organization, and such a dynamic performer before the cameras, that it's really a pity—for the art of the film, as well as for the sake of the world—that he didn't just limit his activities to film work!

Leni Riefenstahl (still spasmodically active) was a popular German actress of the twenties and thirties who specialized in the mountaineering adventures so beloved of German audiences. But as a producer/director/editor of the grand-scale documentary (she also made the superlative record of the 1936 Olympics) she was in a class all her own, as distinctive as Griffith or Eisenstein, and by far the most dynamic of the few women (Lois Weber, Ida Lupino, Dorothy Arzner) who ventured into film direction.

In recent years, Triumph of the Will has been made available to the producers of *20th Century* and other TV series doing documentaries on the Nazi era. All of them naturally and justifiably have been violently anti-Nazi in tone, and have utilized, out of their original context, shots from the Riefenstahl film to illustrate Nazi "barbarism" and "mass hysteria." Unfortunately, the heroic nature of the original images still survives—and despite newly-shot surrounding footage of storm-trooper brutality, and harsh music, the original beauty can't be distorted. Perversely, it has the effect of looking as though inspiring non-propaganda footage is being distorted by TV into decidedly propagandist channels!

When current documentarians don't actually like the footage, they often borrow its ideas. A case in point is offered by a recent USIA documentary. The opening of Triumph of the Will is a brilliantly stylized sequence which starts with mystical cloud formations, as the narrator tells of the misfortunes and disgraces that have befallen Germany since the first World War. Gradually, a plane appears. Finally, in a beautiful optical effect, the curtain of clouds clears, and we see Nuremberg below. The plane lands, and Hitler emerges—seen none too clearly at first. We see him in long-shot, or from the rear, accepting the tumultuous applause of the crowds, before we get a clear look at his face. The overall impression of a godlike saviour descending to deliver his people is unmistakable, even though never put into words. Quite obviously a USIA documentary man, assigned to cover President Kennedy's arrival at a Latin American town, has seen *Triumph of the Will* and, with the sincerest motives in the world, felt that a pictorial idea that had worked for Hitler (who hardly deserved it) might work even better for President Kennedy. Unfortunately, even though he tried meticulously to follow the original format, it didn't work out. The President arrived not in a gleaming plane, but in a workmanlike helicopter. His cheerful grin was democratic rather than godlike. The undisciplined crowds were more like eager fans than reverent worshipers. And there's nothing wrong with this, of course—except filmically: The director, having to work with existing and pre-shot footage, just couldn't divert it to the propagandist ideal he had in mind. Thus Riefenstahl's in a sense "faked" sequence seems true and inspiring and is still a memorable episode, whereas the Kennedy arrival—far more honest in its filmic reportage—is trivial, uninspiring, and already forgotten. At a time when the U.S. image abroad seems somewhat in need of bolstering, perhaps the USIA might do well to swallow its pride a little, and offer Miss Riefenstahl the job of propagandizing us to the world at large!

If so, I hope the presidents and statesmen involved will have the wit to leave in the possibly unflattering but humanizing little touches that Miss Riefenstahl wisely didn't edit out of her films. One of the highlights of *Triumph of the Will* is a brief, almost imperceptible vignette lasting less than a second. The mob roars approval of one of Hitler's speeches. Even he is a bit surprised at the enthusiasm. There is a slightly smug, cocky, self-satisfied nod of his head, and a suggestion of a smile which says, more clearly than reels of film, "Boy, I've got them just where I want them!" Of such moments is the real truth of history, and some of the most valuable moments of film documentary, composed.

The Camera Reconnoiters
by Ben Belitt

This survey by the poet and critic, Ben Belitt, originally appeared in The Nation (New York), November 20, 1937.

It used to be the travelogues, not so long ago, that were being written "with gun and camera"; today it is history. Our chroniclers are already among us. At Corning they have been polishing the great lenses soon to be trained upon interstellar darkness; nearer home their lenses are fitted to motion-picture cameras and are trained upon contemporary chaos.

There have been many, of late, to point out that the camera eye is an organ of which Hollywood seems so far to have discovered only the hypnotic possibilities. Certainly since the time of Griffith it has not ceased to propound triangles and transform Cinderellas in lethal double features throughout the nation, and has paused only rarely for experiments in realism like *Fury* and *The Informer,* or the more synthetic *Zola, Dead End,* and *Winterset.* Its answer to the distress of our time has been the neighborhood bank night and the newsreel potpourri edited down to the perfunctoriness of a news flash. In the course of less than half a century it has not only exhausted its mythology but lost touch with reality.

Hollywood's answer to its doldrums, apparently, is three-dimensional films, features in technicolor, and a revolving belt of imported profiles; and with such projects it keeps complacently occupied. Six months ago, however, a group of scenarists and cameramen came forward with an answer of their own—the independent, non-profit organization known as Frontier Films. At their head is Paul Strand, whose memorable *The Wave* was an indication of what may be expected of this enterprise. His colleagues and advisory staff include, among others, Joris Ivens, pioneering producer of *Borinage* and *Spanish Earth,* Ralph Steiner, Leo Hurwitz, John Howard Lawson, Elia Kazan, Vera Caspary, David Wolff, Malcolm Cowley, John Dos Passos, Lillian Hellman, Archibald MacLeish, Lewis Milestone, and Clifford Odets. Their purpose is to bring to bear on the contemporary scene an organized group of professional scenarists, directors, and cameramen who will faithfully transcribe that scene in terms of its drama, and "wield this power consistently on the side of progress." To this end they have said their farewells to Hollywood, to reconnoiter on their own for themes which American life today has flung squarely before their cameras.

Moviegoers throughout the country have already participated in the scouting experiments out of which the venture emerges. By the hundreds of thousands they have found their way to the independent motion-picture houses to appraise, many of them for the first time, a new type of "documentary short" combining drama and the morning's headlines. In *The Plow That Broke the Plains,* a WPA undertaking, they witnessed the spectacle of American land erosion as recorded by the cameras of Ralph Steiner, Paul Strand, and Leo Hurwitz. In *Spanish Earth,* Joris Ivens, Ernest Hemingway, and Archibald MacLeish, working together as the "Contemporary Historians," unfolded for them the portent of the Loyalist struggle in Spain. In *Spain in Flames* and *Heart of Spain,* the latter a Frontier release, pertinent phases of the same conflict were again touched off; and in the newest Frontier offering, *China Strikes Back,* the lens has documented China's reply to the challenge of man's fate in the Far East.

Spanish Earth invites particularly close inspection. Already in its third month in New York, it is scheduled, in spite of overwhelming competitive odds, for appearance in some sixty key cities throughout the United States, and according to its distributors will have rolled up a total of at least 800 theaters and 2,000 extra-theatrical exhibitions before its run is completed. The figure admittedly dwindles if entered on the records alongside the nation's 17,000 film houses; nor is the sum total of 1,600,000 paid admissions to be compared with the paid-admissions count of the country, which weekly runs to more than 80,000,000. It becomes impressive, however, when one recalls that the totals which are being compared in each case represent the initial triumph of a pioneering venture over a tightly monopolized commercial machine which for more than a quarter of a century has been adding theater to theater in producer-distributor circuits hitherto considered impregnable.

It is the plan of Frontier Films to utilize those outlets of which Hollywood takes no cognizance, as well as the commercial movie houses. "We have," it is explained, "appealed so far to the 'subway circuit' of motion-picture houses, for the most part independently owned and exhibiting the finer foreign films throughout the country. We propose now to open up new channels which will embrace the greatest potential theatrical and extra-theatrical audience for living and purposeful films that exists in America. Our facilities are already at the disposal of responsible agents which cut across the bias of modern life—the trade unions, the cooperative societies, educational institutions, social-welfare groups, peace organizations, public forums, churches of whatever denomination, schools, and the like. We hope to utilize all these channels in the regular distribution of our films. In time we expect to include an even more widely scattered audience in a program of organized roadshows which will tour the farming communities and mill towns of the nation." It is expected that many progressive organizations, particularly trade unions, will follow Europe's example of sponsoring realistic documents in which the problems peculiar to their respective groups will be candidly and dramatically transcribed in the language of their respective trades. A film portraying the unionization of John Doe, automobile worker, is already under consideration.

This concern of experimental photography for events close to our own time and society is not a fad, but a flowering. Many of its practitioners are drawn from the ranks that created the Group Theater. They are the same group, substantially, who several years ago organized the Film and Photo League to produce "stills" and motion pictures which would take stock of modern life in America, which would report the events of the day in newsreels that stayed for an answer where the commercial product looked askance. They are the group who in 1932 trained their cameras on the East Side Hoovervilles, the Washington hunger marchers, and the Scottsboro case. And it was from this group, finally, that the Nykino workshop emerged in 1933, in response to the need for a craftsmanlike unit to effect a vital rapport between the camera and the materials with which it was concerned.

What is the documentary film? It is more, says Paul Strand, than a purely informative chronicle of things and events, a mere journalistic diagram of reality. "The problem which the makers of documentary films must solve," he declared, "does not end with the problem of how an audience may be informed. They must devise legitimate techniques for moving an audience by projecting the basic dramatic meanings implicit in the documents." The reportorial coverage of weekly newsreels and travelogues is only one element in the documentary film and is distributed in strategic sequence-patterns to achieve effects of drama and emphasis that the commercial news-cameraman cannot take into account. In the same way, the March of Time releases are foreign to the technique now under consideration, although they have combined reporting with another significant element of the documentary film—the enactment of the drama. Frontier Films is frankly concerned with the problem of involving its audiences in a context of specific responses to the material with which they are being presented. Unlike the March of Time productions, however, whose chromium-bright polish is in its way as much a matter of pace and façade as the factory product of Hollywood, it prefers to deduce both pace and drama out of the real scene and the real protagonists. It is interested, for example, in the story of Myles Horton, who gave up a career in the ministry to found the Highlander Folk School in a small Cumberland Plateau mountain community near Chattanooga. The resulting moving picture, based on a script by Elia Kazan already recorded in film by Ralph Steiner, will be released shortly. It presents the literal story of a community enterprise filmed in the midst of its own mined-out and lumbered-off poverty, with its own protagonist in the "title role" and native miners, lumbermen, and textile workers enacting the drama that at one time was their experience. "The world," Mr. Steiner declared, "is our studio. One works with life itself here, not with fabrications of it. And there's no more exciting material in the world for a man who wants to run a camera."

Leading directors, cameramen, and writers have affirmed this enthusiasm and are engaged in similar ventures on both sides of the Atlantic. In France, Ciné Liberté, under the distinguished leadership of Jean Renoir, director of *The Lower Depths,* has produced *La Vie est à nous* and *La Marseillaise,* the latter sponsored by the Front Populaire and financed by popular subscription. In England, independent filmmakers like Paul Rotha have organized Strand Films and Realistic Films, which are turning out not only educational films but trade and government documents on such diverse topics as building and malnutrition.

Frontier Films plans to release in the immediate future, in addition to the Highlander School and automobile-worker items, a feature-length picture on child labor called *Pay Day,* prepared by George Sklar and Vera Caspary with the directorial collaboration of Paul Strand, William Watts, and Leo Hurwitz, to be followed later by a shorter film, *Labor Spy,* based on the violations of civil liberties revealed by the La Follette committee investigation, with a script by David Wolff. The cost of a documentary film is naturally dependent upon the exigencies of production. Such a picture as the automobile worker's film requires at least $7,000 to complete, while the current three-reeler, *Heart of Spain,* which was first compiled on the scene in loose photographic sequence by Herbert Kline and Geza Karpathi, and later built into a dramatically moving film in the cuttingroom by Strand and Hurwitz, reached the projector's booth at a cost of only $5,000.

Up to the present, the camera has attempted to make visible only what the public, because of its conditioning, has wished to believe. Just recently the production chief of a major Hollywood film factory announced the picture schedule for the forthcoming year with the manifesto: "With the whole world in a crazy turmoil, people's nerves are too taut to stand the strain of serious drama. War is already under way in the Orient; Europe is on the verge of war; and here in the United States labor troubles and political dissension have everyone on edge. . . . So 1938, like 1917, 1918, and 1919, will see the rise of many new comedy stars."

We need to be delivered from our spellbinders. History by hearsay is yielding place to history by eyewitness, and our roles are already being thrust upon us. It remains for actors to be united with their drama, for the involvement as a whole to be envisioned in terms of its portent. For this purpose the documentary film, as Peter Quince once observed, offers "a marvelous convenient place for our rehearsal."

Land Without Bread and Spanish Earth
by Basil Wright

These two reviews appeared as part of a longer article in World Film News (London), December 1937. Mr. Wright was one of the important British documentary filmmakers of the period.

The depression deepens as we approach *Land Without Bread*. An extraordinary film. Directed by the screen's quondam prophet of surrealism, Luis Buñuel, it achieves in visual simplicity not the imaginative creativeness which is supposed to be the hallmark of documentary, but a stark presentation of actuality which certainly deserves the title of document.

This complete volte-face made by Buñuel, who hitherto had specialized in shots of dead donkeys ensconced in a grand piano, led him to a little known and remote district of Spain, inhabited by people known as the Hurdanos. In stony and infertile uplands they are born to a lifelong despair, martyrs to malnutrition, to goiter, to tuberculosis. Generations of inbreeding have produced a high percentage of cretins. Generations without hope have lost even the art of decent house-building. Children lie down in the street in a coma, cannot be moved, die. Their only hope is death.

Such are the facts that Buñuel's camera quite unemotionally presents. They are presented without sympathy and without rage. He was there with a camera; he saw these things; he photographed them. That is all.

Unfortunately, someone (presumably not Buñuel) has added to the film a wearisome American commentary, plus the better part of a Brahms symphony. As a result, picture and sound never coalesce, and it is only the starkness of the presented facts which counts.

Sincere, truthful, moving, *Spanish Earth*. So you can guess that our old friend the censor had to have a go at it with his emasculating scissors; cutting out "horror" shots and removing tactless references to German and Italian intervention. But with a film like this the impotence he would inflict returns upon himself. Snip he never so furiously, he cannot destroy its strength.

It was made by Joris Ivens and Ernest Hemingway; and those who complain that Hemingway's work is falling off had better prepare to eat their hats, for he has written the best commentary in the history of the sound film. As the pathetic little groups of six men go out across the quiet fields to the attack (a scene photographed with all the restraint which, not merely through the physical compulsion of flying bullets but also through Ivens's sense of filmmaking, gives this film a quality of greatness), as they go out across the fields they used to till, Hemingway's voice—for he speaks the commentary himself—cuts through the sounds of crackling battle, "This is the moment which all the rest of the war prepares for, when six men go forward into death, to walk across a stretch of land, and by their presence on it prove this land is ours."

It is not merely fact that this film presents, but emotions and moods which build up for the first time a true picture of what war is really like. But it presents more than this—it presents the face of Spain and the faces of its people, proud and remote until bombs drop or shells shatter, then in panic and tears; women who trip and fall in their run for the safety of the Metro station, women who gasp and weep in that horrible vacuum which follows the destruction of the home they have lived in so happily until two minutes ago; ordinary men who have become soldiers almost imperceptibly, who will fire a fieldgun every so often at the ruins of their great university which, thanks to the treachery of fellow countrymen and the mercenary troops of Italy and Germany, they must bring even further to destruction; and, worst of all, the faces of children who cannot understand, but are afraid.

Villages, cities, churches, fields—they are all here—a picture of Spain itself. There is no sensational cutting and no coruscating camerawork; but there is the observation of men who can imaginatively observe, can feel and express the implications of what they see. "Man cannot act before the camera in the presence of death," says Hemingway, as a frieze of magnificent faces of Government troops swing past the camera; but here is something more than acting.

We can only hope that the well-meaning Left and Liberal press has not, by screaming to the rooftops that the censor has mutilated the film, put people off going to see *Spanish Earth*. Ignoble cuts count for nothing when you are watching a great film.

Films Without Make-Believe
by Herbert Kline

*This appraisal of the problems of documentary filmmaking is
reprinted from* The Magazine of Art *(New York), February 1942.
Mr. Kline's most recent film is* Walls of Fire, *a feature-length
documentary on Siqueiros, Orozco, and Diego Rivera.*

I did my first day's filming in a hospital for women and children
wounded by fascist bombardments in besieged Madrid. I began
work in films in the belief that the sight of these innocent victims
of explosive bombs could do more to damn fascist aggressors than
all the tirades in the world. I didn't know much about filmmaking
then. But I knew from the first that the filming had to be done in a
way that would make audiences feel that no camera crew had been
present, that life had just unfolded on the screen. As if the vivid
writings of one of the great foreign correspondents had come to life
without the slightest suggestion of movie atmosphere or make-
believe.

My purpose from the first was to go beyond surface reporting of
events to the higher role of interpreting the full meaning of the
scene taken in by the camera. Just as books like "Personal History"
and "Days of Our Years" have gone beyond the daily news reports by
interpreting world events in works of high literary distinction, so
too have I and my documentary film colleagues set ourselves the
task of digging deeper than the newsreelmen, of becoming "the
foreign correspondents of the screen." And now I have been asked
to tell how I got into the exciting life of making films like *Crisis* and
Lights Out in Europe, which critics have compared with the writings
of men like Vincent Sheean, Pierre Van Paassen, and others, for
their values in interpreting mankind's fight for life against fascism.

I grew up in Davenport, Iowa, and never dreamed that I could
some day do what we called "artistic work" out our way. I'm thirty-
two now, and living in Hollywood for the time being, after years in
cities like Madrid, Paris, Prague, London, Warsaw, Moscow,
Mexico City, and New York. Long before I started traveling around
the world filming civil wars and blitzkriegs, I was just as restless as
I am now. I started running away from school and home when I was
fourteen. While other Davenport kids were content with reading
about Valley Forge, Mount Vernon, Niagara Falls, and New York

City in school, I went to see those places by bumming my way. I also went to sea, working my way via the "blackgang" around Cuba and Panama to California. I met all sorts of people—miners, sailors, bootleggers, hoboes, thieves. And I liked bumming around so much that it took me seven years to get through high school. I didn't get much formal education, but I learned a lot about what life was like outside my comfortable middle-class home. And all the while I read, under the influence of an older and wiser brother, the books he told me about: Whitman, Crane, Bierce, Norris, Sinclair, London, Heine, Gorki, Tolstoy, Dostoevski, Balzac, Ibsen, Ellis, Hemingway, Joyce, Dos Passos, O'Neill, Anatole France. These were my university, a regular Modern Library education in an environment that might well be described as an "intellectual Sahara."

I looked up to writers and artists as the great people of a world I'd never know. And then the crisis struck, in 1930 when I was twenty-one. All the misery and poverty I had seen on the road began to strike at the lives and happiness of people I knew. I reacted by joining the intellectual groups that took the side of the unemployed, the dispossessed, and the disinherited. I helped organize and wrote sketches for labor theaters, and began to contribute articles and book reviews to the little magazines that published what we then called "the literature of social protest." I wrote a play about the Negro legendary hero John Henry, and sent it to a Broadway producer who had advertised for plays dealing with social problems. The producer called me to New York to make revisions and promised to produce the play immediately. But a few days after I arrived he lost all his money on another production. Although my play was not produced on Broadway it was staged by several labor theaters, and got me a chance to work in what was then called "the new theatre movement." There I met and helped discover and stage the first plays of Clifford Odets and Irwin Shaw. I worked with John Howard Lawson, Harold Clurman, Albert Maltz, John Gassner, Molly Thacher, Mordecai Gorelik, and others connected with the Group Theatre, the Theatre Union, and the Theatre Guild. I thought and wrote about the creative problems faced by the theater and film artists who were my associates and thus, without realizing it at the time, I prepared for facing similar problems in far-off lands. Then the Spanish fascists attacked the Republican Government, and I left theater work to do my bit for the Loyalist cause.

My film career began in Spain. It happened like this. In February 1937 I was working in Madrid as a writer and speaker for the Loyalist radio station EAQ. Late one night a Hungarian still photographer named Geza Karpathi [later known as the film star Charles Korvin], whom I had met quite by chance in Paris a few weeks before, came to my door and yelled, "Open up—it's me, Geza, from Paris. I've got a film for us to make."

Just like that luck came to my door and I found myself about to become a filmmaker. Because I had chanced to meet Karpathi through a mutual friend, and we had spent several evenings talking about how we would like to make a documentary film together in Spain, if only we could get the opportunity. And because Karpathi had had the luck shortly afterwards to meet Dr. Norman Bethune, the Canadian who had won fame as head of the Loyalists' mobile-transfusion service in Madrid.

Karpathi told his story quickly. Dr. Bethune had engaged him to make a film that would help raise money for the hard-pressed Loyalist medical service. No, of course, he hadn't confessed that he was a still photographer and didn't even know how to load a movie camera. But Karpathi was sure that his filming would be as good as his still photography. And if I would write a scenario for him along the lines we had discussed in Paris, he was sure he could make a worthwhile film.

After a few days watching the Canadians save lives of civilians and soldiers in Madrid and at nearby fronts, I wrote the first idea of the film that became *Heart of Spain*. It had a crude thread of a story showing how one of Madrid's mothers who gave her blood as a volunteer donor meets the young soldier whose life was saved by her blood. It was to be filmed without actors, and with the citizens, doctors, and soldiers of Madrid as its principals. Dr. Bethune and Karpathi liked the idea so much that they asked me to direct the picture.

Since no one more experienced was available, I accepted. And that same day, Karpathi and I went to a film lab and told them something was wrong with our Eyemo camera. While the puzzled technician checked the camera trying to find something wrong, Karpathi and I watched how he put in the film and learned how it was done. There isn't space to tell of the many things we did wrong, or how we fumbled our way through "discoveries" known to every cameraman and director since the days of Billy Bitzer and D. W. Griffith. But we plugged away, and Karpathi did a fine job under the circumstances. In midsummer we turned over the scenes we had made to experienced filmmakers in New York. They revised the crude scenario and cut our technically· imperfect but humanly appealing material into *Heart of Spain*.

Thus I became a writer and director of documentary films. By luck! I wasn't even sure that I had the talent for the work, and some of the professionals who saw those first crude rushes assured me I didn't. But Joris Ivens, Dudley Nichols, Meyer Levin, Ralph Steiner, and other experienced directors and writers encouraged me to continue. *Heart of Spain* was enthusiastically received by public and critics alike. It received a special award of merit from the Loyalist Government, as did *Return to Life,* a second Spanish war film which I worked on later in 1937, as collaborator with the French director, Henri Cartier[-Bresson]. Since then I have produced and directed films like *Crisis, Lights Out in Europe,* and *The Forgotten Village.* Together with my wife Rosa, and my main collaborator, the Czech director of photography, Alexander Hackenschmied, I developed ideas on documentary film direction that were greatly encouraged by the critical reception of our films. *Crisis* was named one of the "Ten Best Films of 1939" by the National Board of Review. *Lights Out in Europe* was named second only to Disney's *Fantasia* among the nonfiction films of 1940. And *The Forgotten Village* has been named by many critics among the best films of 1941. Thus my collaborators and I had the pleasure of finding our work regarded as important contributions to the screen, as well as valuable indictments of fascism.

Now that I am working at Metro-Goldwyn-Mayer Studios in Hollywood many people have asked me if I regard studio directing as more difficult than documentary. I would say that both are difficult, in different ways. As I see it, the main difference is this. It is the job of a studio director to make actors seem like real-life characters, while it is the job of the documentary director to prevent real-life characters from acting falsely by imitating their favorite actors.

Of course the actual filming circumstances of the documentary director are much more difficult. It's easier and healthier to film a fascist "fifth column" composed of Hollywood extras than the real Henlein-Hitler "fifth column" in Sudetenland, as we did in *Crisis.* And it's a lot easier and healthier to film an imitation blitzkrieg on a backlot at MGM than the real thing with Nazi planes divebombing and strafing you, as in the Polish Corridor scenes of *Lights Out*. On the other hand, it's hard to gain the artistry and technical knowledge that will turn make-believe into the kind of realism found in the best pictures of men like John Ford, Lewis Milestone, Fritz Lang, King Vidor, Orson Welles, and others.

The role of the director in documentary films is frequently misunderstood. Many people assume that the director's task is merely that of selecting and reproducing the most interesting scenes one comes across. While it is true that many excellent scenes are filmed "candid" just as they happen before the camera (particularly scenes of violence and fighting), it is also true that the majority of documentary scenes are "directed" in a way that resembles studio location work.

In making a straight documentary like *Crisis* or a story documentary like *The Forgotten Village,* you seldom find a real-life scene the way you want to film it. While you can't re-arrange either an air attack or a street riot, you can arrange and re-arrange every scene that is not dependent on candid camera reporting. And, despite the fact that your people are "non-actors," you can rehearse them as long as they are willing and you feel that their real-life performances can be improved.

The effectiveness of your scenes depends finally, of course, on the skill with which you use your camera. But first comes the script which gives you the key to how you will film the scenes you plan to get. And then the direction which transfers the ideas from paper to film.

Documentary methods must be adapted to the particular circumstances. If you happen to be filming in a democratic country, you can explain your purpose openly to the civilians or soldiers whom you want to have behave in a certain way. But directing Nazis in territory they control is quite a different problem, and one has to be as much a diplomat as a director.

In making *Crisis,* for example, I had the idea of filming a Nazi "fifth column" in action as a warning to America of things to come. It was impossible to do this without the cooperation of the Sudeten Nazis who controlled the German sections of Czechoslovakia beyond the "Language frontier." My collaborators, Hackenschmied, Hans Burger, and my wife, Rosa, all agreed that we would have to bluff our way into getting filming permits. We decided that my wife and I would have a chance to use our American passports to help in getting Nazi cooperation. Accordingly, we went to see Herr Ullrich, the Goebbels of Czechoslovakia, at Brownhouse headquarters of Henlein's Sudeten Deutsche Partei. Ullrich fell for our line completely, as did his Gestapo associates. We listened with interest and apparent approval to Ullrich's ideas about Jews, Roosevelt, and Americans. And, despite my *verboten* racial origin, we had no trouble in persuading him that scenes showing how Sudeten Germans supported Henlein and Hitler would be helpful to the Nazi cause. The next day Ullrich sent us into Sudetenland with a notorious Storm Trooper named Rhodelbach as our guide, and with his aid, we succeeded in filming scenes of Nazi violence against the Czechs and German democrats of the area.

There isn't much space to recount the hundreds of adventures that we had in the months of troubles and martial law leading up to Munich, but the following illustration from one of our scenes will indicate how we worked. If, for example, our scenario called for shots showing SA men going through the streets of a Sudeten city grimly routing prospective voters out of their homes, we filmed the actual scenes. But if we needed additional shots to tie up these scenes with others, we had to ask the SA men to cooperate with us. And we were faced with the fact that our Nazi "friends" wanted us to film them smiling their prettiest. Since this would never do for the shots we needed, we would explain what we wanted in terms appealing to Nazi minds. A well-presented argument that their smiling looked undisciplined and hardly respectful toward the Fuehrer would change our grinning Nazis into the goosestepping, *heil*ing, mean-visaged threat that they were when photographers were not around. It seemed strange for one of my *verboten* and despised racial origin to have a troop of SA men to do my bidding, and march, and *heil* and shout as they were told.

Our scenario called for cutting from the scenes of Nazi violence to Czech soldiers waiting on the frontier for the attack that Hitler had threatened and that everyone expected at any moment. Our idea was to contrast the violence of the Nazi scenes with quiet sequences showing the resoluteness of the Czech army. At first, the Czech officers objected to our filming their soldiers in any but the most orderly military positions. But when we explained our purpose, and that we wanted to "cut" the quiet courage of the democratic Czechs against the hysterics and bluster of the goosestepping Nazis, the Czech officers got the point and allowed us to arrange the soldiers as we pleased. The final cut was from a mass of *heil*ing, shouting SA men to one lone Czech soldier, calmly smoking a cigarette, while waiting rifle in hand behind his barricade facing Germany. This was ten times as effective as a "cut" to a conventional shot of marching Czech troops would have been. And by beginning with shots of individual Czech soldiers and small groups of determined men, we were able to present the men of the Czech army shown in later mass scenes as being substantially different from the robots of the German army mass shots used later in the film.

Vincent Sheean in his commentary for *Crisis* and James Hilton in *Lights Out in Europe* added greatly to the values of each scene by writing in such a way that words fitted the images without describing them literally. Thus they avoided the common error of telling the audience what it already sees and understands, instead of interpreting the scene and enriching the emotional reaction. For example, commentary describing the facts of our scenes of Polish civilians mutilated and murdered by strafings from Nazi planes would only interfere with the effectiveness of these terrors. However, a repetition of Hitler's pledge, "I will not bomb women and children, Herr Hitler said," succeeded in adding full meaning to our shots of dead and dying women and children.

Of course, the *Crisis* or *Lights Out in Europe* type of straight documentary is much more elementary work than producing and directing a story film like *The Forgotten Village*. John Steinbeck's script dealt with a remote and backward village. It dramatized the conflict between the local *curandera,* or witch doctor, and the government doctors of the Servicio Medical Rural, who seek to bring modern medicine to the forgotten villages where women and children die by the tens of thousands each year under treatments the same as their ancestors knew in the days of the Aztecs.

We decided to cast the film, not with actors, but with village Indians, most of whom couldn't read or write. At first, the village children ran from us in fright and hid in the fields. And though the older people treated us courteously, they were suspicious of the *gringos.* None of them had ever seen a movie camera before. The rumor spread that it was a surveyors' device and that we were not people who made photographs, but were out to survey the land and take it away from its rightful owners. We finally won over the majority of those who doubted us, and the village elders gave us permission to film anyone we could persuade to work in our picture. But when we went about trying to cast Steinbeck's characters, we found that we were in real trouble.

The story called for a peasant family and required very careful casting to live up to the full values of the story. The man we wanted to play "Ventura, the father," agreed to do so, then backed out when he learned one scene called for him to hold "Esperanza, the mother," in his arms. He said the woman's husband would get drunk at the *pulquería* one night and kill him for touching his wife. When the woman who agreed to play "Esperanza" heard how neighbor women were gossiping about her, even before the filming started, she backed out too. And the mother of the boy we had selected to play "Paco, the little brother," was frightened when she heard her boy was to be shown as sickening and dying. For she feared, as many primitive people do, that the impersonation of sickness and death might lead to the real death of the child.

We felt with good reason that we were up against tougher casting problems than those faced by Selznick for *Gone With the Wind.* Finally, we got the idea of looking for our principal characters among Indians who had had some contact with city people and even—in markets and roadside village—with *gringos* like us. We found our film mother selling squash flowers in a market, our father working as a gardener, our children and schoolteacher in government schools, and our doctors and nurses in real-life service with the government's rural medical units. Then we took our made-up family out to our main village locations and let them get acquainted with the villagers. After a few days they made friends. And when the real villagers saw that no harm came to the simple peasants in our cast, a number of them agreed to work with us. Even Trini, the village *curandera,* consented to enact her real-life role in a film which was aimed at convincing the peasants that they should put their trust in modern medicine instead of witch doctors. The old lady put her greed for pesos in the hand ahead of her fears for competition in the bush. Besides, as we learned later, the peasants generally had more faith in *curanderas* than in doctors, and would continue with Trini's herbs and magic at the same time they were being treated by modern scientific methods.

One illustration of how we got the script on to film will tell more about our methods of work than any amount of theory that I might write. In a key scene, we had to show the birth of a baby, Aztec fashion. The baby is literally squeezed out, with *curandera* and a woman relative pulling a reboza or head shawl tight around the mother's belly and squeezing her to force the birth. To us Americans it was a terrible scene. To peasant women embarrassed by the presence of strange white men, it was something to laugh about. They would begin the scene seriously, then get embarrassed and break into laughter. Pleading and scolding did no good. They thought it was funny that we educated Americans wanted to make pictures showing how their babies are born. We tried to make the women behave by telling them why we were making the scene, that we wanted to show city people how the village women suffered and thus shame them into sending medical aid to all the forgotten villages in Mexico. That didn't work, because sickness and death were accepted as God's will, and Trini's skill was given credit in the cases of the women who did not die in childbirth. We were at a loss what to do.

Finally we recalled stories we had heard from Trini, Esperanza, and the others, of relatives who had died in childbirth. We asked our women about their lost ones. This made the film mother recall a young and dearly loved sister who had died in childbirth. The film relative remembered a sister she had lost and a daughter. And Trini had lost a daughter and two nieces under her own care. As the women poured out their stories, their feelings changed from resigned reminiscence about their loved ones to genuine grief. We were troubled with laughter and embarrassment no longer. The whole atmosphere changed. And when we called "camera," there was left only sadness and heartfelt concentration on reliving the scene all these women had experienced time and again. The *curandera* got so wrapped up in the reality of her birth practice that she completely forgot the camera and the lights. Of her own accord, she began the ancient Aztec birth chant, "Now it is forming, now it is conforming, now it has feet, now it has a head, now it has eyes," and so on. The faces of all the women reflected Trini's belief and we got the most gripping and effective scene of our film. We had directed our Indians so they achieved what Stanislavsky calls "actors' faith."

In each shot we were up against the same problem: how to make "non-actors" believe in what we asked them to do with such concentration that they would be able to overcome their natural embarrassment and self-consciousness. Sometimes it was difficult. But we learned that, whatever the difficulty, there was no excuse for the director in blaming the actors. Somehow, if we were patient and analytical and ingenious enough we could find a key to the problem. And in the end, we would always find some hidden memory or some physical action or some trick that would help our peasant friends relive the bit of life we had set before our cameras without allowing them time to think that they were "acting."

Now my partner, Alexander Hackenschmied [now known as Alexander Hammid], and I are at MGM facing very different problems of acting and directing. We hope for film assignments that will allow us to make use of our previous filming experience, and enable us to do films worth writing articles about. And now that Madrid and Munich have led to Manila, we are looking forward especially to making films, either in Hollywood or on the firing line, that will use the great medium of twentieth-century art as it should be used—in the fight for a better world!

Joris Ivens: Artist in Documentary
by Sidney Meyers and Jay Leyda

This study appeared in The Magazine of Art (New York), July 1938. Mr. Leyda, the well-known film scholar, is the translator of Eisenstein's writings on film theory.

The emergence of a masterpiece like Joris Ivens's *Spanish Earth* causes the critical mind to wonder at the passion yet balance of a work that was born under bombardment. Great epochs in history, tragic events like the Spanish War, events that touch closely the conscience of the world, seldom receive immediate transmutation into works of art. Perhaps this cultural aesthetic lag can be best explained by what Wordsworth called the necessity for "emotion remembered in tranquility," "the long view" that we would all like to have. It is pertinent to note that two generations had to elapse before the Napoleonic era could be summed up in Tolstoy's "War and Peace."

In the graphic arts, however, the immediate transference of the artist's troubled age to his medium has been accomplished with greater success. Goya produced the "Horrors of War" with the stench of destruction in his nostrils, and Daumier faced Louis-Philippe's dungeons every time he approached the lithographic stone. But, although the graphic arts present the artist with a swifter instrument for the transference of reality and the stuff of history, they require the same discipline, the same integrated version of life that determine the value of all art.

The film, for example, holding within itself the potentialities of rendering actuality most truthfully, has known an endless abuse since its invention by the failure to bring to it a valid viewpoint. Yet Joris Ivens, even in the heat of battle, has known no such failure. In him we encounter a complete socially integrated artist, one whose great craft is stimulated by a deep sense of unity with his fellow human beings. He has brought to his work an instinct for thoroughness, for order, and the profound social alliances which we have encountered before in artists of his native Holland. Here is a great sympathy with the oppressed which we feel in the pictures of Bruegel and Rembrandt, which we find in the work and life of Van Gogh.

Ivens's early education was scientific. He spent a year in the

Zeiss factory in Jena after studying to be a photochemical engineer, with a special concentration on physics and economics. His first job was in his father's photo-supply shop in Amsterdam. Young Ivens found himself wishing to take the step from the chemistry of photography to the excitements of motion picture photography itself. But there was no film industry in Holland. He looked about with his friends for a means of establishing contact with the rich avant-garde movements in Germany and France. To escape the oppressive commercial flood from Hollywood and the Berlin studios, and to show themselves examples of the best European noncommercial work, they organized the Film Liga.

The first Liga programs featured the films of Richter, Ruttmann, and other German filmmakers, produced under the influence of the De Stijl school of abstract design. It was also under this influence that Ivens made, in 1928, his first film, *The Bridge*. It is important to emphasize, however, that, abstract though his earliest film was, it chose for its basis the functional movements of real objects. Outside of Rotterdam is a railroad bridge that swings aside to let the river traffic pass. Ivens fixed upon this simple action for the substance of his first work. From *The Bridge*, Ivens acquired confidence in manipulating the basic materials of his craft, but more important was his discovery of his special feeling for movement, as necessary to the film artist as a painter's feeling for color, or a musician's for sound.

Although aware of *The Bridge*'s value to him, Ivens did not, like many avant-garde contemporaries, confine himself to the methods and purposes of purely experimental work. He aimed higher, being conscious of the lack of human content in *The Bridge*, and reached out for contact with more living reality. He accepted an offer of literary assistance from the Dutch writer, Franken, and the result of their collaboration, *Rain*, perceptibly advanced Ivens toward his eventual goal.

The Bridge and *Rain* were the school in which the Ivens of *New Earth* and *Spanish Earth* studied. Here were learned the lessons of selection and flexibility of camera viewpoint. For example, the process that Ivens was to call "cutting with the camera," by which he means a subtle correspondence between the movement of the camera and the photographed object, can already be found in *The Bridge*. Unknowingly, Ivens was preparing himself for the day when he and his cameraman, Ferno, were to be on a roof in a Spanish village threatened with aerial bombardment, matching the terror of the swooping and wheeling enemy planes with the responsive movement of the camera. When we catch a revealing glimpse of the anxious face of the woman waiting for a streetcar in *Rain,* we see Ivens preparing himself for the deeper anxiety of the refugees being evacuated from Madrid. The hardly perceptible change of focus from wet roof to wet window in *Rain* was to wait for more exciting use of this effect in *Spanish Earth* when University City comes into focus in the broken mirror of the forgotten dressing table. The poetry of wet cobblestones and single drops from an umbrella prepared him for the more pathetic poetry of a beaded lamp swinging from a remnant of ceiling in torn Madrid. These are examples of the continued accumulation of experience that Ivens insists on as the first requisite of the filmmaker. In normal times and under unexciting conditions, he must prepare his art for the emergency that will come.

With *Rain,* Holland was beginning to know that it had another artist to boast of—and to use. The huge Philips electrical industry invited Ivens to add prestige to its products and to make his first sound film. Ivens doubts that the resultant film, *Philips Radio,* materially helped their sales, because he was more interested at the time in putting into practice the lessons he was learning in the Dutch museums, in front of the men and women of Bruegel and Rembrandt. First the critics, then Philips itself, felt uncomfortably cheated by Ivens's preoccupation with the workmen. The critics found their evidence in the terrific activity of the glassblowers—cheeks puffed out to inhuman proportions, the tremendous palsy of work to manipulate the glass forms, the great sweating face of the blower as he stares into the lens. This was not what the Philips Company had expected from their superficial examination of *The Bridge* and *Rain.* You couldn't sell radios by shocking the audience out of the complacency with which it formerly regarded the glittering finished product. Complaints rained in from the Philips offices throughout Europe and Asia. But in Paris more discriminating critics, disregarding entirely its origin as a sales film, named it *Industrial Symphony* instead.

No Ivens film is exactly like its predecessors in motive, in range, or in method. There is a nervous, fluid quality in *Industrial Symphony* that results from the task that Ivens set himself—to create a total impression by means of a continuously passing chain-belt of relevant detail, as seen by a keen-eyed visitor to the Philips factory.

While he was still at work on this film, the Building Trades Union invited Ivens to supervise the filming of one of the great industrial projects of the world—the draining and filling of the Zuider Zee. Ivens undertook the assignment and, with his assistant, Helen Van Dongen, and a third cameraman, John Ferno, began the film recording of this engineering work.

The Film Liga, already a stronghold of the European experimental film movement, had invited foreign filmmakers to speak at their programs. It was as the direct result of Pudovkin's and Eisenstein's visits to the Film Liga that Joris Ivens, as the most talented documentary filmmaker in the West, had been invited to bring his films to the Soviet Union in 1930, lecturing with them. After the completion of *Industrial Symphony,* Ivens received a second invitation from the Soviet Union—this time to make a feature film of the work of the Komsomols at the Magnitogorsk plant in the Ural Mountains. Leaving his group in charge of the growing Zuider Zee record, he went to Russia to work in 1931 on *Komsomol,* or *A Song of Heroes.*

Ivens's steady adherence to the idea of collective work can be seen in his insistence that he be accompanied to the location, not only by his cameraman, Shelenkov, and the scenarist, Skliut, so that the scenario could grow through constant contact with the people about whom the film was being made, but also by the composer, Hanns Eisler, so that his music could come directly from the sounds of the forges and the worksongs. In *Komsomol,* Ivens acquired certainty under the most adverse conditions. He reveled in the opportunity to overcome new difficulties, and filmed from moving machines and derricks, from airplanes, from between blazing furnaces.

Komsomol pushed Ivens far from any previous notions he may have had of a documentary as a minor observational form, giving him a broader conception of the use to which his talents should be put. Ivens returned to Holland, conscious that epic work awaited the documentary form in Western Europe.

He had succeeded so well in establishing a collective in Holland that, although he remained in the Soviet Union for almost a year, Helen Van Dongen and Ferno had continued to keep a thorough record of the Zuider Zee project. When Ivens returned, he brought with him not only a print of *Komsomol,* but a healthy new outlook on the future of the documentary film. Originally the Zuider Zee films, made up into separate short films—*Zuiderzee, We Are Building* (on Dutch industrial architecture), *Pile Driving,* etc., were intended to be confined to local industrial documentation, but, by the time Ivens returned to Holland, the worldwide depression had reached there, affecting the huge project. The idea of its construction was a noble one—to wrest the land from the sea. But Ivens returned to Holland to find that the strong fresh grain grown on the newly reclaimed earth was being thrown into the sea to keep up the prices of wheat in the world market. In these facts, he found a theme to give depth and unity to the separate Zuider Zee documentations.

New Earth, which Ivens based on the Zuider Zee films, is cast in a form as direct and terse as a social-reform tract. Like the tract, *New Earth* also is an expression of indignation, but without the impersonal generalized character of this form. The model for such a film form did not exist for Ivens to turn to. In a sense, it was new earth for Ivens himself. It was a new type of documentary, broader than any filmmaker outside the Soviet Union had conceived it—namely, the theme-documentary. Although Western European documentalists had graduated from the travelogue to impressionist reportage, beyond that they had not traveled far, not further than the abrupt economic conclusion of Grierson's *Drifters.* The subject of *New Earth,* the shattering contradictions between the worlds of production and consumption, involved Ivens in the discovery of new film grammar and vocabulary.

At the outset of the film's shaping, Ivens demanded from himself as much, and more, of the creative imagination and fantasy as goes into the conception of an enacted film. To achieve the greatest pliancy of the many elements that go into the physical making of a film, Ivens had to break with the accepted limitations of sound-film structure. Instead of the accepted conception of the sound film, in which the image takes paramount importance to the neglect of sound, Ivens evolved a flexible contrapuntal style, equal to any need of his many-sided theme. Sound or music could assume leading roles for as long as they gave a kind of strength not possible in the image. The combination of these elements played on all the senses of the spectator. This contrapuntal style, besides giving the filmmaker an instrument equal to anything he would ask of it, provided him with the means of maintaining a varied and unrelaxing grip on the concentration of his audience. Thus he evolved a style that progressive documentary filmmakers the world over were to draw upon because it pointed the way to the solution of their greatest problem—how to compete with dramatic films in sustaining audience interest. Ivens accomplished this end by placing the spectator in an intensified atmosphere of reality, in closeness to the concrete materials of the film and in keenly felt observation of every working action and gesture. When, after a showing of *New Earth* at a workers' club in Holland, a stonemason commented on the correctness with which Ivens had shown men at work, Ivens explained that he had lifted the granite himself, to discover the manifestation of strain, in order to find the proper camera positions.

New Earth was the first film to gather up all the threads of Ivens's development and bind them into an emotional whole. In it were contained the sensitiveness to textures and tones that were noticed in *Rain,* the functional interest of *The Bridge,* the human beings who played an ever-increasing role in all his films, and, most important and significant, a theme that touches the fundamental character of a world in transition. Henceforth, Ivens was to be "troubleshooter," to be found wherever the illnesses of the world cracked it wide open.

Ignoring the critics shocked by *New Earth,* he threw himself into many-sided social work, using films as his instrument, training a group of youngsters to put together short films of ideas under any pressure. For an election period or an economic crisis, the group had equipped themselves to turn out sharp, directly relevant films that were immediately exhibited at mass meetings and workers' clubs throughout Holland and Belgium. Out of this atmosphere of emergency films of hunger-marches and harsh depression contrasts came an idea to do a film about the Borinage, as much of a mining hellhole in 1933 as it had been when Van Gogh preached there in 1879. Van Gogh then wrote to his brother: "Most of the miners are pale and thin from fever and look tired and emaciated, weatherbeaten and aged before their time, the women as a whole faded and worn. Around the mines are poor miners' huts with a few dead trees black from smoke, and thorn hedges, dung hills, and ash dumps, heaps of useless coal. . . ."

The single glaring fact of human suffering conditions all aspects of Ivens's *Borinage*. From it comes the extraordinary simplicity of this film's photography (in which he collaborated with Henri Storck) and of its journalistic, expository structure, wherein the circumstances of misery encircle the spectator. This film's function is simpler than that of *New Earth*. The former's elaborate interplay of sound and sight is here replaced by an almost exclusively visual manifestation of things to which he leads one by the hand, and points to—directly.

The singleness of purpose with which Ivens approached his subject, and his intense adherence in filmic method to the simplest and most direct presentation of material, makes *Borinage* an unforgettable work. For sheer impact of truth and the poetry of its human intimations *Borinage* is without an equal in documentary.

Today, Ivens feels that *Borinage* thrust aside too drastically the formal beauties of cutting, photography, and sound that his former work had developed. But it is difficult to admit the justice of this self-criticism in the face of the film's significance to the development of Ivens himself and to the development of the documentary picture. From a photographic and technical point of view *Borinage* represents a complete break with the decorative, purely compositional tendencies then dominant in the European movements. In a larger and more important sense, *Borinage* advances the documentary toward its true goal and its true subject—the depiction of the state of man.

In 1935 the New Film Alliance of America invited Joris Ivens to show his films throughout the United States. The trip from coast to coast was something of a triumphal tour. From New York, where the National Board of Review voted *New Earth* the best foreign film seen here in 1935, Ivens crossed to California, lecturing at universities and film societies on his way. In Hollywood he and his films brought a rare breath of fresh air to the technicians. He stayed there for a few months, studying modern equipment and production methods. In the spring of 1936 Ivens aided in the formation of Frontier Films and became a member of its staff. This group, comprising several of the finest creative talents in independent films, exemplifies a point Ivens has always emphasized. He invariably points to the non-exceptional character of his activities. All over the world, in Holland, France, England, America, groups of filmmakers are arising, whose aims and social grounding are similar to his. This to him is the most important portent of that time when the film shall assume its rightful place as the prime artistic instrument for the presentation of reality.

In July, 1936, with the flaring of Spain's Civil War, all of Ivens's plans for work in America were forced aside by the necessity he felt of presenting the issues of the war to American audiences. In New York, Ivens, Lillian Hellman, John Dos Passos, Archibald MacLeish, and Ernest Hemingway organized themselves into a producing group known as Contemporary Historians. After several anxious months spent in conjuring the necessary finances and writing a scenario, Ivens left for Spain. The original scenario was based on the experiences of a village that had been captured by the Franco forces and then freed by the Loyalists. It soon grew apparent that his story structure was unrealizable. Ivens found a total unwillingness and inability of the villagers to recall the occupation. The old life had been forgotten. All energies were bent to building for the future, to reinforcing the front. In his search for a more suitable theme, Ivens came upon a small village, Fuentedueña, engaged in an irrigation project. If the earth were made more fruitful there would be more food for the besieged friends in Madrid and for the soldiers at the front. Ivens recognized his theme at once. After a hurried meeting with Ernest Hemingway in Paris, it was decided to scrap the old scenario and build a new one in this village, letting the filming expand under the circumstances of war.

Spanish Earth is a work largely planned and executed under fire. The sacrifice and heroism of men defending their land permeates and conditions the film. The intense discipline required to move almost instinctively under shellfire—and still come away with art—could come only from a sense of dedication to tasks and a degree of consciousness that we find in the greatest artists.

Nowhere before has been sought and expressed the face of men going into battle so truly as in this film. Did you ever see in a film before the actual recoil of a rifle butt biting into the neck and shoulders? Here you feel it yourself. Although the soundtrack was composed and synchronized back in New York, with Irving Reis and Helen Van Dongen, it could only have been directed by a man who had himself been in danger from shells and airplane bombs, which we hear from the soundtrack and instinctively shrink from. Cameraman Ferno's sensitiveness to a wide range of scene and action deserves particular attention. Whether he is showing the

Spanish earth peacefully plowed or brutally bombed, his photography finds the exact tone to communicate each atmosphere.

In *Spanish Earth* Ivens had realized himself most fully. The static and insulated quality of many documentaries is challenged by every detail of the film. Ivens has not only fixed his attention upon his central concerns, but, illuminatingly, upon all the objects and movements that surround them. This rich body of selected observation, which occupies all planes of every shot, and leads, at each viewing of the film, to fresh discoveries, mounts to a tremendous total effect. Each new-found touch leads, not to distraction, but to completer understanding of his subject—the tragedy and heroism of a people torn from the soil.

The greatest single section of *Spanish Earth* begins when we see below us in a village an old woman come out into her yard. Hemingway's voice: "Before, death came when you were old and sick. But now it comes to all in this village. High in the sky and shining silver it comes to all who have no place to run, no place to hide." We hear a frightened cry: *"Aviación."* Another voice, a child's, thin, poignantly young: *"Aviación."* The planes are overhead. The camera spins propeller-wise and locates them. The bombardment comes. The bombs are on us. A mother runs toward us. Someone's younger sister looks about uncomprehendingly, dazed, her hand pressed against her body. "They strike us here." When the dust of explosion settles, a voice is raised in funeral song. We find ourselves beside the dead, touching their feet, meeting their unseeing eyes. In one house, burst open by a bomb, the camera descends to the broken bed.

Such scenes are at the apex of documentary filmmaking—subtle craft at the service of Ivens's conviction—the climax of ten years of seeking. *Spanish Earth* is a complete affirmation of Ivens's intentions. There has been no documentary that so combined exquisite tenderness with consummate craftsmanship, that was so full of humanness, that has been so surely made for broad audiences. The next step taken by this extraordinary, clearsighted artist depends on history. Today, on the battlefields and in the villages of China, he is filming the hopes and struggles of the Chinese people. Wherever out of the clash of old and new worlds emerges human tragedy and nobility, there Joris Ivens will be.

War Is, Was, and Always Will Be, Hell
by Julien Bryan

*This report of documentary filmmaking under fire originally
appeared in U. S. Camera, February-March 1940. Mr. Bryan is
a distinguished pioneer of the American documentary.*

For ten years I have traveled throughout the world taking pictures.
The one thing that made it fun and gave it zest and importance
was that back of it all there was a story to tell and my pictures
helped me do it. If at any time I could have told the story better
with the printed word or over the radio I should have stopped
telling it with pictures.

Just as a foreign correspondent might write a book on life in
China or Japan, giving the background of the people and showing
clearly their economic and social problems, I decided to do much
the same thing with motion pictures. These were not to be routine
travelogues. Far from it. They were intended to show clearly the
trials, the errors, and the misfortunes as well as the progress of the
countries in which they were made.

I visited Russia and Siberia, Turkey, Finland, and Poland,
China and Japan, Mexico and Nazi Germany. All this in peacetime, working slowly and deliberately to obtain an honest and
balanced story of normal life throughout the world.

In July 1939, I visited Holland and Switzerland to make a
series of educational films. In August the situation in Europe was
becoming serious and the sensible thing would have been to return
home at once as other Americans were doing. But, having considerable faith in the Polish Army, I decided to slip into Warsaw
by the back door, through Rumania, and to stay there long enough
to obtain a good back-of-the-lines series of photographs.

At that time few, if any, of us realized that Poland would
collapse completely in three short weeks. In my book "Siege," soon
to be published by Doubleday-Doran, I describe at considerable
length my long trek in getting to Warsaw. There is no occasion
here to go into such detail but only to mention that I arrived in
Warsaw on the morning of September seventh.

It was some time before I realized the full gravity of the situation. Here I was with two Bell & Howell Eyemo cameras, a movie
tripod, six thousand feet of film, two Leicas, and plenty of film

for still pictures in both black and white and color. Everything seemed fine except for the remarks of the few remaining consuls at the American Embassy which were not very reassuring. The city was being bombed dozens of times daily, several thousand people had already been killed, and it looked now as though the Poles would not give up until every stone in Warsaw had been battered down. I was cheered only by the fact that all of the other correspondents and photographers had left Warsaw two days before. This looked like a grand scoop—to be the only one on hand to get pictures of this tremendous siege. But as I began to think about it later, what good would all the pictures be if I could never get out alive?

During those first few days I spent a great deal of time in the hastily constructed dugout of the American Embassy. There were constant bombings and air alarms sounded many times each day. Often we would sit there for hours. We were a woebegone, frightened bunch. It wasn't until later that I learned two very important lessons about war. The first is that everyone is afraid, many people much more so than you are. When I made this discovery it bucked me up no end. Secondly, and this is even more important, most persons are less afraid when they are actively engaged in some useful task rather than sitting mournfully in a cellar. I watched the stenographers and telephone operators at work, and the cook and the janitor and the newsboys. They were worried, of course, but they were much better adjusted and happier when they were busy. So, I followed suit and put my camera to work.

But what was to be my theme in Warsaw? I decided to do just about what I had always done, except that this time it was to be a story of people at war. What happened to them? How were they killed and wounded? Where did they sleep? Above all what happened to them inside? And would the camera register the fear, sorrow, strain, and horror which the faces of these men and women so clearly showed? I didn't know, but I believed that my camera could do this.

I had gone to considerable trouble in getting to Warsaw and so I was greatly disturbed when it was announced over the radio that all photography was forbidden and that any person found on the street with a camera would be arrested and probably shot. The job then was to get proper credentials. This seemed impossible.

Warsaw was in a state of siege and practically all Polish officials had fled the city. But luckily Stefan Starzynski was still in town and acting as Civilian Commander. He and his staff stayed on bravely until the end. Starzynski was delighted when I visited his office, and he agreed to cooperate with me in every way. He furnished a military guide, an interpreter, and a car. To him and his staff this photographic project became of immense importance. They realized that it might be the only photographic record of Warsaw's destruction to reach the outside world.

How to begin a motion picture record of such a siege? It wasn't hard. The Nazis were bombing three principal bridges over the Vistula, so I got that. But it was not enough merely to show a bomb or two exploding in the distance. I took medium shots and close-ups of the great craters which had been formed at the base of the bridge; then the bridge itself, still in use in spite of frequent bombing, with a stream of civilian traffic; close-ups on the bridge, of holes made in it and of torn iron railings; close-ups of refugees, mostly on foot, as they struggled pitifully across the bridge with their bedding, a loaf of bread, whatever they had saved. One woman was carrying a live chicken under her arm. A man walked by with a six-foot picture of Venus on his back.

Praga. Fifteen or twenty blocks burned to the ground. Acres and acres of gaunt brick chimneys towering shakily over the ashes of what had been homes only a few hours before. Now the simplest thing would have been to stay five minutes in each place, taking two or three shots and then go dashing on to another exciting spot. But from past experience I felt that it was much better to stay in one locality and stay there long enough to do a complete job. For example, here in this Warsaw suburb, one could have used thirty feet of movie film on one refugee family and then moved along. But to me it seemed wiser to spend half a day in the same neighborhood and show not only this family in the pitiful ruins of their home, but also their neighbors, the dogs and the cats, the will to survive, the fear written on their faces, the bedclothes, the food, the ruined little church and the great hospital nearby which had also been bombed. If these were pictures done and done well, they would have a unity and a naturalness about them which they would not have if I went to fifty different localities in Warsaw and in each one took only thirty or forty feet of exciting but unrelated sequences.

I had one chance to photograph a maternity hospital. My interpreter and my military guide were anxious that I make two or three quick shots and dash on to another part of the city, to a jail where German prisoners were being held. For a while it looked as though I would never get the pictures of the German soldiers, and I was deeply disappointed, for this was to be a fundamental part of the story. However, I stuck by my cameras and remained for three hours at work in the maternity hospital.

More than fifty mothers and new-born infants had just been evacuated from the maternity ward on the second floor to the great cellar below. This meant no safety in case of a direct hit, though at least it was better than the exposed floors above. But there was no light. Luckily, I always carried with me three No. 2 photoflood lamps. These I managed to screw into a couple of empty sockets and succeeded in getting amazingly well exposed negatives.

Changing film was difficult, especially in the districts which had been razed by incendiary bombs. It was bad enough during the daytime when the smoke would blow into your eyes and the ashes into your camera. But at night it was worse, for then ashes and cinders were constantly falling and it meant a bad film jam if they landed inside. Now and then I had the cover off the camera and was in the midst of loading film when shells landed dangerously near. This is a nice problem for a photographer. Should one drop the camera and film like a hot potato and make a dash for the nearest cellar, or sit calmly on the doorstep and finish loading? Despite these, and other difficulties, I took over sixty still photographs and four hundred feet of movie film in this one location. Perhaps it was too much, but I think not.

The Kodak laboratory was still open. My interpreter left me at the laboratory while he drove off in the car with several friends to get some food for their families. By this time half of Warsaw was standing in breadlines. The two laboratory men at Kodak were eager to help and we had a long talk about developing the film. We finally decided on using Eastman D76, which is standard for motion picture work. Although it does not produce especially fine grain, we decided to use it for the six Leica rolls of still pictures. We put the film in the soup at four-thirty and I left the laboratory and walked home. It was about a mile and a half, but the trip seemed endless, because the principal streets were now subject to heavy strafing from small artillery.

Back in the Kodak laboratory. The two assistants took my films out of the developing tank at five o'clock, put them into the hypo, and at five twenty-five had just placed them in a tank of water for washing. For a minute or two both men left the room. While they were gone, at five-thirty, a six-inch German shell made a direct hit on the laboratory, smashed in the entire wall, and completely ruined the developing tank. By an amazing stroke of luck the tank in the corner of the same room, only six feet away, in which my film was being washed, had not even been scratched.

I finally reached the Embassy on foot. But it was a hair-raising walk. I decided after this that I would always go by car, if I could. Actually it was just as dangerous in the car but somehow it seemed safer, and beside that, I had the comforting feeling of the person with me being just as frightened as I was.

But I never saw my little car again. I waited for Thaddeus, my interpreter, until late that evening, surprised and worried, for he had agreed to come as soon as he had obtained the food for his family and their friends. At last, long after dark, there was a timid knock at the door. It was Thaddeus. He was wounded. His arm was bandaged and there was a small hole in his uniform on his left shoulder. There was blood on it. I was, of course, startled and terribly worried. But Thaddeus had come only to apologize and to tell me how sorry he was to be late for his appointment. It turned out that he was only slightly wounded. But all four of the men in the car had been badly injured, one of them fatally. And then from Thaddeus came the news that my car, which had taken us so bravely into every district of Warsaw, was destroyed. After that, we had to do most of our work on foot. It was bad enough moving about under fire in the car; it was much worse when we had to carry the cameras and film ourselves.

Perhaps the most discouraging of all my photographic adventures in Warsaw occurred one day when a squadron of thirty German planes flew overhead. The clouds were magnificent. I had a 23A filter in readiness and my six-inch telephoto lens was installed on the turret. Conditions couldn't have been better for one of the great aviation pictures of the war. Just as I was about to start shooting, my camera jammed. I jerked it from the tripod, threw it into my black silk changing bag, pulled off the lid, adjusted the film where the loop had slipped down, and in a flash had the camera back on the tripod. The thirty Nazi planes were still there. But luck was against me. The camera jammed again. I was heartbroken, for this was my best movie camera. If it could not be fixed at once I was in a bad way for getting any more movies. I had only one other camera and this was not so good.

I went at once to the office of Eastman Kodak. It was closed, but I managed to get in the back door. Four or five of the clerks and laboratory workers were sitting about. I told my story quickly and they said that there was a skilled motion picture mechanic still in Warsaw who might help. They tried to get him on the telephone. Not only did the telephone work, which was surprising, but the mechanic was at home! Even though the shelling was bad he came on foot to the office, worked all night, and the next day gave me my Eyemo in good working condition. I paid him $20. It was cheap at that.

But I couldn't forget my unfortunate experience with the thirty German planes. I had seen them, but hadn't a single photograph to prove it. Days went by and I began to feel that my one big chance had slipped by.

One day I climbed up to the roof of the American Embassy with no particular thought of taking pictures. It was a quiet day. There were no planes in the sky and there had not been any for many hours. Suddenly from nowhere, with no sign of an air alarm, three great Heinkel bombers flew over the Embassy. They were about ten thousand feet in the air. Two were well in advance, heading in the direction of the River Vistula and the last great bridge. The Polish anti-aircraft batteries got to work and soon a whole string of red phosphorous tracer ribbons streamed across the sky. At the end of each streamer, some ten thousand feet high, was a small black flower, a puff of smoke where the shell had exploded. In the days gone by I had seen at least a thousand such puffs from anti-aircraft, but the planes seemed always to get away. I had never seen a direct hit. Now I saw nine little puffs of smoke, and then the tenth. It was a direct hit! My camera was in the box beside me. Instinctively I grabbed it and pointed it to the sky. There was no time to set for distance or to adjust the diaphragm. I held it there for twenty seconds while the broken bomber fell helplessly and in flames to the ground. When we developed the film later we discovered that the exposure and the distance had, luckily, been correct.

Toward the end of the siege, I was again on the roof of the Embassy. The city was in the throes of a great aerial pageant, probably the largest mass bombing which the world had ever known. But it was impossible to stay in the cellar. It was too fearful and horrible there. We were probably going to be killed, so why not be outside and see the show? Hundreds of planes were in the skies at once. Not one was Polish. Practically every Polish airport had been bombed out of existence. The landing fields of those that remained were pitted with shellholes and no planes could take off.

As I stood there on the roof, the noise from the motors of these great bombers as they powerdived from two miles down to five hundred feet was like a great, mad heavenly orchestra playing in the sky. It was bigger—it was louder than anything I had ever heard.

It was so exciting and thrilling that I quite forgot my fear. During the next half-hour I took three hundred feet of film as Nazi planes dove down within a few hundred yards of the Embassy roof seeming, through my viewfinder, to be almost upon me. I was able to get both telephoto and 50mm. shots of this amazing sky carnival.

Now came the problem of developing the film. I shall never forget that trip to the laboratory bearing our precious burden. Shells seemed to fall in a steady torrent around our car. It was a miracle that we escaped. We developed the film, made two extra prints (a precaution against the negative being lost or destroyed). These prints were buried secretly in widely separated spots.

Now the screening. Outside, German artillery had gone methodically to work again. Every few seconds a shell burst. But we were so intent on seeing the pictures that we hardly noticed the real action going on around us. Maybe the developer had been wrong. Perhaps some hidden defect in the camera would spoil the entire film. Mostly I worried because the photographer himself had been scared and might have ruined the job through some careless oversight. Then to the sound accompaniment of artillery fire (which at times seemed almost to synchronize) we screened the first five reels. Not bad, we thought. There was some camera motion, to be sure, and weaving. Here and there, evidence of underexposure; but everything considered, it wasn't a bad job. Above all here were the pictures I had set my heart on getting—people in war. Strain, fear, despair, horror, anger showed in their faces. This was the document I had wanted to make.

The biggest problem remained. How was I to get out of Warsaw with the pictures? The city was now surrounded by the German army. There seemed to be no chance—except by air. And this was a long chance at best. The Germans had moved up to within a half-mile of the last remaining airport. To leave in daylight was out of the question. My military guide was a captain of aviation and a splendid flyer. He and his staff decided the risk was worthwhile. The pictures must get to America and the outside world. So he set out that night to get our plane. He never returned. Next day we learned that the Nazis had moved up during the night, captured the airport.

I was discouraged—more than that, I began to feel responsible for this man's death, though he seemed all along to welcome the chance. He was not doing this for me, personally, he was doing it for Poland, to get these pictures to the outside world.

I cannot tell here of the long horrible days that followed. Finally, on September 21, there was a 3-hour truce during which a few hundred citizens of neutral countries were permitted to go through the German lines. After what seemed an interminable length of time we arrived in Königsberg, East Prussia. I would have felt safer back in Warsaw. The Nazis had no love for me. I had spoken freely over the Warsaw radio of the brutalities I had seen. I had lectured all over America about Nazi Germany. Here I was with my incriminating Warsaw document; the consequences of being caught with it were fearful. But somehow, I can't tell how, I managed to get through—even more exciting, the pictures got through, too—through the German lines—more than 5,000 feet of 35mm motion picture film, hundreds of Leica negatives, and a few Kodachromes.

The motion picture film is being shown in most of this country's largest cities. Some people call it "vicious propaganda—inciting this country to war." Others say that they are so terrifying that they will best serve the cause of pacifism and will help keep us out of war if enough people see them. What effect they will eventually have, I do not know. It is not for me to draw conclusions. My job is to make pictures and this I have done. I have brought back, from a world gone mad, a record of war and what it does to people. This is my story.

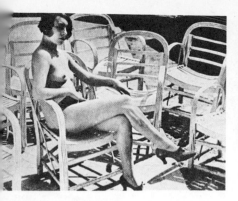

propos de Nice (1930),
ected by Jean Vigo

Three Songs About Lenin (1933-4),
directed by Dziga Vertov

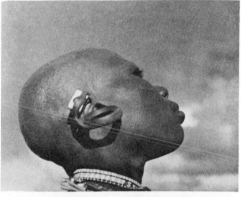

Contact (1932-3),
directed by Paul Rotha

Song of Ceylon (1935),
directed by Basil Wright

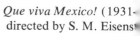

Que viva Mexico! (1931-
directed by S. M. Eisens[

The Wave (1934-5),
directed by Paul Strand and Fred Zinnemann

Night Mail (193
directed by Basil Wr[
and Harry V

...isis (1938),
...ected by Herbert Kline
...d Alexander Hammid

Man's Hope (1938),
directed by Andre Malraux

Spanish Earth (1937),
directed by Joris Ivens
and Ernest Hemingway

The River (1937),
directed by Pare Lorentz

Return to Life (1938),
directed by Henri Cartier
and Herbert Kline

A Selection of Documentaries of the Period

The Adventures of Chico,
Stacy and Horace Woodard
(1938)

Aero Engine, Arthur Elton (1933)

America Today, Workers' Film
and Photo League (1933)

A propos de Nice, Jean Vigo
(1930)

Autumn Fire, Herman G.
Weinberg (1930)

B.B.C.: The Voice of Britain,
Stuart Legg (1934–5)

Borinage, Joris Ivens and
Henri Storck (1933)

A Bronx Morning, Jay Leyda
(1931)

China Strikes Back, Harry
Dunham (1937)

The City, Ralph Steiner and
Willard Van Dyke (1939)

City of Contrasts, Irving
Browning (1930)

Coal Face, Alberto Cavalcanti
(1936)

Contact, Paul Rotha (1932–3)

Crisis, Herbert Kline and
Alexander Hammid (1938)

Cry of the World, Louis de
Rochemont (1932)

Dark Rapture, Armand Denis
(1938)

Easter Island, John Ferno and
Henri Storck (1934)

Enough to Eat, Edgar Anstey
(1936)

*Enthusiasm (Symphony of the Don
Basin),* Dziga Vertov (1931)

The Face of Britain, Paul Rotha
(1934–5)

The Four Hundred Million,
Joris Ivens (1938)

Gorges of the Giants, Bonney
Powell (1933)

Granton Trawler, Edgar Anstey
(1934)

Hands, Ralph Steiner and Willard
Van Dyke (1934)

Heart of Spain, Herbert Kline and
Geza Karpathi (1937)

Hopi, Lewis Jacobs (1934–5)

Housing Problems, Edgar Anstey
and Arthur Elton (1935)

*"Hunger": The March to
Washington,* Workers' Film and
Photo League (1932)

Imperial Valley, Seymour Stern
(1931)

Industrial Britain, Robert J.
Flaherty (1933)

Kuhle Wampe, Bert Brecht and
Slatan Dudow (1932)

Land Without Bread, Luis Buñuel
(1932)

Lights Out in Europe, Herbert
Kline and Alexander Hammid
(1939)

Line From the Tschierva Hut,
Alberto Cavalcanti (1937)

The Londoners, John Taylor
(1939)

Les Maisons de la misère, Henri
Storck (1937)

Man of Aran, Robert J.
Flaherty (1934)

Man's Hope, Andre Malraux (1938)

Men and Dust, Sheldon Dick (1939)

Le Métro, Henri Langlois and Georges Franju (1934)

Millions of Us, American Labor Films (1936)

New Earth, Joris Ivens (1934)

The New Generation, Stuart Legg (1932)

Night Mail, Basil Wright and Harry Watt (1936)

North Sea, Harry Watt (1938)

Olympia, Leni Riefenstahl (1938)

People of the Cumberland, Sidney Meyers (1937)

The Plow That Broke the Plains, Pare Lorentz (1936)

Que viva Mexico!, S. M. Eisenstein (1931–2)

Redes, see: *The Wave*

Return to Life, Henri Cartier [-Bresson] and Herbert Kline (1938)

Rhapsody in Steel, F. Lyle Goldman (1935)

The River, Pare Lorentz (1937)

Shipyard, Paul Rotha (1934–5)

Siege, Julien Bryan (1940)

The Silent Enemy, H. P. Carver (1930)

Song of Ceylon, Basil Wright (1935)

Spanish Earth, Joris Ivens and Ernest Hemingway (1937)

Tabu, F. W. Murnau and Robert J. Flaherty (1931)

Taxi, Nancy Naumburg (1932)

This Is America, Gilbert Seldes (1933)

Three Songs About Lenin, Dziga Vertov (1933–4)

The Transfer of Power, Arthur Elton (1939)

Triumph of the Will, Leni Riefenstahl (1936)

Tsar to Lenin, Max Eastman (1936)

Used Cars, Julian Roffman (1939)

The Wave, Paul Strand and Fred Zinnemann (1934–5)

We Live in Two Worlds, Alberto Cavalcanti (1937)

Weather Forecast, Evelyn Spice (1934)

The Wedding of Palo, Frederick Dahlsheim and Knud Rasmussen (1937)

The World Today, Nykino (1936)

The Yellow Cruise, Léon Poirier and André Sauvage (1936)

PART THREE / 1940–1950

Siege (1940),
directed by Julien Bryan

"Why We Fight" Series (1942-3),
directed by Frank Capra

The Military Experience and After
by Lewis Jacobs

The whole art of the documentary-journalist is in the skill with which he shows and tells us about human beings in conflict, not in the skill with which he can make us forget that we are watching a reconstruction.

A. WILLIAM BLUEM

With the outbreak of World War II, documentary films became a part of the all-out mobilization of national resources. Propaganda films were nothing new in Germany, of course, but now Britain, in particular, set forth on a program of inspirational films aimed at shoring up its war effort.

Britain's *The Lion Has Wings* (1940) showed the courage of the RAF in the face of great odds. *London Can Take It* (1940) documented the doggedness and dignity of Londoners during a day-and-night air raid. *Target for Tonight* (1941) dramatized the valor of British air crews during a raid over Germany at a time when a shaken Britain desperately needed a show of hope.

Listen to Britain (1942) was a lyrical study of the nation's day-to-day routine of wartime living, told concisely, sensitively, and with unusual regard for the use of sound and image in counterpoint. Perhaps the most powerfully inspiring of these early British war films was *Desert Victory* (1943). This picture documented the Eighth Army's pursuit of Rommel's Afrika Korps from El Alamein to Tripoli, some 1300 miles, and brought home to English audiences the first evidence that a turning-point in the war had been achieved.

In Germany, national pride was invoked by *Baptism of Fire* (1940) and *Victory in the West* (1941). The first presented a terrifying account of the Nazi blitzkrieg of Poland; the second used the collapse of France to portray the triumphant face of German might looking forward to greater conquests. Special versions of these Nazi documentaries were used by the Third Reich to emphasize its military invincibility and to impress foreign governments with the futility of resistance.

Canada, also concerned with creating and maintaining the morale necessary for war, had brought John Grierson over from England to head its War Film Production Activities. His series, "The World in Action," reported and analyzed the conflict abroad. *Churchill's Island* (1941–2), the first documentary to be recognized with an Academy Award; *This is Blitz* (1942), and *Food—Weapon of Conquest* (1942) spoke to the people of the Dominion for an all-out effort against brutal aggression.

During the early period of the war in Europe, American isolationist sentiment, pacifist groups, and the government's pledges of neutrality proved a powerful restraining force on American filmmakers impelled to deal with the dangers of fascism. The few prominent documentaries that appeared, *Power and the Land* (1940), *Valley Town* (1940), *The Fight for Life* (1941), and *Native Land* (1942), had a particular relevancy to the domestic issues of the thirties. They were distinguished reminders of another cause.

By 1940 the temper of the nation changed. Under the agonizing radio and newspaper reports about the successes of Axis armies, documentaries depicting the inequities of American society had lost their urgency. Then, as military events in Europe gained momentum, bringing the war fever closer to the United States, a few films of fact appeared that showed Americans what the war overseas was really like. In *The Scuttling of the Graf Spee, The Siege of Narvik*, and *Retreat from Dunkirk*, tragic events found a medium eminently suited to convey their impact on those who had no part in the proceedings. Never before had the elusive reality of combat and destruction been reported with such graphic insights into war's terrible reality.

With the shattering retreat of the remnants of Britain's army from Dunkirk, the last vestiges of American neutrality collapsed. A growing belligerency replaced it, giving rise to two documentaries that focused on the need for a forthright preparedness to go to war "against the old enemy."

In *The Ramparts We Watch* (1940), the producers, The March of Time, included a foreword that read: "The war we so thankfully consigned to history—the World War we wrapped in old newspapers and laid away for posterity to look back on—has suddenly become very much alive." The film itself—a "compilation" documentary—was composed of old newsreels and shots from Army archives, interspersed with scenes of prominent personalities of World War I and sequences staged with non-actors from various occupations and social spheres in a typical American community. Its tone of objectivity intended to give viewers "a clearer understanding of where America's foot belongs in the world today."

The same theme was reinforced in *The World in Flames* (1940), made by Paramount Pictures as a "documentation of events which set the stage for the present struggle." As with its predecessor, the past here was arranged in a perspective intended to give the public a "visual concept of the war's background" and make clear the urgent necessity for Americans to arm in defense of a democratic way of life.

After the Japanese attack on Pearl Harbor, most of America's documentary and fiction filmmakers became totally engaged in the obligations and demands of a government at war. From 1942 until the end of the war, American documentaries served as a potent instrument of national policy.

Documentaries by the hundreds were produced by or under the supervision of the U.S. government and distributed without profit by the motion picture industry throughout the nation and to hundreds of training and combat areas all over the globe. There were training films for the civilian and soldier that ranged from *How to Build a Trestle Bridge* to *Resisting Enemy Interrogation;* incentive pictures to influence the fighting man's attitude toward combat, and toward civilian workers, allied nationals, and minority groups, and documentaries that dealt with the progress of the war itself, good-neighbor relations between America and her Canadian, British, and Russian allies, and between North and South America. Then there were the orientation films. These were prepared by experts in history and psychology to explain the ideological issues of the war to the soldiers and the general public. Not since the documentary form was developed had it been used on such a gigantic scale, or employed so deliberately to serve a single purpose.

The decade preceding Pearl Harbor was graphically covered in *The World at War* (1943), a feature-length documentary compiled by playwright and screenwriter Samuel Spewack. This led into perhaps the most exciting and impressive of the war documentaries, the "Why We Fight" series produced under the supervision of Lt. Col. Frank Capra, with the assistance of skilled Hollywood and documentary craftsmen.

The series included *Prelude to War* (1943), *The Nazis Strike* (1943), *Divide and Conquer* (1943), *The Battle of Britain* (1943), *The Battle of China* (1944), *The Battle of Russia* (1944), and *War Comes to America* (1945). These documentaries presented powerfully the War Department's "interpretation of the causes of war, the evidence on which the interpretation was based, and the events which combined to produce the present state of conflict." They set a challenging standard for their contemporaries in the fiction field.

The Capra series was made in the belief that if a man knows his enemy, the reasons for war, and why he is fighting he will make a better soldier. Similar viewpoints and ideas were expressed in related films produced by the War Department, Army Pictorial Services, the AAF First Motion Picture Unit, the U.S. Navy, the U.S. Marine Corps, and the Office of War Information in cooperation with the British Ministry of Information. Among the best documentaries produced by these services were William Wyler's *Memphis Belle* (1944), John Ford's *Battle of Midway* (1944), *The Battle for the Marianas* (1944), John Huston's *The Battle of San Pietro* and *Let There Be Light* (1945), and *Fury in the Pacific* and *To the Shores of Iwo Jima* (1945), both by the U.S. Army, Navy, and Marine Corps. All were striking studies of men preparing for and engaging in combat.

Crowning the many documentary triumphs of the war years were two that resulted from Anglo-American collaboration: *Tunisian Victory* (1944) and *The True Glory* (1945). The first dealt with the enormous logistical problems of planning and coordinating the landing of over eight hundred troop and cargo ships converging in darkness for the Tunisian campaign. The second was an account of D-Day, the Allied landing in France. Each presented a vivid and comprehensive record of a huge military action with a breadth of vision and a sense of understated heroism that touched on eloquence.

The vast upsurge of documentary films in World War II gave the genre a special prominence. Millions of people in and out of the armed services had become accustomed to seeing thought-provoking pictures. Government agencies, related services, educators, journalists, and others involved in communication fields who had worked closely with filmmakers acquired a respect for the medium and learned to use it effectively. A presumption developed that the end of the war would bring a continued expansion of documentary production by these groups and others attempting to reach the public with new ideas. But with the withdrawal of government support the reverse happened. Military film programs terminated, related sponsorship dribbled off. The "documentary movement," as its members liked to think of it, did not see the anticipated outburst of production. Instead, it came to a dead end.

The war had supplied the filmmakers with a positive point of view and an aggressive purpose. With the end of the conflict and the termination of military film programs, the documentarians were faced with the necessity of reexamining their aims. A period of dislocation and readjustment followed. Unsupported now by the sense of being part of a great cause, they scattered, seeking new opportunities to practice their craft in private ways.

Some formed small production companies to compete for instructional and public-affairs documentaries. Willard Van Dyke, Irving Jacoby, and Henwar Rodakiewicz—all formerly involved in turning out first-rate documentaries for the OWI Overseas Branch and other government agencies—pooled their talents and turned to making films for the State Department, such as *Journey into Medicine* (1947), and for education groups, *Osmosis* (1946) and *Subtraction* (1947), aimed at teacher training.

Other documentary filmmakers with a strong individualistic outlook struck out as independent operators. Perhaps the most important documentaries of the post-war years were Robert Flaherty's *Louisiana Story* (1948) and Sidney Meyers's *The Quiet One* (1949).

The two pictures drew their material from different kinds of sponsorship, opposite sources of reality, and uniquely personal creative visions. Yet common to both was the choice of a main character: a lonely Cajun boy was the protagonist of the first, a lonely Negro boy of the second. The effort in both was to blend storytelling with an awareness of the depths of human personality.

Louisiana Story was made with money supplied by the Standard Oil Co. ($258,000). It told a thin romantic tale of an Acadian family living primitively in the bayous of Louisiana, accepting the intrusion of a modern oil-drilling operation. The action is shown through the eyes and emotions of the young son, watching the strange men and machines with wonderment, and in the end coming to an understanding with these forces from an industrialized outside world.

The real strength of *Louisiana Story* lay in the descriptive sequences. These were constantly more striking than the attempted characterization of the people. Flaherty's appreciation of natural beauty and his special feeling for atmosphere was more than a sentimental taste for the picturesque. It was rather an extraordinary responsiveness to the personality of a *place,* which undoubtedly came from his experience as an explorer and his profound intuitive understanding of primitive man in relation to his environment. The most memorable scenes in the picture were those in which the director created a half-real, half-imagined world as his fluid camera followed the boy hunting and fishing, capturing the strange beauty of floating shapes of plush Spanish moss, cathedral-like swamp cypress, shimmering pools crowded with lily pads, and the denizens of land and water—water moccasins, alligators, and even a playful raccoon. All this was limned in the silence and suspense of a wilderness that seemed created through measureless past ages and now being discovered as though for the first time by an extraordinary eye through the dramatic use of light and shade.

More complex than Flaherty's film and less of a conventional narrative, *The Quiet One* was a harsh and forthright study of a lonely unloved Harlem boy of ten who gets into trouble and is sent to an interracial school for maladjusted and neglected children, where he gradually acquires a sense of confidence in himself. The boy's blackness was not given any special significance. It was rather through what happened to him, and the ways in which the school tried to help him, that an identification was made with the central character. The theme of the film was the tragedy of many such boys—regardless of race or color—whose hostility and dislocation are rooted in the despair of broken homes, rejection, loneliness, and the impoverishment of ghetto life.

Meyers's approach to his material was that of a moralist. He used his story as a way of exposing the very smell and feel of a kind

of life experienced by a particular child scarred by the brutal indifference of his parents and the community, who as a result turned
destructively in upon himself. In the clarity of his human and social
insight, and aided by a poetic narration by James Agee, Meyers
achieved a deeply moving document.

Louisiana Story and *The Quiet One* brought the forties to an
end with two of the most lauded films of the decade. The theme of
self-discovery which ran through both pictures reflected a turning-
away from the large social issues that had served documentary so
eminently in the past, and forecast a different kind of documentary
that was to begin in the fifties. Different, and yet in its special way
no less cogent.

Lorentz's *The Fight for Life*

by James Francis Crow

*This review originally appeared in The Hollywood
Citizen-News on June 27, 1940. Mr. Crow was one
of that newspaper's film critics.*

Last night's preview of *The Fight for Life* was especially sponsored
by the Academy of Motion Picture Arts and Sciences because *The
Fight for Life* is an especially worthy film. It is the third picture
made for the Federal Government by Pare Lorentz, the writer and
producer of *The River* and *The Plow That Broke the Plains*.

Like its two precursors, *The Fight for Life* deals with an American problem. This time it is the problem of childbirth, which still
claims more lives than cancer. It is, of course, a problem for science
and medicine. It is also, however, a problem of living conditions in
general—a problem of the slums. And thus Lorentz tells his story
from the viewpoint of the welfare workers and doctors at a maternity center in the heart of an American tenement and factory
district.

The picture is, as you can see, a documentation and not a piece
of commercial entertainment. But never think that it is not dramatic.
It is most powerfully and mercilessly dramatic. It has the drama
that arises out of the dogged, bitter, selfish, thankless, unremitting,
and eventually triumphant "fight for life" waged by stubborn young
doctors and scientists. It has a kind of cinematic poetry, too—a
poetry that is expressed in the awe-inspiring music of Louis Gruenberg, and in the gravely intoned narration that overlies the action.
And it was fitting that the finest artists and technicians of Hollywood were present at last night's showing to applaud the film.

The story begins with a mother's death in childbirth at a great
city hospital. Then it becomes concerned with the troubled young
doctor who had attended her. It follows him to the slums maternity
center where he devotes himself to the search for every bit of knowledge that he can obtain about childbirth. It shows the helpless
trusting plight of the slums mothers as new members are born to
their already numerous and starveling broods. It shows the homes
in which they live, broken, twisted, hideous homes which are symbolical of broken, twisted, hideous lives. You could walk among

such homes in this city, or any other city of America, and never really *see* them. But this little film, an hour long, will make you see them so that you will never forget them.

Obviously there are too many problems posed in the picture for a young doctor to solve. But he works faithfully and well in his sphere. By the end he has done away with his doubts and his rationalizations: he has come to the conclusion that this "fight for life" is as worthy a fight as a man could find. And the film which starts him with a defeat leaves him with a victory.

Most of the time the picture is wordless. But Floyd Crosby's camera is always eloquently communicative, and so is Gruenberg's awesome music, with its strange thump-thumping theme that rises and subsides and recurs, that stops altogether at death, and goes on steadily with life—the thump-thumping of the heartbeats of mother and child. For decent minds, the picturization of the childbirth scenes is always decent, but withal straightforward, candid, realistic. The acting—most of it is by Myron McCormick, Storrs Haynes, Will Geer, Dudley Digges, Dorothy Adams, Dorothy Urban, and Effie Anderson—is simple and direct. For minds that are alert to the unusual, and that are able to discard, at least momentarily, the attitude proper to the acceptance of commercial entertainment films, *The Fight for Life* offers not only so much education, but also a rare and memorable emotional experience.

Joris Ivens's *Power and the Land*
by Mary Losey

This selection is reprinted from Direction magazine (New York), November 1940. The author was instrumental in organizing the Association of American Documentary Film Producers in 1939.

There are working in American documentary today more first-rank filmmakers than ever before. And I say *working* advisedly. Since we are reminded daily that the Americans are now one big happy family, not to break the spell I will include Canada and the South American countries in this report.

As we go to press RKO is shipping 100 prints of Joris Ivens's new film, *Power and the Land,* to local distributors. *Power and the Land* is a film describing the need for the rural electrification program of the Department of Agriculture. The critical approval which greeted its premiere in St. Clairesville, Ohio, brought it to RKO's attention. Now it will reach audiences in nearly 5,000 theaters. This is not the first time that a government-sponsored film has had major distribution, but it is one of the rare occasions and reason for rejoicing. What is important is that such a film will play not to self-conscious art-theater audiences, but to the millions of ordinary film fans who go to the movies for the fun of it and won't mind a bit if they learn a little something in the process. It is important because *Power and the Land* will play to thousands of farmers who will come away from the theater with a new realization of what electricity might mean to them and with some idea of how to get it. This is a documentary film which really helps to solve the problem it presents.

Three documentary units are roaming South America compiling the film notes which it is to be hoped will eventually bring the face of the southern continent out from under its black mantilla. Herbert Kline is in Mexico, where with a script by John Steinbeck he is recording the lives and times of the Mexican people in 1940.

Completion in six weeks of the National Youth Administration's *Youth Gets a Break* is a noteworthy item of documentary-film history. For a long time now there has been a tradition which attaches itself to documentary production: that a film which starts out to be a $10,000 two-reeler on stamp collection will almost inevitably become, before it reaches the screen, a $100,000 spectacle on the romance of paper. *Youth Gets a Break* was not even a gleam in anyone's eye until August 15, 1940. On that day Joseph Losey began discussions with representatives of the administration about a film which should show the need for and some of the achievements of the NYA. The film was budgeted at $14,000 and was needed for release by the first week of October. On September 1st three crews with shooting script were on location from Maine to Georgia. On October 7th the finished film was previewed in New York. To those who know the reputation of inefficiency under which documentary producers have labored, *Youth Gets a Break* gives us a fresh start.

Other productions of varying ambitions have come from cutting-rooms during the summer months. *Day after Day,* a film for the Henry Street Nursing Service, has just been completed by Sheldon and Lee Dick's unit, Dial Films. A picture on Negroes with particular reference to educational problems in the South has been released by Film Associates. Frontier Films, which has been in business steadily since 1936 and can still boast the most popular labor film ever made, *People of the Cumberland,* has turned its talents to a new field, the scientific film. Its first production in the genre is *White Flood,* a precise, yet dramatic, discussion of the earth's surface. The film is doubly interesting because it marks the first of the experimental work in film music which is being done by Hanns Eisler under a grant from the Rockefeller Foundation.

And release has at last been announced of the three films which were made last spring by the Educational Film Institute: *Valley Town,* by Willard Van Dyke, *And So They Live,* by John Ferno and Julian Roffman, and *The Children Must Learn,* also by Van Dyke.

Indeed, the last six months have marked the debut of a number of American composers into film music. The score of *One Tenth of a Nation* is by Roy Harris, Douglas Moore has written for both the Ivens film and *Youth Gets a Break,* and Paul Bowles provided the music for a study of the Indians of the Southwest, *Roots in the Earth.* This swells the ranks which already included Aaron Copland, Marc Blitzstein, and Virgil Thomson.

Canada's new Film Commissioner is John Grierson, whose name has become synonymous with the practice, not the theory, of documentary-film production. Already ten films have been finished in Canada and at least another ten are in work. Under the omnibus title of War Services, the working lives of every section of

Canada's citizenry are coming to the screen. Films in French Canadian produced by French Canadian units are discovering that the Province of Quebec is more than a quaint collection of pre-revolutionary peasants. The fishermen of the Grand Banks, the wheat farmers of Manitoba, the hockey players of Ontario are all already on celluloid. Some of the films, particularly those which may be of interest to American audiences, are being made by American crews, Irving Jacoby on the ice hockey, Roger Barlow on *Air Youth,* and others.

Add to all this the fact of the arrival in this country of a dozen filmmakers who formerly worked in Europe, among them Victor Stoloff, John Ferno, Alexander Hackenschmied, Hans Burger. Each of these has his films, his talents, and his work to add to the general effort.

The documentary film movement is on the march.

The Ramparts We Watch
by Pare Lorentz

Mr. Lorentz, one of the country's leading film critics
before becoming the outstanding government
documentarian of the Roosevelt Era, wrote this review
for the October 1940 issue of McCall's magazine.

The three most important pictures of the season are about war: the full-length March of Time, *The Ramparts We Watch;* the British propaganda picture, *Pastor Hall;* and Alfred Hitchcock's romantic melodrama, *Foreign Correspondent.*

The March of Time's first full-length picture is an attempt to show us how we went to war in 1917, and to do it in a factual, reportorial manner, and, besides justifying our participation in the last World War, it practically urges us to plunge into this one.

As a motion picture, *The Ramparts We Watch* is extremely interesting. The editors have done a superb job of matching old newsreels, in which the characters walk and talk in the speed of the old silent movies, with dramatic interpolations played by a group of amateur professionals.

These ten amateurs, and the hundreds of bit players—citizens of New London, for the most part—are remarkably refreshing on the screen.

They are homely, yet simple and attractive; the youngsters are bright, intelligent, and not in the least self-conscious; the streets and homes of New London look like the streets and homes of a small city, and the editorial staff of The Day looks like the editorial staff of a newspaper.

Thus, the producers have shown Hollywood that intelligent amateurs can give you better verisimilitude on the screen than ambitious extras and bird-witted cuties who overact in every scene no matter how unimportant they may be to it. They have achieved what the directors of the old Russian pictures brought off: a naturalness and simplicity of group scenes.

The producers were awkward in their direction; most of the dramatic interludes are too slow and are not edited to match the speed of those scenes which are narrated, an error that occasionally leaves the actors wandering around with little to say or do for seconds at a time.

Allowing for this dramatic awkwardness, *The Ramparts We Watch* is a full-length picture with no stars; a factual, panoramic story, partly narrated, and partly dramatized, which on the whole comes off as a unified chronological drama, and provides another proof that the Hollywood star plot, the Hollywood dialogue technique, and the expensive, artificial Hollywood sets are not fundamentally necessary to the production of interesting motion pictures.

As an accurate interpretation of the events leading up to our entrance into the last World War, *The Ramparts We Watch* has a hundred mistakes—errors, for the most part, of omission.

Simply, their story is that we were patient and forbearing, until the Germans became so arrogant we couldn't stand it any longer and went to war to make the world safe for democracy.

In the last twenty years we have had a hundred books a year attempting to explain the economic background of the war, to fasten the war guilt on the proper parties, and to interpret those complex influences that led us to go to Europe.

I will not attempt to sum up these volumes. I do know that I lived in a small town not unlike New London, and that during the years shown in *The Ramparts We Watch* we were brought to a dangerous pitch of hatred and hysteria by an extraordinary propaganda campaign. What led my town to kick the German professor out of the college; to burn the German books; to ban German music; to accuse old settlers of being pro-German for idle statements made down at the post office, were the atrocity stories of women being mutilated, of babies being bayoneted, of wells being poisoned, of dead soldiers being used to make glue, etc.

There is nothing of this in *The Ramparts We Watch.* There is no mention of the bumper cotton crop of 1914; the hungry farmers of the South and Middle West. There is nothing of William Jennings Bryan, or of Colonel House, of Walter Hines Page, of Robert M. LaFollette, Sr., or of Charles Augustus Lindbergh, Sr.

More extraordinary, in a conclusion that brings us up to date, the editors simply say that Manchuria was invaded in 1931 as the beginning of a sowing of the whirlwind; that Ethiopia was invaded; that Germany re-armed, and that now we are faced with a necessity of preparing to go to war again.

There is no mention of the Chamberlain government; of the Blum government; of Anthony Eden, of war in Spain, of the non-intervention agreement; no mention of a number of things that Vincent Sheean, and John Gunther, and Jay Allen, and half a dozen other foreign correspondents have been reporting in our daily press for years.

I feel, then, that *The Ramparts We Watch* is not an accurate report of the real events that sent us into the first World War; and it certainly gives us no quick summary of the events that are leading us into the next one.

By the time this is in print, we may be at war, so it is a little late to dwell upon any explanation of what caused it. You will not, however, find any reasons in *The Ramparts We Watch*.

The Giant Shinnies Down the Beanstalk:
Flaherty's *The Land*
by Theodore Strauss

This interview was originally published in The New York Times,
October 12, 1941. The author was a staff writer on that newspaper.

The giant was in a jovial mood. Despite the fact that a commiserating waiter was bringing distressing minute-by-minute reports on the backward progress of the Dodgers, Robert Flaherty continued to scatter his dollars like chaff—probably to bolster his own failing confidence—in even money on "dem bums." But when the cataclysmic blow finally fell, Mr. Flaherty's shaggy white head was only momentarily bowed. Raising his flagon with a full-blooded oath that would have rent the veil in a tabernacle he was shortly launched on the reasons why Hollywood morticians are the wiliest entrepreneurs at large. Laughter shook his mighty frame like an inner tempest. The Dodgers had lost? "I am absolutely heartbroken," he said sincerely, but already his mirth was erupting. He had thought of another story.

Listening to Robert Flaherty one listened to a great romantic and a great romancer. Put him in a cassock and you might have had Friar Tuck—a great tumbling man with massive red cheeks, brilliant blue eyes, and the sharp profile of an eagle. His size was matched only by the exuberance of his wit; he tossed ideas like an agile bull lifts the matador. A born raconteur, he talked fabulously out of a memory shot full of colorful, bawdy, and heroic reminiscence of all the places he had ever been from the dangerous straits of Hudson Bay to the fragrant islands of the Pacific, from Mysore and the elephant hunts to the Aran Islands where they shoulder the northern sea. He talked like a man who had just finished a long and grueling job.

In fact he had. It is nearly two years since Mr. Flaherty was summoned by Pare Lorentz and the then existing United States Film Service to make *The Land,* nearly two years since he returned to his homeland for the first time in a decade of wandering. It is nearly a year and a half since he loaded his cameras in a station wagon and set out to "rediscover" America. "It was really an exploration," he said.

To be sure, his journeys constantly "on location" were but part of the long, exhausting struggle that goes into the making of a Flaherty film. There were endless conferences with Wayne Darrow, head of information in the Agriculture Department, who, as Mr. Flaherty gratefully remembers, told him, "Take your time and don't pull your punches." There were talks with such interested parties as Milo Perkins, and after traveling 25,000 miles and exposing 100,000 feet of film began the cutting with Helen Van Dongen and the writing of the narration with Russel Lord—a task which Mr. Flaherty said had to be so accurate "that only an expensive corporation lawyer could write it."

"Actually," he said, "there wasn't any story. They gave me a camera and threw me out into the field to make a film about the land and the people that live by it. I was fresh and had no preconceptions whatever; I was so sensitive you could hear me change my mind. So I merely groped my way along, photographing what seemed to me significant; it was only later that we began to see the pattern. The film is different from my others. It isn't a romance. It hasn't any specific solution for what the camera sees, but it is often critical. And that perhaps is the most amazing thing about it, that it could be made at all. It shows that democracy can face itself in the mirror without flinching."

For what Mr. Flaherty met and saw and heard and photographed was often grim. He saw eroded, desolate lands nearly equal in area to the size of Germany, France, and England combined. From the rich harvests of the Minnesota river valleys he turned southward, where the long dusty roads were often clotted with migrants too weak to work even if they found it. Elsewhere, in the midlands, he met farmers who boasted of having worn out five or six farms in their lifetimes—and then he saw farms that had been left behind, the rat-infested shells of empty houses. And again the straggling pilgrims on the dusty roads.

But just as ominous was the terrible face of the machine. He watched the automatic cornhusker that robbed the rows with blind efficiency, the cotton picker, watched by awestruck workers who hardly surmised its impact on their way of life, which did in twenty minutes what it took a man two days to accomplish. In Minnesota he saw an angle-dozer which cleared an acre of wooded, boulder-strewn land in an hour. The farmer who owned it had paid $6,000 for it, cleared new land for his neighbors at five dollars an hour, and was so proud of his machine that he wore a yachting cap at work.

"It is incredible," said Mr. Flaherty. "With one foot in Utopia, where the machine can free us all, we have yet to dominate it. That is the problem of our time—to conquer the machine. With it new modern countries have been developed in a matter of generations rather than centuries. In 1855 Japan, an almost medieval country, sent its first Ambassador to the Court of St. James attired in a suit of chain mail. Today it is one of the most highly industrialized countries in the world. The progress in this country is something that neither Washington nor Jefferson could have dreamed of. Today we stand at the threshold of a great calamity or a great new era. The decision is ours."

Did we say Mr. Flaherty was a romantic? He is. His feet still wear seven-league boots and there is still the aura of legend about his massive shoulders. He still hopes that a kindly deity will allow him some day to wander to the Mountains of the Moon, to the Himalayan back-country and China. But beneath his great gusto Mr. Flaherty has changed. His "rediscovery" has left its impress upon him. In facing what is the most primitive and most modern of our problems he has not escaped unmoved. Out of the seared hinterland of America he has emerged with what he believes to be his deepest and truest film.

An Angry Film: *Native Land*
from Time

This review appeared, unsigned, as was the custom,
in the Cinema section of Time, June 8, 1942.

Native Land (Frontier Films) is an angry picture. Its wrath is directed at violators of U.S. civil rights, especially those vested interests who struck down American working men in the labor turmoil of the recent 1930s. Unashamedly pro-labor propaganda, it is, nevertheless, an eloquent indictment of acts of injustice and intolerance which did happen here and might again.

Most of these acts are taken from the files of the U.S. Senate Civil Liberties Committee. Producers Leo Hurwitz and Paul Strand have dramatized them in sequences bound together by straight documentary interludes, highlighted them with perhaps the finest spoken commentary (Paul Robeson) ever recorded on celluloid and an effective musical score (Marc Blitzstein) accompanying the Robeson songs. The result, better as episodes than as a whole movie, is a shocking, stinging picture whose realism could never have been achieved in soft-stepping Hollywood.

Like some of the early Soviet films, *Native Land* is charged with power by its in-line, unswerving theme. It opens softly with a camera portrait of the U.S. which free men have built by virtue of the Bill of Rights, veers suddenly into an outrageous violation of those rights: the murder of a forthright farmer (at Custer, Mich., in 1934) for presuming to speak his mind at a grange meeting.

From that incident until the final reel, *Native Land* seldom lets down. With a fine feeling for suspense and violence, it re-enacts the vigilante pursuit (in 1936) and murder of a pair of Arkansas sharecroppers who wanted a trivial raise, the Ku-Klux flogging of Joseph Shoemaker and two companions (in 1935, on a road north of Tampa, Fla.) for almost defeating a Klansman in the city elections, the untidy tale of a company labor spy, etc.

These savage episodic passages receive the full benefit of Producer Strand's sensitive, pointed camera work, and of the remarkably natural performances of Fred Johnson (farmer), Art Smith (labor spy), Housely Stevens (sharecropper), *et al.*

Native Land's fervent faults are the faults of propaganda. It fails to identify the violators of its civil liberties, save by implication and by frequent mention of big business. It ignores the flies in labor's own ointment, advocates militant unionism as the future guarantor of the people's civil rights, almost forgets the Administration's efforts on behalf of organized labor, and displays small interest in union means or ends beyond an economic security guaranteed by organized mass membership.

Although it was designed to plead labor's cause and harps on a few notorious cases of injustice, *Native Land* is incidentally a powerful reminder of the necessity for guarding the Bill of Rights as a protection for those people who are wantonly crushed in all kinds of struggles. Despite its partisanship, it is as vitally American as Carl Sandburg.

Film and Reality: The Background
by Richard Griffith

*This selection appeared in Cinema 16 Program Notes (New York)
for June 1962, and is reprinted here by permission of Amos Vogel.*
Film and Reality *was produced by the National Film Library
of the British Film Institute from footage selected by
Alberto Cavalcanti and assembled by Ernest Lindgren.*

Though little known and less seen in the United States, this is one of the most controversial films ever produced. Passions still run high in its country of origin whenever this apparently innocuous film-history-on-film is mentioned.

Ernest Lindgren, Curator of the National Film Library of Great Britain, conceived the film as an adjunct to the work of his institution; he wished to provide British film societies with an outline of the history of the fact film (the only branch of cinema in which Britain can be said to have excelled) made up of excerpts from important films in the Library's collection. As adviser on the project, he selected Alberto Cavalcanti, a French director of Brazilian origin, who made that famous ancestor of the documentary film, *Rien que les heures* (1926). Subsequently, Cavalcanti had descended to third-rate commercial production in France, whence he was rescued by John Grierson, after the latter's well-known fashion of absorbing into the British documentary film movement whatever appropriate talent and experience lay at hand. Cavalcanti contributed notably to the technical development of British documentary, particularly in the field of sound and in connection with such outstanding films as *Night Mail* and *North Sea.*

Despite the esteem in which he was held by his colleagues in documentary, they were not entirely comfortable with the news that he was to preside over the making of a film which might well be their monument. "Such an attempt at contemporary historical record," said Documentary News Letter, "was felt to be a task better suited to a production committee than to an individual. Attempts were made by the Association of Realist Film Producers, the documentary movement's representative organization, to influence the production, but without success." That being the case, the resulting brouhaha was inevitable.

Basil Wright, director of *Song of Ceylon,* was selected to write the documentary movement's official review of the film. His criticisms were specific and more or less tactful, referring only once to Cavalcanti's "preoccupation with aesthetics" as against those sociological aims which were the guiding spirit of British documentary as a whole. But once was enough: Lindgren immediately and furiously replied, indicting the documentarians for "narrow parochialism bordering on intolerance," and for a "contempt for technique which, under Grierson's influence, has permeated all the writing of the British school in recent years." The ensuing argument on both sides bogged down in the verbal confusions which generally attend such controversies. Cavalcanti subsequently withdrew from the documentary scene and the controversy subsided. After making fiction films in England (*Dead of Night*), Cavalcanti recently returned to Brazil where he apparently intends to set up a production unit.

Is there anything of interest to be drawn from this ancient quarrel, and what can be our verdict on the film itself, as history, after nine years? As to the latter, it can only be said that the National Film Library, for reasons best known to itself, selected an individual filmmaker to chronicle his own extremely populous field —a filmmaker, moreover, whose penchants and prejudices were at odds with the purpose which many felt to be the essence of the documentary idea. That high purpose was all Cavalcanti's colleagues had to warm them through many a cold and hungry year, and it was unbearable to them that it should be shoved aside in favor of what they regarded as a purely aesthetic approach.

Unclear though it may be from the above confused alarums of struggle and flight, there was something at stake. Cavalcanti, in his commentary to the film, says: "Film technique has been developed mainly by seeking to represent reality. Because the filmmaker's material is not make-up and scenery, but photography and sound-recording, the best work in the cinema has been done by those who have remembered what the first inventors never doubted, that the essence of cinematography lies in its power to represent reality." This statement may seem obvious to those for whom the old issue of film *vs.* theater is long since dead and buried out of sight. But within this context there is still another conflict: is the art of the film an art of observation, in which the photographed material properly dominates the artist and leads his hand and eye?

Or is it an art in which the artist strives to manipulate the material he photographs, to make it express and project his own desires, dreams, fears, obsessions? This controversy still rages, not infrequently in these very notes and in this very hall. Cavalcanti's film gives it fresh fuel, for, from tempermental bias, he has sought out those films which impose an aesthetic pattern upon reality, instead of those which prompt the spectator to exclaim "how true!" rather than "how beautiful!" Combatants may step outside in the lobby immediately after the performance.

British Documentaries in the War
by H. Forsyth Hardy

This selection is reprinted from "20 Years of British Films"
(Falcon Press, London, 1947). Mr. Hardy, editor of "Grierson
on Documentary," and long the director of the Edinburgh Film
Festival, is director of Films of Scotland.

When the war began documentary had passed beyond the experimental stage. There was a solid body of achievement to justify Grierson's belief in the documentary idea. Some 300 films had been produced, portraying the life and purpose of Britain with truth and imagination. The battle for authenticity had not been won without at least a skirmish or two. The most notable was the controversy on the subject of what British films should be sent for exhibition at the New York World's Fair in 1939. The issue was summed up in Grierson's phrase: Knee breeches or working clothes—in other words, the tradition and pageantry of the British Council films, or the story of Britain's social aims and achievements as told in the documentaries. Public opinion in the U.S. did secure exhibition for the social documentaries; and there were other evidences of international recognition of the worth of the British documentary movement.

At first there seemed no doubt about the role documentary was to play during the war. The G.P.O. Film Unit, with Cavalcanti as producer, made *The First Days,* brilliantly interpreting the atmosphere of London during September 1939. Filming freely in the streets and parks, cameramen registered the calm determination of the Londoners, the feeling of friendliness, the sense of unity in a common cause. Omitting Korda's curious compilation, *The Lion Has Wings* (which Vincent Sheean reports having seen run as a comedy—in Berlin!), the next film to appear was *Squadron 992* (1940), Harry Watt's dramatic reconstruction of the Firth of Forth raid in the early weeks of the war and the defensive role of the balloon barrage. It was a brilliantly arranged and exciting film, with a warm human quality we were beginning to think of as characteristic of Watt's work. In the final analysis it was a defensive film, like *Britain Can Take It* (1940), and others similar in theme to follow; but, as a dramatic episode, it would have taken its place naturally in a film program where the compensating aggressive notes were struck elsewhere—if there had been such a program.

It was many months after the outbreak of war before the Ministry of Information suggested that it had evolved a policy which would make adequate use of the documentary movement. The leaders of the movement themselves were in no doubt that a magnificent opportunity was being frittered away. In issue after issue, Documentary News Letter underlined its criticism of lost opportunities. Perhaps it was difficult for the Government, when the future of the country hung rather delicately in the balance, to devote much attention to a policy for documentary. Perhaps their very eagerness made the documentary producers protest overmuch. Whatever the reasons and their justification, it is true that documentary began only gradually and fitfully to make its contribution to the war effort.

That the documentary producers did protest is proof of the seriousness of their sociological purpose. Consider, for example, the following quotation from Documentary News Letter for July 1940: "It may be argued that it is now too late to inaugurate a plan of long-term democratic propaganda, that our public information and propaganda services must now devote all their energies to the immediate needs of a desperate national fight for life. Yet a nation fighting desperately to defend the present, lacks the inspiration which springs from a vision of the future. Now, more than ever, it is necessary to repair past errors and fortify national morale with an articulation of democratic citizenship as a constructive force which can mould the future."

With Jack Beddington in charge of the Films Division at the Ministry of Information, progress began to be recorded, although there was as yet no evidence of consideration of long-term issues. A series of five-minute weekly film messages, to be shown in cinemas all over the country, was announced, and a good beginning was made with J. B. Priestley's *Britain at Bay*. Before these films were replaced by monthly issues of fifteen minutes in length, over eighty were produced. They varied widely in subject matter and in quality. There were Government appeals: *Salvage with a Smile, Mr. Proudfoot Shows a Light,* and *The Nose Has It* (Arthur Askey cleverly adapting Benchley's lecture technique). There were films of Britain on the defensive: *Dover Front Line, Words for Battle,* and *The Heart of Britain.* There were recruiting films: *A.T.S., Hospital Nurse,* and *Land Girl.* There were reports from the war fronts, notably Harry Watt's *Lofoten.* And films reflecting the Allied war effort: *Diary of a Polish Airman* and *The Five Men of Velish.*

In addition to these short films, which were the main documentary activity for over two years, there were a number of more ambitious products made by the G.P.O., or the Crown Film Unit, as it was now known. The first of these was *Men of the Lightship* (1940), produced by Cavalcanti before he went to Ealing Studios and directed by David Macdonald. Its story of a Nazi attack on an unarmed lightship was still the "Britain Can Take It" theme; but it succeeded significantly in stimulating a feeling of active protest. This was followed by another story of the sea, *Merchant Seamen* (1941), whose theme was the hazards of the Merchant Service and its ability to hit back. The story was told through the experiences and personalities of a group of seamen who are torpedoed but escape to serve again. Directed by J. B. Holmes, this was a mature and effective film, notable technically for the handling of the players. It was followed in a month or two by Harry Watt's *Target for Tonight* (1941), which remains the best-known documentary made during the war or before it. This account of a raid over Germany came at the right psychological moment, when we were wearying of the "Britain Can Take It" idea and longing to hear of aggressive action. Watt's film caught the drama of what was then a large-scale raid and the dry phrases of the official communiqués came alive.

The success of *Target for Tonight* with audiences both in this country and abroad had a sharply stimulating effect. The graph of film production at the M. of I. rose steadily. Many of the films had purely utilitarian purposes: films on how to dig and how to deal with a fire bomb, how to get more eggs from your hens and how to enjoy a Woolton pie, how to keep rabbits for extra meat and how to get orange juice for the children. The documentary units, now growing fast in numbers, lent their skill, often with ingenious result. to the making of these films of advice or exhortation. They were shown for the most part on the nontheatrical circuit built up by the Ministry's 150 traveling film units.

In addition to these instructional films, there were others in the style and on the scale of *Merchant Seamen* and *Target for Tonight,* dealing with campaigns or Service achievements. *Ferry Pilot* (1942), directed by Pat Jackson, told the story of a service vitally important in the early years. *Wavell's 30,000* (1942), first of the campaign films, described Wavell's advance into Libya. *We Sail at Midnight* (1941), directed by Julian Spiro, told the story of the operation of the Lease-Lend arrangement in terms of the supply of essential tools to a British tank factory. J. B. Holmes's *Coastal Command* (1942) described the patient and tireless work of the R.A.F.'s coastal patrols. In this film in particular, the understatement characteristic of documentary was carried to such an extreme that the story failed to come alive on the screen: it described but failed to reveal. Its chief virtue was its magnificent aerial photography. *Operational Heights* (1943) supplemented *Squadron 992* by telling the story of one of the balloon ships guarding vital stretches of the sea approaches. *Close Quarters* (1943) suffered from the disadvantage of reaching the cinemas two months after the studio-produced story of submarine patrol work, *We Dive at Dawn*, but otherwise demonstrated the greater power inherent in the imaginative use of real material.

Malta G.C. (1943), a tribute to the island's heroic role in the battle of the Mediterranean, was an appropriate forerunner of the series of combat films. The standard was at once set high by *Desert Victory* (1943), which told with simple lucidity and sober pride the story of the advance from El Alamein. The film rested firmly on the basis of the material shot by the combat cameramen: legitimate additions were the animated diagrams explaining the tactical aspects and a staged sequence depicting the Eighth Army's night attack. *Tunisian Victory* (1944), a joint British-American production, enjoyed the advantage of a campaign which offered a perfect scenario, and made the most of it, despite the interpolated nostalgic sequences. With *Left on the Line* (1944), the battle scene moved to Europe and the story of the British and Canadian drive from the Normandy beaches to Brussels was told with restraint. *The True Glory* (1945), most ambitious of the series of war films, also adopted the most ambitious shape. It told the story of the invasion of Europe and the victorious campaign in the West in the terms of the men who fought and won the battles. Directed by Carol Reed and Garson Kanin, the film sustained a fine balance and only the passages of declamatory commentary earned criticism. Finally, *Burma Victory* (1945), by David Macdonald and Roy Boulting, succeeded both in making clear the confused phases of the Burma campaign between 1942 and the end of the Japanese war, and in being a good film, intelligently constructed, vivid and compact.

An important addition to these war films was *Western Approaches* (1944), the Crown Film Unit's most ambitious production and its only picture in Technicolor. Written and directed by Pat Jackson, its aim was to bring alive the drama of our struggle against the U-boats. The strength of its story of a torpedoed crew, rescue from a convoy, and the destruction of a submarine lay in its authenticity. Here was a magnificent justification of the documentary method.

Drama on the home front was not neglected. Several of the films were made by Humphrey Jennings, the unrepentant impressionist of the Crown Film Unit. Experiments in *Spare Time* (1939) and *Listen to Britain* (1942) were followed by the more ambitious *Fires Were Started* (1943), which told the story of the blitz by focusing our attention on a single incident. By making us familiar with the routine of the station and the individual firemen, he added to the suspense and excitement of the action during the raid. Jennings's developing skill and versatility as a director were further demonstrated in *The Silent Village* (1943), a memorial to the people of Lidice, played out against the sympathetic background of a South Wales mining village; and in *The True Story of Lili Marlene* (1944), in which much technical skill and ingenuity were squandered on trying to find some significance in the popularity of a Nazi song. *A Diary for Timothy* (1945) attempted a survey of the last six months of the war, and despite the controlling influence of Basil Wright as producer, Jennings's flair for impressionism again diverted him from the exacting demands of his theme.

With war demands pressing increasingly, there was little opportunity to continue the social documentaries of the immediate pre-war period. *The Harvest Shall Come* (1942), directed by Max Anderson, told the story of the decay of British agriculture over the past forty years and posed the problem of farm labor when the policy of importing the bulk of the nation's food was resumed. Like *North Sea*, it was a genuine story film made with a documentary purpose. *Children of the City* (1944) discussed the reasons for the war-time growth of child crime and the constructive measures taken in Scotland to deal with the problem. In *Tyneside Story* (1944), Gilbert Gunn examined sympathetically the post-war outlook for shipbuilding and the shipyard worker. Ralph Keene's *Proud City* (1945) took as its theme the opportunity war has presented for rebuilding London. More important than any of these films, however, were Paul Rotha's two productions, *World of Plenty* (1943) and *Land of Promise* (1945). The first dealt with food—pre-war distribution and consumption, the effects of war and the possibilities of control and fair distribution after the war. It was a masterly piece of exposition, a milestone in the development of the factual film. *Land of Promise* dealt similarly with the problem of houses and homes, proceeding as in the food film by question, argument, and the calling of evidence.

If, at the outbreak of war, the documentary movement was underemployed, by the end of 1945 too many films were being made and standards suffered accordingly. Only the exceptional productions could compare with the best work done in the immediate pre-war years. There were two main reasons for this decline in quality. One was the restraint inevitable under Government sponsorship. To see a film through the protracted processes of investigation and production, with endless reference back, called for toughness and integrity rarely found in adequate combination. The other reason was the tiredness of directors, who had no time and little inclination to bend imagination to the work in progress and make their films reveal as well as describe. Too many documentaries in the later war period were little more than pictures held together by commentary.

Despite this tendency, noted with regret both inside and outside the movement and possibly inevitable in the conditions prevailing, documentary emerged from the war with a greatly enhanced reputation. Documentary had become familiar to audiences in every part of the country, from London's West End to isolated village audiences in the Shetlands. If documentary did not play the part which the most enthusiastic members of the movement hoped it would during the war, it was not because of their lack of enthusiasm but because of restricted opportunity. Let me close this survey with an apt comment of Grierson's, made following a visit to this country toward the end of the war: "It has been a wonderful thing to see, in spite of the war and the special difficulties of film making in Britain, the documentary people there have remembered the essentials of social reference. They have not been fooled into the fallacy that fighting films give anything more than one layer of the present reality. But I keep on feeling that the documentary group as a whole is not at the center where political and social planning is being thought out and legislated, or not close enough to the center. It is not good enough to be on the outside looking in, waiting on someone else's pleasure for an opportunity to serve social progress."

One for the Ages: *Desert Victory*
by Manny Farber

*This review is reprinted from the New Republic, April 12, 1943.
The author was for many years the regular film critic of the
magazine. His work has been collected in a volume titled
"Negative Space" (Praeger, New York, 1971).*

The British government's documentary, *Desert Victory,* is a pleasure and an excitement. It is a real documentary, not a newsreel assembly that jumps from one minute part of one event to another minute part of another event until two reels are over. *Desert Victory,* in fact, puts you inside the North African campaign where it was last October, and allows you to see it as it progresses, from the beginning to the end. At the start the British Eighth Army was barely holding a thirty-mile front between the Qattara Depression and the sea, and at the end British tanks are passing, thirteen weeks later and 1,300 miles further west, through the gates of Tripoli.

This is the first time a movie has been the original source for the clearest account of an event. The filmmakers of the British government were obviously as well prepared for the attack that came in the night of October 23 as was the Eighth Army under Montgomery. The photographing of this attack is so successful that the soldiers come as close to being movie players, without being, as is possible—this while clawing their way forward through barbed wire, or fishing anti-tank mines out of the sand, or as their bagpiper plays while walking with the Highlanders, stiff-legged and sweating, through their own land mines. Seconds before the signal for attack is given the screen goes bare and silent, and then explodes in your face as British artillery laid down the barrage that shook buildings outside of Alexandria, sixty miles away. So that here, for the first time, is a sustained record on film of an attack, as it was being made—the entire scope of Montgomery's plan is studied as it unfolds. Incredible photography was almost underfoot of the advancing Highlanders, up ahead clearing the way with the heroic sappers, with the air force that was strewing the desert with Axis wreckage. There was even a photographer to run around with the dour, angular-faced Montgomery. Everywhere the event is examined with the completest curiosity of which the camera is capable (from Rommel's viewpoint as well).

Desert Victory contains the two great ingredients of the English movie tradition: slow, lucid, beautifully modulated photography, and nearly perfect film editing. The photography sees the outside world of texture and light values in the same way as the human eye, leaving the business of drama and working up of emotions to the content of the event itself. (The opposite of this method, of course, is that of Orson Welles, whose camera is used to fix mood artificially.) While English photography seeks the clarity of the eye, English editing tries to follow the demands of human instinct, that is, to approach the heart of an event and to stay with it as long as one's curiosity holds out. This technique, as applied in *Desert Victory,* is in contrast to the flickering, choppy aspect of the Russian war documentaries, where the heavy hand of moral and purpose is always teaching you your lesson—this scene is to show that the Nazis destroy art, that one that the Russian pianist raises morale, the other that Russian women work in coal mines, etc., and never is the continuity controlled by the unpredictable progress of the event but by a program of secondary meanings. This is not in any way to condemn the brilliant work the Russians are doing in covering their war, but only to say that emotion and interest in a film have more chance of taking hold when the event is shown at such length that it can speak for itself.

The longest chase in history, that of Rommel from El Alamein to Tripoli, is in the film sketchily, mostly signposts and a touch at each stop—Tobruk, Bengazi, El Agheila—to watch the crowds lining the street as the British go through. But the main purpose of the film has already been accomplished, to a thorough degree, and that rare thing, a perfect movie, has been made. Col. David Macdonald, of the Army Film and Photographic Unit, directed twenty-six men in making *Desert Victory;* four were killed, six wounded, seven captured. It is a fact that Tobruk was actually taken by the British film unit, which arrived some hours in advance of the fighting forces.

World War II: Armed Forces Documentary
by Richard Dyer MacCann

This chapter is taken from the author's doctoral dissertation,
"Documentary Film and Democratic Government." Prof.
MacCann is also the author of "Film and Society" and "Hollywood
in Transition," and editor of "Film: A Montage of Theories."

In World War II, the War Department managed to establish a continuing and relatively satisfactory relationship between the government and Hollywood. Like most rapprochements, this one was attended by suspicion, hesitancy, and missteps, but in the end considerable confidence was established and some outstanding movies made. There was a very real fear on the part of some Hollywood people that a corps of filmmakers would be built up by the Signal Corps and become a threat to Hollywood itself. On the other hand, many said, and probably rightly, that there would be little art and no public interest in any war films turned out by Signal Corps "technicians." The eventual compromise, which involved putting directors, producers, writers, and technicians in uniform, did not threaten Hollywood commercially but did undermine some familiar movie habits—and this was all to the good.

By virtue of the tough, continuing requirements of working together on real problems, another kind of rapprochement took place. The factual needs of Washington and the dramatic experience of Hollywood met and mingled and found reason for mutual respect. The generals found that they could not get by with a forcible injection of knowledge. The directors found that making up a story was not necessarily the best way of doing everything on the screen. The people in the Pentagon, seeking the physical response of obedience, became more aware than ever before that they had to deal with what was going on in the minds of soldiers. The people in Hollywood, seeking to reach soldier's minds, became aware that well-ordered facts were the most persuasive dramatic material they had. When the films began to be made more and more for public showing, this kind of rugged honesty persisted and resulted in achievements of enduring greatness.

The product which came out was documentary, but it was documentary under pressure. Working with limited goals in mind, though not altogether without a sense of their place in history, men like

Capra, Zanuck, Ford, Wyler, Kanin, and Huston could do very little planning. They could not direct the shows they photographed. They couldn't even direct what the combat cameramen were going to do. Sometimes cameramen had to throw grenades. Thirty-two of them died on the western front alone. Only toward the last did a new writing technique come to full fruition in *The True Glory,* using the idiom of the soldier himself in combination with the filmed events of epic size. For the most part the makers of government war films were simply film editors.

A priority list of film needs had been set up by arms and services in accordance with a letter from the Adjutant General on April 23, 1940, but after Selective Service began to bring men in in great numbers, the problems became more acute. Subjects of basic usefulness to the army as a whole were sought, and *Articles of War, Military Courtesy, Safeguarding Military Information, Sex Hygiene, Personal Hygiene* were among the earliest of these. Hollywood made them, and Darryl Zanuck, vice-president in charge of production at 20th Century-Fox, accepted two scenarios before any terms were arranged.

On November 26, 1940, Y. Frank Freeman, then chairman of the Motion Picture Production Defense Committee, wrote a letter to the Secretary of War concerning arrangements about training films. He had talked it over with the Chief Signal Officer (Major General J. O. Mauborgne) and with industry representatives. He proposed production by the industry for the War Department on a nonprofit basis. On December 12, Secretary Stimson accepted this offer and an Advisory Council to the Chief Signal Officer was set up; Nathan Levinson was commissioned a colonel in the Signal Corps reserve and assigned to the War Department Liaison Office in Hollywood. Shortly afterward Darryl Zanuck was appointed to the Advisory Council and made a lieutenant colonel in the reserve.

The nonprofit arrangement had its advantages and disadvantages but finally broke down under the weight of increasing demands and increasing costs. A year after Pearl Harbor a straight contract plan was worked out.

Things moved fast after the Japanese attack. There already existed a Training Film Production Laboratory at Fort Monmouth, New Jersey, in addition to the Army War College photographic laboratories. The need for a big central source of training films finally became not only apparent but compelling. One of the leading reasons was the increasing quantity of confidential and restricted information which had to be taught to specialized troops. The War Department bought outright the old Paramount studios at Astoria, Long Island, and moved in equipment and personnel from Fort Monmouth. The Signal Corps Photographic Center was activated on March 30, 1942, and by December all training films for ground forces were being made there. People from Hollywood now started coming to New York in greater numbers.

By the middle of 1942, training needs already began to yield to more dramatic subject matter. "Highest priorities will be given to those pictures which present instruction directly concerned with combat operations." In September, a new series called "Fighting Men" was announced, which would be "short, highly dramatized, and hard hitting. Presentation will in general be by a soldier speaking typical soldier language." This was immediately inspired by a speech of Lieutenant General Wesley McNair at the Army War College, in which he called for greater toughness in training and a realization that the soldier must either "kill or be killed." The resulting pictures emphasized that treachery was to be expected and the ethics of the playing-field did not apply. In *Kill or Be Killed,* a Nazi soldier gets an American to reach for some water for him and shoots him in the back for his pains. Demonstrations of brutality were predominant and Life commented that "the trainee can almost hear the crunch of flesh and bone."

Meanwhile, at another level, the Signal Corps was soliciting the services of a popular Hollywood director whose films had been full of the irrepressible faith and humor of middle-class America. Frank Capra was at the very height of his success when the Signal Corps requested him to apply for a commission on December 8, 1941. The response to *Meet John Doe* had been less than unanimous, but the titles of his previous films, year by year, represented a veritable gallery of popular triumphs: *Lady for a Day, It Happened One Night, Broadway Bill, Mr. Deeds Goes to Town, Lost Horizon, You Can't Take It With You, Mr. Smith Goes to Washington.*

The War Department was already well aware that morale was not exclusively a matter of chow and letters from home. It also had to do with a sense of direction on the part of the individual soldier. Pearl Harbor helped, but there could be no forgetting the pre-Pearl

Harbor threats of OHIO ("Over the Hill in October")—the widely publicized manifesto of the drafted boys who thought one year was enough. General Marshall had already called a conference on November 18, 1941, which resulted in an orientation program throughout the army on the reasons for military service—a program which was assigned to the Bureau of Public Relations.

Thus, "Why We Fight" became the next film need. Capra was brought in as a major for the specific purpose of producing the orientation films which became the most famous film achievement of the War Department. General Marshall called in Capra and Major General Frederick H. Osborn, head of the Special Services Division, and talked with them for an hour about the problem of maintaining morale and instilling loyalty into a civilian army. He told them he wanted motion pictures to help with this job, gave them a general order to go ahead, and asked them to hurry.

The series of films was based directly on a series of lectures prepared by the Army Bureau of Public Relations which were being delivered to troops. These apparently left something to be desired in the way of motivation. General Marshall had occasion to give a public appraisal of the effectiveness of those lectures when the first film *Prelude to War* was under attack on the floor of the Senate:

I want to say this: That I personally found the lectures of officers to the men, as to what they were fighting for and what the enemy had done, so unsatisfactory because of the mediocrity of presentation that I directed the preparation of this series of films.

Some day there will be an extended depth analysis of the themes and purposes of these films. It can only be said here that, in general, they attempted (1) to destroy faith in isolation, (2) to build up a sense of the strength and at the same time the stupidity of the enemy, and (3) to emphasize the bravery and achievements of America's allies. Their style was a combination of a sermon, a between-halves pep talk, and a barroom bull session. Capra and his staff searched for pictures to illustrate certain ideas; then the commentary was tailored to fit the pictures which were actually found; the words were kept simple, direct, hard-hitting, with plenty of time allowed between statements to permit both statements and pictures to sink in deeply.

However familiar its message was by 1943, there can be no doubt that *Prelude to War,* which was shown to total troop audiences of 9,000,000 by 1945, reinforced and sharpened the lessons of the thirties. Its purpose was to describe "the causes and events leading up to our entry into the war." The film made plain that the war did not begin at Pearl Harbor. The "other world" of totalitarianism had made a choice between democracy and force: its "tragic mistake of choosing the second course" meant that "demagogues" gained power in Italy and Germany. In Japan it was "not one man but a gang," backed by the secret Black Dragon society. But "no matter how you slice it, it was plain old-fashioned military imperialism."

In the beginning, Capra pictured not only our own early leaders, and the Declaration of Independence, along with people like Lafayette and Lincoln who fought for freedom, but also claimed that the belief that all men are created equal went back to old-world leaders as diverse as Moses, Mahomet, Confucius, and Jesus. The nations of the "other world" had now surrendered their liberties. Throwing away their human dignity, they "became part of a mass, a human herd." Their leaders were now public enemies. "Remember these three faces"—Hitler, Mussolini, Tojo. "If you ever meet them, don't hesitate."

Following this came the actual picture story of the giving up of liberty, told in a kind of three-way counterpoint. Crowds yelling "Sieg Heil!," "Duce!," and "Banzai!" approved the giving up of free speech, assembly, press, and courts, along with labor unions and bargaining rights. The Matteotti assassination, the killings of Japanese statesmen, the Nazi murders of Roehm and others were seen as a pattern. Sneers at culture, destruction of religion, and perversion of truth in the classroom all come to a climax in scenes of children marching. The sinister comment is: "I want to see again in the eyes of youth the gleam of the beast of prey."

"What of our world?" We weren't so smart, ourselves, because we were preoccupied with our own little problems. "Let Europe fight her own battles." We turned our backs on the League of Nations and put up prohibitive tariffs. It was true that John Q. Public ran the country; he read what he pleased and attended any church he pleased. But he didn't pay much attention when the German children drilled; he didn't know about the Japanese Tanaka plan for conquest. When the war actually began on September 18, 1931, it was impossible to convince a city busdriver or a midwestern farmboy that a mud hut burning in Manchuria was a threat to his life.

Ethiopia came and went, with "Mussolini beating his chest like Tarzan," and, though Roosevelt and other leaders gave warnings, we were still hypnotized by our two oceans. But now the two worlds are lined up, the chips are down, and it's "us or them."

There can be no doubt of the effectiveness of such a film as this for young men and women who had lived through the thirties— simply as a reminder, for some, but more particularly as a forceful organizing of loose thoughts for those who had never bothered to work things out in their minds. This single film may not have deeply affected fighting motivation. Research Branch reports, using questions of doubtful relevance, tended to discredit the effect of the film. But it strengthened those who were most in agreement with the opinions of waverers. A propaganda film could not expect to do much more. And the most typical comment on *Prelude to War* was: "It's propaganda, all right, but it's good propaganda."

Soon after, came *The Nazis Strike* and *Divide and Conquer,* which dealt in much the same way with Germany's aggression eastward (including Austria and Czechoslovakia) and westward (up to Dunkirk). *The Battle of Britain* was followed by *The Battle of Russia,* which depended heavily on reenactments directed by Anatole Litvak in Hollywood, and which received considerable critical approval when it was released, as was *Prelude to War,* for public showing. *War Comes to America,* also publicly released, was the last of the series and did not appear until 1945, some time after *The Battle of China.* Neither of the last were as widely seen as the first five, which were all shown to Army personnel for the first time in 1943. They were required seeing. They were supposed to be viewed, and notation made on the service record, before any soldier went overseas.

Eight million men were supposed to have seen *The Battle of Britain.* Pictorially it was probably the most impressive of the group; it is dramatic and inspiring history even today. It starts with pictures of Hitler in Paris. "Where Napoleon failed, I shall succeed; I shall land on the shores of England." As the audience becomes accustomed to thinking in terms of 1940, and the hopeless prospect which then confronted the world, the Nazi plan is ticked off: Phase One—Knock out the Royal Air Force and destroy communication and transportation; Phase Two—Dive bombers and paratroops; Phase Three—Invasion. After that, the United States.

Then the British preparations are described—the army dragged from the sea at Dunkirk, one tank for every thousand square miles, one machinegun for every 1500 yards of beach, men working 70 hours a week, defense maneuvers which were permitted to use one shell at each practice. But, though they were outnumbered ten to one, the British "also had an air force."

We hear Churchill's magnificent words and feel the force of his spirit, and then we watch what happens. The great gulf between the printed page and the film has never been better illustrated than here, for the raging inferno of London in August and September can only be named, not reproduced, in words. The film reproduces it. The film gives meaning and depth to the statistics—the 26 major attacks in the first ten days, the 697 German and 153 British planes lost, the 500 bombers and fighters overhead on September 15 and the 185 shot down, the 50 million pounds of bombs in 28 days. And then in October the night attacks. In November, Coventry. On Christmas night, the fire bombs.

The outnumbered people and the little air force are the steady heroes of this remarkable moving picture. No thoughtful American could watch this dramatic and terrible story without a sense of wonder and gratitude that this thing could have been done on this little island in 1940.

Signal Corps cameramen were also writing history as well as informing the troops. *The Liberation of Rome* was as much for posterity as for the encouragement of the common soldier or the information of the American public.

Of the 200,000 feet of film which came into New York each week from overseas crews, not very much went into Information-Education films. More, for instance, went into weekly issues of "Combat Bulletins," which were less confidential versions of the "Staff Film Reports." The practical value to the Army—as well as the other services—in having film records of military operations to study filled an important function in officer training. This short-term historical value was no less important than the long-term value of history as a means of instilling pride.

But somewhere in the middle distance, between these two values of immediate training and historical record, was the value of public information. Some of the most memorable motion pictures of the Army were made with public relations firmly in mind.

The first big undertaking of this kind was in November and

December of 1942, when Darryl Zanuck, on leave as head of production at 20th Century-Fox, and 65 other army and navy cameramen took pictures at Algiers, Oran, and Casablanca, and in Tunisia. The immediate outcome was a production called *At the Front in North Africa,* toward which there were mixed critical reactions. This pioneering effort was nevertheless a first evidence of what might be done in the way of reports from battlefields, and was an important response to the early leadership of the British in this respect.

The star of this later phase of military documentary turned out to be John Huston. He made only three short pictures, but two of them were among the finest documentaries ever filmed.

In *Report from the Aleutians* he brought back too much material and used too much of it—especially for a campaign which was over so soon and out of the limelight. But, if the film had been cut, the sacrificed parts would probably have been the very incidentals which give it flavor. *Report* contains one of the best shots ever made of an army mailcall, for instance, and some of the introductory data on changing weather included pictures of planes landing on the runway in half a foot of water. There were remarks about that runway: all one and a half million square feet of it were put down—"by the infantry, of course"—in 36 hours. Such remarks foreshadowed Huston's uncompromising treatment of war in his next film, but there were softer highlights, too, as when he played his camera on the faces of individuals in the bomber crews and caught something of their team spirit, or when the narrator says against the roar of returning motors: "The ride *back* from Kiska is the most beautiful ride in the world. It doesn't matter if there's a big piece of daylight pouring through your wing—there's just something about the scenery. . . ."

The Battle of San Pietro was simply a grim statement of how war looked to the infantryman in Italy. Richard Griffith says that this result was unwelcome in the Pentagon—that later pictures were not permitted to be so outspoken nor so "anti-war"—and such may well be the case. But *San Pietro* does not have enough excitement in it to be dangerous. There is acid comment on a bombed church: "Note interesting treatment of chancel." There is dreary despair: "Each river seemed like five, each peak a little higher than the last." It rains at H-hour. The enemy observation is excellent. Somewhere among the faceless hills a battalion keeps sending out patrols, and "not a single member of any of these patrols ever came back. . . . Many companies lost all their officers, and enlisted men came forward as inspirational leaders." It is a peculiarly inconclusive story, despite the introduction of liberated Italians at the end. It is as close to the real feeling of daily battle on the ground as any film since *All Quiet on the Western Front.*

Huston's third contribution to an understanding of war was never made available to the public. It concerned the treatment of psychiatric cases in a veterans' hospital and not all the subjects of these unposed scenes were willing to see them released. *Let There Be Light* is nevertheless one of the most deeply moving of all documentary films. That it was not shown widely at a time when many young men were returning from experiences of terror, is a thing to be regretted, for its spirit of compassion is such as to leave almost any audience chastened and changed. Regardless of the specific healing methods shown, and their effectiveness—and it apparently is true that the comebacks shown in the films were not all permanent ones—there is gained through watching these tortured men, with their torn memories and their longing for safety, a new awareness of the damages of war and the strange paths some men must walk when they return to peace.

Probably the most important sequences from a documentary point of view of psychology are the group-therapy sessions which the concealed camera caught with such steady honesty. The things these men share with each other about their early lives reveal the frankness and understanding the psychiatrists have achieved in working with them. It becomes very clear that not only the war, and not only themselves, but also the people who have lived near them, are responsible in part for their sicknesses. "Not all the learning in all the books is half as valuable as to find someone you esteem—someone you can feel safe with—someone who gives you the feeling of being important. Knowledge alone is not enough."

The final scene is the equal of anything in fiction films. The boy who has been freed from paralysis by the removal of a mental block and the boy who has surmounted incoherent speech by surmounting his terrified memories of German SS's are both playing ball in the hospital yard. The paralyzed boy is running the bases; the stutterer is umpire.

The largest achievement of wartime documentary was the presentation on film of the campaign in western Europe. It is difficult to assign credits for this achievement, since its British-American director-editors were Carol Reed and Garson Kanin, its scenario was constructed by five people in and out of the forces, and it was produced by the Office of War Information and the British Ministry of Information. But the greatness of this film lies primarily in the pictures, which were taken by 1400 Allied cameramen on the western front, of whom 101 were wounded and 32 killed. This extraordinary testimonial to the bravery and toil of the men who fought in France and Belgium and Holland and Luxembourg and Germany was based on 6,500,000 feet of film. It is a worthy testimonial to the men who took the pictures that the editing was done with skill and the narrative written with originality and warmth.

Of the technique of this narrative, Iris Barry wrote:

> The vernacular of a polygot Allied Army forms an integral part of *The True Glory,* a rough and rich cross-section of recent European and human history. The natural speech of the men, typifying those who wrote that history, enhances the message of the hundreds of battle pictures which compose the substance of the film. Blank verse, less effective but helpful as punctuation to mark the successive stages of the story, chimes in and, on yet a third level, the voice of General Eisenhower lends authority or adds elucidation to the saga. The whole is a broad, eloquent canvas compressing and suggesting much more than the visible facts, and doing it in a manner possible only to the motion picture: nothing else has so fully sustained or recorded the heroic story from D-Day to V-E Day.

Certainly one of the enduring values of this powerful film is its reflection of the way Anglo-Americans thought and acted in this war of the 1940s.

"We didn't think we'd spend fifteen days in the same field outside of Caen . . . each side mortaring each other all the time. . . . You get tired of being mortared . . . you think every one's coming straight for you."

"We thought: God, are we going to have to go right across the world doing this to beat 'em? . . . Then we heard that the Third Army was taking off. . . . They'd pulled a rabbit out of a hat—and what a rabbit! A rabbit with pearl-handled revolvers."

"Mortain . . . was where I got hit. . . . I get a belt in the face, left side, and I keel."

"I just kept 'em covered. . . . It wasn't my job to figure 'em out.

. . . But, brother, I never gave 'em more than the Geneva convention, and that was all."

There were many examples of dangerous photography in this motion picture: one of the most intense is the matter-of-fact recording of that long moment when the side of the LCI goes down and the men start clambering out on to the Normandy beach. You have seen their faces before, but now you see only their backs and you strain your eyes ahead, as they do, to see what is beyond.

In that moment, an infinitesimal trace of the fear and darkness of war is shared. To have shared even so much with a wondering and uncomprehending public, was the glory and achievement of those brave men who happened to carry cameras. *The True Glory* is eighty minutes of priceless film. Along with its final message addressed directly to the public—"It is not the beginning but the continuing of the same, till it be thoroughly finished, which yieldeth the true glory"—this motion picture stands as one of the enduring artistic monuments to men at war.

The Negro Soldier: A Challenge to Hollywood
by Virginia Warner

This selection, the first of a series, originally appeared in
The People's World (San Francisco), April 8, 1944.

The War Department doesn't confine its history-making activities to the battlefields, but has lately been making motion picture history, too. *The Negro Soldier,* to be released this month, is a 40-minute documentary which plows through the ruts of old conventions and outworn prejudices in the handling of the Negro on the screen, and lays the groundwork for a new approach to the Negro in the motion picture industry.

True there has been increasing awareness in Hollywood that a new approach to this group of the American people was necessary, and there have been occasional dignified and worthy roles for Negro actors in recent films. However, the industry as a whole has been held back by lack of understanding, by the chains of old habits, by fear of making a break with the past, by uncertainty as to what kind of characterizations should replace the old stereotypes of clowns and mammies and Uncle Toms.

The Negro Soldier shows what can be done by simply approaching Negroes as Americans, and being concerned with what they really do, how they do it, and how they feel about it. Every one of the old stereotypes has its opposite—and true—face in *The Negro Soldier.* Instead of the fat mammy with a bandanna around her head, an accent you could scoop up with a spoon, and a worship of the white family she serves, we have a mother who dresses and speaks like hundreds of other American mothers, and has the same pride and love for her boy in the service. The part was played by Bertha Wolford, a Hollywood extra, who has a son in the army.

Instead of the eye-rolling, ghost-fearing buffoon, we have an intelligent, patriotic young GI who qualifies for officer training. This part was played by Lieutenant Norman Ford, who was picked out of a regiment in one of the camps where *The Negro Soldier* crew was taking pictures. Lieutenant Ford has since been overseas, where he fought well and was seriously wounded.

Instead of the superstitious, uneducated, and subservient preacher, we have a young, vigorous man in the pulpit of the Negro church, who is leader of his people in their participation in their country's war effort. The part which takes the place of a narrator is very ably handled by Carlton Moss, who also wrote the script. It recalls the vital leadership of such Negro churchmen as A. Clayton Powell in New York and Clayton Russell in Los Angeles.

Instead of crap-shooting, loudly dressed young comics, we have hundreds of boys in uniform, doing those uniforms honor.

In a word, we have Negro Americans taken from life. This is a challenge to Hollywood to go to the same source for the Negro roles in its pictures.

This film offers a proving-ground for audience reaction, for although it cannot be expected to get the reception of a feature with popular actors and all the trimmings, it can provide a barometer for public acceptance of Negroes in dignified roles. Already the press reaction in both Negro and white press has been almost universally favorable.

In order to make full use of this film as a pioneer in preparing for further steps in the direction of screen reflections of national unity, it should get sufficient publicity to guarantee its showing at a large number of "white" theaters. The film itself deserves such showings, and they can do much to strengthen appreciation of the contribution to the war being made by Negroes.

Unfortunately, Hollywood has not availed itself of the usual channels for making such use of this picture. It is being distributed by the war activities committee of the industry, but instead of being handled by one major studio, who would then exploit it as, for example, 20th Century-Fox did with *Battle of Russia,* it is being handled by a different company in each section of the country and, far from being pushed and advertised, is simply available to exhibitors on request.

However, the picture has not yet been released, and the motion picture industry can still prove the good intentions it has expressed on occasion, by giving the film a proper sendoff with a preview in a Los Angeles theater.

On the Pacifiic Coast *The Negro Soldier* is being distributed by the Warner Bros. exchange, and those who wish to see it can not only request it from their local exhibitor, but can also write to Warners, urging that it be shown in every Warner house, and given ample publicity.

A Diary for Timothy
by Iris Barry

This review is reprinted from Film News (New York), November 1945. Miss Barry was the founder of the Museum of Modern Art Film Library, New York.

During six years of wartime filmmaking, Humphrey Jennings has steadily matured as a director. His films include *Listen to Britain, Silent Village, Words for Battle,* and *I Was a Fireman.*

Each of these films employed experiments which culminate and fuse in his latest film. *Listen to Britain* used no commentary and developed an imagist approach to his subject by which discrete images were linked in idea and bridged by music and effects in counterpoint to the picture. *Silent Village* was an experiment to re-create in film the mystery play in which the "rude mechanicals" reconstructed in all veneration the tragedy of Lidice. *Words for Battle* was an anthology of prose and verse of many centuries commented upon by contemporary visuals, and *I Was a Fireman* realistically, in picture and vernacular dialogue, reconstructed one night of the London blitz.

A Diary for Timothy emerges now to combine these experiments in a film of rare beauty and great certainty of directorial touch. The story of the film is ordinary enough. A child is born on September 3rd, 1944, the fifth anniversary of Britain's entry into the war and approximately nine months before V-E Day. The commentary of the film is a diary for the boy, which will tell him of the world he was born into. The diary tells him something of the bravery and the courage, something of the despair and something of the sacrifices of the days which make up his first six months on earth. It tells him, too, something of the new feelings of justice and equity in his country, something of the quiet beauty of England, something of the new hopes in people's hearts and something of the old fears.

Long a disciple of T. S. Eliot, Jennings continues to employ an imagist quality closely related to Eliot's. He takes the worn phrase and counterpoints it with the new thought or the new sound. In doing so, he brings new meaning to the archaic and new connotation to the novel. This can be well illustrated from a sequence in the film of John Gielgud playing Hamlet. The stage scene is crosscut with modern action. The gravedigger's discussion of suicide is replaced by a 300-years-later discussion of the flight of a rocket bomb. Yorick's comment on the folly of my lady to paint an inch thick falls over a scene of a bombed house in which a woman is buried. In a handful of images and a brace of lines the mind of Shakespeare illumines today and these days become as rich and spacious as those of Elizabeth.

228

Rouquier's *Farrebique*
by William Whitebait

This appraisal of the first French feature-length dramatic documentary, originally published in The New Statesman (London) and later in Documentary 1947, is reprinted here from the latter publication. Mr. Whitebait was a member of the staff of The New Statesman.

With the exception of *Rien que les heures,* Cavalcanti's impression-ist reporting of a Paris day, *Farrebique, ou Les Quatre Saisons,* is the first considerable documentary yet made in France. Why should there have existed, until now, this gap in the most intelligent and realistic of all cinemas? The answer is partly to be found in the very realism that has always distinguished French films; the lessons of documentary—I think of Renoir, Vigo, Carné, etc.—had been learnt, without the method. Nevertheless the omission remains strange. *Farrebique* may be regarded either as a further delving into the regional life reflected by such films as *Goupi-Mains-Rouges* and *L'Atalante,* or as closing a gap between science and poetry, in which, for some reason, French films had lagged. They had pre-ferred a poetry of the comic and fantastic.

Rouquier calls his film *Farrebique, ou Les Quatre Saisons.* He owes something, as must every filmmaker who takes peasants for his theme, to Dovzhenko's *Earth.* To begin with, the treatment is less specatcular. A tall square farmhouse rises with its almost win-dowless stone on a hill. The valleys over which the sun casts its quick shadowplay reside—we discover gradually—in that south-western district known as Guyenne. Breadmaking, the oxcart, the plough, the sacred dungheap, the vine; so, prosaically though with beautiful definition, this Georgic begins. But it takes us deeper, in a couple of directions, than we expect. First, the people themselves are no mere puppets, and during the course of four seasons we get to know them as intimately as characters of fiction, though in different ways. The children grow up a little; another baby is born; electric light is laid on; a young man strains his back at harvesting, and be-gins to make love; the old grandfather, who in the field has twiched flies off the bullocks' eyes with a hazel branch, is himself dying, with a fly crawling over his temples, and an old friend bends over to ask,

"How goes it then?" The complaint against documentaries that they miss the spark of living cannot be made here.

Then, secondly and more surprisingly, Rouquier learns brilliant and varied ways of developing his scene. He has a wonderful eye for detail: innumerable flashes—of a cartwheel turning, a lizard bolting into shade—of a hare leaving prints in the snow—of the evening shadows lengthening along a slope—reveal an almost Debussy-like sensibility to Nature. Sometimes, to emphasize the passing hours, the shadows will drop swiftly down a wall; we see the white roots of corn or maize wriggling in the soil, flowers bursting open; natural sounds of all kinds, from the human voice and footstep to the shrill cicada, are given their full value, while in a lyrical movement music and image alone will entrap the senses. And these are not mere tricks to distract, but the expressions of a vigorous imagination.

Flaherty's *Louisiana Story*

by Harold Clurman

This review originally appeared in the October 1948 issue of Tomorrow magazine. Mr. Clurman is the distinguished theater director, critic for The Nation (New York), and author of several books on the theater.

Robert Flaherty, who is one of the fathers of the documentary film and the creator of *Nanook of the North, Moana of the South Seas, Man of Aran,* has made another picture in a somewhat similar vein called *Louisiana Story.* The difference between *Louisiana Story* and the older pictures lies not only in the fact that it employs speech and a semblance of plot, but that it verges on a "purpose."

The Standard Oil Company paid for the making of *Louisiana Story.* Although it did not issue any orders to Flaherty except to show some of the process by which oil is brought from the earth, one is a little troubled by a sense that in some subtle way we are supposed to decide whether the discovery of oil on the land of simple inhabitants of the bayou country in Louisiana is a boon or a bane for them: we cannot tell which. If the picture has a serious flaw, it is that it seems to have a point which is not demonstrated, a meaning that eludes us.

Nothing in the picture's very bare dialogue would lead us to believe that any sort of "propaganda" is intended, but for the first time Flaherty is dealing with two orders of reality—the industrial as well as the natural. The juxtaposition may in itself provoke an unconscious demand that something be said about it. The flaw we suggest may be due as much to something that we, perhaps unjustifiably, expect as to something that Flaherty actually planned.

If the picture says anything at all on the score of industry and nature, it derives from Flaherty's special vision rather than from anything he may believe. For, in *Louisiana Story,* industry is seen as a phenomenon as "natural" as nature itself. If the machinery that the oil company sets up in the waters of the bayou appears a terrible threat to human life, it is less so than the huge alligator that glides through the same waters, fascinating as evil itself. Is Flaherty saying that all life has its innocence and its menace, that the alligator and the oil drill existing side by side with almost equal inevitability are things man may have to guard against equally? This doesn't seem probable, but questions such as these keep obtruding in the spectator's consciousness.

The greater part of *Louisiana Story* is a photographic poem which relates it to the best of Flaherty's work. Flaherty's genius lies in his effort to rediscover nature, so to speak, at its source. This does not imply softness or sentimentality. Struggle and pain are always present in nature and Flaherty observes these with just as patient and loving an eye as its more smiling aspects. In all of Flaherty's films nature is shown in its fathomless loveliness, mystery, and grandeur, together with people toiling to live within the pull of its fierce dialectics. Flaherty is so aware of this duality that where nature is at its gentlest, as in the South Seas, he dwells at length on the rite of tattooing in which the natives symbolically enact the pain of life by actually inflicting it on themselves in order to remind themselves that without it men cannot attain their full stature. In the opening sequence of *Louisiana Story,* the camera flows through the inlet and describes its intimacies of strange foliage, delicate wild life, wondrous gestation, beautiful efflorescence of nature's joyous and tender secrets together with the ominous presence of the monster that is as much a part of all this glory as the rest.

Are there villains in biology? Drama there certainly is. The drama becomes most poignant with the entrance of man. A boy of about eleven is the "hero" of *Louisiana Story*—the fleshed counterpart of Flaherty's spirit. He is as beautiful as anything in nature; indeed, he and almost all the people we see in the picture are very much like natural objects. Some of these people look like animals, others like trees, still others are akin to stones.

The boy in *Louisiana Story* expresses himself in sounds (part American, part French) that remind us of the birth of speech at a time when man was very close to the other creatures of the earth. The boy is strong, sweet, eager, unafraid, curious, ready to do battle to protect what he loves. The great events of his young life are his fight with the alligator and the advent of that other monster, the machine.

We never see the boy's ultimate conquest of the alligator—only the first thrilling skirmish. We never find out whether the other actor in the drama—the mighty instrument that rises fabulously over the water's surface and digs deep below it—brings the boy the same satisfaction as his triumph over the beast of the bayou. We see unforgettable episodes in the boy's life, and we are left to conjecture if they have any significance beyond the amazement they provide our eyes and the stimulation they offer our imagination.

In the end *Louisiana Story* remains a happy event on the primitive level of Flaherty's pure—we might say boy's—vision that disturbs us by suggesting another dimension which Flaherty either does not recognize or does not consider his province. The miracle of Flaherty's simplicity remains, offering us the opportunity to penetrate where we have long ceased to look, inviting us to journey into a free domain where we may relax our constricted spirits with fresh delight. And Virgil Thomson's superior score helps emphasize what is easy, open, bright, clear, and graceful in the film. Without problems or proofs *Louisiana Story* is a treasure.

Sweden's Arne Sucksdorff
by Arthur Knight

*This study of the Swedish director, written when the author was
assistant curator of the Museum of Modern Art Film Library,
New York, appeared in The New York Times, November 21,
1948. Mr. Knight, author of "The Liveliest Art" (1957) and a
critic for Saturday Review, recently published "The Hollywood
Style," in collaboration with the photographer Eliot Elisofon.*

To the current crop of new film talents must be added yet another
European, Arne Sucksdorff. Sucksdorff, a Swede, has already
gained some recognition abroad. His pictures won an award at the
International Film Festival at Cannes, and two "Charlies"—the
Swedish equivalent of the American "Oscar"—in his own country.
They were applauded at the Brussels Film Festival last year, and at
the Edinburgh Festival this year. Other filmmakers have begun to
study his pictures to see how he gets his effects. And 20th Century-
Fox has just purchased a group of them for distribution in this
country.

What makes this recognition so remarkable is the fact that all
of Sucksdorff's films to date have been "shorts." Longer films can
quickly gain attention for their makers, as witness Rossellini with
Open City and *Paisan*. But "shorts" and their directors are generally
ignored together. Yet when *Symphony of a City,* the first of
Sucksdorff's films to receive general distribution here, was shown
recently at the Roxy, virtually every metropolitan critic added a
paragraph of praise for the "short" to his review of the feature
picture.

Sucksdorff, a sturdy, handsome man now in his mid-thirties,
studied to become a naturalist, but soon discovered that he preferred
to paint and draw. In 1937 he went to Germany to study art, and
there picked up photography as a hobby. A series of Rolleiflex
studies of Sicily won him first prize in a Swedish magazine competition. While still in Germany Sucksdorff began to acquire the magnificent camera equipment that makes his pictures possible, and in
1939 made his first film, *A Summer's Tale,* which not only brought
him his first "Charlie," but also a job with Svensk Filmindustri, the
leading Swedish film studio. He has been with that same studio ever
since.

His films are perhaps closest in feeling to those of the veteran American documentary filmmaker, Robert Flaherty. Like Flaherty, Sucksdorff seeks the far-off places. Like Flaherty, he shows man against nature, or records a remote pattern of life untouched by civilization. The same kind of camera perception, the ferreting out of detail, the anticipation of movement—marks the work of both men. The similarity cannot be pushed too far, however: Flaherty, a moralist, shows in his films how things should be; Sucksdorff shows how things actually are.

"This is life," he says, "and whether we like it or not, this is the way life goes on."

His films emerge as highly individual, highly personal. Whereas most directors merely supervise what goes into their films, Sucksdorff is at once scenarist, photographer, editor, and even technician. He has built some of his equipment with his own hands. His films, on which he may work as long as six months for a single reel, are planned out in advance.

He writes for them a conventional scenario, then goes on location—more often than not in some wild and lonely place—and lets the country itself suggest whatever changes are to be made. Patiently then he photographs the footage he will need, often shooting hundreds of feet to procure the few frames that will be "right" for his purpose. Sound, too, is recorded on location.

Returning to the study at Stockholm, he painstakingly assembles his material, shaping it to his plan. Dialogue is rare in the Sucksdorff films. Natural sound is used imaginatively and suggestively. A sparse commentary fills in the details. In the American versions, the commentary is dispensed with entirely in favor of a brief written foreword stating the theme. To score his films he has turned to several of Sweden's foremost young composers, Erland von Koch, Stig Rybrant, Yngve Sjöld, and Hilding Rosenberg. Their work is as integral to his pictures as his own photography.

Sucksdorff generally draws his themes from nature, fascinated equally by the good and the bad he finds there. In *The Hunter* he shows us the good—a hunter who stalks for the chase, not for the kill, a hunter who, like Sucksdorff with his camera, derives his pleasure from the beauties of nature pulsing and alive. In *Shadows on the Snow* he shows us nature triumphant—the hunter forced back from his prey by fear of the shadowy night and a bear's superior cunning in the wilderness.

Struggle for Survival, a study of wild bird life on a Baltic island, reveals nature at its fiercest as the creatures rear their young despite preying gulls and unyielding ground. Nothing could be crueler than the single close-up of the herring gull's cold, unblinking eye, nothing more frightful than the fledglings plunging to death on the rocks below in their first attempt at flight. Yet this too is life, an aspect that the naturalist knows best.

Symphony of a City, although the first of Sucksdorff's pictures to be released here, is actually his most recent film. In it he has uncharacteristically turned his back on nature to present an impressionistic study of Stockholm. Oddly enough, while praised over here, some Swedes have not liked it. They found it beautiful, but said in a way they could not understand. Its mood seemed alien to them.

But again Sucksdorff was photographing life as he saw it and, as the body of his other work explains, the crowds, the rush, and the impersonality of the city are not for him. The precarious angles of his close-ups of faces mirror his distaste. His most positive expression is one of wonderment, which he shares with a small boy who wanders through the city, gazing roundeyed at the streets, the docks, and the solemn grandeur of a Stockholm cathedral.

All the Sucksdorff films are marked by the man's familiarity with his material, and his own willingness to let it speak through him. His technical skill, which is tremendous, is never used for pyrotechnical displays, but rather to facilitate the passage of his material to the screen. His uncanny ability to use animals, untrained people, and mere things as actors, the product both of prodigious patience and ingenious editorial manipulation, enhances his films with a new kind of visual excitement.

The American moviegoer is fortunate now in having this unusual series of "shorts" to break the routine monotony of travelogues and trailers among the "selected short subjects."

Some Aspects of the Work of Humphrey Jennings
by Lindsay Anderson

*The author, who was to go on to become a distinguished
director himself, wrote this appraisal of the* oeuvre *of
Jennings for Sight and Sound (London), April-June 1954.*

It is difficult to write anything but personally about the films of
Humphrey Jennings. This is not of course to say that a full and
documented account of his work in the cinema would not be of the
greatest interest: anyone who undertook such a study would certainly merit our gratitude. But the sources are diffuse. Friends and
colleagues would have to be sought out and questioned; poems and
paintings tracked down; and, above all, the close texture of the films
themselves would have to be exhaustively examined. My aim must
be more modest, merely hoping to stimulate by offering some quite
personal reactions, and by trying to explain why I think these pictures are so good.

Jennings's films are all documentaries, all made firmly within
the framework of the British documentary movement. This fact
ought not to strike a chill, for surely "the creative interpretation of
actuality" should suggest an exciting, endlessly intriguing use of the
cinema; and yet it must be admitted that the overtones of the term
are not immediately attractive. Indeed it comes as something of a
surprise to learn that this unique and fascinating artist was from the
beginning of his career in films an inside member of Grierson's
G.P.O. Unit (with which he first worked in 1934), and made all
his best films as official, sponsored propaganda during World War II.
His subjects were thus, at least on the surface, the common ones;
yet his manner of expression was always individual, and became
more and more so. It was a style that bore the closest possible relationship to his theme—to that aspect of his subjects which his particular vision caused him consistently to stress. It was, that is to say,
a poetic style. In fact it might reasonably be contended that Humphrey Jennings is the only real poet the British cinema has yet
produced.

He started directing films in 1939 (we may leave out of account an
insignificant experiment in 1935, in collaboration with Len Lye);

and the date is significant, for it was the war that fertilized his talent and created the conditions in which his best work was produced. Watching one of Jennings's early pictures, *Speaking from America,* which was made to explain the workings of the transatlantic radio-telephone system, one would hardly suspect the personal qualities that characterize the pictures he was making only a short while later. There seems to have been more evidence of these in *Spare Time,* a film on the use of leisure among industrial workers: a mordant sequence of a carnival procession, drab and shoddy, in a Northern city aroused the wrath of more orthodox documentarians, and Basil Wright has mentioned other scenes, more sympathetically shot— "the pigeon-fancier, the 'lurcher-loving collier,' and the choir rehearsal are all important clues to Humphrey's development." Certainly such an affectionate response to simple pleasures is more characteristic of Jennings's later work than any emphasis of satire.

If there had been no war, though, could that development ever have taken place? Humphrey Jennings was never happy with narrowly propagandist subjects, any more than he was with the technical exposition of *Speaking from America.* But in wartime people become important, and observation of them is regarded in itself as a justifiable subject for filming, without any more specific "selling angle" than their sturdiness of spirit. Happily, this was the right subject for Jennings. With Cavalcanti, Harry Watt, and Pat Jackson he made *The First Days,* a picture of life on the home front in the early months of the war. On his own, he then directed *Spring Offensive,* about farming and the new development of agricultural land in the Eastern counties; in 1940 he worked again with Harry Watt on *London Can Take It,* another picture of the home front; and in 1941, with *Heart of Britain,* he showed something of the way in which the people of Northern industrial Britain were meeting the challenge of war.

These films did their jobs well, and social historians of the future will find in them much that makes vivid atmosphere and manners of their period. Ordinary people are sharply glimpsed in them, and the ordinary sounds that were part of the fabric of their lives reinforce the glimpses and sometimes comment on them: a lorry-load of youthful conscripts speeds down the road in blessed ignorance of the future, as a jaunty singer gives out "We're going to hang out our washing on the Siegfried Line." In the films which Jennings made in collaboration, it is risky, of course, to draw attention too certainly to any particular feature as being his: yet here and there are images and effects which unmistakably betray his sensibility. Immense women knitting furiously for the troops; a couple of cockney mothers commenting to each other on the quietness of the streets now that the children have gone; the King and Queen unostentatiously shown inspecting the air-raid damage in their own back garden. *Spring Offensive* is less sure in its touch, rather awkward in its staged conversations and rather over-elaborate in its images; *Heart of Britain* plainly offered a subject that Jennings found more congenial. Again the sense of human contact is direct: a steelworker discussing his A.R.P. duty with his mate, a sturdy matron of the W.V.S. looking straight at us through the camera as she touchingly describes her pride at being able to help the rescue workers, if only by serving cups of tea. And along with these plain, spontaneous encounters come telling shots of landscape and background, amplifying and reinforcing. A style, in fact, is being hammered out in these films; a style based on a peculiar intimacy of observation, a fascination with the commonplace thing or person that is significant, precisely because it is commonplace, and with the whole pattern that can emerge when such commonplace, significant things and people are fitted together in the right order.

Although it is evident that the imagination at work in all these early pictures is instinctively a cinematic one, in none of them does one feel that the imagination is working with absolute freedom. All the films are accompanied by commentaries, in some cases crudely propagandist, in others serviceable and decent enough; but almost consistently these off-screen words clog and impede the progress of the picture. The images are so justly chosen, and so explicitly assembled, that there is nothing for the commentator to say. The effect —particularly if we have Jennings's later achievements in mind— is cramped. The material is there, the elements are assembled; but the fusion does not take place that alone can create the poetic whole that is greater than the sum of its parts. And then comes the last sequence of *Heart of Britain*. The Huddersfield Choral Society rises before Malcolm Sargent, and the homely, buxom housewives, the black-coated workers, and the men from the mills burst into the Hallelujah Chorus. The sound of their singing continues, and we see landscapes and noble buildings, and then a factory where bombers are being built. Back and forth go these contrasting, conjunctive images, until the music broadens out to its conclusion, the roar of engines joins in, and the bombers take off. The sequence is not a long one, and there are unfortunate intrusions from the commentator, but the effect is extraordinary, and the implications obvious. Jennings has found his style.

Words for Battle, Listen to Britain, Fires Were Started, A Diary for Timothy. To the enthusiast for Jennings these titles have a ring which makes it a pleasure simply to speak them, or to set them down in writing; for these are the films in which, between 1941 and 1945, we can see that completely individual style developing from tentative discovery and experiment to mature certainty. They are all films of Britain at war, and yet their feeling is never, or almost never, warlike. They are committed to the war—for all his sensibility there does not seem to have been anything of the pacifist about Jennings—but their real inspiration is pride, and unaggressive pride in the courage and doggedness of ordinary British people. Kathleen Raine, a friend of Jennings and his contemporary at Cambridge, has written: "What counted for Humphrey was the expression, by certain people, of the ever-growing spirit of man; and, in particular, of the spirit of England."

It is easy to see how the atmosphere of the country at war could stimulate and inspire an artist so bent. For it is at such a time that the spirit of a country becomes manifest, the sense of tradition and community sharpened as (alas) it rarely is in time of peace. "He sought therefore for a public imagery, a public poetry." In a country at war we are all members one of another, in a sense that is obvious to the least spiritually-minded.

"Only connect." It is surely no coincidence that Jennings chose for his writer on *A Diary for Timothy* the wise and kindly humanist who had placed that epigraph on the title page of his best novel. The phrase at any rate is apt to describe not merely the film on which Jennings worked with E. M. Forster, but this whole series of pictures which he made during the war. He had a mind that delighted in simile and the unexpected relationship, "It was he," wrote Grierson, "who discovered the Louis Quinze properties of a Lyons' swiss roll." On a deeper level, he loved to link one event with another, the past with the present, person to person. Thus the theme of *Words for Battle* is the interpretation of great poems of the past through events of the present—a somewhat artificial idea, though brilliantly executed. It is perhaps significant, though, that the film springs to a new kind of life altogether in its last sequence, as the words of Lincoln at Gettysburg are followed by the clatter of tanks driving into Parliament Square past the Lincoln statue: the sound of the tanks merges in turn into the grand music of Handel, and suddenly the camera is following a succession of men and women in uniform, striding along the pavement cheery and casual, endowed by the music, by the urgent rhythm of the cutting, and by the solemnity of what has gone before (to which we feel they are heirs) with an astonishing and breathtaking dignity, a mortal splendor.

As if taking its cue from the success of this wonderful passage, *Listen to Britain* dispenses with commentary altogether. Here the subject is simply the sights and sounds of wartime Britain over a period of some twenty-four hours. To people who have not seen the film it is difficult to describe its fascination—something quite apart from its purely nostalgic appeal to anyone who lived through those years in this country. The picture is a stylistic triumph (Jennings shared the credit with his editor, Stewart McAllister), a succession of marvelously evocative images freely linked by contrasting and complementary sounds; and yet it is not for its quality of form that one remembers it most warmly, but for the continuous sensitivity of its human regard. It is a fresh and loving eye that Jennings turns on to those Canadian soldiers, singing to an accordion to while away a long train journey; or on to that jolly factory girl singing "Yes, My Darling Daughter" at her machine; or on to the crowded floor of the Blackpool Tower Ballroom; or the beautiful, sad-faced woman who is singing "The Ash Grove" at an ambulance-station piano. Emotion in fact (it is something one often forgets) can be conveyed as unmistakably through the working of a film camera as by the manipulation of pen or paintbrush. To Jennings this was a transfigured landscape, and he recorded its transfiguration on film.

The latter two of these four films, *Fires Were Started* and *A Diary for Timothy*, are more ambitious in conception: the second runs for about forty minutes and the first is a full-length "feature-documentary." One's opinion as to which of them is Jennings's masterpiece is likely to vary according to which of them one has most recently seen. *Fires Were Started* (made in 1943) is a story of one particular unit of the National Fire Service during one particular day and night in the middle of the London blitz: in the morning the men leave their homes and civil occupations, their taxicabs, newspaper shops, advertising agencies, to start their tour of duty; a new recruit arrives and is shown the ropes; warning comes in that a heavy attack is expected; night falls and the alarms begin to wail; the unit is called out to action at a riverside warehouse, where fire threatens an ammunition ship drawn up at the wharf; the fire is mastered; a man is lost; the ship sails with the morning tide. In outline it is the simplest of pictures; in treatment it is of the greatest subtlety, richly poetic in feeling, intense with tenderness and admiration for the unassuming heroes whom it honors. Yet it is not merely the members of the unit who are given this depth and dignity of treatment. Somehow every character we see, however briefly, is made to stand out sharply and memorably in his or her own right: the brisk and cheery girl who arrives with the dawn on the site of the fire to serve tea to the men from her mobile canteen; a girl in the control room forced under her desk by a near-miss, and apologizing down the telephone which she still holds in her hand as she picks herself up; two isolated aircraft-spotters watching the flames of London miles away through the darkness. No other British film made during the war, documentary or feature, achieved such a continuous and poignant truthfulness, or treated the subject of men at war with such a sense of its incidental glories and its essential tragedy.

The idea of connection, by contrast and juxtaposition, is always present in *Fires Were Started*—never more powerfully than in the beautiful closing sequence, where the fireman's sad little funeral is intercut against the ammunition ship moving off down the river—but its general movement necessarily conforms to the basis of narrative. *A Diary for Timothy,* on the other hand, is constructed entirely to a pattern of relationships and contrasts, endlessly varying, yet each one contributing to the rounded poetic statement of the whole. It is a picture of the last year of the war, as it was lived through by people in Britain; at the start a baby, Timothy, is born and it is to him that the film is addressed. Four representative characters are picked out (if we except Tim himself and his mother, to both of whom we periodically return): an engine driver, a farmer, a Welsh miner, and a wounded fighter pilot. But the story is by no means restricted to scenes involving these; with dazzling virtuosity, linking detail to detail by continuously striking associations of image, sound, music, and comment, the film ranges freely over the life of the nation, connecting and connecting. National tragedies and personal tragedies, individual happinesses and particular beauties are woven together in a design of the utmost complexity: the miner is injured in a fall at the coal face, the fighter pilot gets better and goes back to his unit, the Arnhem strike fails, Myra Hess plays Beethoven at the National Gallery, bombs fall over Germany, and Tim yawns in his cot.

Such an apparently haphazard selection of details could mean nothing or everything. Some idea of the poetic method by which Jennings gave the whole picture its continual sense of emotion and significance may perhaps be given by the sequence analyzed and illustrated here, but of course only the film can really speak for itself. The difficulty of writing about such a film, of disengaging in the memory the particular images and sounds (sounds moreover which are constantly overlapping and mixing with each other) from the overall design has been remarked on by Dilys Powell: "It is the general impression which remains; only with an effort do you separate the part from the whole . . . the communication is always through a multitude of tiny impressions, none in isolation particularly memorable." Only with the last point would one disagree. *A Diary for Timothy* is so tensely constructed, its progression is so swift and compulsive, its associations and implications so multifarious, that it is almost impossible, at least for the first few viewings, to catch and hold on to particular impressions. Yet the impressions themselves are rarely unmemorable, not merely for their splendid pictorial quality, but for the intimate and loving observation of people, the devoted concentration on the gestures and expressions, the details of dress or behavior that distinguish each unique human being from another. Not least among the virtues that distinguish Jennings from almost all British filmmakers is his respect for personality, his freedom from the inhibitions of class-consciousness, his inability to patronize or merely to use the people in his films. Jennings's people are ends in themselves.

Other films were made by Jennings during the war, and more after it; up to his tragic death in 1950; but I have chosen to concentrate on what I feel to be his best work, most valuable to us. He had his theme, which was Britain; and nothing else could stir him to quite the same response. With more conventional subjects—*The Story of Lili Marlene, A Defeated People, The Cumberland Story*—he was obviously unhappy, and, despite his brilliance at capturing the drama of real life, the staged sequences in these films do not suggest that he would have been at ease in the direction of features. *The Silent*

Village—his reconstruction of the story of Lidice in a Welsh mining village—bears this out; for all the fond simplicity with which he sets his scene, the necessary sense of conflict and suffering is missed in his over-refined, under-dramatized treatment of the essential situation. It may be maintained that Jennings's peacetime return to the theme of Britain (*The Dim Little Island* in 1949, and *Family Portrait* in 1950) produced work that can stand beside his wartime achievement, and certainly neither of these two beautifully finished films is to be dismissed. But they lack passion.

By temperament Jennings was an intellectual artist, perhaps too intellectual for the cinema. (It is interesting to find Miss Raine reporting that "Julian Trevelyan used to say that Humphrey's intellect was too brilliant for a painter.") It needed the hot blast of war to warm him to passion, to quicken his symbols to emotional as well as intellectual significance. His symbols in *Family Portrait*—the Long Man of Wilmington, Beachy Head, the mythical horse of Newmarket—what do they really mean to us? Exquisitely presented though it is, the England of those films is nearer the "This England" of the pre-war beer advertisements and Mr. Castleton Knight's coronation film than to the murky and undecided realities of today. For reality, his wartime films stand alone; and they are sufficient achievement. They will last because they are true to their time, and because the depth of feeling in them can never fail to communicate itself. They will speak for us to posterity, saying: "This is what it was like. This is what we were like—the best of us."

The Quiet One: A Milestone
by Walter Rosenblum

This selection, by the photographer Walter Rosenblum,
appeared originally in Photo-Notes (New York), Spring 1949.

There were headlines in the newspapers recently about a group of kids in Harlem who fought one another from roof to roof, using homemade guns as their weapons. There was nothing wrong with their unhappy craftsmanship, for one boy was killed. The reason for their mutual form of self-destruction is no secret. They had no homes to speak of, and the kind of jobs available to them were dictated by their color and not their ability. Unable to understand the cause of their misery, they turned their hatred against one another, street against street, white against Negro.

One would think that our great motion picture industry might find these problems source material for their films. After all, these incidents are not isolated phenomena. Hollywood has but to turn the corner to Los Angeles to find all the drama its cameras could use. Yet what have our movie moguls ever shown us but a spurious group of Dead End Kid films? Hollywood, interested only in escapist films, is busy drowning itself in the clichés of "pure" entertainment.

Four young people have evidently been dissatisfied with the Hollywood product, for they have made a film of their own; their inspiration, America 1949. Dick Bagley, Helen Levitt, Janice Loeb, and Sidney Meyers have made an epic on a shoestring. Starting with $30,000 and a desire to say something about the neglected "one-third of a nation," they have made a film richly deserving of the superlatives Hollywood has coined but so rarely earned.

As their protagonist, they have chosen a Negro boy, Donald Thompson, about ten years of age, born and raised in Harlem. We watch him through the film, being robbed of every vestige of human dignity, by a cancerous slum environment. The boy has never known his father, never known the meaning of emotional security. His mother remarries when he is but an infant, and he is forced to live with his grandmother, a tired, beaten woman, incapable of supplying Donald with the love for which he is starved. Desperately in need of affection and human warmth, Donald searches the streets of Harlem looking for someone to befriend him. He tries to buy friends with money stolen from his grandmother, and he even re-visits his mother. But nowhere does he find understanding and love. And all along the road, Donald pays heavily for each emotional defeat. He is backward at school, unable to learn to read or write. He plays hooky, steals, smashes windows, bashes in car fenders, and winds up being arrested. Fortunately he is sent to Wiltwyck, a progressive school for delinquent children, where an attempt is made to bring him back to mental health. The school tries to provide the love and understanding that was denied to Donald by the laws of the jungle in which he lived.

There have been other films about delinquent children. The Soviet *Road to Life* was a classic of its kind. But the wild boys of the road in that film were the innocent victims of a gigantic economic and political upheaval. In *The Quiet One,* we see neurosis engen-dered in our children as a daily part of "normal" life in America today. The film shouts no slogans. It recreates our childhood, identi-fies Donald's fears with ours as children. We feel strongly about Donald because we know him, and love him as a brother or son. He is part of us, part of our lives. As long as he faces destruction we know that we can't be free.

The Quiet One uses every cinematic device to bring us closer to the core and meaning of the film's content. The camera, as it ex-plores the streets of Harlem, intensifies our vision, forcing us to take cognizance of an environment to which we might otherwise be blind. The use of dubbed-in sound, which was a financial necessity because of the small film budget, is itself turned into a virtue. Sound is used to highlight the visual image, and the emotional impact of its use is always overpowering. There is one scene where Donald, while walk-ing through Central Park, comes upon a crying child who is being comforted by an anxious mother. In his own frustration, he mimics the child, crying mama, mama, mama. And as he walks away from the mother and child, he enters a tunnel. The reverberation of those sorrowful words bouncing off the tunnel walls multiplies his an-guish a thousandfold. This complete unity of sight and sound is a feature of this film.

Each of the four who made *The Quiet One* was relatively new to his job. Yet the camera work of [Richard Bagley,] Helen Levitt, and Janice Loeb is characterized by great spontaneity, a complete integration of the people to their environment, and a candid quality which is able to reveal the people in their most expressive moments. Sidney Meyers, in his first directorial assignment, works miracles with a cast made up almost entirely of non-professionals. Under his direction, they portray the most complete mental torturings, acting feats which would be cause for alarm to the most experienced professionals. His editing of *The Quiet One* is on the same high level as his directing. It is with a great deal of pride we note that Sidney Meyers was one of the original members of the Film and Photo League and is part of the documentary tradition it developed.

The performances in this film are not merely true to life, but distill the essence of each enacted scene. The actors have caught the fervor of the film's message and deliver stunning performances. There is always complete identification with the necessity of the emotional moment. They are beautifully supported by the musical score of the young Negro composer, Ulysses Kay, the commentary written by James Agee and narrated by Gary Merrill.

The Quiet One rescues the documentary film from the hollow shell that Hollywood was forcing it into. The ratchet voice of those films which stole the form of the documentary but rejected its content should be shamed into silence by the intensity and integrity of this film.

The Quiet One raises its voice against poverty and despair. It fights for the rights of every child to a full quota of love and understanding. Four people have used their art to smash away at the jungle of slums that litter this country of ours. Their film is a weapon for decency, a milestone in cinema art.

Progress in Documentary
by Warren Miller

This selection appeared originally in Masses and Mainstream (New York), March 1949. The late Mr. Miller was a novelist and critic.

It seems clear by now that if the American film has any future at all, it lies not in Hollywood but with the independent filmmakers. It is these men, unrestricted by banks, motivated by artistic need and the social quality of their thinking, who may bring the film to a place in art and give the neighborhood movie-house a value and importance in the lives of people—an importance it now completely lacks, being only a dark place seldom illuminated by the light of truth and art.

Two independent films recently made in New York and currently playing are Leo Hurwitz's *Strange Victory* and Sidney Meyers's *The Quiet One*. Both were directed and edited by two men who were responsible for, and the product of, the old Film and Photo League—a group that included Irving Lerner, Van Dyke, Steiner, Lionel Berman, Jay Leyda, Lewis Jacobs. Virtually unrecognized is the fact that, by and large, the history of American documentary is these men; and, but for Jacobs and Leyda, this country's contribution to the literature of film would be nonexistent.

The Hurwitz film opened last summer and played but a short time; it received reviews that were both favorable and cool. The impression given seemed to be this: that Hurwitz had done well a job that needed doing, but that was no reason for people to go see it. And some who went to see it were made uncomfortable by the film's refusal to compromise with fact: the fact of the exploitation and oppression of the Negro people in America, the fact of anti-Semitism, of native fascism; and the disquieting idea that the recent war had indeed produced a strange victory, the values of the loser being adopted by the victor.

To accept the film's message as a valid one meant that one had also to accept the responsibility for doing something to end that condition. Some found an easy out for conscience in criticism: there were too many babies, it was too long, and besides we all know these things anyway—as if the critic's sole job was demolition.

The film has since been reedited and worked to a tight finish. Its structure is so complex that it would require diagrams to describe it. It twists in on itself, coils, and then springs with tremendous force. It is not, as has been charged, repetitive—unless you find a Bach fugue repetitive. There is reiteration and variations on a single theme. It has been and, I am certain, will be criticized by those who miss the larger structure which holds it all together, enforces and molds it.

The construction of the film gives it the density of a poem. I do not mean that it has the levels of meaning of, say, a poem by Yeats; the meaning, as it should be, is clear and explicit. Here, the density is a matter of relationship of one image to another, of juxtaposition, of the purposeful harmony and discord of cuts, of the theme briefly stated and then taken up again in another context, seen from another perspective, in a different light.

Aware of the easy road that racism travels, Hurwitz juxtaposes a COLORED ONLY sign with a tattooed number on the arm of a Nazi victim. The Russian woman grieving at her husband's coffin; the emaciated, twitching child with swollen body; the horrible corpses at Auschwitz—these are seen to be the victims of this singularly undangerous looking man in the conservative business suit.

In this film Hurwitz had to be both director and editor. Indeed, in such a film the distinction is almost meaningless. The task that faced Hurwitz as editor was a staggering one: organizing thousands of feet of assorted shots taken by nameless Army cameramen, as well as the sequences, staged and unstaged, specifically prepared for the film. Of course, this is the problem of every editor with any film. But seldom is the task so immense and seldom is it carried off with anything like the artistry and power achieved by Hurwitz.

It should surprise no one that every company from MGM down to Film Classics has refused to release this film in the United States. It will have to play at those houses not owned or controlled by the major companies. Meanwhile, it is playing to large audiences in England, France, Czechoslovakia. In Italy, in towns where theaters are not available, it is shown on street corners and town squares by those who recognize the film's value and importance.

Sidney Meyers's *The Quiet One* is a brilliant, moving film about a boy, insecure and unloved, mentally disturbed by the conditions of his existence. That the boy is a Negro is not invested with special significance; yet, in our society, the choice of a Negro child as hero has, inevitably, extensions of meaning that go beyond the framework of the film. What Meyers has achieved here is a total identification with his central character; one makes no reservations. It becomes, therefore, more than the story of a boy's sickness and partial recovery; it shows, as it must, the environment that makes love difficult and security impossible. Its meaning then is social, and the simple story of a disturbed boy becomes a document of the power of knowledge and love.

The film was made in cooperation with the Wiltwyck School for Boys, a place where mentally disturbed children, of all races, are given guidance, care, and, if they permit it, love. The film might easily have fallen into an old trap: that psychiatry alone is the answer. But the intelligence that went into the making of this film, from producer to cameramen, did not permit this. And this intelligence operated on every level of the film: it is for this reason that *The Quiet One* is the best film exposition to date of psychiatric treatment. There is no magic, the cure is not found suddenly in Ingrid Bergman's lovely eyes; it is depicted for the first time as the slow and painful process that it is.

There are three major sequences in the film. The editing of the first is as good as anything that has ever been done in this country; and the last, the boy's flight from the Wiltwyck School, approaches the grand work of the European masters of montage. The first sequence is the boy's search for love; his wandering through the streets of Harlem; the faces that smile, but not to him; the bought companions who leave him; the pregnant woman whose secret is not his; the spurned gesture of helpfulness; the mother who walks out on him. All of this builds in tenseness and is broken off at precisely the right moment. He is about to throw a rock at a plate-glass window; the rock is thrown and at that instant the film cuts back to the countryside around the Wiltwyck School—the rock falls in a pond and the wavelets circle out, touch the shore.

In his flight from the school, the boy, Donald, walks along the railroad tracks. Startled by an oncoming train, he leaps to a rockface and holds himself pressed against it while the train goes by. At this point occurs the most brilliant editing in the film. The terribly abused device of flashback is here used validly—valid because it functions organically in the film and is not imposed on it between fadeouts or by means of some artificial transition gimmick. As each car of the train passes, there is a flash of light on Donald's face and, seemingly, it is within the time-space of the flash that his mind relives incidents from the past, scenes with which the audience is already familiar. This gives it an intensity the flashback rarely has, since it is usually employed to inform the audience of an event it has no knowledge of; here, we relive it, too.

The camera work of Helen Levitt, Richard Bagley, and Janice Loeb contributes enormously to the success of the film, particularly Helen Levitt's outdoor shots. Some of the Harlem exterior shots are so brilliantly composed as to seem to change, for a moment, the proportions of the frame. The score by the Negro composer, Ulysses Kay, like that of David Diamond's for *Strange Victory,* is excellent. James Agee's dialogue has a highly charged poetic quality. . . .

The Quiet One simply could not have been made in Hollywood. The few men capable of conceiving a script like this have been fired from their jobs, and no director now functioning there has the talent to put it on film. And no producer with the courage or moral energy to sponsor it.

Documentary Technique in Film Fiction
by Parker Tyler

*This selection by Mr. Tyler, the American film critic
and theoretician, originally appeared in the Summer
1949 issue of the American Quarterly magazine.*

The ideal of documentary as a film form drew its main impetus from two sets of pioneer filmmaking: Robert Flaherty's earliest travel films, *Nanook of the North* and *Moana* (1922 and 1926); and the Russian propagandistic films, Eisenstein's *Potemkin* and *Ten Days That Shook the World* (1925 and 1928) and Pudovkin's *The End of St. Petersburg* (1927). Naturally, it was the "fact-reporting" of the ordinary newsreel that appealed to the men who visualized the documentary style. The one man most responsible for the development of documentary as a form to transcend the workaday newsreel is John Grierson, a Scotsman, who gave Great Britain her early lead in the documentary field. It was Grierson who was individually inspired by Robert Flaherty's travel films and who termed his other chief source of inspiration, *Potemkin,* a "glorified newsreel."

The rise of a film style that should, in essence, glorify reality has been going on steadily for some time, not only in England and Russia[1] but also in the United States. A very recent, outstanding example of serious documentation in film fiction came from Australia, *The Overlanders,* concerning a famous cattle trek across country. The tendency, as writers have frequently remarked, has been to consider British film as generally characterized by a realistic style related to Grierson's long championship of documentary. Indeed, it would seem true that the treatment of even such melodramatic entertainment as England's *Odd Man Out,* with its careful and varied social faceting, was influenced by the documentary ideal.

It must be noted that the development—or more or less imperceptible infiltration—of "newsreelism" in film fiction took place as the result of educational aims in filmmaking, extending to the propagandistic. This was true in different senses of England, Germany, and Russia, and comes under the heading of general propaganda, both foreign and domestic, including the effort to create good will in other countries by a factual rendering of the native people and institutions rather than a fictional rendering.[2]

Mr. Grierson has clearly stated his ideal concerning documentary in his collected film writings, "Grierson on Documentary".[3] It is, in brief, to draw men together into a homogeneous global group by portraying them so that the essential humanity of each nation will shine through its strange clothes and exotic habits. I do not have in mind the social and political significance of this ideal, despite the large group of films encouraging moral reforms by various means, but rather its aesthetic importance to film as form. Grierson has been responsible for a great deal in the artistic application of film style as a means, as attested by documentaries as diverse in subject matter as *Song of Ceylon* and *Night Mail*. The latter introduced into the narrative of the fast mail train between England and Scotland both verse and music as highly modulative elements, which would mean, as to aesthetic surface, the reverse of documentary into fiction. The most important aspect of the subject, however, is signified by the the question: In what way does documentary differ in its basic technical premises, its aesthetic theory and practice, from straight film fiction? It is the large frame of the latter into which documentary has lately been trying to fit.

We may strike at the heart of the matter without delay by going back to some of the earliest films made, to, indeed, that French precursor of the "glorified newsreel" *Potemkin,* depicting the same event—the insurrection of the sailors on the Russian battleship of that name and the massacre on shore of the sympathizing townspeople by the Czarist troops. This now thoroughly anachronistic film was made shortly after the event took place (1905) and therefore was in effect, especially since so brief, a *fabricated newsreel.* While its sets were painfully artificial and its acting unbelievably awkward, it probably thrilled movie patrons of that time. As with *Intimate Scenes of Convict Life,* made in France the same year and ostensibly portraying conditions on Devil's Island, the primitive French version of the Potemkin affair sought to fulfill the function of a visual newspaper, to tell a true story in animated pictures rather than in words. The modern journalistic parallel of these films is that presentation of "fact" still to be found in Hearst news supplements. Indeed, the formula may be expressed as a neat blend of Jules Verne with simple reporting. At once, then, we see what the ideal of the visual newspaper came to be: a variety of information that would be the more palatable the more decorative and exotic or sensational it was. The seeds of fiction were planted early in documentary, those of documentary late in fiction.

Yet going behind this inevitable ideal of the earliest filmmaking, we come to the one essential fact—rather than ideal or moral aim—at the base of the documentary conception. This fact was nothing but the photographic image itself, whose chief distinction (even when not yet in motion) was its "factual" or "truth-telling" nature: "The camera does not lie." At this late date we can deal with this axiom with the proper scientific skepticism. But at one time it was mainly because first the still and then the moving camera were innocently supposed to duplicate reality that movies achieved their later fame. Thus, even though the Potemkin incident took place at a faraway Russian seaport, it was deemed veracious to represent it as *actualité,* the modern French term for newsreel film being *actualités.* Briefly, it was a reconstruction of the form of truth known as history.

Now this was precisely the premise—I may say the aesthetic premise—of Eisenstein's own later film, the classic *Potemkin.* For the incident was a historical classic of revolutionary Russia and all that Eisenstein did was to reconstruct it on the basis of the authenticated and manifest record of the events. A simple visual problem presented itself to the Russian director, that of fabricating a spectacle which should have every aspect of being the real thing, in other words, as the Potemkin affair might actually have taken place. Therefore, the scenario or shooting script of Eisenstein's *Potemkin* merely had to graft itself as a story of visual action on a "slice of history," or more accurately, on a given, or prior, reality which it sought ingeniously to duplicate as though the narration were that of a gifted and peripatetic eyewitness. In the same manner the happenings of Hiroshima might be cinematically reconstructed with John Hersey's eyewitness report serving as scenario.

So what may be termed the eyewitness character of film is a scientific element relating automatically to the documentary technique and inseparable from it. The film eyewitness would thus be a *sine qua non* of documentary: a theoretical safety valve on propagandistic aims, since what the movie camera sees must be *actualité* in the raw, not in any sense a fabricated *actualité* like the primitive French *Potemkin.* For the modern newsreel to be authentic, then, it must have been "on the scene of the crime." Hence there are newsreel scoops of great catastrophes and singular events as an automatic adjunct of journalism. The importance of the eyewitness element to the film public was observable during World War I, when various war films advertised as "taken at the front" were questioned as frauds or as largely fabricated.

When Grierson applied the qualifying adjective "glorified" to the noun "newsreel" to describe *Potemkin,* just what did he signify by it? He was making an important observation because the glorification consisted not only in the elaborate detail that made Eisenstein's film so convincing, but also in the elevation of newsreel events to that level of dignity we conceive as the category of history. *History* implies not only recorded events but furthermore a narration of events having form—that is, a beginning, middle, end, and a coherent outline. Clearly, the newsreel form as a variety of documentary does not satisfy the category of the history form chiefly because the *actualités* it shows are out of narrative, or meaningfully factual, context. In short, we cannot make proper judgments of events in terms of cause and effect unless we see them in a sizable abstract perspective, that is, a narrative perspective combined with a logical perspective or one of ideas. In regard to public events the annals of history automatically supply such a perspective.

Here time itself must enter as an aesthetic element in our consideration of documentary technique. Obviously, the snapshot quality of regulation newsreel journalism tends to make actuality seem (in terms of formal significance) fragmentary, superficial, and even trivial. So the documentary ideal of film technique is this: the aim of presenting formal wholes above a minimum of factual significance, taking the alternate forms of *narrative* or, as in films of scientific subject matter, *logical exposition.* The latter, too, in the special shape of laboratory processes would be narratives of a sort, like the biological narrative of tracing the chicken from ovum to hatching and beyond.

Yet aside from all such formal considerations or aspects of photographic technique alone, one indispensable factor is to be admitted to the ideal of documentary, and this is the principle of sub-history to be termed, as previously mentioned, *actualité;* that is, prior reality as a rigid logical premise, that reality of which documentary is to be conceived as merely the photographic reflection. Thus, in our own *March of Time* glorification of the newsreel, certain scientific or informational subjects, such as classic American jazz and the pulp-paper industry, are conceived as formal wholes, *actualités,* and on a rough narrative basis are presented as they developed from their origins to their present status. Naturally, in the formal sense, more or less fabrication or fictitious duplication of reality is necessary in such film processes, depending on the specific character of their subject. But if intelligently conducted according to the historic or authenticated facts, the *March of Time actualité* is to be accepted as true, accurate, and essentially real. As a purely rhetorical category, this form of subhistory would be *scientific knowledge.* We realize, of course, that levels of depth and points of relevance qualify all scientific knowledge.

We must turn now to an ineluctable aesthetic axiom. When it is a question of formal representation, where deliberate choices must be made as to emphasis and logical omission as well as commission, not only can mechanical error creep in, but also psychological prejudice or so-called distortion of the facts may operate. The artistic or creative ideal of form is that, while literal facts in their apprehensible forms are ignored, the *actualité* is knowingly, purposefully sacrificed for the synthesis known as the higher truth of art, or to echo Keats's paradoxical formula, as the "beauty" of "truth." Thus, at its most "actual," art can claim no better than a *rearrangement of the facts.* Naturalistic techniques in the novel and in painting relate themselves to this rearrangement of the facts.

It is this very borderline between art and actuality that the documentary seems to straddle, for primarily documentary must aim at the economically logical arrangement of a given order of facts in line with the category of scientific knowledge just mentioned. At times, however, as we see from the most imaginative documentaries, the logical arrangement of facts becomes a rearrangement, producing what is almost a poetic rather than logical order—an order, one might say in literary terms, of high descriptive prose in factual narrative. It was such an eloquent descriptive prose of film in Flaherty's early work that attracted Grierson's admiration: a sense of dealing with a beautiful, not merely a true, subject matter. In terms of poetic presentation the montage (or severely technical) creation of such films as *Song of Ceylon, Easter Island,* and *Black Friendship* (to cite three of the very best) outstrips Flaherty and compares with Eisenstein's own documentary montage; of course, these later films have the advantage of the audio-visual presentation, including music and verbal commentary.

It is on considering such a film as the ill-fated *Que viva Mexico,* which Eisenstein made on the actual scene and which was issued only in commercially butchered versions, that we may arrive at one key to the documentary technique in recent film fiction. By the same means we can understand the trend that recently has sent companies to Mexico itself to film fiction stories having that locale. A perfectly natural bridge lies between documentary and creative film: the existence of specific places and their verifiability beyond the fiction convention. The factual time element of history or true event (consider *Potemkin* or others) is theoretically equivalent in documentary to the factual space element of true place or scene. The suitable combination of these elements would be the ideal toward which documentary should strive.

While the scene of *Potemkin,* Odessa, changed in time, so to speak, it remained the same in space. As a place, Russia, although it underwent a historical transformation, remained the same as physical background.[4] So background, or place, is a more permanent and reliable factor than history, or time, with its fluctuation and complex modes. We recall that whereas the classic *Moana* of Flaherty had no fictitious element of narrative, no story beyond the daily routines of its South Sea islanders, Flaherty's Eskimo classic, *Nanook,* literally had a triangle drama, a love story. Yet *Nanook* was in the same documentary category at Eisenstein's *Que viva Mexico,* which also contained a love story, because it placed so much emphasis on natural background, or true place, as well as on native customs. Ethnologically and scenically, despite its fictitious vein, *Que viva Mexico* maintained the category of scientific knowledge.

Art, in the creative or fictional sense, deals with time and place only indirectly or incidentally; its direct subject is life—a permanent and universal reality, a dimension theoretically immeasurable in any factual sense and visible only in symbolic form. Although the scene of a novel may be Paris or New York or Scotland, what we experience aesthetically when reading it is not the essence of these scenes as physical places in which various and numerous people live from day to day, which other people visit and leave, but only a segment of particular human behavior within these places and the moral significance of this behavior; such specific human significance exhausts the reality of the art form.

Now the ideal of film documentary may be taken as, in one respect, the antithetic complement of such artistic reality. In presenting man, in Grierson's phrase, "here and now," documentary—even at its most poetic—supplies a version of the implicit residue or natural background of art works; it supplies man as a permanent human society delimited formally by geology and nation, social custom and government. In the documentary or super-newsreel perspective, human society in all its diversity exists as an unbroken or global nature, partaking of all living visible forms from the amoeba to man; today, documentary has actually amassed a record of these very forms. Here the law of the photograph operates and—in what may be called the ideology of aesthetic—transcends film fiction by positing a theoretical *actualité* behind every effect of action, lighting, and makeup in creative film, no matter how melodramatic, formal, or artistic such effects may be.

Consequently, no matter how ingenious as to scenario, or artificial as to presentation in montage technique, a film such as *Song of Ceylon* or *Que viva Mexico* may be, the aesthetic emphasis remains documentary because such a film posits an actual, photographable, and unfabricated nature as the background against which men inevitably act and from which, in the ethnological sense, men just as inevitably draw some of the meaning of their acts. It is true that the civilized backgrounds of cities, an agglomeration of so many kinds of buildings, imply much less ethnic unity than the crude natural backgrounds of primitive societies, and so are less significant as clearcut, dominant presences; a failing in civilized life of which Mr. Grierson, incidentally, is very sensible, and to the remedy of which he has directed much documentary energy. But to isolate the principle: the eyewitness camera, no matter how fictitious the narrative it photographs, provides unavoidably (according to the documentary thesis) the telltale or statistical evidence of the real world, in which the spectator no less than the actor moves.

By the path of such a basic film principle, what I may term journalism has crept into the techniques of American and British film fiction. Despite what film virtues the documentary may encourage in general, and whatever it may accomplish conclusively on its own ground, its techniques, as absorbed into fiction forms, are obviously subject to various aesthetic hazards. As for Russia, it has slighted its propaganda documentary for straight propaganda fiction even in its historical films such as Eisenstein's own *Alexander*

Nevsky and *Ivan the Terrible* (Part 1). During the war *The Hitler Gang* was American propaganda fiction about the enemy.

If we glance at literature for a moment we can observe the growth of a documentary feeling not only in the naturalism of Zola and Flaubert, with its emphasis on environment and contemporary *actualité,* but even in Tolstoy's "War and Peace," where the historical facts of the Napoleonic war in Russia hover behind the fictitious narrative as a time-space entity virtually as independent as though it were actual historic record. Modern civilization itself came in for some documentation with such a novelist as Arnold Bennett, whose chief objective in "The Grand Babylon Hotel" was to depict the organism of the great hotel of our times, something echoed in film fiction by the Grand Hotel genre of movie (one of them called, oddly enough, *Hotel Universe,* while during the war there was a *Hotel Berlin).*[5] Larger attempts at special group portraiture of the human race have been made; outstanding, no doubt, is Jules Romains's "Men of Good Will," the epic of twentieth-century Paris and France, a great part of which is an urban portrait corresponding to Eisenstein's rural portrait of Mexico. As in the latter film and in Flaherty's *Nanook* and *Man of Aran,* the background of human and natural or architectural mass, as well as social institution, merges imperceptibly in Romains's novel with the account of imaginary characters. The documentary form as personal memoir entered prose fiction with Proust's "Remembrance of Things Past." In documentary we may note that the generic becomes a value in itself, the human genus being as palpable as any human individual, just as the city landscape of Paris becomes an important in Romains's long novel as the home of any individual character.

Wars, especially while in progress, provide ideal media for the quasi-documentary fiction writer, who thus takes advantage of something in the very air. Inevitably, the documentary received new impetus in the last war and approached a prose poetry of form in such a technicolor film as *The Memphis Belle,* about flying fortresses and their missions. But war is a tremendous group activity rather than a background, and must fade in time as soon as it is over. What remains? Literally, espionage remains as the inter-bellum activities of government agents in counteracting foreign spies, the native land being a background continuous both in time and space. How logical it was, then, for producer Louis de Rochemont, trained by the *March of Time* documentary, to conceive the pioneering spy films, *The House on 92nd Street* and *13 rue Madeleine*, both "based on files of the F. B. I." An American precedent for these films was *Confessions of a Nazi Spy* (1939), based on a supposedly factual book of that name. The documentary idea is hit squarely in the center by the street names and numbers, which take their cue from the highly documentary "10 Downing Street."[6]

Grierson would be shocked at what he might term a sheer distortion of documentary method in these American films. The stories themselves have the same melodramatic plots as hundreds of previous American films less conscientious about realistic backgrounds and details. During the last war Noel Coward conceived a fiction film, *In Which We Serve*, utilizing documentary in a manner which probably won Mr. Grierson's approval. It afforded a good example of the British film style previously mentioned: a realism of documentary character. The national cohesion of the British makes such a fiction style possible, although I think it incorrect that anything significant as art has been achieved with it. For example, the feeling of a documentary morality, amounting to an assertion of national character in terms of history, appears in a more recent Coward film, *This Happy Breed*, a latterday *Cavalcade* that is the story of a middle-class family from 1919 to 1939. An ingenious scenario and excellent acting make this modest social cycle into quasi-documentary; added to the London background, we have the moral backbone of the British people. However sentimental this movie in actual substance, the new *form* is there.

It remained for American film, however, to create a sense of invading the very heart of fiction by documentary devices. The most obvious was the choice of well-known or identifiable backgrounds, filmed on the original spot. *Boomerang* has a small Connecticut town where the actual murder case of the story actually took place, and *Kiss of Death* has New York City, where an ex-convict tries to go straight while mingling with crowds about such landmarks as the Chrysler Building. Among recent efforts dignifying the crime and detective story, the most significant perhaps is *Boomerang*, with its hark-back to a structural device exploited by Orson Welles in *Citizen Kane*.

Not only did Welles's objective in this sensational film about a millionaire youth who became a famous publisher and capitalist smack richly and specifically of *actualité*, but also he was clever enough (how deliberately, I cannot say) to adopt a pervasive attitude of journalism toward his story, even to encompassing that basic element of the camera's newsreel veracity. Rather than photograph the world in its true way, however, Welles imitated *actualité* with various technical devices. He erected his story on the premise that his famous man had a sort of Freudian secret, transpiring in his deathbed utterance of the word "rosebud"; the mystery of this little word so piques a newspaper reporter that he embarks on a private search to solve it. The narrative, thus, is told in a series of flashbacks, testimony by the people who have been intimate with the famous dead man. Several shots in emulation of newsreel cameramen "on the sneak" aesthetically bolster the effect of verisimilitude, as likewise do backstage opera shots facing the glare of the footlights. By tracing an inner secret, available from the dead only as data is available, the amateur detective-reporter becomes a kind of census taker, and signally fails, as though such a secret would not yield itself to the inquiring reporter line of research. But as a matter of fact, by a tour de force, the camera eyewitness is enabled technically to solve the search of the reporter. We learn the origin of the mysterious word when the camera eye, a more privileged documentary agent than any human being in the film, floats over the mountains of Kane's posthumous bric-a-brac to focus on a small sled just as it is being put into a furnace; painted on the sled is "Rosebud." Apparently the sled symbolizes Kane's parents, from whom he was separated by his mother's decision to give him a new life with his inheritance.

It was entirely through technical devices of photography that Welles reinforced the identifiable public myth implicit in his story. These later melodramas, on the contrary, rely almost wholly on official document, identifiable actual background, and realistic detail in acting and story. Yet the eyewitness personality of the camera was crucially exploited by a film called *The Lady in the Lake,* in which the camera eye is identical with the eyes of the detective involved. The camera itself is a pun for the detective's body, moving forward when he moves forward, and so on. We see the world through his eyes and glimpse his face or figure only when a mirror happens to come in line with the camera's vision (that is, when he sees himself) or when he extends an arm or leg in front of him. The obvious documentary value of this device is its very indirectness and fragmentation of visibility, because the vision of an individual is equated with the universal vision of the camera, thus limiting the latter's scope arbitrarily. Moreover, the story implicitly says: This is the visual evidence, which you are privileged to see with the detective; he saw no more than you see. What is a technical handicap for the sake of the spectator's fun becomes a scientific virtue; it is also an experiment in competitive detection or logical reconstruction.

Unfortunately the eyewitness camera behaves as independently of human agency in *Boomerang* as it does in *Citizen Kane*. In the latter the human agent fails in his factual search, and in the former the district attorney, while brilliant, honest, and energetic, fails to catch the true criminal, succeeding only in exonerating a man falsely accused and almost railroaded by some crooked politicians. Here, then, is one of the main aspects of the application of documentary technique to the fiction type known as detective story. It is a method paralleling the experimental method of science itself; a tentative, and not always successful, search for the relevant, conclusive facts. The most remarkable novelty about the newer documentary fiction is the extension of Welles's tour-de-force camera-eye detective to *Boomerang*'s semi-omniscient, roving eye of journalism.

In this way what may be termed an irresponsible narcissism of the documentary view emerges. That is, the presumably mechanical reproduction of the moving photograph has, implicitly, a kind of mystical power to reveal what nothing else can, even if that power is not always available or operative through human eyes. This hypothesis would account for the scientific vanity and pretentiousness of Robert Flaherty that his filmic invasion of the island seen in *Moana* solved an anthropological problem, whereas self-evidently his theory is only a rationalistic, layman's sort of fiction. One might say that Welles's impersonal eyewitness camera had the same vanity as Flaherty's abstract theory, as though its catching the word "Rosebud" on the burning sled per se solved some Freudian problem; all it really did, as a lucky roving reporter might have succeeded in doing, was to catch a piece of photographic evidence far more melodramatic than conclusive. Likewise with the literal detective-camera in *The Lady in the Lake,* which symbolically justifies the mythic claim of private detective agencies to be an "all-seeing eye."

Within the context of so much verifiable reality (that is, the Chrysler Building and Connecticut actually exist), it is strange to observe that the documentary eye of film thus assumes a certain inexplicable, selfish knowingness. The point is that we are implicitly reminded in various ways of the camera's presence as a documentative agent. Whereas this very knowingness would seem technically quite natural in straight fiction, no matter how implausible the story, it is structurally at variance with the documentary form as soberly, technically conceived. True science does not boast; it is modest, tentative, conscientious, even as the talented Connecticut district attorney. In *Boomerang* the penetrating omniscience of the camera eye lacks the pedantry of Welles's coyly clever camera. It does operate, however, to make the audience acquainted with a structural element of which those in the movie are ignorant. This is an interview which the to-be-murdered priest has with a guilt-ridden man who seeks his advice and to whom he recommends a mental institution. Because this harassed being believes the priest means having him "put away," it is apparently he who later shoots him. Although this conclusion is made possible by the camera's later identification, it will be observed this unofficial testimony is not absolute, conclusive. The man who has secretly interviewed the priest faithfully attends the trial of the accused man, who, with melodramatic anticlimax, is finally exonerated by the fearless district attorney. A newswriter who figures in the story observes the said individual nervously hanging around the courthouse and subconsciously notes, it would seem, his resemblance to the accused. But after the acquittal the guilty-looking lurker speeds out of town in an auto and dies in a smashup. When the newswriter sees his photograph in the paper reporting the incident, a vague idea seems to dawn in his mind . . . but here the movie ends.

It might be argued that the ostensibly guilty man is never apprehended in the film because the moviemakers wished to remain true to the record of the case in the files of the Connecticut courthouse—a record whose contents are made known to us by the voice of narratage accompanying the film off and on throughout. This voice of the news commentator is, of course, pure newsreel-documentary. The case was one in the early career of Homer Cummings, who later became United States attorney general. So here the documentary technique rises toward the previously mentioned ideal category of history. *Somebody,* a scriptwriter might argue, killed the priest, and it would merely be robbing the customers to keep his identity the total secret that real circumstance kept it. So a red-hot suspect is filtered skillfully into the facts of the fiction to give the man in the audience an "in" on the actual, hidden circumstances.

Another name for verisimilitude in art is probability. Owing, in *Boomerang,* to the positive yet mistaken testimony of five identifying witnesses, it was *probable* that the falsely accused man must have borne a close physical resemblance to the real murderer, and this resemblance was supplied by the film fiction in the manner given above. But in the strict documentary sense probability is disqualified; certainty is the cornerstone of the reflected image of life, and it was by creating the reasonable certainty of the accused man's innocence that the district attorney won his acquittal. The main dramatic invention here would seem an error of the documentary-fiction cult through overzealousness.

I have mentioned the documentary as equivalent to the generic, the archetype or prototype of human society; one such prototype is unquestionably the criminal, whose mythical first father was Cain. A way of emphasizing this incontestable reality is to photograph specific and actual prisons, literally identifiable buildings, not only the Chrysler Building, as in *Kiss of Death,* but also the Tombs and that cradle of crime, the New York Lower East Side. The real fugitive camouflages himself daily with such perennial realities. Consequently, links of greater or lesser specific character appear between action and scene in the latterday documentary thrillers.

Inseparable from crime is the investigation of the police department, a civic institution with its varied public edifices, both judicial and punitive. A famous prison official, Warden Lawes, lent his personal documentation to a movie once by appearing in it himself. At the same time (as we learn from *Boomerang*), police investigation is subject to a human limitation and error inconsistent with what might be termed its architectural surface. This could seem a documentary demerit. And all documentary realism—from the mere title, *Alcatraz,* and a few shots of Sing Sing from the outside, to the presence of Warden Lawes himself—might seem designed to lend credibility not only to obviously false sets and transparently hopped-up stories but also to the reality of the axiom that Justice is often blind.

The case, however, is more subtle than that. If the fiction of a melodrama, as lately, is worked into a hybrid recipe of fact and fiction, if the crimes treated are, literally or symbolically, already on the books, the verisimilitude tends to compass the fiction itself. For this simple reason: the murderer as individual is technically a fiction until legally convicted; even a suspect, as we see vividly in

Boomerang, is a legal-fiction criminal only, as anxious as a certain group is to consider him a real one. This theoretically imbeds fiction in the chosen theme of fact. Crime detection is therefore allied to the method of scientific knowledge already mentioned as a category of documentary. The whole process of apprehension and trial is an experiment conducted to make a present hypothesis secure in a past fact by connecting, beyond any reasonable doubt, the doer with the deed.

Could it not be maintained that the latest exhibits of detective-film fiction are manipulated to suggest lessons in crime detection and conviction? Assuredly the documentary feeling has also entered via the psychiatric clinic and we receive lessons, however dubious, in apprehending the guilty elements of dream. Significantly, *Spellbound* combined the murder story with the clinical drama, as did also *Shock.* In *Crossfire* one catastrophic result of a great social problem, race prejudice, yields to the scientific method of the police. Though the abstract "edifices" of both private morality and social justice are so insubstantial, the institutions devoted to upholding them are built on the supposedly solid ground of scientific method.

We may conclude that the police detective as an agency in real life has been identified, à la documentary, as the potential or would-be eyewitness, and that, as the pursuit of the criminal advances, we come nearer and nearer (how literally through the detective-camera pun in *The Lady in the Lake!*) to legal, or quasi-scientific, fact. We are permitted to reconstruct the crime in the well-known manner of real as well as storybook detectives, so that we see paralleled, in terms of method, the specific reconstruction of history entailed by a historical documentary such as *Potemkin,* except that, to begin with, we deal with an imponderable, an X-factor: the identity of the criminal that may or may not be revealed. If our thrillers have a journalistic sensationalism, it may be argued that newspapers, if not themselves scientific instruments, are on the documentary side of science; however approximately, however propagandistically, they deal with facts.

Crime detection in film, being a sort of scientific experiment, logically draws to its means not only photography (actual photographs, of course, play a scientific role within crime detection) but also the backgrounds of *actualité*. In the labyrinth of a city the criminal hides as effectually as the hunted animal in the labyrinth of the forest or the guilty impulse in the labyrinth of the private self. But in the abstract or universal picture of all things (and reality finally is "all things") the criminal cannot totally efface himself. Since he exists somewhere—often, presumably, in the "vicinity"— the material camouflage of the very walls of buildings implicitly documents his existence. If these walls are identified as actual, if they are on 92nd Street, the criminal's reality is that much more authenticated.

The infiltration of documentary into film fiction, whatever the artistic worth of its results, must be gauged as part of the over-powering forces of a technological era, in which film is still the important scientific discovery it once was hailed as. Scientific techniques, after all, have a secure and unchallenged place in modern social ethics. "The basic force behind documentary," to quote the historical statement of John Grierson, "was social not aesthetic." But there is another side to "the picture."

The hit film *Naked City* clearly shows that the documentary vogue in fiction has brought Grade B movies up to Grade A stature. This means only one thing: the crime melodrama without star actors. In *Naked City* it is Manhattan Island and its streets and landmarks that are starred. The social body is thus, through archi-tectural symbol, laid bare ("naked") as a neutral fact neither, so to speak, good nor bad, but something which, like the human organism itself, may catch a disease—the criminal—and this disease may elude its detectors. A good piece of intuition, in this light, was the incident near the end, the turning point, when the criminal in full flight bumps against a blind man and his seeing-eye dog; the mur-derer's sadism flares, he fires his revolver at the annoying dog, and his pursuers are led to him by the report. In the same way the sick body blindly reacts to the hidden disease in it, and then draws the vigilant "police of the blood" to help fight the disease.

I don't think this analogy is a coincidence. The fact is that the vastly complex structure of a great city, in one sense, is a supreme obstacle to the police detectives at the same time that it provides tiny clues as important as certain obscure physical symptoms are to the trained eye of a doctor. As I have observed, the ideal of sci-ence dominates the fiction documentary in film, and the latter's tech-nique is strictly analogous with the method of logical deduction (the abstract) as well as with the method of seeking out and following up clues (the concrete). Of course (and here the point presses against all the problems of true art), this film vogue is another modern means of avoiding the basic problems of the human spirit and of human society; in brief, it is a journalism of science as well as of fiction.

NOTES

1. It gained headway in Germany between the two wars.

2. The British Information Film Service offers this country a variety of documentaries on social problems, including juvenile delinquency.

3. Compiled and edited by Forsyth Hardy (New York, 1947).

4. The same is not true circa 1949.

5. The latest example of this genre specified an actual hotel, *Weekend at the Waldorf*.

6. Although not detective stories, two recent films naming streets in their titles, apparently to aid authenticity of plot, were *It Happened on Fifth Avenue* and *Miracle on 34th Street*.

The Fight for Life (1941),
directed by Pare Lorentz

Land (1941),
ted by Robert J. Flaherty

Fires Were Started (1943),
directed by Humphrey Jennings

The Silent Village (1943),
directed by Humphrey Jennings

Memphis Belle (1944),
directed by William Wyler

Fury in the Pacific (1945),
directed by U.S. Army, Navy and Marine Corps

Tunisian Victory (1944),
directed by Hugh Stewart and Frank Capra

The True Glory (1945),
directed by Carol Reed and Garson Kanin

Western Approaches (1944),
directed by Pat Jackson

Desert Victory (1943),
directed by David Macdonald

Valley Town (1940),
directed by Willard Van Dyke

A Place to Live (1941),
directed by Irving Lerner

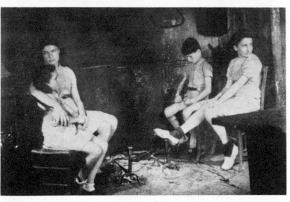

Farrebique (1946),
directed by Georges Rouquier

The World Is Rich (1948),
directed by Paul Rotha

Forgotten Village (1941),
ected by Herbert Kline and Alexander Hammid

The Quiet One (1949),
directed by Sidney Meyers

Louisiana Story (1948),
directed by Robert J. Flaherty

A Selection of Documentaries of the Period

El Agente agronomo, Julien Bryan (1945)

Attack! The Battle for New Britain, U.S. War Department (1944)

Autobiography of a Jeep, Joseph Krumgold (1943)

Baptism of Fire, German Army film (1940)

The Battle for the Ukraine, Alexander Dovzhenko (1942–3)

The Battle of Britain, Anthony Veiller (1943)

The Battle of China, Frank Capra (1944)

Battle of Midway, John Ford (1944)

The Battle of Russia, Anatole Litvak (1944)

The Battle of San Pietro, John Huston (1945)

Blood of the Beasts, Georges Franju (1949)

The Bridge, Willard Van Dyke and Ben Maddow (1944)

The Capital Story, Henwar Rodakiewicz (1945)

Children of the City, Paul Rotha (1944)

Children on Trial, Jack Lee (1946)

Churchill's Island, Stuart Legg (1941–2)

Creation According to Genesis, Paul Burnford (1949)

The Cummington Story, Helen Grayson (1945)

A Diary for Timothy, Humphrey Jennings (1945)

Desert Victory, David Macdonald (1943)

Divide and Conquer, Frank Capra and Anatole Litvak (1943)

A Divided World, Arne Sucksdorff (1948)

East by North, Henwar Rodakiewicz (1946–7)

Farrebique, ou Les Quatre Saisons, Georges Rouquier (1946)

Feeling All Right, George Stoney (1949)

The Feeling of Rejection, Robert Anderson (1947)

Fellow Americans, Garson Kanin (1942)

The Fight for Life, Pare Lorentz (1941)

The Fighting Lady, Edward Steichen (1944)

Fires Were Started, Humphrey Jennings (1943)

First Steps, Leo Seltzer (1947)

The Forgotten Village, Herbert Kline and Alexander Hammid (1941)

Fury in the Pacific, U.S. Army, Navy, and Marine Corps (1945)

The Gates of Italy, Stuart Legg (1943)

High Plain, Julien Bryan and Jules Bucher (1943)

Hymn of the Nations, Alexander Hammid (1945)

Ice Patrol, Henwar Rodakiewicz (1947)

The Illegals, Meyer Levin (1947)

Indonesia Calling, Joris Ivens (1946)

Journey into Medicine, Willard Van Dyke and Irving Jacoby (1947)

The Land, Robert J. Flaherty (1941)

Let There Be Light, John Huston (1945)

Letter from Camp, Raymond Spottiswoode (1940)

Library of Congress, Alexander Hammid (1944)

Lili Marlene, Humphrey Jennings (1944)

The Lion Has Wings, Alexander Korda (1940)

Listen to Britain, Humphrey Jennings (1942)

London Can Take It, Harry Watt and Humphrey Jennings (1940)

Louisiana Story, Robert J. Flaherty (1948)

Make Way for Youth, Robert Disraeli (1948)

Memphis Belle, William Wyler (1944)

Muscle Beach, Joseph Strick and Irving Lerner (1947)

My Father's House, Herbert Kline (1947)

Naissance du cinéma, Roger Leenhardt (1946)

Native Land, Leo Hurwitz and Paul Strand (1942)

The Nazis Strike, Frank Capra and Anatole Litvak (1943)

The Negro Soldier, Stuart Heisler (1944)

Nettezza urbana, Michelangelo Antonioni (1948)

One God, Nicholas Farkas (1949)

One Tenth of a Nation, Henwar Rodakiewicz and Joseph Krumgold (1940)

Osmosis: Mysterious Passage, Irving Jacoby (1946)

The Overlanders, Harry Watt (1946)

The Pale Horseman, Irving Jacoby (1946)

Paris 1900, Nicole Védrès (1948)

People in the City, Arne Sucksdorff (1947)

People to People, Henwar Rodakiewicz (1944)

The Photographer, Willard Van Dyke (1948)

The Pirogue Maker, Arnold Eagle (1949)

A Place to Live, Irving Lerner (1941)

Power and the Land, Joris Ivens (1940)

Prelude to War, Frank Capra (1943)

Private Smith of the U.S.A. Slavko Vorkapich (1947)

The Quiet One, Sidney Meyers (1949)

The Ramparts We Watch, Louis de Rochemont (1940)

Report from the Aleutians, John Huston (1943)

Return (Le Retour), Henri Cartier-Bresson and Richard Banks (1946)

The Roosevelt Story, Julian Roffman and Ben Kerner (1947)

A Salute to France, Jean Renoir and Garson Kanin (1944)

Le Sang des bêtes, see: *Blood of the Beasts*

The Secret Land, Orville Dull
(1948)

Seeds of Destiny, David Miller
(1946)

Siege, Julien Bryan (1940)

The Siege of Leningrad, Lenfilm
Newsreel Studios (1942)

The Silent Village, Humphrey
Jennings (1943)

Steeltown, Willard Van Dyke
(1943)

Storm Warning, Paul Burnford
(1941)

The Story of Lilli Marlene, see:
Lili Marlene

Strange Victory, Leo Hurwitz
(1948)

A Summer's Tale, Arne
Sucksdorff (1943)

Target for Tonight, Harry Watt
(1941)

They Also Serve, Ruby Grierson
(1940)

A Time for Bach, Paul Falkenberg
(1949)

To the Shores of Iwo Jima,
U.S. Navy, Marine Corps, and
Coast Guard (1945)

The Town, Josef von Sternberg
(1944)

The True Glory, Carol Reed and
Garson Kanin (1945)

The True Story of Lili Marlene,
see: *Lili Marlene*

Tuesday in November, John
Houseman (1945)

Tunisian Victory, Hugh Stewart and
Frank Capra (1944)

Valley Town, Willard Van Dyke
(1940)

Valley of the Tennessee, Alexander
Hammid (1944)

Victory in the West, German
Army film (1941)

War Comes to America, Anatole
Litvak (1945)

Western Approaches, Pat Jackson
(1944)

"Why We Fight" series, Frank
Capra (1942–3)

Window Cleaner, Jules Bucher
(1945)

With the Marines at Tarawa, U.S.
Marine Corps (1944)

The World at War, Samuel Spewack
(1943)

The World in Flames, William C.
Park (1940)

The World Is Rich, Paul Rotha
(1946–7)

World of Plenty, Paul Rotha (1943)

PART FOUR / 1950–1960

Jazz on a Summer's Day (1959), directed by Bert Stern

Waters of Time (1951), directed by Basil Wright

The Turn Toward Conservatism
by Lewis Jacobs

Documentary films are defined as those dealing with significant historical, social, scientific, or economic subjects, either photographed in actual occurrence or re-enacted, and where the emphasis is more on factual content than on entertainment.

Special Rules for Documentary Awards,
Academy of Motion Picture Arts and Sciences

The 1950s were prosperous but uncertain years for Americans. The economic climate was one of increasing gains, with employment rising to an all-time high. "Eisenhower prosperity" created a living standard far beyond anything America had ever known. But at the same time the nation faced the depressing effects of the Korean War, the Cold War, and McCarthyism. An atmosphere of conservatism set in and dissent became hazardous.

The American documentary of the fifties clearly reflected these conditions. Its outlook on life revealed itself in a neutralism that offered no challenge to the national temper.

In general the films contributed no startling innovations of technique or unique ideas, but in many cases a high degree of professionalism shone through. There were three broad groups of films: those serving the special interests of sponsors; those made for art's sake, and, finally, the films seeking to make—without stridency—some meaningful observation about the human condition.

The largest number of documentaries were those made by an affluent new breed of sponsors representing big business, big non-profit organizations, government information services, and television companies. These groups gave the medium a slick facade, a new purpose, new subject matter, and new audiences. They also provided it with extravagant budgets, "name" directors, writers, and narrators, and original music scores.

The latest advances in science, medicine, sociology, psychology, education, and personal relations were brought to public attention in a vast variety of factual films that attempted to vitalize textbook information. The best of these documentaries, with a sense of topicality, campaigned for improving man's knowledge of himself.

Steps of Age (1951) and *A Place to Live* (1955) defined the problems of the aged and their needs. *The Princeton Story* (1950) evoked the gifts of learning through the memories of alumni who met for a class reunion. *That All May Learn* (1951) stressed the evils of illiteracy. *Battle for Bread* (1950) documented what was being accomplished by the UN to improve the production of food. *The American Road* (1952), *Decision for Chemistry* (1953), and *The World That Nature Forgot* (1956) told of the achievements of American industry in upgrading living standards. *Angry Boy* (1951) showed how to cope with the fears and hostilities of children. *The Lonely Night* (1954) dramatized the benefits of analytical psychotherapy. *All My Babies* (1953) described the training and skills of a Negro midwife in rural Georgia. *The Bridge* (1950), one of a series of films made by the Community Education Film Division of Puerto Rico, reconstructed the communal activity of villagers who, faced with periodic floods from an overflowing river, built a bridge to allow their children to attend school on the other side with safety. *Project for Tomorrow* (1950) and *Adventure in Sardinia* (1951), two of forty-five Marshall Plan films, emphasized the individual's stake in his nation's economic recovery.

Among the credits of these films could be found such important documentary filmmakers as Alexander Hammid, Irving Jacoby, George Stoney, Ben Maddow, Sidney Meyers, Henwar Rodakiewicz, and Willard Van Dyke. Though they served the goals of audiovisual education, these men of talent avoided the pitfalls of educational didacticism and their films were as good as anyone could wish. They kept alive the consciousness of the medium in a period of cautious "disengagement."

Film as art, rather than education, inspired the second group of filmmakers. Young and new to the documentary genre, and working at another level of achievement and within narrower limits, they made films on low budgets and high hopes. *Jazz Dance* (1954) by Roger Tilton and *Jazz on a Summer's Day* (1959-60) by Bert Stern dramatized with style and distinction the atmosphere and personalities found in the better shrines of the jazz world. *Weegee's New York* (1950) by Weegee, *N.Y., N.Y.* (1957) by Francis Thompson, *Highway* (1958) by Hillary Harris, and *Bridges-Go-Round* (1957) and *Skyscraper* (1959) by Shirley Clarke were impressionistic, semi-abstract profiles of the metropolitan scene.

For the most part, the films in this group were conceived and executed by one person for the purpose of self-expression. The main thrust was not journalism or polemics, but "pure cinema." It was a commitment to a plastic order that often called upon distortion lenses, prisms, special mirrors, multiple images, and rhythmic cutting syncopated to jazz or rock-and-roll scores, for a minimum of meaning and a maximum of effects. Nearly all of the films contained sequences that were dazzling, witty, and engaging. Animated by a drive toward cinematic virtuosity and the belief that film was the true art form of the time, these filmmakers aimed at personal statements, not about their subjects, but about their medium.

What distinguished the third group of documentaries was a new type of city film—one that was not derivative, as city films had been since *Mannahatta* and *Rien que les heures*. There was no impulse toward the abstract, impressionistic, or experimental. Instead, these new city documentaries were straightforward accounts of a particular milieu examined with honesty and compassion, and often emphasizing the aloneness of the individuals.

Lionel Rogosin's *On the Bowery* (1957), for example, eavesdropped on the derelicts of New York's Skid Row by following an ex-lawyer who, unable to cope with the city's pressures, sought escape in alcohol. The story of this man was the basis of the film's narrative structure, which documented the isolation and despair of broken, stumbling men sleeping out the remaining days of their alienated lives in the anonymity of flophouses and cheap ginnmills.

The critical judgments in *On the Bowery* were implicit; the film didn't preach or clamor for change. But it stirred the conscience of the viewer with a grim relentlessness.

The same humanism and directness marked Rogosin's second film, *Come Back, Africa* (1959), made secretly in and around Johannesburg and smuggled out of the country under the guise of a musical. The film used a combination of improvisation and hidden-camera techniques to tell a kaleidoscopic story of a simple African from Zululand who had come to "South Africa's city of a million dreams." There, with growing bitterness, he learned what it was like to live under the restrictions and indignities of apartheid. The black man's search for a complete self in a white-oriented world was a story of frustration and tragedy.

The theme of alienation also governed *The Savage Eye* (1959), a documentary shot in Los Angeles by Sidney Meyers, Ben Maddow, and Joseph Strick. Its story moved on two levels: a subjective one—the "savage eye" of the protagonist, a recent divorcee who has drifted into an aimless existence in a world of drifters; and an objective one —a violent, intense, bitter, and often pathetic view of the raw underside of a modern city inhabited by sleazy promoters, strippers, addicts, transvestites, and faith-healers.

The relationship between character and milieu was expressed through an interaction that juxtaposed the personal and social symptons of dissociation. The girl's urgent need for self-integrity, mired in feelings of confusion, isolation, and inhibition, was significantly placed in a setting of spiritual poverty and brutality. The effort by the girl to rationalize and accept the false appearance of personal love failed. This led to attempted self-destruction—cause and consequence of a divided self succumbing helplessly to the forces that acted upon her.

The Savage Eye brought together all the isolated insights of city films made before and, in combining them with a deeper and more coherent social vision, became perhaps the best American example of a more profound kind of city film. At the Edinburgh Film Festival the film created such a sensation that, instead of being shown only once, it had to be repeated eight times.

In the fifties the documentary suddenly became a staple item on the television screen. But despite the great activity in television, documentaries of genuine worth were rare. The "Victory at Sea" series (1952-3), *The Murrow-McCarthy Debate* (1954), *Nightmare in Red* (1955), and *The Twisted Cross* (1956) were landmarks among the hundreds of forgettable telecasts.

Working in a confining social atmosphere, television documentaries were neutralized by sponsors and further diminished by television producers whose horizons had been shaped by radio programs and still photography. Complex issues requiring research were avoided in favor of material that could be manufactured in front of cameras: press conferences, sporting events, parades, and the like.

British documentary after World War II wasn't much better than the American product. The vital themes of social reform the British movement had pursued in the thirties and forties were replaced by glossy industry-sponsored films calculated to sell goods and services.

Norman Wilson, chairman of the Edinburgh Film Festival, expressed a growing concern of many filmmakers in the publication Documentary 51: "Documentary has fallen on evil days," he declared, "without a sense of urgency or belief. There is no more fire, no more guts . . ."

Elaborating on Wilson's views in the same magazine, John Grierson said: "The people who sponsor its ultimate shape and qualities do not care a damn for the purpose it once professed and the ends which gave it its larger life . . . They are stifling a great public asset and serving this country ill."

Grierson's anger was echoed in the pages of Sight and Sound (July-September 1952) by Basil Wright, who called for "an attack on the sponsorship bastion" and protested that "documentary could only be revitalized by an individual sense of adventure."

In the same issue, Stuart Legg offered another appraisal. "Much of what documentary was advocating in the thirties has now come to pass," he said, "not only by social sanction but by legislation. The pleas of a minority have gained majority acceptance. Documentary ought to be looking for a new point of departure . . . for the themes which it is urgent to bring forward now will become crucial tomorrow."

Despite the criticism of such distinguished veterans, it would be wrong to conclude that documentary's "vital impulse" had disappeared. There were sporadic signs of continuing vitality. Basil Wright's *Waters of Time* (1951) and Humphrey Jennings's *Family Portrait* (1951)—made in honor of the Festival of Britain—harmonized complex historical ideas with warm human feelings. More allusive than dramatic, their euphonious lyric style was modulated with subtle perceptions, only too rare in documentary. But because these were not documentaries that "attacked," some British observers labeled them effete.

More topical films, in the "committed" sense, were provided by a number of other documentaries whose focus fell more sharply upon the harsher realities of the modern world. Their vigor came from a compassionate involvement with the problems of human beings: disabled war veterans *(The Undefeated,* 1950, Paul Dickson), children without hearing who were learning how to speak *(Thursday's Children,* 1955, Lindsay Anderson), or worldwide victims of malnutrition, illiteracy, and disease *(World Without End,* 1954, Basil Wright and Paul Rotha).

Perhaps the most challenging expression of the new nonconformist documentary outlook the older generation had asked for was in some of the Free Cinema films produced by the British Film Institute's Experimental Committee, "created to sponsor experiments by young talent . . . and to support ideas unlikely to find sponsorship under ordinary commercial conditions." Of special interest were *O Dreamland* (1953) by Lindsay Anderson, *Momma Don't Allow* (1956) by Tony Richardson and Karel Reisz, *Nice Time* (1956) by Claude Goretta and Alain Tanner, *Every Day Except Christmas* (1957) by Lindsay Anderson, and *Together* (1956) by Lorenza Mazzetti and Denis Horne. Dealing honestly and affectionately with the familiar world of everyday British experience, the Free Cinema films suggested that a new level of personal response had been reached in the art and character of British documentary, enabling it to achieve images charged with feelings and means registered with greater sensibility.

French documentaries, unlike the British and American films, rarely fell into clearly defined groups; the sense of social commitment was diffused in the varied differences of individual filmmakers, rather than concentrated in cinematic schools. The only unity that could be found in the movement was of an intellectual and aesthetic order. As such it fitted in easily with the demands of a style with which many of the best French filmmakers seemed to be imbued.

During this period the imprint of a personal style had appeared in a small number of documentaries exquisitely refined and polished and informed with consummate skill and power to evoke the purpose for which they were made. First among them was Alain Resnais's *Night and Fog* (1955), a cool, grave semi-compilation film on the Nazi concentration camps, made in collaboration with Jean Cayrol, the novelist and poet, himself a former camp prisoner, and Hanns Eisler, the composer and former associate of Brecht, who had been driven from Germany by Hitler. The poetic intensity of *Night and Fog* sprang from a sophisticated humanism and a scrupulous concern for style. The film not only revealed the truth about the horrors of Auschwitz, but—because of its construction, moving in a purposeful counterpoint between the tragedy of the past and the forgetfulness of the present—energized a form that became a constant reminder that the past was always present, and a warning of what everyone was capable of in a society that did not respect the elementary rights of all its citizens.

Polish and refinement fortified the substance of Chris Marker's

Sunday in Peking (1955) and *Letter from Siberia* (1957) and Agnès Varda's *L'Opéra-Mouffe* (1958). These were documentaries of compelling style and richness, composed from the subjective and impressionistic explorations of the most ordinary material selected from everyday life, but given shape by an attitude and a respect for formal qualities that had been determined, in Marker's case, by his exceedingly sophisticated range and style as an essayist, and in Varda's by her accomplished background in still photography.

An equally marked preoccupation with style was reflected in another group of French films, though they were divergent in their conceptions of cinema and opposed in their views of the world. Georges Franju's *Hôtel des Invalides* (1952) was a lucid and bitter documentary that debunked institutions and traditions and represented an individualist revolt against the myths of patriotism and the glories of war. Nicole Védrès's *Life Begins Tomorrow* (1952) explored the present and the future of the atomic age in a highly original and witty fashion that offered an image of hope by some of France's most prominent thinkers. Jacques-Yves Cousteau's *The Silent World* (1956) revealed the strange surreal universe beneath the sea with a dazzling beauty that yielded exquisite fragments of a fantastic world seen before only in dreams.

Outside of France, the documentary of personal statement was less common. Belgium, Holland, Sweden, the two Germanys, Italy, and Russia, during the postwar years of the 1950s, had all become centers of documentary production. Yet, despite the vast production of factual films, few were notable. At the apex of a mountain of competent documentaries dispensing information, education, advertising, and propaganda were (from Sweden) Arne Sucksdorff's *Indian Village* (1951) and *The Great Adventure* (1953); from the Dutch émigré Joris Ivens, *Song of the Rivers* (1954), made with Vladimir Pozner, and, with Cavalcanti, *The Wind Rose* (1957); (from Holland) Herman van der Horst's *Houen Zo* (1953) and Bert Haanstra's *Glass* (1958).

What made these and the more impressive achievements from France, Britain, and America in these years stand out—despite a cautious orthodoxy—was a creativeness, intellectual conviction, and zest for individualism that could not be submerged. These personal qualities, combined with a reawakened critical attitude toward modern life, would in the next years add a further vitality to the documentary idiom.

Through the Psychiatric Looking Glass
by Cecile Starr

This review of three mental-health films appeared in
The Saturday Review of Literature (New York),
May 12, 1951. Miss Starr was the magazine's critic of
nontheatrical films. She is the author of "Ideas on Film."

Angry Boy

The importance of the child guidance clinic to young Tommy Randall and his family is presented in story form in this new Mental Health Film Board release. When Tommy was caught stealing money from his teacher's purse his mother could hardly believe it, for Tommy was always "a good boy." Referred by the school principal to the guidance clinic, Mrs. Randall and Tommy begin their regular interviews with the social worker and the psychiatrist. The film shows how the clinic staff works with them.

We also see into the Randall home, where Tommy is caught up in the confused hostilities and jealousies of his parents' world. "There is a lot of hate in Tommy," the psychiatrist admits to his staff, "and it won't disappear overnight." Scenes of Tommy's later sessions with Dr. Marshall show some of that hate coming to the surface. As the hatred is released and Tommy begins to see that Dr. Marshall is really his friend he begins to be less afraid of himself and of the people around him. When children are denied the affection they need they react with fear and anger, the film states.

This brief description does not do justice to *Angry Boy*. All three of the films reviewed here could be more easily described in pages instead of paragraphs, for they reach out in many directions and each has its important overtones. *Angry Boy* has several notable virtues (in addition to its editing by Aram Boyajian): its people are "real" people, the action and symbols in the film are neatly interwoven, and there is depth to every situation and sentiment. There are some weak scenes, too, for unfortunately the members of the professional staff at the clinic are not always as relaxed before the camera as they should be; but on the whole this is a worthy and significant film. The role of Mrs. Randall is especially skillfully written, directed, and acted. Tommy himself is probably one of the most appealing children ever seen on any screen.

Steps of Age

Problems of growing old are movingly set forth in this film which was produced and edited by two of the people responsible for *The Quiet One.* Most of the story takes place as Mrs. Potter, a sixty-two-year-old widow, climbs the long stairs up the hill to her daughter's house. Her spoken thoughts and flashback recollections as she goes up the symbolic stairs serve to summarize her plight.

"When do you begin to learn to grow old?" she asks at the beginning. "You wake up one day and realize that your husband is dead and you are living with your married daughter and now you are old and lonely and face to face with all the mistakes you ever made."

From the top of the hill a child drops a ball and Mrs. Potter stoops to pick it up. "When I was young I could run all day and never get tired," she says. She remembers when her husband died—though he had really stopped living the day he locked himself up in the crane and wouldn't come down, that day he was retired from his job at the factory. When he died in reality she went to live with Emma. ("Of course we need her," Emma had said to her husband after a spat with her mother one night, "but can't she help without eating us up alive?")

Awaking from her reverie of loneliness, futility, and guilt, Mrs. Potter reaches out to hand the ball to the little girl on the stairs. "Maybe you start with this," she tells herself, "that you're alive—that every twig and every stone and every second is so precious that nothing like it will ever happen again."

Hope for a happier future is indicated in a brief final sequence when Mrs. Potter arrives back at Emma's. The children are in the front yard, and from the window Emma calls out and says she needs some help with the roast she bought for dinner. With tears in her eyes Mrs. Potter starts into the house.

There will be a few tears shed in the audience, too, I suspect, for this is a remarkably touching story, the larger aspects of which are beautifully and sensitively presented. The role of Mrs. Potter is exceptionally well acted and the photography is at times inspired.

While it does not present as concrete a solution to mental health problems as *Angry Boy,* it is provocatively important in its own way.

Feelings of Depression

Like the earlier films of the Mental Mechanisms Series (*Feeling of Rejection, Feeling of Hostility,* and *Over-Dependency*), this is a concise case study of a disturbed personality. John Murray thinks that his deep depressions are the result of business reverses, but his wife and his business partner think that his feelings are excessive, that he is sick and should see a doctor. The film goes back to scenes of John's earlier life and explores his contented infancy, later jealousies of his baby brother, guilt about his mother's ill health, loneliness after her death, over-idealization of his father, and the inevitable letdown when his hopes and dreams fail him. Suppressing his feelings of loneliness and neglect, John added to his already overloaded emotional stresses by "becoming a father" to his younger brother after their father's death. As John dedicates himself more and more to his self-imposed responsibilities his periods of depression become more frequent, while his brother is finding the happiness he seeks. The film ends with a summary of the presentation of John's problems, and it adds that psychiatry could help him find a richer life in his own right, with his own work and his own wife.

Intended primarily for use by psychiatrists as a stimulus to discussion with groups of patients, *Feelings of Depression* is a penetrating hard-hitting film, though general audiences left to their own resources may fail to understand it fully. For that reason the producers—and this reviewer—recommend that it be shown only when a competent professional person is on hand to guide discussion and answer questions. This is not a poetic picture—its plainness is in fact one of its chief virtues—but it is singularly well organized and well planned. Its serious and systematic presentation, its well-paced action and effective commentary, and its unprettified charm place *Feelings of Depression* with the best of mental health films.

*   *   *

All three of the films reviewed above shed a warm light on some of the shadowy personal conflicts which can distort reality, impoverish the spirit, and destroy free communication and trust among people, even those nearest and dearest to each other. In producing them the sponsoring agencies are declaring not only that such problems do exist and can be alleviated but that they do not have to exist. In other words, children can have an excitingly wholesome relationship with their parents, old age need not be a synonym for uselessness, we can all gain from facing and accepting our individual and common hopes, our disappointments, fears, and desires.

It is only four years since the National Film Board of Canada first released *The Feeling of Rejection* in this country. Its producer-director, Robert Anderson, had worked previously on a number of Canadian Army films, among them one entitled *Psychological First Aid,* which dealt with problems of fear and anxiety among soldiers. Counterparts of this film were also produced by other governments, but Canada was the first to experiment with the psychiatric film for civilian use. Since 1947 over 600 prints of *The Feeling of Rejection* have been purchased in the United States alone, an enviable record among the small group of worthwhile postwar documentaries.

Not only was the subject of *Rejection* new to nontheatrical audiences, but the film treatment was also different. It was a document of one person's life rather than a way of life. There were nonprofessional actors, who didn't "act"; they acted like the people we all know, like the people we are. The story and situations and settings were equally familiar but they appeared with new meaning in the film. And there was an added quality of sincerity, sadness, and hope. In the foreground the reassuring voice of the narrator interpreted what was shown and said and pointed out relationships between one event and another. The film held our attention to the very last scene; then all we could do was wish for more.

And before long there was more. The National Film Board, again with Robert Anderson as producer-director, made two more films much in the same pattern—*Hostility* and *Over-Dependency.* So beautiful a film as *The Quiet One* turned a sensitive eye to a human predicament, and a poetic ear caught the throb of sorrow beyond sorrow. The film *Preface to a Life* attempted to simplify the ingredients of parent-child relationships, but the results were more complex and confusing than illuminating. *Palmour Street* took a low-budget stab at presenting family problems in a Southern Negro community, and it ended with a large question mark to a question which was never clearly asked. Films on problems of marriage, child care, adolescence, and the like were produced for special use in high school, college, church, and so on.

The Mental Health Film Board, formed in 1949 to collect money, skills, and knowledge for a continuing series of mental health films in this country, now has released its first two productions. Almost simultaneously the fourth in the Canadian series is also available. Five other Mental Health Film Board productions are in various stages of completion—on children's fears, primary education, adolescence, family life in Puerto Rico, and a sixty-minute general mental health film now being shot under the direction of Irving Jacoby and Willard Van Dyke.

Robert Anderson, back in Canada after a year in the U.S. with the Mental Health Film Board, has completed *Breakdown,* the story of a girl who gets sick, goes to a mental hospital, gets well there, and goes home again.

This is sufficient indication that we shall be well supplied with mental health films in future. But we need better films as well as more. We need those that are carefully planned and integrated, a real series of mental health films rather than a string of titles. Without such planning and integration there is the danger that, like the travelogue, the mental health film will become a cliché even before it has been well defined and understood. When the first travelogue films were made audiences were enchanted with the new and delightful things that came to life before their eyes. But before long these same audiences began to wince at the painfully inadequate formula—exotic costumes and dances, lists of exports and imports, beautiful mountains and lakes, the inevitable setting sun. Travel films potentially have much to show about people and places, but after seeing half a dozen of them we can't distinguish one from another. One may be about Ceylon and one Norway. But they are conceived in a vacuum; like Alice's Wonderland adventures, they are completely simple in what they say, devilishly confusing in what they fail to say or to imply.

Similar dangers are all too possible for the mental health film. The first step to ward off this threat would be for psychiatrists and filmmakers to do some preliminary paperwork and set down a few tenable principles on which a series of planned and related mental health films can be based. On such a foundation production can continue on a progressive rather than a haphazard basis, and the films can show life not only sliced into labeled segments, as scientists conveniently study it, but also as it is lived—fluid, fluctuating, and whole.

Mere excursions are not enough—whether they be to the exotic lands of Siam or Alaska or Haiti, whether they be to the troubled lives of Mrs. Potter or Tommy Randall or John Murray.

The Lonely Night: Dramatic Power
by Martin S. Dworkin

*This is the concluding section of an article, "Movie
Psychiatrics," first published in the Antioch Review, December
1954. Mr. Dworkin, is general editor of "Studies
in Culture and Communication" for Teachers College Press,
and advisory editor of "The Literature of Cinema" for
Arno Press/The New York Times.*

An engrossing example of the dramatic power of imaginative documentary is *The Lonely Night,* written, directed, and produced by Irving Jacoby of Affiliated Films for the Mental Health Film Board. This film excited such interest in its initial nontheatrical showings that it is being put into commercial distribution, and will be booked into "art" theaters around the country, as well as into regular nontheatrical channels.

The story it tells is fiction, but is not false. It is good to understand at once that documentaries require as much creative imagination as do formally dramatic films. There is no "reality" anywhere simply awaiting cinematic record, no representation of locale, behavior, and events that does not involve selection, organization, and technical manipulation. Documentary is a style, as is fictional drama. Both can be true or false—to their own respective conditions and criteria. The case of Caroline Cram, the disturbed young woman in *The Lonely Night,* is a typification, a sensitive recreation that distills the qualities of many instances; more than this, the case has been imbued with an essential dramatic personality: the generalization has been given particular life.

The film portrays the young woman's disturbance undogmatically, as a matter of mental health, rather than as an epic symbolizing ancient instinctual agencies. Her problem is revealed in notably realistic interviews with her analyst, and in flashbacks to the childhood experiences in which her personality took form. In contrast, we are also introduced to the Dunnes, who seem to be making a life with their three young children in which the ordinary frictions of daily living are dealt with wholesomely, in a climate of love and mutual respect. Their present life is unlike Caroline's past; their future will not be her travail now.

The film doesn't preach. The narrator Frank Silvera is no omniscient priest of some scientific certainty. If it had not been intro-

duced as dealing with modern psychiatry, one could regard most of
the film's lessons as articulate expressions of old wisdoms. No
miracles occur in the analyst's office. In fact, the sequences there
stress the slow, often agonizing process of self-discovery, the extraordinary patience of the conscientious psychotherapist. Nothing is
oversimplified, yet the film is wholly clear according to its point of
view—without the weight of masses of theory or findings. One reason
for this is that the film limits itself to a few basic principles of mental
health. Another is that it doesn't try to make propaganda for an
ecumenical scientific discipline, and can spend its time making
itself clear.

But *The Lonely Night* is noteworthy not only for a clear, sensitive script—or, by the way, its fine, unexaggerated music, composed
by Mel Powell and played by the New Music String Quartet, with
Benny Goodman. The film has moments of high drama; those in
which Marion Seldes appears as Caroline are especially moving.
Miss Seldes, daughter of mass-media expert Gilbert Seldes, gives
a performance of astonishing skill, projecting a characterization
that is truly profound and wholly credible—so much so, in fact,
that one is aware of an especially intense response on the part of
some of the audience. Women who watch the film seem particularly
moved, as if they have been unprepared for this synthesis of documentary realism and dramatic characterization. They cough, they
fidget, reaching interminably in their handbags for unneeded things.
If they were watching Joan Crawford, Bette Davis, or Barbara
Stanwyck in one of their familiar vehicles, they could traverse with
greater equanimity spiraling passions and hysterical ecstasies, arriv-
ing at the closing denouements of romantic detumescence with
dampened handkerchiefs, but elevated emotions.

The Lonely Night is intended to move people, but to move them
to *do* something. It is meant to teach, not to blow up gusts of ready-
made passion in studio windmachines, providing easy catharsis for
costive spirits. The neurotic behavior dramatized by Miss Seldes is
plainly unhealthy, not idealized to inflict vicarious tortures. The
psychological drama of the film relies neither on romantic alchemies
nor on psychological magic. The audience learns that there is hope
for Caroline—not in manipulating a jargon, nor in some happy
ending, comfortably inevitable, but in a painfully slow attrition of
irrational responses. It also learns something of a kind of world in
which children can be brought up to self-respect and reliance, to

mental health without need of therapy.

The entertainment film has tried to dramatize psychotherapy without alloying it. *The Snake Pit,* it will be recalled, followed Olivia De Havilland through a psychotic crisis, even into a mental hospital, exposing some of ineptitudes and inhumanities of institutional care. Miss De Havilland's travail, in fact, seemed even more severe than Miss Seldes's, involving a more violent withdrawal from reality, requiring shock treatments and other radical therapy. If the film commendably did not make Miss De Havilland's sickness seem trivial and her cure easy, it could not, nevertheless, avoid psycho-analytic pontification or some fairly sticky theatricalism—such as a scene in which the patients at a mental hospital joined in singing "Going Home," to the Dvorak music. The point of the scene was to play up the poignancy of the desire to go home, to be free, to join the world again. But cheap tears for the audience were bought at the cost of good taste and credibility. The singing patients might have been air cadets, or sea cadets, in some familiar movie potboiler about *esprit de corps,* the honor of the old academy, or some such like. Psychotherapy was given a theme song, put across in a production number—as if to show us that we were watching something made to entertain us, after all.

Of course, movies have to entertain. When they do not, the theaters are empty and discussions of their effects become academic. And psychiatry is no more sacrosanct a subject for the movies than is religion. As for the latter, the recent *Martin Luther* demonstrated that even theological debate can be made fascinating. The problem is not one of inherent complexity of subject matter, although the ponderous jargon of psychiatry can make it appear so. Here *The Lonely Night* offers ample proof that films can inform people about principles of mental hygiene without first inculcating a faith in a particular scientific ritual, with its own esoteric language, under-stood only by initiates.

There may be fundamental opposition between the ideas of entertainment and of education—when the former is defined in the practical, popular sense of passive amusement. If so, there are limits to what can deliberately be taught in the fictional entertainment film—although, of course, the attitudes the audience may develop from films are incalculable, and unpredictable. Popular entertain-ment, moreover, characteristically builds upon notions which have been accepted so widely and for so long, that they are assumed to be certainties—although many may be mutually contradictory. Popular entertainment does not teach, but reassures—which can be construed as bad teaching, to be sure. It is a commonplace admonition to aspiring creators of fiction for popular magazines, radio, films, and television that their stories had best illustrate some old maxim; if they choose to challenge old ideas in some way, they had better write for media reaching a smaller, more receptive audience. One difficulty, then, of the psychiatric film designed to entertain is that it must establish its assumptions, giving them the force of old ideas. A way of doing this is to couch them in a familiar form, such as the common melodrama with its accustomed opposition of good and evil, and its happy outcome. But the results are inevitably dubious, if for no other reason than that the theories and findings of science are not certainties, and may not be proposed as comforting axioms. The movie psychoanalyst usually sermonizes in the same kind of masquerade as does the "doctor" in the cigarette or toothpaste advertisement. He either simplifies to the point of falsehood, or juggles the colored balls of a jargon to mystify the onlookers.

The Lonely Night does not start out to "entertain" in the popular sense. It teaches, and the audience learns. There is a story that is absorbing, although it does not follow conventional fictional patterns. The film is simple, yet subtle, holding much to interest even those sophisticated enough to raise questions or qualifications. It is popular, yet not popularized; comprehensible without debasement. It engrosses, hence its demands upon the audience are met with interest and participation. This can be a definition of "entertainment," too.

Films in the 'Truth Campaign'
by Thomas M. Pryor

*This report on films as a weapon of psychological warfare is
reprinted from The New York Times of March 25, 1951.
Mr. Pryor is now editor of Daily Variety (Hollywood).*

Specially prepared documentary motion pictures and newsreels are
playing an increasingly important role in the world information
and education program through which the State Department hopes
to counteract in some measure the anti-United States propaganda
flowing out of Moscow.

The film program, designed to strengthen Washington's "Campaign of Truth" abroad, has been stepped up sharply during the
last six months and is expected to perform a vital service for
democracy by reaching the minds of millions of illiterate persons.
Educators have long since discovered the basic truth of the old
Chinese adage that a picture can be worth ten thousand words,
and now the State Department's information specialists recognize
that the "Voice of America" radio network cannot accomplish the
whole job by itself.

Plans for the production this year of 400 two-reel films, explaining the Government's foreign policy and showing how the
average American actually lives, are well underway, according to
Grant Leenhouts, associate chief of the International Motion Picture Division, Department of State, and head of its central production and distribution office, located at 165 West 46th Street.

Aside from these and other special-purpose pictures, tailored
to demonstrate the benefits offered through the Point Four Program
of technical assistance to underdeveloped countries, the film bureau
turns out a weekly newsreel called *News of the World* and a more
comprehensive pictorial news "magazine" which is released monthly.
The movie bureau also has a supplementary backlog of more than
1,000 films inherited from the defunct Office of War Information
and the Office of the Coordinator of Inter-American Affairs. All
of these subjects have been re-edited and brought up to date with
new commentaries.

The newsreel and the majority of the other pictures now in
circulation have soundtracks in as many as forty different languages

and dialects. At present these State Department movies reach an estimated audience of 10,000,000 monthly in practically every country in the world. On a few rare occasions certain subjects, described by Mr. Leenhouts as being of "a purely educational nature," have been shown upon request behind the Iron Curtain—in Hungary and Poland as well as in Russia.

The content of the films produced by the I.M.P.D. is determined by State Department policy experts who in turn are guided by reports from special film officers and other information personnel attached to all United States embassies and consulates. Frequently the same subject is filmed on different intellectual levels, Mr. Leenhouts explained, one version being aimed at informed people, such as government officials, educators, and other leaders of public opinion, while the other film is designed for the uneducated masses. In preparing the last type of film experts in anthropology, such as Dr. Margaret Mead, associate curator of Ethnology of the American Museum of Natural History, are consulted.

Every means available for showing pictures is used, such as commercial theaters, schools, churches, civic and fraternal organizations. Town halls, or other gathering places, also are rented.

In addition, a vast network of 16mm mobile projection units also are operated and maintained by the I.M.P.D. to reach people in remote areas where there are no theaters or suitable substitute facilities for exhibiting movies. There are more than 1,200 such mobile units scattered throughout the world at present and more will be added if the budget now being sought for this activity is granted by Congress.

Since 1947, when the State Department enlisted movies as a diplomatic aid, the budget for the International Motion Picture Division has marched slowly upward. In 1948 $332,257 was appropriated for this activity, and for 1952 the requested budget is $13,074,035. The figure represents an increase of $1,271,035 over the current fiscal year's appropriation.

Nobody knows how the cost of the State Department's film propaganda activity compares with that of Soviet Russia, but the Russians are using movies extensively, especially to spread their doctrine among the illiterate masses, whose imaginations respond more readily to pictures. Moscow's agents are particularly busy peddling movies in the Near East, the Far East, and in Southeast Asia. American film representatives, who use jeeps to cart their projection equipment and films, including screens, are extra aggressive in those areas.

Although the State Department is close-mouthed about details of its film operations, reports from field representatives have made abundantly clear that this is by no means a striped-pants or kid-glove contest that is being waged between the pressagents of democracy and communism. The men who carry our movies into isolated hamlets, where the people assemble in the village square and see the movies under the stars, must be prepared to face physical dangers.

Reports, even from areas with sizable populations, have told of instances where the opposing forces have arranged demonstrations involving physical violence as well as costly vandalism. Theater screens have been destroyed by knife-wielding demonstrators and theater operators have been threatened with personal harm.

Despite such inspired disturbances and other less openly strong-arm methods which are employed in the attempt to shut out America's information movies, the films are steadily reaching out to larger audiences and their overall reaction has shown marked enthusiasm. According to Mr. Leenhouts, it is not unusual for foreign government officials to make requests to United States representatives for further showings of films. Usually the State Department's film people can meet any demand, for the subject matter of the available pictures ranges from matters of purely local interest to world events.

An important function of the State Department's film program, says Mr. Leenhouts, is to create a closer feeling of kinship between the average foreigner and his American counterpart. In this regard the Government feels the need to correct generally the romanticized impression of life popularized by Hollywood's entertainment films. On the other hand, the State Department's film officers give whatever extra push they can to those Hollywood pictures which are regarded as being helpful in advancing the "Truth Campaign."

Although the International Motion Picture Division has its own camera crews in different parts of the world, they are not numerous enough to fill the demands for pictorial matter. The unit, therefore, has contracted for the services of regular newsreel photographers and, in addition, gets film from the motion picture divisions of the United Nations, the Army Signal Corps, the Air Force, the Navy, and the Marines.

Other sources of supply include libraries of stock film footage owned by newsreel companies, local companies which specialize in producing commercial and industrial films, and the studios of Hollywood. A large proportion of the State Department's films are a composite of stock footage and specially photographed material. The I.M.P.D. also obtains without cost, or for payment of $1, various types of pictures from large industrial concerns. All advertising is removed from such pictures, says Mr. Leenhouts, and they then are equipped with new narrations.

Actual production of pictures is farmed out on a contract basis to companies producing commercial and industrial films and to various Hollywood studios. The I.M.P.D. has engaged the services of nine laboratories in this city and two on the West Coast, on an annual contract basis, to process its films and turn out prints. Similar agreements have been made with five local sound-recording studios and with four title and optical-effects concerns. Currently the unit is shipping about 2,500 prints of films a month, averaging six to eight different subjects.

Although picturemaking is a comparatively slow process, the I.M.P.D. manages by going on a round-the-clock basis to get important declarations by President Truman or Secretary of State Acheson on film without undue delay, considering the normal red-tape that is involved in any Government operation. For instance, when Mr. Truman made his last major pronouncement on foreign policy, 1,000 prints of films in thirty languages were processed and ready for shipment throughout the world in less than ten days.

The Hot Documentary
by Marya Mannes

This selection appeared originally in The Reporter
magazine (New York), November 17, 1955.
Miss Mannes is the novelist and social critic.

For years in the entertainment business, "documentary" has been a dirty word. The observation of reality, a deterrent to the enjoyment of illusion, has been considered dull. "Documentary" is still a dirty word: Now it has been discovered that the observation of reality can be dangerous.

The network heads, the agency heads, the wise guys had almost killed off the documentary business in the last decade on the basis that people didn't want to learn. First the newsreels were virtually squeezed out of the motion-picture theaters, then the factual shorts; and it was not until Disney, in such films as *Beaver Valley* and *Seal Island,* showed reality as marvelous that the documentary—now called "feature"—became acceptable again. That is not only because these films concerned beautiful things beautifully put together; it is because the natural world is uncontroversial. It fascinates without worrying. But when Edward R. Murrow presented his visual essay on Joseph McCarthy, people began to feel the intense emotions which facts, used as the instrument of art, can stir. It set up a reaction in the industry of television that is gathering momentum daily.

The reaction is twofold and conflicting. One is the belief among people of intelligence and vision in the mass media that the observation and interpretation of the real world can be valuable as knowledge and powerful as entertainment. The other is the suspicion of the sponsor that the impulse to think is not necessarily compatible with the impulse to buy. Controversy may lead to enlightenment but not to sales; and tempting as it may be to call Big Business chicken-livered, its paramount function is to sell. It cannot sponsor for its health or ours. The tragedy is that this abstention of business from controversy leads in the end to a kind of censorship through omission that no intelligent society can afford.

If this seems farfetched, you have only to examine three recent events in the documentary field. Alcoa gave up its sponsorship of

Murrow's "See It Now" last spring and General Motors' Pontiac Division bowed out last month. Maybelline, Columbia Records, and CBS-Columbia sponsored his *Vice-Presidency* program of October 26, but the series as a whole has been reduced from a weekly program to several shows a year, as yet unsponsored. Pontiac has also pulled out of the sponsorship of Project 20, the big NBC series of documentaries made by the "Victory at Sea" team of Henry Salomon, Isaac Kleinerman, and Richard Hanser, with future sponsorship expected but undefined as of this writing.

Both Alcoa and Pontiac have consistently denied that the element of controversy has in any way prompted their decisions, but it seems hard to believe that a sponsor as powerful as General Motors would withdraw from programs of such acknowledged prestige if it did not believe that in the long run sales would suffer from public reaction to them. Add to this that the sponsorship and even the presentation itself of Eric Sevareid's proposed new Sunday period of commentary and film are very much in doubt, and a pattern emerges. Murrow and Sevareid are not only first-rate technicians in the current-events documentary field; they are fearless men who call the shots as they see them. Only Henry Salomon, the brilliant young producer of "Victory at Sea" and *Three, Two, One, Zero,* has managed, up to now, not to stir up controversy. There are not two ways for Americans to view our naval triumphs in World War II or the scope and gravity of atomic power.

Yet Mr. Salomon seems to be in trouble at last. After an announced presentation of *Nightmare in Red,* his documentary on the Russian Revolution, for November 13, the withdrawal of Pontiac as the sponsor for this and others of the series has postponed it until next year. "Although offering no explanation to NBC for asking out," Variety reported, "informed persons on Ad Row have no doubts in their mind that General Motors is adopting discretion as the better part of democratic valor and future trade. . . . General Motors is a world-trading outfit and has been in the forefront for over 30 years of efforts to reduce barriers to business among nations. In coming face to face with the possible political embarrassment of *Nightmare in Red,* General Motors was completely consistent."

If there is any truth in this (and there appears to be sense), then the irony is exquisite. Salomon's indictment of the Soviet system might endanger the sales of Pontiacs to the Soviet state. What is bad for General Motors is bad for us. Don't let's be too beastly to the Russians—if trade is at stake.

When a preview of *Nighmare in Red* was shown at the Overseas Press Club in New York, Salomon said in the prologue, "We are not preaching or propagandizing or judging. We are just showing things objectively, as they happened." One club member ventured to suggest that *Nightmare in Red* was hardly an objective title, while another (Victor Lasky) said, "For my part, the title isn't half strong enough." But there was no disagreement on the impact of the film itself. It was a shaking experience, masterfully evoked by three men who knew what to do with the material they had. This was no longer a documentary in the old sense. "We will not be reporting," wrote Salomon of Project 20, "nor will we unreel history by the yard. . . . (We) will attempt to give twentieth-century man the opportunity to stand apart from himself, for a long look at himself, ànd the world in which he lives. . . . If we do our work well, our drama will be so alive in its impact that its meaning and emotions will echo and re-echo in the viewer's mind long after the sight and sound of the programs have disappeared. . . ."

The Salomon team did find history by the yard, and it will be hard to forget such sights as these on the accelerated yet remarkably clear film of that time: Czar Nicholas II and his family roller-skating on the decks of the royal yacht; the Czar taking snapshots of his four children playing tag; the Czar being kissed on both cheeks by a long file of officers; the Czarina in heavy-flowered hat permitting her hand to be kissed by a line of curtsying little girls. There is glimpse after glimpse of this futile court, playing in the sun while the frightful darkness gathered. And then, Lenin: dictating with jerky intensity to his bug-eyed fanatic wife; haranguing a crowd, his face precise, irresistibly urgent. Kerensky, then Trotsky and Stalin—not the old pseudo-benevolent Stalin of his later deification but the pockmarked black-haired political thug. A younger Vishinsky, icy and alert, in remarkable newsreels of the purge trials, the old revolutionaries confessing their sins with dreadful submission. Then, worst of all, a sequence made of several executions by Red Army squads: the condemned stood up before a trench; the grotesque leap of limbs and flight of caps as the bullets hit them and they fall backward out of sight; the laughing inspection of their riddled bodies in the trench.

These and many other celluloid ghosts were found in a six-month search of seventy-six sources: the contacts of the International Federation of Film Archivists in London, the Paris flea market, a castle on the Rhine near Wiesbaden, the private collections of White Russians here and abroad, a barn in New Jersey, the dusty files of the defunct leftist French newspaper Journal-Eclair. Can after can of film, stored, hidden, forgotten, or jealously guarded, was ferreted out by Salomon and his cutter, Isaac Kleinerman, who knew what they wanted and were determined to find it.

Some things, of course, they could not get, so they borrowed scenes of the revolution from two Russian film epics directed by Eisenstein, *Potemkin* and *Ten Days That Shook the World,* splicing them so deftly with the "live" reels that only an expert could separate the two. But even such material as this would not have had its cumulative power without the structure and rhythm imposed on it by Salomon and Kleinerman; without the score of Robert Russell Bennett, who borrowed freely and rightly from Russian folk music and the Tschaikovsky idiom; without the text of Richard Hanser, who not only uses words poetically but knows when and where to borrow. Accompanying a sequence showing peasants in the final stage of liquidation by deliberate starvation are these words from "Richard II": "Let's talk of graves, of worms and epitaphs; make dust our paper and with rainy eyes write sorrow on the bosom of the earth. . . ."

Documentary? No, perhaps not. Dangerous? Yes, in the wrong hands. Another team could have made a different picture from the frames on the cutting-room floor, for what is omitted is as significant as what is shown, and the order of showing as important as the content. If there were any criticism of this particular film, encompassing the Russian agony from 1917 to 1945, it would be that it is not the whole truth. It is not the whole truth because there is no way of showing what went on in Russian minds and hearts during those convulsive years and what it is that has kept Communism alive and strong through horrors and injustices that should long since have shriveled these minds and hearts entirely.

Nightmare in Red shows with searing finality the evil of totalitarianism. But it does not show what makes a people accept totalitarianism: a want and a weakness within as responsible for their captive state as the force from without. Briefly the film's creators indicate the deep, continuing need of the Russian people for a "Little Father," be he Czar or Stalin. But do we not ourselves want that to some degree? *Nightmare in Red* may show what Communism does; it does not show what Communism is. To make clear the seduction that leads to destruction—this is the next job at hand.

But who will sponsor such pictures if business does not pick up the tab? Who will see to it that this growing and infinitely useful new form of art—the documentary in depth—becomes a part of the American diet, still so deficient in the vitamins of thought? The British have answered this, but in a manner unacceptable to our system. Their government-subsidized BBC has made the documentary a daily food, nourishing and sustaining. But government has never been our answer in such dilemmas; we turn inevitably to private sources.

One cannot help wondering whether the logical patrons of public stimulation and enlightenment are not the big foundations, those enormous accretions of wealth, which, if they are to remain tax-free, must be dedicated to the service of society. They could not serve it better, surely, than by guaranteeing the limitless productivity of such guardians of the public conscience, such extenders of the public vision, as the Murrows and Sevareids and Salomons.

The Documentary Heritage
by Burton Benjamin

This selection is from Television Quarterly, February 1962.
Mr. Benjamin is senior executive producer of CBS News.

This is to be the year of the documentary. Every advance indication points to an unprecedented level of factual programming by the networks and a concomitant upsurge on the local level. Whether the documentary will prove to be a great whale of an idea or merely a "minow" in a sea of mediocrity remains to be seen. One thing is reasonably certain: a mere numerical increase in such programs will not in itself provide salvation or solution for television's ills.

Not that the documentary is a come-lately to be thrust into the video limelight, feet-scraping and abashed. The documentary is a proud and established movement that did not need television to give it birth but did need television to give it support, circulation, and vital impetus. It is interesting to note that the documentary movement is said to have been born in 1922 when Robert Flaherty made his masterpiece, *Nanook*. This was exactly one year before V. K. Zworykin invented the iconoscope. The documentary was an art when television was still a laboratory phenomenon.

Yet, in its relatively short life span, television has done more for the documentary than the motion picture industry did in six decades. The documentary was the stepchild of the commercial cinema, particularly in this country, where it was patronized as a "selected short subject." With the notable exception of *The March of Time,* which flourished theatrically from its inception in 1935 until the end of World War II, the documentary in this country generally was economically beset and sustained chiefly by the ingenuity and dedication of its practitioners. Films were intensely personal creations. A man made a film—not a company, network, or "team." Audiences were small and frequently as loyal and dedicated as the filmmaker himself. It was a far cry from the television producer today who in answer to the inevitable question, "How many saw your show?" may count ten, twenty, even forty million viewers.

In those days the only solution was government subsidy, which made possible such films as Pare Lorentz's *The River* and *The Plow That Broke the Plains* in this country, and the notable films of John

Grierson in Britain. World War II provided another sort of subsidy and resulted in such memorable films as Frank Capra's series, "Why We Fight," John Huston's rarely seen but unforgettable *Let There Be Light,* and William Wyler's *Memphis Belle.*

At war's end, government subsidy tapered off to practically nothing. The theatrical market all but vanished. *The March of Time* and *This Is America,* which had been conceived by Frederic Ullman, Jr., became victims of that theatrical abomination, the double feature. Film costs rose sharply and union restrictions stood in the way of the personal filmmaking of the 20s and 30s. It required the public-spirited largesse of an oil company to enable our greatest documentarian, Robert Flaherty, to complete his last film, *Louisiana Story.* The documentary seemed to have reached dead end.

Then along came television with its bright new future, its voracity for product and, most important, its ability to reach a vast audience. Its owners and managers came from radio and had an appetite for better things. They were interested in news and its adjunct, the awkwardly named "public affairs." They were certainly a more responsive and amenable group than the theatrical distributors and exhibitors, who had kept the documentary confined to the art houses and film societies for so many years. It can be argued that without television the documentary would have been hard put to survive in the postwar years.

The current season is a case in point. It is difficult to calculate how many millions the three networks will pour into documentary programming. If figured on a "time-and-talent" basis, it is not inconceivable that it would pay for all of the documentaries of Flaherty, Grierson, Rotha, Wright, Legg, Lorentz, Van Dyke, Cavalcanti, Ruttmann, and Eisenstein. These gentlemen, all active in the 30s, would have found the present documentary scene unbelievable. They might not have found it entirely attractive, but the budgets would have been irresistible.

Despite its current affinity for the form, television did not invent the documentary, as some of its practitioners today maintain. It did recast it sharply and will continue to mold it in its own image. "The documentary of today will be unrecognizable in ten years," writes John Crosby, and all of the evidence seems to prove him right. The television documentary is constantly evolving; this is a mark of its vitality. Yet it was not born without an umbilical cord. It does have a heritage.

One of the landmarks of the television documentary as it evolved was the bold and brilliant Murrow-Friendly series "See It Now." It had its roots in *The March of Time* as pictorial journalism, making free use of natural sound and selecting provocative subjects. But "See It Now" really began where *The March of Time* left off. With a better method of transmission and a weekly, rather than a monthly, dead-line to meet, it moved its materials from scene to air with incredible speed. It made *The March of Time*'s vaunted journalistic pace seem oxlike. It wisely eschewed *The March of Time*'s contrived dramati-zations, stuck to the facts, and was tough and unrelenting in its reportage. It approached controversy with appetite. Where *The March of Time* had tackled Huey Long and Father Coughlin, "See It Now" took on Senator Joe McCarthy in his heyday. There had been nothing like it before, and there has been nothing like it since.

Other documentary film forms, familiar in the 30s and 40s, came to television to be developed and refined. "Victory at Sea," the history of the U. S. Navy in World War II, had its roots in such splendid wartime documentaries as Capra's "Why We Fight," as well as *Desert Victory, Fighting Lady, With the Marines at Tarawa, The Battle of San Pietro,* and *The True Glory.* Richly produced by the late Henry Salomon, it had a score by Richard Rodgers, a fine script by Salomon and Richard Hanser, and masterful editing by Isaac Kleinerman. Again, television had not created the form but had enormously enhanced it.

The same might be said for the use of still pictures, rather than motion-picture films, in television documentary, a technique utilized by Project 20 in such programs as *Meet Mr. Lincoln* and *The Coming of Christ.* As Louis Stoumen pointed out recently in The New York Times, the approach is hardly new, having been pioneered by men like Curt Oertel and himself in the cinema. It had been ex-ploited in superlative fashion by the Canadians, Walter Koenig and Colin Low, in *City of Gold* for the National Film Board of Canada. It has certainly been advanced by television, not only in execution but in the scope of its subject matter.

The historical documentary or compilation film is another case in point. It is most regularly represented on television by the series which I have been producing, "The Twentieth Century." It is also represented on an irregular basis by Project 20. It is a documentary form created, before television, in such films as de Rochemont's *The Cry of the World, The Ramparts We Watch,* and *The Golden Twen-*

ties; in *This is America,* the 1933 feature produced by Fred Ullman and Gilbert Seldes; in Nicole Védrès's remarkable *Paris 1900;* in the postwar German film *In Those Days;* and in British Pathé's "Scrapbooks."

Television, in my judgment, has contributed a great deal to the advancement of this form. If nothing else, it has produced for the ages an invaluable record of our times, not only in its broad, sweeping outlines but in its significant details of the men and the events that have shaped our times. It is living history in its most dramatic form. Some critics have on occasion criticized those compilations—ours and others—as "just a collection of newsreel clips," which only demonstrates a rather painful lack of understanding of just how these films have to be made. The historian preparing a book on Woodrow Wilson today must begin with the realization that he cannot interview his subject. He must go to the libraries of the world, collect all of his material, organize it, digest it, give interpretation and point of view to it, and then write it. The historical filmmaker has an almost identical problem. He cannot photograph his subject. He must collect all the materials on him—namely library film—organize it, digest it, give it interpretation and point of view, and then produce his program. If the compilation film is "just a collection of newsreel clips," then the history book is "just a collection of library clips," and no history makes any sense.

The thesis here is that television has materially advanced the documentary art but owes a debt to its past. It is because of this that I am impatient with those in television today who want to call what they are doing by another name. There are two schools of thought on this. There are those who maintain that the documentary was born with television—"we have discovered all of this, before us there was nothing"—and those who maintain there is an onus attached to the name documentary.

"Documentary," Grierson wrote, "is a clumsy description but let it stand." For years there have been those unwilling to do so. At one time Bosley Crowther suggested "think films." Jean Benoît-Lévy plumped for "films of life." The semantic argument persists. Not long ago, a quite prominent documentary producer was complaining to a New York television critic that the label had to be changed. It frightened viewers, inhibited sponsors, and made network executives see red ink. His recommendation: nonfiction programming. A newspaperman pointed out that this would also fit "What's My Line?"

Other producers have suggested "telementaries," "docudramas," "factdramas," and "actuality dramas with a hard spine." All of these are a bit Orwellian, but understandable in a medium where an hour show is an hour show and an hour-and-a-half show is a spectacular. With television's flare for euphemism, ballet could be changed to "grace dance" and serious music to "non-jazz." Let us all look forward to the day when the major concern will be the contents, not the label on the can.

One innovation television has brought to the documentary is the star—the reporter-narrator. In the 30s and 40s the star was either the subject of the film or the producer. The narrator was a disembodied anonymity. Westbrook van Voorhis represented the unknown voice of doom on *The March of Time*. Unless you recognized his voice you would not have known that Walter Huston was the narrator of *Let There Be Light*. Beginning with Mr. Murrow—through Messrs. Cronkite, Huntley, Brinkley, Smith, Sevareid, McGee, and others—television has changed all of that. The reporter-narrator-star is a fixture on the video scene—and screen.

What about tomorrow? Producers asked this question often deal with it technically. They talk of new lightweight portable cameras, vestpocket sound-recorders, the infinite capacities of video tape, and global communications via satellites. They are understandably fascinated by the instruments or tools that will contribute to the swifter, more lucid and more penetrating telling of the documentary story.

Perhaps this observer will be forgiven, if instead of looking forward, he glances backward. For there is a kind of film that we are not making today and which I think we ought to be making, for it is a part of our heritage. It is the "little" film about man himself.

It may be said that the issues of our times are too cataclysmic for us to deal with the life of an Eskimo in Canada. We are dealing with war and peace, life and death—with survival. We are dealing with emerging nations and the billions of Asia and Africa. The problems are so large, and the people seem so small.

But are the people ever small? Look at Flaherty's *Nanook, Moana,* or *Man of Aran* today and ask how many of the documentaries we are making will survive this test of time. Can it be that we are so absorbed with viewing the world from the outside in, we have no time to look at man from the inside out?

As Frances Flaherty wrote of these three films by her husband: "[They] are three films on the same theme, a theme as old as man and as new as the atom bomb: the spirit by which a people comes to terms with its environment. What he is saying in these three films is that the spirit by which these primitive, machineless peoples come to terms with Nature is the same spirit by which we in our turn shall come to terms with our machines—that the continuity of history throughout its changes is written in the human spirit, and that we lose sight of that continuity at our peril."

Is this too small a theme for our times? Hardly. It is a theme that gets to one of the basic issues of our times. It derives from our documentary heritage as so much of what we have done and are doing derives from it. What I am suggesting is that in the months ahead we explore man against his world, rather than the world against man.

Filming Skid Row
by Mark Sufrin

This report, reprinted from the Winter 1955-56 issue of Sight
and Sound (London), tells of the filming of On the Bowery,
produced and directed by Lionel Rogosin, written by Mr. Sufrin,
photographed by Richard Bagley, and edited by Carl Lerner.

The Bowery, the infamous street of derelicts in New York, is a syndrome of human blight, waste, and decay; misused and shabby men living in a stale tenement city-confusion. At the turn of the century, the Bowery was a high-life district; it has long outlived its reputation, with only faded memories of that kind of vitality remaining. For years the street has been a refuge for the marginal people —the homeless and friendless, the alcoholic, the dope addict, the mentally ill, the prostitute, the aged, the petty thief, the uneducable and unemployable, the occasional railroad worker and seaman—a sociological underground that moves in and out of city hospitals and prisons, welfare offices, grinding jobs, domestic courts, seedy employment agencies, and all the gray, antiseptic-smelling unprivate places. It is a sifting down to the bottom level—the sediment of a society that is inexorably carried down to this last place to exist. And beyond all the other poignancies and rationalizations is the salient impulse of drink and the fact of drunkenness—stale beer, cheap wine and whiskey, the harsh, blinding liquid squeezed from canned-heat, and the ingenious extraction of alcohol from any source.

In our experience and knowledge, this would be the first attempt to make a feature-length film about a skid row. How to make such a film? To deal with it as a few city blocks of physical and social decay, spanned by a dark and dirty elevated train, with stratifications of alienation, would be merely an experiment in urban sociology. It had to be individualized, and this was difficult not only in terms of dramatic action but of the kind of people to use. Looking at the men on the street, their grubby sameness, it seemed as though there were some correlation between body structure and misfortune. However, this snobbery was the beginning of our education. It was decided to make a film about a few men—alcoholics (a sociological and psychological abstraction, but in human terms a suffering personality) on the very level and the place in which they lived.

What we wanted to avoid was cheap melodrama 'set against "real" or "documentary" settings. What we intended was to extract a simple story from the Bowery itself. Not a "typical" or "symbolic" story, but an essence of truth of the place to expose (not dramatize) the hopelessness, the aimless dread and fear of such lives—without an arrogant sentimentality or too-generous morbidity on our part. For the other side of the Bowery is what men live in all places of the world: they fraternize, banter, work a little, and feel not too sorry for themselves.

For months we observed and talked with the men, drank in the bars, walked the streets, visited the missions and flophouses, before deciding what shape the film would take. The Bowery is not a bizarre sin-street of women, lewd gratification, or illegal dissipation; but a furtive night-street of men and sleazy bars, huddled and broken figures in doorways, shattered men who wish to paralyze in themselves with drink and senseless violence what human beings desire most to keep alive. We decided to make the film as we saw the street. It would be photographed as exactly as we could while the cycle of each numbing day followed another; action would be recreated only within the frame of the script and precisely as we knew it transpired. Our actors were taken from the street and would speak in their own argot, with guides of what to say only for story purposes. Direction on our part would try to define the action, but not gesture or inflection, to fit a man to a specific role. But, more than selecting "real" people to play "real" people, we evolved the roles as a synthesis of the Bowery. Then we proceeded to look for men who would not only *be* what they were supposed to be *acting*, but men capable enough to perform before a camera. In any other milieu this would not be too difficult a task; but here was the added problem of the psychologically unstable character of the population.

The actual *mise-en-scène* of the Bowery was perfect; but there was some hesitancy on our part. As we conceived the film, we were uncertain whether we were telling the truth about a place or merely presenting an outsider's version of what the Bowery is. As we selected the players we became certain of the approach and the insight gained. Standing on a corner where the younger men looked for a day's work on passing trucks, we spotted what looked like a perfect choice for one of the main characters—physically he was all that could be asked. When we approached and talked to him, we were amazed and delighted with the almost exact duplication of his own story to ours. If this seems a little juvenile or naïve, permit me to explain. It is one thing to "write" a role and then cast it—even with a nonprofessional. It is quite another to give a man a specific age, appearance, occupation, sectional origin, a set of circumstances, then to walk a street corner and say "that looks like him" and then discover that he is precisely what you said, right down to the sum of money (almost to the dollar) he earned and threw away drinking. With the other leading character it was the same story, although some of the features of his shrewd and alcoholic fantasist's personality were pieced out scene by scene so that he was never quite aware, until the end, that it was *himself* on film and not someone else he was purporting to play.

The "supporting" cast was a gift of the street itself. The Bowery is a spectrum of a thousand personalities, stories, and lives. There are gnarled, lumpy workers' faces; wilted, aged, seamy faces; haggard, pouchy, teary alcoholics' faces; and there are bright-eyed old seamen, hard ferret-faced drifters, and pimply young *Luftmensch*. And there is a comic tatter about the place. It is a babel of accents, dialects, and twangs; men from all over the world with stories and personal misfortune of every kind and experiences beyond the knowledge or desire of most people. They walk the street—men with ego-supporting fantasies and childlike temperaments; violent bruisers, and poor muttering dolts and psychotics—with the license of a culture unwilling or unable to care. Most of the population of thousands are harmless but themselves are harmed, holding on to an existence that means loneliness, terror, and death in some alley or flophouse at the end.

Very few, once they hit the Bowery, ever leave, are reclaimed, or rehabilitated. These are the people who "just don't give a goddam" any longer. Free of the whip of normal ambition, responsibility, or demands (though they live lives of ritualized retreat), their only imperative is the need for alcohol. The need to buy it and to sleep it off. Outside of the relatively small percentage of occasional or non-drinkers, it is all the same to the Bowery "wino"—night, early morning, rain, winter and summer, listening to the agonized jump of the jukebox or walking through the street which contains all the elements of normal city life—they respond to an intense inner compulsion. They are men too concerned with the fracture of their own personality (though they are only conscious of its demands).

Outside of the mechanical details, not too much pre-production planning could be done. Since we did not wish to commit ourselves beforehand, no bar or flophouse owner, none of the furtive side of the Bowery, was contacted. We did a certain amount of research at Yale University and with physicians connected with Bellevue Hospital, where clinics have been established for the study of alcoholism. The officials of the Bowery Mission promised their cooperation, and with this we were ready to start. The script was written, locations chosen, and arrangements for a crew made. For the bulk of the film, it would consist only of Lionel Rogosin, who produced and conceived the idea of a film on the Bowery, myself, Richard Bagley (who photographed *The Quiet One*) as cameraman (there was little specialization among us, the functions of story, script, and direction mutually shared with each taking a little more responsibility in one area), and Darwin Deen as assistant cameraman. Each of us also handled a second camera at times. The small size of the crew was a necessary element of making the film. We were going to do a good deal of the filming from a car or in a very rapid, mobile method when out on the street itself; we didn't want the commotion and sprawl of a regular production setup. It put a tremendous strain on us, each trying to perform many functions plus added hindrances that such a place presented. Just about the time we decided to start filming, the city went ahead with its plans to tear down the elevated structure that has shadowed the Bowery for so many years. In the end, it would mean death to skid row, but the disadvantage of working under these conditions would have compensations in this last (and probably only) record of an infamous place.

Ugly, blighted buildings that degenerated to ruin in fifty to a hundred years—without grace, without history, and, soon, without function. Only here and there a Victorian exuberance, Georgian stateliness, a dark and empty Gothic savings bank. Cracked sidewalks; cobbled streets with rusting, unused trolley tracks, pawnbrokers with their mean, mildewed harvest; restaurant-supply houses; the "horsemarkets" where the Bowery eats; furniture stores with gaudy, chromium novelties; and the lofts of cheap garment factories and ragpickers—these are the other parts of the mosaic that make up the Bowery. The men stand about in groups, talking, cursing, muttering in drunken triumph or agony; a flurry of fists, a traffic accident, a figure collapsing to the pavement, occasionally breaking the monotony (but even the violence, the bleeding and

cracked faces, the drunkenness, is so much a part of ritual and routine as to be monotony itself). Beyond all this was the phenomenon
that can frighten and shatter the person who walks with "somewhere
to go," who knows a home and a job, whose horizons extend beyond
a few city blocks—the hesitant, shuffling, reeling walk of the men
up-and-down the street, their hands clenched rigidly, or violently
declaiming counterpoint to their babbling. This, and the endless parade of bodies sitting, slumped, stretched prone in drunken release
—nothing to do, nowhere to go.

The cast, at least those figuring in the story element of the film,
had to be coddled, cajoled, and watched. Over the months it gave
us the personalities of nursemaids, social workers, psychologists, and
jail turnkeys. A few turned out to be belligerent drunks who disappeared from the "set" at the most inopportune intervals and could
be found only after a diligent search of the bars (from where, surprisingly, they allowed themselves to be led quite amiably). Another
was taken in a police raid, sent to a city prison where his full gray
beard was unceremoniously shaved and his clothes burned. At approximately the same time (despite dire warnings), the two leading
characters decided to get their hair cut, though the previous scenes
showed them as somewhat shaggy (the entire action of the film takes
place over three days). What more elemental blow to a filmmaker?
What more, we were soon to discover. This threw our already hazy
schedule completely off, and ensuing weeks had to be spent in the
proverbial "shooting around." After that, we shaved them, trimmed
their hair, and took their "costumes" from them after a day's work,
complicating our burden.

The bulk of the film was shot in the midst of the hottest summer
in the history of New York (than which there is nothing hotter,
more humid, and more unpleasant outside a tropical rain forest).
After a few weeks of long hours crouched like duck hunters under
the searing steel top of the automobile, our physical energies began
to deteriorate and the strain to tell in almost constant fatigue and
short tempers. We recognized what was happening, but because of
the nature of the film and the way it was necessary to shoot, dedication, enthusiasm, and nervous energy displaced the grievances.

A new problem presented itself: over-inquisitive police (or, shall
I say, police with a rather decorous sense of duty?) stopped us constantly to investigate the black sedan with four stealthy ill-dressed
young men with a mountain of suspicious-looking boxes and cam-

eras. They would listen to our variously concocted stories with a sardonic indifference that New York City police have cutivated to a fine art—and then we would have to move on. Or, again, we would have our camera on a scene and a policeman would come along to break up that particular group and we wound up with half-finished action (to be repeated another day and another day when we had new scenes and an entire backlog to do). After we had been surrounded late one evening on a lonely street off the Bowery by a covey of patrol cars who thought we were thieves, and stopped a few days later by detectives looking for dope or some contraband, we resorted to using official permits that would allow us comparative freedom. It had become a necessary gesture, though we sought as little publicity and truck with red-tape and officials as possible.

By this time our bearded actor, once again sporting a luxuriant growth, was picked up by police in another roundup. Frantic tracing via a neighborhood police precinct, a court, and a city prison, located him through a sympathetic warden, who promised not to shave him (by this time, his clothes were safely put away each night). At the end of his sentence, we met him at the ferry that brought prisoners from the island, brought him down to the Bowery, installed him in one of the "hotels" (he had formerly slept the year around on the sidewalk in front of a furniture store), and doled out only enough money daily to keep him out of trouble. At this stage, we supplied each of the cast with letters to the police requesting them to contact us in the event of the bearer of the letter being found drunk, etc.

Filming proceeded for as long as two days with no incidents. Then one morning we arrived to find demolition crews at work on the elevated structure. Our "set" was being torn away before our eyes, and long before we had finished with our exteriors! After a few days of exploratory surveying and inspection, the crew moved further uptown, but another plague took their place. To prepare for the further rehabilitation of Third Avenue (of which the Bowery is a very small section), the streets were being widened. This presented a knotty problem in shooting schedules. Where we had shot before, nothing would match the mounds of dirt and wood barricades, and we had to occupy ourselves in those sections that remained untouched while we waited for the pipes to be relaid, the trenches refilled, and the paving applied. After a time the demolition crews returned, and throughout the rest of production we dodged the shower of sparks from acetylene torches, became snarled in the murderous traffic jams that the demolition caused, and watched the somber and symbolic process of parts of the wormy old structure being swung away on giant cranes.

Photography was a problem that was always with us. The heavily latticed windows and sunlight under the elevated, the patches of sunlight in the middle of the sidewalk, the dark areas near the buildings and the inky alleyways, the ebb and flow of the men, made lens reading, focusing, and framing a nightmare for the kind of candid work we were doing. On the street at night, it was only in the tiny areas outside the bars, or under hotel and moviehouse signs that we could work at all. (Later, when we had exposed ourselves and our purpose, we brought in small portable lights.) This is what usually happened: the camera would be set up and focused on a particular scene; then we would be discovered by the subjects, the police, a bar owner or storekeeper who didn't want his place of business in the background, or the group would shift and disappear completely. Back the camera would swing into the interior of the car, facing innocently away from the window. Another waiting period ensued until we saw what we wanted, and the entire complication of focusing, framing, getting a meter reading (obtained by sauntering somewhere near the subject) would begin again.

The demands of the film brought us further and further into the open and we became an added part of the daily scene. Traffic and onlookers became a serious problem. We would decide on a shot, jump out of the car, set it up as quickly as possible, place the actors if that was necessary, and in a somewhat high-handed way fend people off from walking through the action. Then, if traffic lights, pedestrians, shopkeepers, dramatic action, and camera coincided, back we clambered into a car and drove off quickly to dispel curiosity and to discuss the next shot. We were reviled as Commies, Daily Worker bums, slobs who traded on the misery of poor unfortunates, slumming probers; to some we were men from the flagrant tabloids, the F.B.I., or television people. (This would seem to be an interesting index of what a certain socioeconomic level thinks of as the proper agencies to collect information or do visual research.) After we became known on the street, the threats, save for one of the demented or aggressively drunk men, stopped, and we began to get more attention and "cooperation" than we bargained for. In the main, we found most of the Bowery inhabitants to be amiable and likable (in the sense that the mass of derelicts seemed less threatening or feckless once an individualized response was sought for). But if they "sinned" less than we imagined, we met with thievery and moral dishonesty on a supposedly more respectable level. Twice, in dealings with a bar and a flophouse owner, we were either held up for money or refused further permission after we had shot thousands of feet of film in both places.

The bar scenes occupied the last week of filming. This was left for the last because it is the structure, the soul, the substance of the Bowery. Some of the filming was secret, involving a camera with an ingenious reflex-finder arrangement, hidden in a bundle (every filmmaker who reads this can appreciate the ludicrousness of carrying a 35mm Arriflex with a 400-foot magazine into a bar). We went into the bars, two at a time, unshaven, dressed in Bowery clothes, feigning drunkenness, forced to swallow glass after glass of the foul, flat beer they serve. Sitting in the midst of the agitated ferment of drunks, we became part of the smell, the gargoyle faces, the wine sores, the sleeping and retching, the whole spasmic disturbance; always imagining that the bartender who glanced over frequently knew that the man with his head down on the bundle was actually a photographer peering through a finder. The other bar scenes were part of a three-day nightmare that blends, in memory, into a psychological indiscretion. Even with the enlarged crew, it almost blew out of control. And that is the irony: the public will never see half of what we captured on film and sound-tape—too raw, too elemental, too brutal, too depressing. And, in some instances, because we know that an audience wouldn't believe it as actually happening, but as a concocted repetition of clichés.

If at times I thought I was being too melodramatic in the writing of this article, something happened to prove the essential truth of what a skid row is like and the inevitability of the alcoholic's death. One of the actors began to grow a tremendous paunch which matched preceding scenes not at all. He attributed it to "gas," while we naïvely attributed it to his tremendous consumption of beer (this was a financial expedient). But no beer drinker ever grew so fat, so fast. When we broached the subject, he would dismiss us with an airy wave and tell us that he would "cut down" and he'd be "oke." We decided to take him to a doctor who told us he was a dying man with cirrhosis of the liver. There were a few strained jokes about getting him on film fast; but actually it was the shock of this one man whom we had come to know, work with, and love a little that threw the truth of the Bowery and all skid rows up in block print. He admitted to the doctor that he had been treated before and warned to give up drinking —even beer. His daily consumption, he admitted, was some forty to fifty glasses. The doctor treated him with mercury shots; and for the rest of the production, some seven weeks, he abstained completely and followed doctor's instructions to the letter. After his last day on the film, we told him that he would be kept on until we could find him a job. He had moved from the Bowery and tried to assure us (with very little success) that he was going to "straighten out"—the eternal paean of the skid-row man. We doubted but we hoped; to see one man come out of that hell would have been worth everything. He seemed psychologically revived by the responsibility of his job and our companionship: it gave him something for the next day, for every day. But what secret impulses of self-destruction lie within the alcoholic, what the end of the film meant and the anomic state it brought him to, is too difficult and painful to imagine. He started drinking again one afternoon, and two days before the writing of this article he was found dead in a Bowery bar (not in the place we knew him to frequent—they had been told about his condition by the man himself to forestall temptation during production. Even on the Bowery a man can want to hide what he thinks is his shame and weakness).

Mr. Rogosin, Mr. Bagley, and I, the three who actually made the film, tried within our resources and the difficulties inherent in the project to make an honest, compassionate record of some human beings in a state of prolonged crisis. If we caught something of the loneliness, the ignorance, the waste and futility of such lives, and communicated it to others, that will suffice.

The morning after the last day's shooting, we three met for a late breakfast. Each of us, in his own way, that previous night had suffered some variety of remorse, of guilt (though we were happy enough to finish the photography). It was rather a strange reaction, even making allowances for the normal letdown. I can explain only my own feeling. At first it was a sense of guilt at having used these men for my own purpose. And as that rationalization wore away, the truth emerged. There was an involvement with humanity here, a profoundly moving experience—and now I had escaped that frightening place. *They* still remain.

316

Cousteau's *The Silent World*
by Bosley Crowther

*This review was written for the September 25, 1956,
issue of The New York Times, for which the author
was then the first-string film critic.*

People who dote on real adventure in the ever-wondrous area of the
sea are in for an hour and twenty-six minutes of pictorial (and
piscatorial) marvels and thrills when they see the new film at the
Paris, Capt. Jacques-Yves Cousteau's *The Silent World*. For this
account of oceanographic exploration on and below the surface of
the sea is surely the most beautiful and fascinating documentary of
its sort ever filmed.

With a sense of the awesome and the dramatic as well as with
technical skill in surface and underwater exploration and color photography, Captain Cousteau and his team of skindivers have produced a marine adventure film that combines the experience of
looking at marvels with a wonderful intimacy.

They have put the personnel of their research ship, the Calypso,
as it ranges the Mediterranean and Red Seas, the Persian Gulf and
the Indian Ocean, in contact with the creatures of the deep in such
a way as to make the contrasts much more striking and wonderful
than would be the mere fascinations if they were simply viewed
objectively.

That is to say, the hardy divers and the operations of the compact little shop, a floating marine laboratory, are established clearly
at the start of the film before the cameras are taken under water to
view the wonders and the beauties that are there. The personal perils
as well as pleasures of free diving with the remarkable mechanism of
the aqualung are brought to the attention of the audience before any
extensive exploration is done. And the span of pictorial observation often is returned to the surface and to the ship, with the men
maintained carefully in the foreground, as the picture flows along.

Thus we go from a brief introduction of divers moving with
phosphorus torches through blue-gray depths to the businesslike
deck of the Calypso where these magical creatures, emerging, are
merely men in scanty swimtrunks and grotesque apparatus that is
dropped as they breathe open air. And then we go back in to the
water to look at fishes and lobsters and coral clumps and to feel a

case of the "bends" with one of these divers, after we have been made acquainted with him.

This intimacy with the explorers, intelligently and humorously set up, is largely responsible for the vivid sense of participation one gets from this film. From the awesome experience of gazing into the purple coils of a sea anemone to the drama of thundering along the surface in a school of mammoth sperm whales, one is there as a breathless companion of the modern mariners in this tidy ship. At the end, you and Captain Cousteau, his crew, and their dachshund are friends.

You have been with the limber skindivers into the dark and haunted holds of a sunken ship and been dragged along with them by scooters, powered with batteries, that bore through the deeps. You have got a close view of racing porpoises from a portholed chamber in the prow of the ship and sat in a steel cage under water and watched sharks attack the body of a dead whale.

All of this and much more, Captain Cousteau and his leading associate, Louis Malle, have filmed with an integrity of events and in colors that are irreproachable. Like true scientists, they've eschewed trickery. When the excellent music of Yves Baudrier is used, it is applied to scenes, however amazing, of authentic occurrence and continuity.

It should be noted that his picture is not a version of Captain Cousteau's book, *The Silent World*, but is a compilation of photographic material obtained on the Calypso-National Geographic expedition in 1954–55. James Dugan prepared the narration, which is spoken in English, mostly by Captain Cousteau.

The only trouble with the whole thing is it makes you want to strap on an aqualung and go!

Four French Documentaries
by Noel Burch

This selection is reprinted from Film Quarterly (Berkeley, California), Fall 1959. Mr. Burch is the author of the book "Praxis of Cinema."

The "serious" French director is unlike his Anglo-Saxon counterpart in that documentary filmmaking as such holds no special prestige for him. Many French directors of the postwar generation have, at some stage in their career, done documentary work (Louis Malle, Pierre Kast, Alain Resnais, Georges Franju) but with very few exceptions they all look upon this field merely as a *bonne école,* a good way to learn their trade; they have always been most interested in *transcending* the subjects they are given to treat (in almost every case their films were done to order for the government or private industry). By this I do not simply mean that they make a very free use of film technique to "get at the heart" of their subject, as does Lindsay Anderson, for example; no, their subject matter interests them *only* in so far as it enables them to develop some highly personal fantasy, generally far removed from what anyone else would consider the "heart" of the subject at hand.

A brilliant exception to this rule is Jean Rouch, who made *Les Maîtres-Fous* and *Treichville (Moi, un Noir),* and who is a true documentarist in the Anglo-Saxon sense; a rather sad confirmation of it is Agnès Varda, whose recent commissioned documentaries are so inferior to *L'Opéra-Mouffe* and *La Pointe courte* (both financed by herself) precisely because her strained efforts to transcend imposed subjects led her into the most embarrassingly mannered preciosity. The most remarkable confirmation of the rule is, of course, Georges Franju, the uncontested master of postwar French documentary. In his case, "transcendence" is a mild word indeed, for did he not turn a film of slaughterhouses into one of the most beautifully antirealistic films ever made (*Le Sang des bêtes*) and a short commissioned by the Defense Ministry into a fiercely pacifistic masterpiece (*Hôtel des Invalides*)? That Franju was never really interested in the Griersonian conception of documentary becomes apparent when one sees all of his thirteen shorts: four of his first five commercial shorts were masterpieces or near-masterpieces, but by the time he had made his seventh he had completely lost interest in the two-reel format and was only biding his time, waiting for his chance to make features; that chance has finally been given him, but it may have come too late.

These are three extreme cases; but the most recent documentary work of Alain Resnais and Chris Marker (who had previously collaborated to make *Les Statues meurent aussi*, still banned by the French censor because of its anticolonialist sequences) provides equally interesting examples of both the healthy and the less healthy results which can come of this typically French attitude toward documentary.

Chris Marker is a personable young man with excellent taste and a fine cultural background (he edits a series of books for that enterprising postwar publishing house, Les Editions du Seuil): in short the ideal young French intellectual. His first film (or at least the first to attract any general attention) was called *Dimanche à Pékin*, and was a prettily impressionistic color-study of "Peking the picturesque."

Now, aside from the rather irritating implications of this de-politicized attitude (Marker is at least a fellow-traveler, and only just a shade more critical than is to be expected), the most distinctive, and no less irritating, feature of this visually handsome little film was its commentary. Written by the director himself, it rambled on from the first frame to the past piling up *mots d'auteur, astuces, calembours,* and every kind of word-play the French language allows, with the most astonishing facility—and self-consciousness.

My first impression on seeing *Lettre de Sibérie* was that Marker must have found Siberia a pretty dull place, or else that his movements were so restricted that he wasn't allowed to film anything of interest; why else had he had to go to such incredible lengths to "jazz up" his film? Because jazz it up he did. The mainstay of this operation was, of course, the inevitable commentary, ten times wittier here than in *Dimanche à Pékin*, ten times faster and denser, too: you've really got to be on your toes, this time. All in all, it *is* a pretty brilliant job of verbal juggling, though a passing attempt to "transcend" his subject by suggesting that *his* trip has something to do with one of Henri Michaux's fabulous journeys (the opening line of commentary is "Je vous écris d'un pays lointain") is rather distastefully inappropriate in view of the willfully superficial, slightly smug, and above all thoroughly unpoetical tone adopted.

I'm afraid, however, that were it not for a few *morceaux de bravoure* which were *not* shot in Siberia, and which I shall come to in a moment, a blind man could have as much fun sitting through a screening of this film as we who have the gift of sight; in fact, he would probably have a better time than I did, for he, at least, would not have his attention continually distracted from Marker's witticisms by the incredibly dead, ugly, grainy images which were, inexplicably enough, all that he and his cameraman were able to bring back from their stay in that "land of contrasts" (to cite the central cliché around which Marker so skillfully wove his commentary). Painfully aware, as I expect he must have been, of the visual poverty of his footage, Marker decided to interlard the purely "documentary" sequences of his film with two or three items shot in a Paris studio and on the animation table. The first of these is a set of animated variations on the theme of mammoth elephants, treated in a rather noisy, UPA-like style which is not unamusing. With the second—a parody of publicity shorts, suggested by the manifold uses to which the Siberian puts his reindeer ("Employez RENNE pour votre lessive!")—the joke begins to wear a bit thin, and as for the third . . . There is, however, one other stunt sequence which I feel is worth describing, not only because it is one of the most amusing episodes in the film, but because it will help to convey the more than ambiguous political implications behind Marker's apparently irresponsible wit.

Not far from the end of the film we are shown a short sequence filmed in a Siberian city under construction: a red bus full of workers drives over an as yet unpaved street, and passes a car driven by some administrative personnel, while nearby a crew of laborers are leveling the street-bed by dragging a heavy timber over the earth. These shots are then run through three more times, each time with a different commentary. First comes the "progressive" commentary (this *modern* bus is red, the *color of the socialist revolution; as we can see, both workers and administrative personnel are motorized; these happy workers are hard at work building their own city, etc.); next comes the "reactionary" commentary (this crowded bus is red, *the color of blood;* automobiles like this one are scarce, uncomfortable, and terribly expensive; the workers leveling the road are being forced to use the most primitive of tools to do so, etc.); and finally we have what Marker calls the "objective" commentary (the bus is just red and is less crowded than the Paris *Métro* at rush-hour; this passing Mongolian worker—described in the reactionary commentary as "sinister"—is merely cross-eyed, etc.) It was actually very funny to see and hear, but in point of actual fact the workers leveling that road may or may not have been supplied by the neighboring "reform through labor" camp, and if they were not, why then this city may or may not be springing up on the site which the former inmates of a recently disbanded camp have "freely chosen" for their new home.

In the end, though, one does have to admit that, by dint of a tremendous amount of brainracking, Marker did manage to turn really deadly material into a fairly entertaining film. Let us therefore hope that the *succès d'estime* this film has earned in Paris (among bourgeois critics) will enable him to have another crack at it, and this time he will employ his wit and resourcefulness behind his camera as well as over his typewriter.

Alain Resnais resembles Chris Marker in many respects. He, too, is witty and cultivated (though a bit less complacent), he, too, is an authentic French intellectual (a rarer quality among French filmmakers than may generally be supposed abroad). But, unlike Marker, he has a deep feeling for specifically cinematic values. Even in such youthful essays as *Van Gogh* and *Guernica* or in the purely pedagogical *From Renoir to Picasso,* his sure sense of rhythm and tone were clearly apparent. His two most recent documentaries (and perhaps his last, since he has just finished his first feature, *Hiroshima, mon amour,* and it is rare that feature directors ever revert to shorts) are two of the most remarkable examples I know of "abstracted" filmmaking, in the same sense that Cézanne in his later years can be said to have "abstracted" landscapes and still-lifes.

The first of these was *Toute la mémoire du monde,* a black-and-white *étude* (with all the musical and pictorial allusions this word implies) on the French National Library.

In my opinion the basic *formal* conception of this work is highly original, and even revolutionary: from beginning to end the film is one long "dolly-shot." On a purely technical level, of course, this description is but a figure of speech; the technique of *Toute la mémoire du monde* has nothing whatever to do with the rather primitive "ten-minute takes" found in Hitchcock's film *Rope.* But, whereas the over-all impression created by Hitchcock's camera as it doggedly followed his characters around the set was an absolutely static one (as a matter of fact, this was the most interesting feature of that film), Resnais produces an effect of absolute dynamism by juxtaposing dozens of highly stylized dolly-shots designed to "describe" the various halls, reading rooms, and stacks of the edifice on the Rue Richelieu.

At the very beginning of the film, a mysterious shot done in a dark cellar of the library sets the prevailing visual and emotional tone; panning upward from a dusty, haphazard pile of old books (which has served as background for the credits), the camera discovers a strange black metallic apparatus with three gaping eyes (it is actually another camera from which the magazines, which might enable the lay spectator to identify it, have been removed), a microphone is lowered into the frame and the narrator's filtered voice begins the weird, evocative commentary.

After the initial shot described above, the camera sets out through the complex "security system"—dozens of heavy gates and grills, sluggish open-work elevators, and an army of vizored attendants, constantly checking permits and turning keys in locks. The formal organization of this sequence is of a controlled complexity practically unparalleled in filmmaking: the various permutations and combinations devised by Resnais in juxtaposing similar and/or contrasting trucking-speeds and trucking-directions, the play of light and shadow and the spatio-dynamic ambiguities within each separate shot, engender patterns of rhythm and tone which are not unlike the free, highly intellectualized structures found in the work of certain contemporary composers. Resnais, who has long been considered one of France's best cutters, does not generally draw up his cutting scheme in the cuttingroom, as do most American directors, nor during the elaboration of the script as most English and many French directors do: he fashions his cutting plan *while he is shooting,* and has a rare capacity for conceiving each shot as a plastic function of the shots which are to precede and follow it in the final workprint. As for the spatio-dynamic ambiguity referred to above, one of the best examples is afforded by a shot in which the camera tracks along a catwalk around the outside of a dome over the main reading room. (By implication the camera's "eye" is that of a guard pacing the prison wall.) Although the audience is conscious of the fact that "they" are advancing along the catwalk, the smooth curves of the dome and handrail, together with the perfectly white sky in the background, create a double impression of absolute stillness and undefinable motion.

Finally, having got past all the barriers separating the "prisoners" from the outside world, we reach the "cellblocks": the stacks, with their long dark aisles filled by the echoing footsteps of invisible guards. Here I should like to say a word about the photography of Ghislain Cloquet (who did the splendid color photography in *Nuit et brouillard*). His accomplishment in lighting the cramped quarters this film was shot in as though he were working on the best-equipped set in Hollywood, the way he managed to dehumanize the library attendants (whom we see constantly throughout the film without ever really seeing them at all) and humanize their prisoners, the books, rank him, I feel, as one of the finest cinematographers in the world.

A word, too, about the score of this film: it is signed by Maurice Jarre, whose remarkable music for Franju's *Hôtel des Invalides* may be familiar to some readers. His music for *Toute la mémoire du monde,* though perhaps a bit over-eerie in spots, evinces the high degree of proficiency he has attained turning out incidental music for the Théâtre National Populaire, and, considering the general mediocrity of film music the world over, certainly deserves praise for its solid orchestration and relatively audacious atonality. (Unfortunately, Resnais was ill-advised enough to ask Pierre Barbaud, whose amateurish music had already substantially contributed to the mediocrity of Chris Marker's films, to do the score for his next documentary, and, except for a few measures written in a fairly successful imitation of Berg's early twelve-tone style, he fared no better on this assignment than he did in Marker's films.)

During the second part of *Toute la mémoire du monde,* we follow a book on its journey back through the maze of corridors and elevators as it rises toward the sunlit reading room for a few hours of blessed freedom, able at last to fulfill its knowledge-giving role, and the film ends with an exquisite combination pan-and-dolly shot beneath the famous vaulted ceiling of the library's main reading room.

Though less ambitious, on the face of it, than *Toute la mémoire du monde,* Resnais's most recent short, *Le Chant du styrène* (first shown publicly in Paris in March of this year), is perhaps even more brilliantly perfect. I say less ambitious because, in a sense, "it has all been done before": *le styrène* is a type of plastic—polystyrene. But rather than an industrial documentary, the film is a synthesis of visual abstraction and verbal lyricism, and as such it has probably never been equalled since the heyday of British documentary. The film opens with a very startling shot done in stop-time photography in which we see strange tentacular shapes of garishly colored plastic "growing" just as plants used to grow in the "Secrets of Life" series or in Rouquier's *Farrebique*. The half-dozen shots that follow are all in the same vein: we seem to be visiting some weird plastic garden or subterranean grotto, and though we recognize some of the objects shown us as knife- and fork-handles or dishracks, there is no doubt but what they are *also* tropical plants or stalactites. This sequence is accompanied with those few measures in Barbaud's score which have some musical stature, and this effectively heightens the sense of strangeness. As an added refinement, the elongated *Dyaliscope* frame is filled in for each shot with fuzzy, hardly visible geometric shapes which blend with the dark-colored background and offer a kind of neoplastic contrast to the baroque vegetation. (*Dyaliscope* is one of the optical processes which the French have drawn from their compatriot Henri Chrétien's original anamorphosing lens. It is far superior to Cinemascope in every respect: clearer image, no distortion in panning shots, etc.)

Suddenly, in the very center of the lower border of the huge screen there appears a tiny red bowl, and the commentator's voice is heard for the first time, making a literary pun which is, in a way, a counterpart to the punning title: "Temps, suspends ton bol." The "scene" changes and we begin to explore, still in tremendous close-ups which destroy all sense of proportion, a factory in which household objects are being manufactured from polystyrene. This is the first stage of the journey we are to take as we follow the plastic backwards from its finished products to its most elementary origins. Stated this way, the schema of this film is very banal, but we must not forget that this schema is to be elaborated upon by Alain Resnais and . . . Raymond Queneau. The author of "My Friend Pierrot" has written for this film one of the most brilliant and witty texts ever spoken on the screen. It is in the form of a long picaresque poem, couched in what I expect are rather free alexandrins, and bears a hilarious resemblance to the long narrative poems of Victor Hugo (a quotation from whose work serves as preface to the film). Unfortunately it is quite impossible to give any idea of the dry humor of this mischievous text, without resorting to long, untranslatable quotations.

Alain Resnais and his cameraman, Sacha Vierny (to whom, inexplicably, was ascribed the miserable photography of *Lettre de*

Sibérie), have performed a veritable *tour de force* in "industrial" camera-work. The acid contrast between candy-colored ribbons, pellets, and sheets of plastic as they pass through the gamut of presses and conveyor belts and the steely grays and browns of the machinery itself, is more than simply striking: it serves to create a perfectly coherent *abstract* universe, in which the sudden appearance of a line of workers shuffling oddly into the factory toward the end of the film—practically the only shot in which the "natural" spectrum is given full play—produces the shock of a rude awakening, as it recalls the irksome presence of mere humanity on the edge of this mechanical fairyland. (This dehumanization is reminiscent of a similar quality in *Toute la mémoire du monde*.) The dynamic use of color is also remarkably refined: the camera is often in movement, but its movements never seem banal or gratuitous as they do in so many industrial films, and the reason is that brightly colored fore- or back-grounds are constantly sliding past steely back- or fore-grounds in breathtaking kaleidoscopic fashion. One remarkable use of color as a dynamic element occurs in a *fixed* shot, in which we see tens of thousands of orange-colored plastic pellets sifting through a steel screen: the blue-gray steel appears in the most unexpected places in the vast frame and seems slowly to devour the brightly colored pellets, for the camera-angle chosen makes it impossible to tell these are simply falling through the holes. *Le Chant du styrène* lasts some twenty minutes, and I should say that, photographically speaking, there is only one shot in the entire film which I have really "seen before" (the classical shot of red-hot slag falling in huge viscous slices into a slowly moving string of gondolas).

The most important element of synthesis in the film is the relationship between the metric structure of Queneau's verse and the relaxed rhythm with which Vierny's startling images are made to succeed one another. In the case of this film, I presume that Resnais's *montage* was, at least in part, conceived after the shooting was over, for the use of the verse meter as a kind of bar-line regulating the leisurely syncopation of the editing is far too subtle to be accidental.

Finally, as Queneau leads us farther and farther back toward the sources of polystyrene—coal, petroleum, etc.—he seems suddenly aware that there is no reason why this account should ever stop, and with a few speculative verses on the prehistoric origins of coal and petroleum he decides, still without breaking the meter, that further investigation is better left "à d'autres documentaires," and this provocative little masterpiece just seems to stop . . . on a close-up of the seething jade-green sea.

Author's note: This article was written in 1959. Some of the views which it contains and, more generally, the critical approach on which it is predicated are no longer subscribed to by the author.

The Current Affairs Documentary
by Norman Swallow

*This selection is taken from the book Factual Television
(Focal Press, London, 1966). The author has long been
prominent in British television.*

In the U.S.A. the gap which followed the end of "See It Now" lasted
only a year. On October 29th, 1959, the first of the new "CBS Reports" was transmitted: *Biography of a Missile,* introduced and narrated by Murrow, which followed the story of a missile from the
drawingboard to the firing-range, and included statements from
Dr. Werner Von Braun and Dr. James Van Allen. Since the "CBS
Reports" has covered subjects as varied as the population explosion,
death on the road, racial tension, the problems of President de
Gaulle, Britain since the war, the world's water supply, East Germany, American conservatism, the European Common Market, the
work of Allen Dulles and the Central Intelligence Agency, the
Congo, South Africa, American undertakers, and the life and times
of Konrad Adenauer.

It has never hesitated to be outspoken, and never seems to be
afraid of supporting unpopular causes or irritating people of influence. *Harvest of Shame* (1960) was an investigation into the sad
condition of migratory farm workers in the United States, *Biography
of a Bookie Joint* (1961) dealt with the operations of an illegal
gambling establishment in Boston. *East Germany—The Land Beyond the Wall* included an interview, rare on Western screens, with
Walter Ulbricht. *Thunder on the Right* was a forceful exposé of
right-wing American political groups. *The Other Face of Dixie* had
the courage to visit four cities which had actually met successfully
the challenge of racial conflict.

"News media," Fred Friendly said, "are often criticized for reporting violence and controversy but not going back to see how the
wounds have healed. This 'CBS Reports' was an attempt to do just
that."

A list of eminent personages who have appeared in "CBS Reports"
reads like a Who's Who of the global Establishment: Ayub Khan,
Willy Brandt, Allen Dulles, the late Hugh Gaitskell, J. K. Galbraith,
President Eisenhower, Averell Harriman, King Hussein of Jordan,

Herman Kahn, President Kennedy, Robert Kennedy, Walter Lippmann, Chief Albert Luthuli, Harold Macmillan, Robert McNamara, Krishna Menon, Guy Mollet, Jean Monnet, Robert Moses, the late Jawaharlal Nehru, Richard M. Nixon, the Shah of Iran, Janio Quadros (then President of Brazil), Nelson A. Rockefeller, Dean Rusk, Bertrand Russell, General Salan, Jacques Soustelle, Generalissimo Trujillo (former dictator of the Dominican Republic), Harry S. Truman, Walter Ulbricht, and Konrad Adenauer.

Ed Murrow left "CBS Reports" in 1960 when he joined the USIA in the Kennedy Administration, but Fred W. Friendly remained in charge of the series until the summer of 1964. At present its permanent team consists of a director of operations, ten producers, an associate producer, six cameramen, six film editors, six sound technicians, a production manager, and the use of more than a dozen reporters. Of "CBS Reports" Fred Friendly himself once wrote:

"It would be simple to provide a prospectus for 'CBS Reports,' listing ten or a dozen subjects on which we are currently working. We are always working on ten or a dozen subjects. Some are completed in a matter of months; some take years; some are never finished. We are essentially a news series. We schedule some topics at the last minute—though never without a substantial portion of earlier research and production—and we do change broadcast dates to accommodate the pertinent developments.

"Every day there is more for the people of the world to know; and every day, what we don't know can kill us. We of 'CBS Reports' believe that our job is to try to cast a little light, create a little more understanding of what bothers people, what helps people, what can kill and what can save. Something that Dr. Frank Stanton said when we were about to start 'CBS Reports' provides the most succinct statement of what we hope has been accomplished and what still remains to be done. 'It is no exaggeration,' Dr. Stanton commented, 'to say that the United States is probably better informed today than ever in history. Nor is it an exaggeration to say that the need has never been greater than today.' "

A few months after the start of "CBS Reports," NBC began its "White Paper" series, produced by Irving Gitlin with the help of Albert Wasserman, and for its first transmission it chose *The U2 Story,* a careful and often exciting dossier of the incident in which an American U2 aircraft was shot down over Russia.

"White Paper" was not as frequent a series as either "See It Now" or "CBS Reports," and from the beginning it aimed to present a sixty-minute program every two months. Its purpose, however, seemed at the time to be more precise, and possibly more fearless, than its rivals': "To point its cameras squarely at some of the major issues, trends, and developments which many fear are sapping America's vitality or may suddenly explode into major threats to our way of life."

Certainly this was a fair description of the second program in the series, shown in May 1960, and called *Sit-In*. This was an analysis of one particular incident in the battle against segregation—the occasion in Nashville, Tennessee, when Negro customers had entered a café and refused to leave. Apart from its fearless honesty (and American television has been consistently outspoken in its treatment of racial conflict) this program, even more than its predecessor about the U2, made fine use of television's ability to counterpoint the present and the past.

Using both news material that had been shot at the time of the incident, and more recent coverage from Nashville which, at least in outward appearance, was calm and settled, it was able to let the present make its own comments on the past, and the past to attach its own moral to the benevolent and sometimes empty phrases of the present. Negro students who had taken part in the "sit-in" not only expressed their considered views on the problem in the light of what had happened, but also described the incident itself, looking back on it as participants. The local mayor, a significant figure in the proceedings, spoke of the present and the future and also, like the students, described the actual incident in his own words and as it seemed to him in retrospect.

In this way *Sit-In* was able to look at the Nashville incident subjectively, through the eyes of those who were personally involved in it, and this device gave an extra dimension to what might otherwise have been just another objective report. There was also a considerable fascination in being able to compare how people said they had thought and behaved in a time of crisis with how they actually behaved.

Occasionally "White Paper," without openly editorializing, has contrived that men should condemn themselves out of their own mouths and by their own recorded behavior, and an excellent example of this was the film about the Negro demagogue, Adam

Clayton Powell. Mr. Powell at one minute was "living it up" with the "Big White Folks," at another was relaxing informally in his Puerto Rican hideout (the implications being that he had chosen it as a way of appealing to the Spanish-speaking population of his Harlem constituency), and at another was behaving like the popular misconception of an American politician among his poorer colored supporters. Every shot in the film was true, every word spoken was authentic (and nearly all of them were spontaneous), and there was no routine commentary to give us an objective view of Mr. Powell. The comment, and it was very powerful indeed, came from the editing, from the juxtaposition of images and speech.

"White Paper," as a series, has also made considerable use of the crosscut interview, using selected sentences from the statements of several people, and crosscutting them into a fast-moving argument. Yet its ambitions and its technique have sometimes been ahead of its subject matter. *The U2 Story* and *Sit-In* were followed by the more routine *Panama—Danger Zone*, and *Angola—Journey to a War*. Although the last-mentioned had considerable scarcity value, and was neatly directed and narrated by Robert Young, these were the conventional themes of roving current affairs series. *Battle of Newburgh* (about local welfare scandals) and *The Business of Gambling* were subjects nearer home, though whether they were explosive enough to be fairly regarded as matters which "are sapping America's vitality" or as "threats to our way of life" must remain a very open question.

A third American network, the American Broadcasting Company, began its own major current affairs series, "Close-Up," in the autumn of 1960, and ran it for three years. Like "White Paper," but unlike "CBS Reports," "Close-Up" occasionally explored the subjective approach, and did so with a thoroughness which was new in American television (where the objective reporter seems in danger of degenerating into a sacred institution). Thus, *Walk in My Shoes,* made by Nicholas Webster, was an attempt to show what life looks like to a Negro.

More significantly, it was ABC which took the considerable gamble of encouraging the *cinéma-vérité* team of Robert Drew and Richard Leacock. Drew and Leacock, perhaps inevitably, also tackled the problem of Negro rights in *The Children Were Watching,* a film about the attempt in 1960 to integrate the public schools of New Orleans. In this film, as in *Walk in My Shoes,* "Close-Up" seemed to be breaking new ground, not only in actual technique but in its efforts to get into the skins of those men and women whose lives were most closely affected by whatever problem the program decided to tackle.

Sometimes these men and women were ordinary and not at all in positions of authority, but at other times they were those who had the responsibility of making delicate executive decisions. *Crisis: Behind a Presidential Commitment,* by Gregory Shuker, was a film which took its cameras into the offices of President Kennedy and his brother Robert during the delicate days when Governor Wallace was threatening to bar Negro students from the University of Alabama. Richard Leacock made *Yanqui, no!* for the "Close-Up" series —a film about the balance between the respective influences of the United States and communism in Latin America. This also was a film which had the considerable merit of avoiding an interviewer (though it had a narrator) and thereby seeming to get closer to its subject matter than has sometimes been the case in "CBS Reports."

C'est la guerre, about the war in Algeria, was another exercise in immediacy, in which the cameras stayed with a patrol before, during, and after a dawn attack. Unfortunately—for this viewer anyway—some of the earlier sequences seemed curiously artificial, and the attack itself looked like any generalized war sequence. Yet "Close-Up," even when least successful, had a recognizable style of its own, and usually had a different look about it; and if its principal producer, John Secondari, had done no more than introduce Drew and Leacock to the television screen he would have amply earned our gratitude.

In referring at such length to "See It Now," "CBS Reports," "White Paper," and "Close-Up" I have selected those current affairs series which seem to me to have been the most seriously significant in American television. It is only fair to say that they are merely the highest peaks in a long range of mountains. "White Paper," for example, followed "Outlook" (by Chet Huntley and Reuven Frank), and both Chet Huntley and David Brinkley, NBC's distinguished pair of topical reporters, for several years have had their own regular half-hour programs. CBS ran its "Eyewitness to History" for several years. ABC runs a thirty-minute "News Report" every Thursday, and all the major networks have recently stepped up their output of news specials, a form of "instant documentary" at which American television is particularly expert, and in which commercial sponsors have lately become admirably interested.

The firm of Xerox, having sponsored an NBC special on *The Kremlin,* agreed to sponsor six more documentaries from the same company. The Humble Oil and Refining Company last year brought 26 NBC news specials and another 25 were bought in advance by The Savings and Loan Foundation. "CBS Reports" is sponsored by Travelers Insurance; ABC's sixty-minute film, *The Soviet Woman,* was bought by Philco. I mention these precise examples as evidence of the growing realization in a hard commercial world that the documentary need be neither dull nor minority. As Mr. Richard L. Tobin put it in the issue of Communications [supplement of Saturday Review] for March 14th, 1964:

"The day of the news commentator is dead. The day of the documentary is at hand. It is at hand because the public tunes in to this sort of news show as it never has before, and with good ratings, sponsorships are easy where once they were pioneering. Ever since that excellent old series *The March of Time,* on radio and newsreel, we must admit to long-term partiality for the documentary as absorbing entertainment. We're happy to have company, and delighted that advertisers are flocking to a worthy standard."

It is possible to admire Mr. Tobin's sentiments without praising his literary style, and the discovery by wealthy sponsors of the news documentary, however belated, is as good an excuse as any for throwing hats in the air along the length of Madison Avenue. Moreover, it is one reason, and arguably the most effective one, why television in the United States has now evolved a logical pattern for its treatment of news and current affairs. The main news programs on the principal networks are now thirty minutes in length, a time which allows for comment on the news as well as the straightforward presentation of the facts.

In addition, the production of news specials has increased dramatically in the past two years; at the time of writing, some 400 news specials, all produced by Chet Hagan, have come from NBC alone. This combination of news-with-comment and special programs mounted at short notice provides a continuous flexibility which at present is one of the main reasons why current affairs coverage in the U.S.A. is able to be both immediate and deep.

Reinforcing this topical activity are the more considered documentaries, and it is in the nature of American television that these should be scheduled as a series, appearing for convenience at the same hour of day and at regular intervals of time (usually weekly). This form of planning combines the maximum of topicality with the maximum of considered comment, the merits of the well-informed daily newspaper with those of the knowledgeable political weekly. For the ideal at which all those concerned with news and current affairs should aim must surely be this: news of the moment, presented at the same times daily, and with one news program at a peak evening hour which can be regarded as the main bulletin of the day; immediate comment on the news, which will fill in whatever background may be necessary, and which will allow time for longer interviews than a normal news program can allow with those who are today making the news; nearly-immediate news-documentaries, for which the most suitable length would seem to be thirty minutes, and which are television's substitute for the topical feature piece in the daily newspaper, and which have time enough to treat each subject in reasonable depth; lastly, the documentary which is not tied to a particular news story on a particular day, but which has been prepared with great care over a longer period of time, yet is neverthelss related to the news by confining its subject matter to those themes which are directly concerned with the continuing issues of the age in which we live.

This ideal pattern may not as yet be perfectly realized in any of the world's television producing countries, but I believe that the United States is closer to it than anywhere else.

New Trend in British Documentary: Free Cinema
by Lewis Jacobs

This selection appeared originally in the
February 1958 issue of Film Culture (New York).

A new kind of film support has appeared in England, offering a wide opportunity for creative independence to British filmmakers, known as "Free Cinema." A special board called the British Film Institute's Experimental Production Committee has been created to sponsor "experiments by young talent in film style, technique or subject; and to support ideas unlikely to find sponsorship under ordinary commercial conditions." The money for these projects has come from a fund derived from a percentage of the British entertainment tax returned to the motion picture industry.

Recently five representative films were presented at the Museum of Modern Art, thanks to the ubiquitous efforts of Cinema 16— that vanguard of film societies—in collaboration with the American distributor, Contemporary Films.

A large audience of filmmakers—documentary, poetic, experimental, TV spots, industrial, animation—turned out despite a furious rainstorm and a subway strike, reflecting the great interest here in the program.

Enlightened patronage has been rare, but in the past it has played an important role in the British documentary tradition. Beginning in 1927–28 and continuing throughout the 30s and 40s, such government agencies as the Empire Marketing Board followed by their government, social, and industrial organizations were uncommonly liberal in their sponsorship of films and in providing opportunities for new film talent. So long as the film's general aim was served and its budget observed, no limits were placed on the filmmaker's artistry. During those two decades the English documentary flourished with extraordinary creative fire and excitement in the works of Grierson, Rotha, Wright, Elton, Lye, Watt, Anstey, Legg, Taylor, Jennings, and others who produced the spate of memorable pictures that placed the British in the forefront of the documentary movement.

But with the postwar social and economic change of climate came a change in sponsorship for the nonfiction film. By 1950 the leading documentary filmmakers had to seek other support. Most of them turned to commercial production for more profitable but, also more cautious clients. The general quality dropped.

Now once again, creative independent sponsorship has come to the aid of the talented filmmaker. *Nice Time, Momma Don't Allow, Together, O Dreamland,* and *Every Day Except Christmas* were presented as ". . . the first signs of a fundamentally progressive approach to exploring contemporary life through the cinema" (a statement by the Committee for Free Cinema in the British Film Institute's program notes). *Together* won a special award at Cannes (1956); *Every Day Except Christmas* received a gold medal at Venice (1957).

The first film, *Nice Time* (Alain Tanner and Claude Goretta), documented a typical Saturday night crowd searching for amusement in Piccadilly Circus. Framed by opening and closing shots of the statue of Eros, which dominates the surrounding streets, are the uninhibited actions of milling crowds, seized upon by a candid camera, with occasional Weegee-like studies of unashamed vulgarity or unconscious pathos. As a whole the film proved to be a loose compilation of colorful characters which was not strong enough in its impact to leave a deep impression.

Momma Don't Allow (Tony Richardson and Karel Reisz) revealed a characteristic evening at a jazz club. A simple storyline followed a butcher, a hairdresser, and a cleaning girl as they met their partners and joined some "Teddy Boys" for an evening of music and dance. The film highlighted a series of slight romantic and humorous incidents. As in *Nice Time,* the camera was a casual spectator, focusing upon the passing moment and letting it speak for itself. The people—the musicians and dancers, the shy, the bold, the slummers—were pleasantly observed but there was a singular note of passivity in the treatment. (Or was it merely British restraint?) Except for a small flare-up of dramatic interest—a mutual misunderstanding by one couple and several touches of humor, particularly a dancing couple preoccupied with continually circling around each other, the result was objectivity to the point of remoteness.

However, underlying the jazz enthusiasm which brought the participants together was a significant commentary: the need of the individual to be part of something vital, to be hep, to belong. But, because of the general lack of definition, the point seemed over-extended and weakened. One is bound to compare the film's lack of forcefulness with the vigorous statement of a previous motion picture, *Jazz Dance* (Roger Tilton), which handled the same material. In this latter film, objectivity was given eloquence by a careful selection of camera angles. In addition, emphasis upon pattern and rhythms of cutting and deeper feeling for cinematic organization helped communicate the point of the film more effectively.

Together (Lorenza Mazzetti and Denis Horne) was a bare, straightforward account of the solitary life of two young men—deaf-mutes. What they saw and did—and by implication, occasionally what they felt—was photographed in a series of diarylike sequences, objective and restrained in tone.

The mutes were shown as outsiders, lonely and misunderstood, living in a narrow world of silence. They moved about their dingy, crowded rented room in quiet routine, ate their meals with the landlady's family in an atmosphere of suppressed impatience, walked through bomb-torn streets subjected to the grimacing taunts of children, did their work in speechless isolation from fellow dockworkers, and at the end were separated by death when one of them was accidentally pushed over a bridge to drown without his companion or anyone else ever hearing his struggles or learning what has happened to him.

The subject was an unusual one, the most personal on the program. The camera detailed the obscurity of the men's lives without slighting one or the other. But what might have been poignant and genuine often emerged contrived and cynical. The cold objective treatment of the characters tended to oversimplify them. They appeared to be aloof, indifferent to their own dilemma. In the filmmakers' ruthless attempt to avoid any narrative or dramatic structure which might have emotionalized the incidents, the scenes became drawn out and monotonous, the tempo tedious; the sequences lacked climax, often ending abruptly.

The one exception to this flat detached treatment was a dream sequence. The younger of the mutes, who had seen a dancer at the fairgrounds and then at a bar, later dreamed of loving and being loved by her. They moved back and forth locked in a tight embrace, round and round, caught up in a rhythmic flow not unlike some primitive ritual. Their scenes ended with the mute awakening to see his companion pouring cold water into a washbasin.

Photographed in a manner that was part real, part fantasy, the sequence was a passage of genuine warmth and poetic feeling. It fused emotion and concept into a unique cinematic expression. One wished the entire film had displayed such feeling, insight, and vividness.

O Dreamland (Lindsay Anderson and John Fletcher) proved to be a sardonic comment upon popular culture. It contrasted the nightmare world of tawdry distractions at an amusement park with the apathetic search of its motley group of pleasure-seekers. People stared aimlessly at life-sized mechanical models featuring Joan of Arc burning at the stake, the hanging of a criminal, the execution of the atom spies, torture devices through the ages, and similar historical horrors.

The pageant of shocking displays was accompanied by the mocking laughter of twitching puppets, frenzied outbursts of grimacing gargoyles, and the strident leers of penny-in-the-slot viewers of suggestive peepshows. The violence of sound and image assaulted the seemingly dead sensibilities of the listless crowds with a kind of perverse pleasure.

In contrast to the mild impressionism of the previous pictures, *O Dreamland* was charged with a rampant emotional expressionism. Camera and microphone were used in counterpoint to bypass the superficial look of the subject and to inject a meaning. Frankie Laine's raucous "I Believe" blasted the ear while the screen showed a lion pacing his cage like some strange animal out of a painting by Hieronymus Bosch. "Kill me—thrill me," passionately pleaded Muriel Smith in a sultry voice, while spaceships darted across each other in frenzied flight and pursuit. Startling camera angles, unexpected juxtapositions of viewpoint, suggestive distortions, deft, on-the-beat cutting, and the emphatic contrast between what was seen and what was heard gave the film a hard-hitting, bravura impact.

Every Day Except Christmas (Lindsay Anderson, Leon Clore, and Karel Reisz) was a portfolio of honest, direct, unsubtle, and sometimes strong portraits of the night workers in the Covent Garden market, a chronological account of the way flowers and produce arrive at the market, are displayed and sold. Men and milieu were handled with sympathy and understanding. But the picture's force was always descriptive. The film moved from person to person and what we got was a series of low-keyed sketches of English workers at the market, sometimes hardly looked at, sometimes more directly glanced at, and occasionally—as in the instances of the old lady porter and the oldtime buyers—really and roundly seen.

Although conventional in treatment, the film was lifted by the warmth and insight of such scenes as those in the restaurant where the merchants gathered for tea-and-sausage breaks and, at the end, where poor street vendors bargained for leftovers.

What stood out above all in these five works of Free Cinema was a real concern for people as individuals. The old guard of British documentary primarily dealt with issues: housing, health, labor, education, politics. Today's British filmmakers focus upon human beings—people who are obscure, lonely, isolated in a world of monotonous routine. What the Free Cinema filmmakers are saying is that these people are trying to make contact with some force that will give meaning and vitality to their lives. (Are they the young angry men of the cinema?) By implication, this emphasis upon the aimlessness in the life of the average man could be regarded as a critical commentary on the current scene. . . .

In terms of individual achievement, *O Dreamland* and *Together* proved to be the most provocative. . . . The platform of Free Cinema is of vital importance and holds out high hopes for the future of creative filmmaking.

Lionel Rogosin's *Come Back, Africa*
by Archer Winsten

This review is from the New York Post, April 5, 1960.
The author is the Post's first-string film critic.

Come Back, Africa, Lionel Rogosin's successor to *On the Bowery,* is a picture standing somewhere between a rich new form and a necessity-ridden best-possible-under-the-circumstances. He went to South Africa to make a picture about social problems there, but it was not possible to have his full intentions known and still gain local cooperation. Therefore he was limited in what footage he could get, in the ways he could proceed in telling his story of white inhumanity to the natives. Pretending that he was shooting a musical travelogue and hiding his camera when shooting in proscribed native areas, he got out before the authorities realized what was being done.

Now the film is here and its opening . . . , not long after the shooting riots in South Africa and the sit-down strikes in the South, could hardly come at a more appropriate time. The handicaps of some dialogue rendered in English subtitles, other English dialogue very difficult to understand, and many sequences of crowds walking in Johannesburg do not permit total identification with those who are suffering. The effort to understand is a serious interference.

Even so, the main story outline is a valid construction. A Zululand husband and father, Zachariah, comes to Johannesburg to work in the goldmines so that he can feed his starving family. A series of mischances in jobs as houseboy, garage worker, waiter, and roadgang laborer reveals the conditions under which a native must function. He goes to a "shebeen" (illegal drinking establishment) where there is a sort of drunken conference on what's wrong with Africa and what should be done. It is at this time that Miriam Makeba, the singer, makes her appearance and sings with the voice that has charmed so many in N.Y.C. nightclubs.

When his wife has gotten a job as a maid, against her husband's wishes, he is arrested for visiting her in her quarters. Then, during his prison term, the wife is attacked and killed by a local hoodlum.

This tragedy seems contrived, at least hastily presented in this film. And it is equally possible to feel that many other sequences in the picture spring at you without proper preparation. People are not adequately introduced or understood. There is frequently an air of hasty, virtually unprofessional storytelling. The performances become those of amateurs standing about, trying to act as natural as possible. It is a rough picture, roughly made. The city streets, the crowds, and the beating musical transitions are not what one is used to in major or even minor film documentaries.

And yet, the picture is all of a piece. That's the way the whole thing is made, and it does, in the end, hang together and make a powerful effect. Therefore, rather than pick at flaws arising out of the production handicaps, let us consider the very real accomplishments of Rogosin's film. It has picked some real types—husband and wife are fine—and it has used them to exemplify the tragedy in which South Africa is presently stewing and which may explode into a catastrophe at any time.

The difficulties of the picture have a way of lessening as you see it more than once, becoming more familiar with its people and better able to understand what they are saying. And, as this happens, the structure and method become not only more apparent but also more effective.

This is not a film to be put aside as being of inferior workmanship. On the contrary, it has a quality all its own, a thing rewarding in itself, as well as this most extraordinary timeliness. If you want to see and understand more of what you read from South Africa, there is no better way to inform yourself just now than to see this picture of Johannesburg, the bitterness of the whites, the growing anger of the Negroes, and the horror of the shacks and tin shelters of Sophiatown slum.

Underside of a City: *The Savage Eye*
by Archer Winsten

This review appeared in the New York Post on June 7, 1960.

The Savage Eye is extremely well named. Purporting to be the experiences and states of mind of a young woman who has just been divorced, it can also be taken as a pitiless view of what is perhaps the worst part of America, Southern California at its worst.

The picture took a long time to make. To put it together three men used their spare time over a period of about four years, $65,000 and a lot of deferred salaries. They are Ben Maddow, screenplay writer of *The Asphalt Jungle, Intruder in the Dust,* and *The Unforgiven;* Sidney Meyers, documentarian who directed *The Quiet One;* and Joseph Strick, director of *Muscle Beach.* This was the picture into which they put everything, then doubled and redoubled.

Last August it hit the Edinburgh Festival with resounding success, winning an award from the specialists. The critics at the following Venice Festival also gave it their award. The British Academy called it the best documentary of the year.

There is no middle ground, no compromise possible at all with this film. Either you think it's tremendous as it knocks you about, or you get up and leave, demanding your money back as you pass the box-office.

A woman, Barbara Baxley, just divorced, comes into the Los Angeles airport where people are greeting one another, all of them kissing. She's alone, and the voice which comments from time to time throughout the film, somewhat grandiloquently orates, "Travelers by cloud, uneasy, grateful, swung on a thread of exploding fire, they step down from heaven, to the great sweaty footbound company of us all."

OK, but this commentator is going to make himself felt now and again, literally lush, pretty good at that, but sometimes just writing away because he's a pro and can't really believe the pictures have told everything as they really have. It doesn't happen so often that it ruins everything. It's just too much, two or three times.

There are great sequences to come, sequences that can become as classic as those unforgettable eating or traffic scenes in *The City.* The beauty and massage section is devastating. They don't forget to include a nose tilting operation. People play cards: "Where one miserable stranger can meet with seven others." They are old faces and hard, rough hands. It's two in the afternoon, four hours to dinner, and this is a bar. People watch a woman on a treadmill, or crowds standing in line for a TV show. There are many old people, the poor and ugly ones, the graveyard for pets, and the love lavished on pets. The commentator aptly remarks, "Pity the pets. They bear more than their natural burden of human love." Auto accidents, people hurt and bleeding, death. We see the hideous spectacle of professional wrestlers, and the more hideous participation of the watchers. Our divorcee is with a man, an older one, married. Nightclub. Strippers. Some pretty hard words about people and what they do.

The scenes of Christmas and celebration come on. The commentator is wound up for one of his sharpest sallies: "On the morning of the sixth day the stars declined, and the sun rose, and out of a handful of fire and dust, garbage and alcohol, God created Man."

Our divorcee remarks, "He made a big mistake."

We come to a faith-healing sequence taken straight from life. Words cannot describe this teetering on the sharp edge between religion in its most manic and/or commercial aspect and insanity. Our heroine has an auto accident—what part of American life could be without it—and we descend into an unconscious of love, blood (of the transfusion), and humanity in all of its least lovely manifestations, even to the homosexual exhibitionistic transvestites, if you need the full title.

The picture ends with recovery through childhood, and on to youthful love, love everything. But it leaves behind its dominantly horrible view of life: the old, the ugly, the unloved, the lonely, the dying, the dead, the depraved.

It is doubtful that any divorcee undergoes a baptism quite so strenuous, but if one cares to sum up the emotional trauma in images, these will certainly suffice. Perhaps they are excessive if we are trying for a real and balanced view. But there is no question about their brilliance and power. This is redemption through suffering, or the path out of emotional Hell through the center.

The Savage Eye is all of one piece, masterfully, artfully wrought by its three makers, a work that must be recognized as great no matter how unlikable, a film that will be seen for many a year no matter who rejects it now.

Thirty Years of Social Inquiry
by Harrison Engle

This abridged interview with Willard Van Dyke, the American
documentarian, now director of the Film Library of the
Museum of Modern Art in New York City, originally
appeared in Film Comment (New York) for Spring 1965.
Mr. Engle is himself a filmmaker.

Willard Van Dyke has been one of America's leading documentary filmmakers for almost thirty years. Born in Colorado, Van Dyke began his career as a still photographer during the early thirties, when he spent several years with Edward Weston in California. During that time Van Dyke had many one-man shows of his photographs, and often he acted and directed with little theater groups. He started in films in 1935, and a year later he came East to serve as a cameraman on *The River*.

Directed by Pare Lorentz, *The River* was a powerful and sweeping film on the human consequences of generations of misuse of our natural resources in the Mississippi basin. As cameraman, Van Dyke was able to apply his photographic talents to a work that expressed his sense of social concern and inquiry. It was also an opportunity for him to participate in evolving a documentary style unique to this country.

Van Dyke's first personal success came in 1939 with *The City*. Co-directed with Ralph Steiner, *The City* was a remarkable film on city planning and was a hit for two years at the New York World's Fair. For perhaps the first time, audiences saw a film about the everyday problem of making our cities livable. *The City* traced the development of our great urban centers and tried to pose a solution to unchecked growth and the threat of megalopolis. It was a disarmingly honest film, and many moments of humor added to its popularity. By bringing wide public attention to the documentary form, *The City* marked a turning point in American film history.

Van Dyke struck off in a different direction with *Valley Town*, made in association with New York University. *Valley Town* dealt with a small Pennsylvania town caught by the Depression and the rising tide of automation. Decidedly European, the film was like a Brechtian poem to the common laborer. Its many musical innovations and almost operatic quality made it especially interesting.

The main characteristics of Van Dyke's work were formed during this early period. His films tend to be rather open, straightforward statements that express his visual sensitivity and sharp humor, his view of man's relation to nature, and, above all, his active concern for human problems. But, with each new film, Van Dyke pursued different subjects and techniques. Thus, from films on unemployment and urban planning, he has progressed to more varied themes—education, agriculture, communications, world travel, and mental health. Because of this diversity, the public perhaps never has been fully aware of Van Dyke's place in American cinema. Nevertheless, he has gone his way, seemingly determined not to be classified. He is one of the few early documentarists who have remained *au courant* in the best sense.

Recently Van Dyke directed three films for CBS Television— *The Mekong River, Pop Buell in Laos,* and *The Farmer.* Also, he has completed several other documentaries on important aspects of modern life. *Rice,* a striking color film on the food shortage in Asia, and *Frontiers of News,* a dramatic treatment of the best news photographs of 1963, have received wide attention and are currently distributed by the Museum of Modern Art.

Van Dyke is a craftsman, in the best sense of the term. Since his directorial debut, in 1935, with a film about self-help cooperatives in California, Van Dyke has made more than fifty films, nearly all commissioned by a sponsoring agency or company, and designed to achieve specific ends. A quick look at his filmography will show the great variety of subjects and themes to which he has brought, over the years, his personality and filmmaking skill.

*   *   *

ENGLE: Why did you leave still photography for films? And why did you choose the documentary rather than the theatrical film?

VAN DYKE: I think the choice came at a time when I was most concerned with social problems. I came to film when two-thirds of the people in the United States were worried about their livelihoods, realistically. It was the Depression period. At the time, Hollywood was not interested in making films of these problems. Because I wanted to be a filmmaker and was interested in social situation, documentary was the obvious way to go. There was no other way.

As time went on I found that I was much more stimulated and interested in *the real situation*—trying to get that on screen in a poetic or realistic fashion—rather than dealing with fictional individuals and their more or less artificial problems. That doesn't mean that I don't enjoy feature films. I do, but I just don't want to make them particularly.

ENGLE: What were your first experiences in film?

VAN DYKE: At the age of twelve, I worked one summer as an extra in Hollywood, in a film called *The Rubaiyat of Omar Khayyam,* directed by Jack Cunningham. I'm sure that Jack Cunningham has long since passed from behind the camera, or from behind the megaphone, but that was my first experience. I never got over it. I remember swiping the little bits of film out of the projection room in the studio and taking them home and running them through a projector, over and over again. I just never got over it, that's all.

The first film I made myself was called *An Automatic Flight of Tin Birds.* I had never seen *Un Chien andalou,* but my film had a rubber glove in it, several eyes I had gotten from a slaughter-house, and a figure of a man on a cross on a hilltop—you know, "the images." They were borrowed, eclectic images—all right for some people, but certainly not right for me at that time. The film was unsatisfying because it didn't express the things that were of concern to me in my surroundings and in my life.

It was then that I became interested in the social documentary, which did not yet exist as a form in any way that I knew about. This was about the time of *Drifters,* but I was not yet aware of what Grierson was doing in England. I got an opportunity to make a film on self-help cooperatives in California. It was a wonderful chance to deal with the problems of people trying to help themselves. Well, this film also left a good bit to be desired. When it was finished, I came to New York to make a film on soil erosion. But that was made by Pare Lorentz instead, and it became *The Plow That Broke the Plains.*

ENGLE: You were drawn to films primarily through concern for social conditions, rather than because of any particular style of cinema?

VAN DYKE: I should add that, when *The Cabinet of Doctor Caligari* came to Oakland in 1922, I saw it almost every day for two weeks. The next film that made a tremendous impression on me was *Variety*. Then *Ten Days That Shook the World* and *Potemkin*. All of this was before I was established as a still photographer. Without being taught, and having no film literature to read, I picked out films that were important for me. Later I left still photography because it could not provide the things that I knew films could provide. I was excited and interested in film as a pure medium of expression, but I was more interested in using it for a social end.

ENGLE: Were you aware of what other socially concerned still photographers were doing at that time—people like Dorothea Lange, who were making social photo-essays?

VAN DYKE: Yes. While I was a still photographer I had a little gallery where I showed photographs and paintings. I had Dorothea Lange's photographs there, and I introduced her to Paul Taylor, who became her husband. He was responsible for the book, combining text and Dorothea's photographs, that used the words of dispossessed people. This was a kind of documentary film, using words and pictures together in a creative, social way. So there was a sort of ferment going on at that time.

ENGLE: Did your work with Pare Lorentz on *The River* help shape your ideas?

VAN DYKE: Pare Lorentz's influence on me was enormous. But this was because he gave me complete freedom to do what I wanted as a cameraman. He never talked filmmaking to me. Instead, he would recount stories that would tell me what his aims and goals were.

Working on *The River* gave me confidence as a young, beginning cameraman. I would see my footage alongside that of such seasoned and terrifically qualified cameramen as Floyd Crosby and Stacy Woodard. Crosby, of course, went on to win an Academy Award for *High Noon*. But before this he'd been with Murnau in the south seas, and he'd won all kinds of honors for his outdoor photography. So this opportunity to do an important job on the second American documentary was one of the most important things that ever happened to me.

ENGLE: How do you define the social documentary?

VAN DYKE: I would say it is a film in which *the elements of dramatic conflict represent social or political forces rather than individual ones.* Therefore, it often has an epic quality. Also, it cannot be a re-enactment. The social documentary deals with real people and real situations—with reality.

I don't think there is any such thing as objectivity in film work. Sometimes a filmmaker will assume that he is being objective, or that his camera is being objective. But any piece of film that comes out of a camera has already gone through a selective process. Also, there are many issues where objectivity is impossible. For example, a filmmaker could not be objective about The Bomb. He has an *attitude* towards it. Furthermore, I think a *filmmaker has a responsibility to express his attitude*. He has a responsibility to take a position in relation to the things in which he believes. Sometimes the responsibility is an awesome one. When a filmmaker begins to deal with problems like the war in Viet Nam or disarmament, he can't treat them lightly. He must think through what he feels about it, and then *execute that feeling with precision*. And he must execute that feeling *with poetry, too*. Because too often we forget what Grierson said about documentary film, that it gives us *the opportunity to make poetry of our problems*.

One of the things that has emasculated some television documentaries is that they try to satisfy everyone. As a result they end up not being anybody's position about anything. A documentary that continually says "on the other hand" is just absurd. One must live up to the responsibility that is laid upon you by using this tremendously important medium. To waste your time, or the audience's time, without taking a position in a film seems to me derelict in your duty.

ENGLE: Do you find this attitude in *cinéma-vérité* and the films of Drew, Leacock, and Maysles? They seem to aim for the truth to come from the material rather than from their own statement about the material?

VAN DYKE: Most of these filmmakers would say that they are not controlling the situation in front of the camera, but that they do control the result. In editing the film they can't help but put it together in a way that expresses their feelings. *And the stronger their involvement with the subject, the more effective it is.* You can see this in *The Chair* or in *Petey and Johnny*, which are among the most successful films in that style.

ENGLE: On this matter of using film responsibly, what do you think about such propagandists as Leni Riefenstahl?

VAN DYKE: A documentary film will treat a subject in depth regardless of the personal statement that is made. Leni Riefenstahl simply seduced us with a slick, superficial approach. *Triumph of the*

Will and *Olympia* were films of spectacle and no more, During the war, at the Office of War Information, we tried to find a way of using captured German film material to make anti-Nazi films. We had a fine-grain of all Leni Riefenstahl's work, and we used to sit night after night screening this material, trying to discover how to turn it against the Nazis. But we never could. The reason was that it was all spectacle, and there was simply no way to make it unattractive.

At the Office of War Information a number of documentary filmmakers, who had really just begun their careers, were gathered to make films on different aspects of American life. The documentary people were Sidney Meyers, Alexander Hammid, Irving Jacoby, Joseph Krumgold, Henwar Rodakiewicz, Irving Lerner, and me. Because documentary was a new thing, and because Hollywood had always been the source of pictures, the OWI got a group of Hollywood writers to write scripts for our films. But a problem arose immediately because these writers would sit together in a room to dream up ideas. They would write from their heads instead of *working with the realities of a location.* And we were never able to get a single script from them that was useful. On the other hand, *Hymn of the Nations* was done by shooting a Toscanini rehearsal, then developing a theme on the United Nations from that. And *Steeltown* was done because of my experience with industrial processes. In both cases the actual situations dictated the form of the film. This experience at OWI solidified the thinking of these documentary filmmakers. It became clear to all of us that direct observation was the only way to arrive at a truthful and successful presentation.

ENGLE: How do you feel today about the ending to *The City?* Wasn't suburbia your solution for megalopolis?

VAN DYKE: Not really, although I must admit many people have read it that way. Our answer was to have planned satellite communities around decentralized factory situations. Well, I'm no city planner, but I do know it just hasn't worked out. Our urban centers have continued to grow, and the problems we showed in *The City* have become accentuated.

Grierson was correct, however, when he mentioned that Van Dyke, as an old villager, should not have left out the smell of fish and chips. What John was saying was that the communities in our film looked sterile and antiseptic. You couldn't believe that there were real people living in them. Everyone was too well scrubbed.

ENGLE: Many of your films have very successful musical sequences—the lunch break section in *The City,* for example. Or the marvelous balletlike sequence with the mill workers in *Valley Town.* How was this unity of image and music created?

VAN DYKE: The sequence in *Valley Town* came about as a result of watching Aaron Copland working on the score for *The City.* Copland brought a piano into the editing room next to the moviola. He'd run a sequence, then try out an idea for it. By running a sequence over and over, he would work out his musical idea in a most direct way. He didn't just create a general character of music. Notes and visual images played in a counterpoint that could have been achieved only through this method.

But music had a more important role in *Valley Town.* Irving Lerner, who edited the film, suggested that I use Marc Blitzstein for the score. Marc had written "The Cradle Will Rock," which also dealt with unemployment in a steel town. So music became a part of the conception of the film. In one sequence a steelworker is walking home after looking for a job. I had planned to use a thought-speech over this section. However, Marc suggested we try a kind of recitative, as in opera, that would lead into a song once we got inside the man's home. We worked closely together this way—the director, the editor, and the composer—conceiving sections musically the whole time. This was especially true with the handmill sequence you mentioned. It was shot as a ballet, edited as a ballet, and scored as a ballet.

During the time of *The City* and *Valley Town,* documentary filmmakers were trying to solve the problem of the narrator. Of course, they still are. But in *Valley Town* the narrator becomes a character. He is the mayor of the town. And the people in the town use song and speech to carry the story forward. The next film I made, *The Children Must Learn,* was shot in the Kentucky mountains and used mountain ballads for the score. The ballads partly replaced the narrator, because they were used to comment on the action. This forced a certain poetic style on the commentary. I wrote the commentary one night during a Broadway show that I was bored with. I wrote it around the edge of my playbill.

ENGLE: In *The City,* the little boy on his way to church runs through a graveyard, and then the camera comes back to examine gravestones. In *Valley Town,* the point of view is from above the town—with the cemetery in the foreground. In *The Children Must Learn,* a graveyard again takes a significant place in the film. Is this a deliberate motif, and if so, how and why did you use it?

VAN DYKE: In time I became a little self-conscious about the fact that this was a repeat motif in these films. But, in thinking about it, I always find that this was used lyrically—in the same way that other natural elements were referred to. Death is a natural process; it is invested with emotion and is just as natural as being born, and so I treated death in these films almost as I would clouds or the sea coming in or any of the things in *Symphony of the Senses* that you look at from the point of view of their beauty and their place in nature.

ENGLE: Your enthusiasm for the underground cinema is well known. What aspects of it interest you most?

VAN DYKE: To say that I am enthusiastic about the underground cinema is perhaps overstating the case. But I certainly am enthusiastic about *some* of the work I have seen that can be called underground cinema. I like it for two reasons. First of all, I'm always interested in efforts to *stretch the medium.* When someone comes up with a new approach to film technique, or with new subject matter, or with something to say that he feels very strongly about, then a vital quality enters the work, although the film may be crude, technically speaking. There is a vitality in some of these films that most Hollywood and television products lack entirely. I respect and I like this vitality. Secondly, I like the *protest* in some of these films. We don't live in the most perfect of all worlds—I don't think we ever will, and I don't think we ever should. But the spirit of protest against commercial values, against injustices, against the middle-class rot that we see so much today, is a necessary thing. When protest dies there will no longer be any hope for America. And although protest in these films may be wildly undisciplined at times, this spirit is essential. It is this spirit that I respect.

And the contemporary European filmmakers interest me also. Antonioni and Bergman, in particular, and Resnais certainly interests me. In *Hiroshima, mon amour* he is trying to get at this thing, the presence of The Bomb. Here is this great overwhelming fact, yet here are two human beings who are exploring it in their own ways. Resnais interests me in *Hiroshima* very much. And Truffaut, too.

ENGLE: Many people, and the government of New York City, have charged the underground cinema with obscenity. What are your feelings about this?

VAN DYKE: Let's take Jack Smith's *Flaming Creatures*. *Flaming Creatures* is a film that was ruled by three judges in New York City to be obscene. They took it as their criterion that a film must not be offensive to contemporary community standards. Now, within that framework, I'm afraid I can't find *Flaming Creatures* obscene. There are some sad moments in the film. But as a whole it is not as good as Jonas Mekas has claimed it to be. I think that—and this is second guessing—Mekas got forced into a situation where he had to stand up for the film long beyond what he would have done if he hadn't been pushed into that position by being arrested for showing it.

Just because Smith shows masturbation in the film, because he shows transvestites, because he shows other sexual activities, doesn't make the film obscene. I am suspicious of this word. I don't understand it. There is no unanimity of opinion on the part of the public or judges or students of words, etymologists, as to what "obscenity" is. Therefore I get a bit nervous when people use the word. I feel that very often what they are saying is that they find the material depicted threatening to them, that their emotions are stirred in a way that they don't like. Basically that's what such critics are talking about when they complain of *Scorpio Rising* and *Flaming Creatures* and a good many of the other underground cinema films. But if a viewer is secure in his own self, in his feelings about the world, in his emotional reaction to things, and if his relationships with other people are mature, then these films will not be obscene to him. If these films appear obscene, it is simply because of the viewer's own lacks and insufficiencies.

ENGLE: Would anything in a film constitute obscenity, in your opinion?

VAN DYKE: Yes—wherever there is no art intention in the film, that is, if the intention of the film is simply to portray sexual acts with the avowed purpose of arousing lustful feelings on the part of the viewer—as in certain stag movies, "blue" movies, and so forth, that are used simply for that purpose in a house of prostitution or to pander to the voyeuristic instincts of guys who are not mature human beings. If a film is made that way, with no attempt to have a deeper meaning or to have an artistic intention, then I think I would call that film pornographic or obscene. I would say that I'm not interested in that kind of film because it's like any other ineptly produced, superficial presentation of subject material.

I think the greatest obscenity is the depiction of violence for its own sake. There are no laws against sadism as far as the screen is concerned. You can portray the most disgusting brutality and there is no law against it. This, in my opinion, is real obscenity, maybe because that kind of violence is shocking to me and because it arouses emotions in me that perhaps I prefer not to acknowledge. I don't know, but I find this shocking. I agree with the Reverend Howard Moody, who feels that the definers of obscenity should not concentrate solely on sex or vulgar language, but on anything whose purpose is the debasement and depreciation of human beings, especially violence.

Despite these abuses of the screen, I'm against censorship of any kind, for any purpose whatsoever. I just don't believe in it. It may very well be that that's Utopian, but I just don't believe that censorship is necessary.

ENGLE: Many of your films have been for television. Does television require changes in your approach to the material?

VAN DYKE: Yes. Television at its best has a feeling of immediacy, a sense of things happening at that moment. Films are less concerned with this feeling. Technically, in television films my takes are longer. There is no attempt at interpretive lighting, because it will be lost on the screen. Nor do I try to choose that moment in the day when the light and the action work together best.

In television, the relationship between the producer and the director is different, too. The producer is responsible for a whole series of programs. Often he has sold the network and the client on thirteen or twenty-six shows, with a certain format in mind. When a director makes a film for that producer he must understand that his approach to the material should fit the format. Also he must realize that the footage he shoots might be used in a different way than he had intended. Sometimes these are serious limitations for the director, but he must accept them or not make the film. Under the best circumstances, I have found this relationship with television producers to be very satisfying.

Among my own television films, I've liked *So That Men Are Free* and the two-part show on Ireland, both for "The Twentieth Century," CBS. I've had a good experience, by and large, working with Bud Benjamin and Ike Kleinerman, especially on those shows.

ENGLE: Did you know Ed Murrow?

VAN DYKE: Yes. Not well, but I knew him and had tremendous respect for him while he was at CBS. One goes back and looks at the films he made and the things he was responsible for there . . . television was different then. One can only hope that it will be as good again sometime.

Collaboration is an essential part of documentary filmmaking. My collaboration with Bill Jersey, for instance, has been very good. This was on *The Procession* and *Search into Darkness.* In *Search,* one thing I wanted was to show engineers and scientists working on problems unselfconsciously, so the viewers would participate in the scientific work even though they didn't understand the details of it. Now this was set up at the very beginning before we began making the film, and this fitted in with Bill's own beginning to explore spontaneous cinema. So I backed Bill in shooting thousands of feet of 35mm with two cameras until he got those moments that were most revealing. The film has several fine sequences where the audience never understands what these scientists are after, but is fascinated to watch the process taking place. Another example of collaboration was with Graeme Ferguson on *Land of White Alice;* I collaborated also with Irving Jacoby on many films; and, of course, to go way back, the collaboration of all of us on *Valley Town;* and the collaboration of Steiner, Rodakiewicz, and myself on *The City* —these are wonderful things to remember. I've mentioned working with Benjamin and Kleinerman most recently. Those were fruitful. The films were better as a result of working together.

I've had some wonderful clients, and naturally some that weren't very good. A good client allows the filmmaker to give him what he needs. And the filmmaker has the responsibility—again that word— to give the client what he needs. The filmmaker also has the responsibility to turn down a project if he doesn't believe in it. To take a film for the money and not do what is right for the client is just dishonest.

ENGLE: What about the client relationship with *Search into Darkness?*

VAN DYKE: That was a very good experience. The sponsor gave us a substantial budget, told us what the film was to accomplish, then left the rest to us. Something like this happened with *Skyscraper,* too. Here there were four sponsors, and the agreement was that no one sponsor would take precedence. That gave us considerable freedom. Both *Search into Darkness* and *Skyscraper* are effective films, and I think they are better for having had a minimum of sponsor supervision.

ENGLE: Several years ago you and Graeme Ferguson made a film, *The American Negro—A Progress Report,* for the U.S.I.A. What was the outcome of this project—was it ever shown?

VAN DYKE: We were trying to make a film about the Negro problem in America that would be effective for overseas audiences, effective in the sense that their conceptions about white-Negro relationships in this country would be improved. But the question was whether we could do this and still be honest. For at that time there was a great deal of publicity about violence and violations of the civil liberties of Negroes. So the problem was how to show these things in the film and still have it acceptable to the government and Congress as propaganda. Well, the film Graeme Ferguson and I made was never released by the U.S.I.A. Perhaps events moved too rapidly.

ENGLE: Many documentary filmmakers have had difficulty transferring their style to color work. How do you find shooting in color?

VAN DYKE: It depends on the film. When Wheaton Galentine and I went to Southeast Asia to make *Rice,* there was never any question but that it had to be in color. This was because we were dealing with earth, with growing things, and with people; and the color relationships between these elements were important to the story. We were very successful when we showed the planting and rich harvests of rice in Asia. But color was harder to handle when we had to explain that one million people are being born there each week, and that rice production must be increased. For example, we would show a crowded street with everyone dressed differently, and the eye would be intrigued by the dazzling colors. This worked against the point we were trying to make. You simply couldn't believe that those clothes were rags and that there were problems to be solved.

Color should be used functionally. Obviously it wouldn't help a film like *Showman.* On the other hand, Antonioni uses color in *The Red Desert* in a functional, interpretive way. It reinforces and adds to the impact of his statement. When an artist like this is trying to express a complex, delicate feeling, he should use every tool available to him.

There's no question that color is in fashion. There is a tremendous pressure to use color today, whether or not it is suitable for the subject. But also color lends itself to the pattern of modern life. Twenty-five years ago, when we made a film, we were clear in stating our message. Lorentz, for example, was very clear when he said that we should stop the erosion of our land in *The River*. The films of those days were rather straightforward statements. But today the issues are not all that clear, and even when they are clear, filmmakers do not want to say things as directly as they used to. Often they want to approach their statement from a tangential position. And color is useful in this respect.

ENGLE: Do you think that the development of lightweight equipment has given filmmakers new themes to work with?

VAN DYKE: It's a whole new approach. But as far as the themes are concerned—no, I don't think they are any different basically. But the treatment of these themes could not have been accomplished in any other way than the way in which practitioners of spontaneous cinema are approaching them. For example, there have been anti-capital-punishment films before *The Chair*, but there's never been a film that approached it in that way.

Regarding Maysles, Leacock, Drew, and some others, I don't think they're even aiming for objectivity. I mean any of the films you can name, made by any of them, is making a pitch. Now, Leacock very often has spoken about the responsibility of the cameraman or cameraman-director in using the spontaneous cinema. These themes of truth or morality, of ethical values, have been the stuff of art from the very beginning. If filmmakers were not dealing with this kind of level, then you wouldn't even notice them.

As for myself, I don't have any style. But I can say certain things about the way I make films that differ from the way others make films. One of these things is my concept of directing. The job of a director of documentary films is to direct the creative energies of the people involved in the film toward the needs of the subject. Now that means that the director attempts to *create a climate in which the participants feel they can reveal the situation in front of the camera* in a significant way through the film. This means you run a quiet set. It means that you don't shout at people. It means you don't get people upset unless this is going to achieve the goal, unless this is going to open up the creative energies of the people. But this latter rarely happens. Mostly, when you express your own anxieties all you do is tighten everybody else up, and the thing can't move in the way in which it has to move. I believe there is a kind of mystic atmosphere that can be created around the act of making films in which people feel comfortable, they feel stimulated, they feel able to give the utmost that they have to the film.

ENGLE: Do you think one of the differences between your films and those of spontaneous cinema is that your films are structured?

VAN DYKE: Sure, that is one of the differences. The kind of documentary films that I make are more explicit than spontaneous cinema. I start out to say something in the documentary film. Cinéma-vérité starts out with a situation and lets that situation lead the filmmaker wherever it's going to go. It has its own logic, so there's no preconceived plan on the part of the filmmaker if it is successfully done. Often this approach is more effective than the documentary films in which you are told how to feel and what to feel. I wouldn't like to say that that rules out all of the type of films that I've made, though. There is room for both things in the world.

ENGLE: Haven't you got a special interest in the film preservation program of the Museum of Modern Art?

VAN DYKE: Oh, film archives are very important. A place like the Museum of Modern Art should be and sometimes is a place where film students can examine the masterpieces of the past. This is our heritage. This is the thing that we rest on, that everything grew out of. Archives like the Museum ought to be expanded a thousand times. There ought to be dozens of little cubbyholes with automatic projectors that can be run back and forth, can speed up and slow down, where a student can spend as much time as he wants to study a film. The Museum ought to reach out to the community and keep it abreast of what is happening in the world of cinema, just as it does in the world of painting, sculpture, and any of the other arts. It has a responsibility to do that and less of it is being done than might be done—because of lack of money.

Now, film is a very expensive medium on any level. To maintain a film archive is an expensive proposition. To keep films in circulation is expensive. To maintain personnel who are skilled and knowledgeable about motion pictures is expensive. I'm sure that many of the film archives that exist—such as Eastman House, the Museum of Modern Art, and now the Hollywood Museum—do as much as they can with the funds available to them. But as students and lovers of our medium, we ought to encourage such places *to extend their activities*. We ought *to help them get money* to do the things that they should do. I can hardly overestimate the value of such places.

ENGLE: Have you had contact with the film schools of Poland and the Soviet Union?

VAN DYKE: When Dr. Toeplitz visited this country, I saw the films that were made in Poland by the film school there. I found them really extraordinary examples of students' work. They were, in some cases, mature works of art. They showed a clear progression from the first sort of student film through films done by graduates. And they had a remarkable mastery of not only all technical aspects of the craft, but also an understanding of the medium from a social point of view, what film's relationship is to the society out of which it comes. I don't know anything about the Russian film schools. I've seen a few films that I assume were made there by students, and I found them very derivative, eclectic films lacking in any real focus, very inferior to the Polish films.

ENGLE: You went to Europe during the first years of your film-making. Will you explain why you went and what you did?

VAN DYKE: I went to Russia in 1935 because I was very interested in theater. I still was acting and directing in little theater, and I went abroad because I could go to the theater every night and see something new and marvelous. Also, I had respect for some of the Russian films I had seen. Especially the films of Pudovkin and Dovzhenko. Eisenstein, also, but perhaps I would put Dovzhenko, Pudovkin, and Eisenstein in that order. Their films meant a great deal to me, so I wanted to see the place where they were being made. But I went in the summer and all of the filmmakers were away to the Crimea. They didn't want to be around Moscow in the summer, and I didn't get to meet any of them. I saw a couple of Russian movies that I could have seen later in New York. So, as far as movies are concerned, it was not very fruitful. In fact, a great revelation to me was the paucity of good documentary film production over there. I came to realize that documentary can become great only in a country that allows free inquiry into problems. I began to understand why England, Canada, and the United States have made the most effective documentaries. On the other hand, I did see Ulanova dance *Swan Lake,* and for the first time I saw ballet in a way that made me understand something about it. The other countries I went to were not very fruitful either, as far as film was concerned. I was in north Europe at the time Hitler was in power. There was nothing happening in German filmmaking that interested me, and I stayed there as short a time as I possibly could and got out.

ENGLE: Why do you travel around the world to make films?

VAN DYKE: To see what's on the other side of the mountain. I suppose that's a facetious reply, but when I was a kid why did I go to the edge of the prairie, climb up the hill, and look down the other side? I don't know. I think that one thing that might be said about me is that I am wide open for any experiences at all and that I welcome new experiences. To travel around the world, to see different people and work with different people, is another way of experiencing new and exciting things. And also, more important, perhaps, it is a way of verifying one's own philosophy, position, ideas, concepts—whatever you might want to call that. Because the more you get to know primitive people, for example, the more you realize the nature of yourself; the more you work with strangers, the less of a stranger you are to yourself.

ENGLE: What are your feelings about Robert Flaherty?

VAN DYKE: Flaherty was never an influence on me personally, though to deny Flaherty's influence on all documentary filmmakers would do him a tremendous disservice. Of course, he was a great influence on *all of us,* but personally, no. Lorentz and Grierson were the big influences on me: Lorentz because he gave me the opportunity and because he was the first American filmmaker to make a social documentary; and Grierson because he was the person who defined social documentary. He was the man who first saw its use and meaning for England, just as Lorentz saw its meaning for the United States. So these were the two prime influences.

But, as far as Flaherty is concerned, I had great affection for him as a person. I didn't know him nearly as well as Leacock did, for instance, or as well as a great many other people. But some of my most wonderful memories are of a period in New York when word would go out that Flaherty was at the Coffee House and that he was telling stories. We'd go down there to listen to these wonderful, marvelous, fluid Irish stories that would go on for hours. This was always a great experience.

I also had a respect for Flaherty's lack of interest in film. I understood this—that he wasn't really very interested in film. I remember a party at my house. There were a lot of filmmakers there, and Flaherty was there. Suddenly I was aware that a wonderful presence was missing at this party. I looked and Flaherty was not around. And I went to the nursery, and here's Flaherty down on the floor with my son Peter, playing with his electric train and having a tremendous time. He was not really interested in all the film talk going on in the other part of the house.

Flaherty was a man with great heart and great affection for people and for life. His influence on American documentary was not as great as it could have been, had he lived longer and been able to continue working, because he was working right up to the very time that he died.

ENGLE: Many people have criticized Flaherty's romanticism and escapism, objecting that he wants to go to the Aran Islands, so to speak, to avoid the problems of contemporary life.

VAN DYKE: I can't agree with them. I think that Flaherty was showing us by indirection some of the problems in our contemporary lives. By going back to the primitive, he helped us to see something that we have lost—direct simple contact with nature, for example. It's perfectly true that Flaherty didn't attempt to examine or unravel the complexities of an automated civilization. But then his simpler, more direct approach to film seems to me to reveal the problems in a more profound way than if he had approached them directly. I'm aware of the fact that even I have been guilty of saying, "There was romantic documentary and that was Flaherty, and there was the social documentary and that's Grierson and Lorentz"—but the longer I look at film, and the more I see of Flaherty's work, the more I realize that it has a profound vision that just goes beyond all this narrow terminology.

ENGLE: Do you find such vision in current documentary films?

VAN DYKE: It's a different thing. Let's just explore it from this point of view: we're dealing today with so many facets of so many problems that it's extremely difficult for a filmmaker to get an over-all view of anything. It becomes oversimplified as soon as he does. You know, you can't make a film about The Bomb, and yet that was the great temptation a few years back, as soon as the terrible fact of this thing became apparent to us. But you might be able to break down some of the *effects* of the discovery of the bomb or the use of the bomb, some of the *effects* on our society, and thus make a film about a small segment of that problem.

But not these great epic themes—the time is not now for those. I wouldn't like to say that the time is past, but I don't think you can deal with them in today's world. Once I tried to formulate this by saying Flaherty's films were films about man against nature; and then Lorentz came along with films that said, "Well, it's not just man against nature, with his own bare hands and with his simple tools, but it's with the aid of science." Then there came another period when we began to make films in which the thing was man against himself; we tried to find out why he needed to destroy himself, why he was fighting himself. I never could quite get this last theme into any real perspective as far as the previous ones were concerned. But I think in there some place is the dilemma. The others were external enemies. The enemy now lies within.

The Undefeated (1950),
directed by Paul Dickson

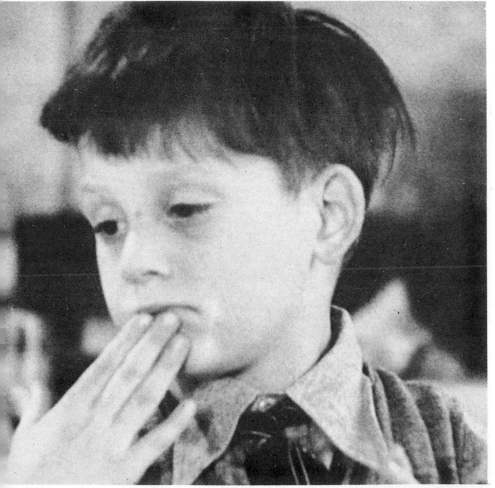

Thursday's Children (1954), directed by Lindsay Anderson and Guy Brenton

Momma Don't Allow (1955),
directed by Karel Reisz
and Tony Richardson

All My Babies (1953),
directed by George Stoney

Sunday in Peking (19
directed by Chris Mar

On the Bowery (1957),
directed by Lionel Rogosin

Letter from Siberia (1957),
directed by Chris Marker

light and Fog (1955),
irected by Alain Resnais

Hôtel des Invalides (1952),
directed by George Franju

Come Back, Africa (1959
directed by Lionel Rogos

N.Y., N.Y. (1957),
directed by Francis Thompson

A Selection of Documentaries of the Period

All My Babies, George Stoney
(1953)

All the Way Home, Lee Bobker
(1958)

Angry Boy, Alexander Hammid and
Irving Jacoby (1951)

Bernstein in Israel, Richard Leacock
(1956)

The Big City, Charles Guggenheim
(1951)

Bullfight, Pierre Braunberger
(1956)

Burden of Truth, Reid Rummage
(1958)

Le Chant du styrène, Alain Resnais
(1958)

Children of Hiroshima, Kaneto
Shindo (1952)

The Children's Republic, Madeleine
Carroll (1950)

A City Decides, Charles
Guggenheim (1957)

City of Gold, Colin Low and Wolf
Koenig (1957)

Come Back, Africa, Lionel Rogosin
(1959)

Coney Island, Valentine Sherry
(1951)

Corral, Colin Low (1954)

The Cry of Jazz, Ed O. Bland
(1959)

Davy, Richard Leacock (1958)

The Day Manolete Was Killed,
Dave Butler and Barnaby
Conrad (1957)

"The Earth and Its Peoples" series,
Louis de Rochemont (1950s)

Echo of an Era, Henry Freeman
(1958)

Emergency Ward, Fons Iannelli
(1952)

Every Day Except Christmas,
Lindsay Anderson, Leon Clore,
and Karel Reisz (1957)

Family Portrait, Humphrey
Jennings (1951)

Feelings of Depression, Stanley
Jackson (1951)

The Film of Holland, Bert Haanstra
(1951)

For the Living, Lewis Jacobs and
Leo Seltzer (1950)

The German Story, Andrew and
Annelie Thorndike (1956)

Glass, Bert Haanstra (1958)

The Great Adventure, Arne
Sucksdorff (1953–4)

Have I Told You Lately?, Stuart
Hanish (1958)

Highway, Hillary Harris (1958)

Holy Week in Popayan, Arnold
Eagle (1959)

Hôtel des Invalides, Georges
Franju (1952)

Houen Zo, Herman van der Horst
(1953)

The Hunters, John Marshall and
Robert Gardner (1958)

In the Street, Helen Levitt and
James Agee (1953)

Indian Village, Arne Sucksdorff
(1951)

Jazz Dance, Roger Tilton (1954)

Jazz on a Summer's Day, Bert
Stern (1959)

Land of Enchantment, Henwar
Rodakiewicz (1952)

Letter from Siberia, Chris Marker (1957)

Life Begins Tomorrow, Nicole Védrès (1952)

The Lonely Night, Irving Jacoby (1954)

Momma Don't Allow, Karel Reisz and Tony Richardson (1956)

The Museum and the Fury, Leo Hurwitz (1955)

Nice Time, Alain Tanner and Claude Goretta (1956)

Night and Fog, Alain Resnais (1955)

Nightmare in Red, Henry Salomon (1955)

Notes on the Port of St. Francis, Frank Stauffacher (1952)

N. Y., N. Y., Francis Thompson (1957)

O Dreamland, Lindsay Anderson (1953)

On the Bowery, Lionel Rogosin (1957)

L'Opéra-Mouffe, Agnès Varda (1958)

Out of Darkness, Albert Wasserman (1956)

Pacific 231, Jean Mitry (1950)

Pantha Rhel, Bert Haanstra (1952)

Paul Tomkowicz, Street-Railway Switchman, Roman Kroitor (1953)

A Place to Live, Lee Bobker (1955)

Pull My Daisy, Robert Frank and Alfred Leslie (1959)

Salt of the Earth, Herbert J. Biberman (1954)

Sausalito, Frank Stauffacher (1953)

The Savage Eye, Joseph Strick, Sidney Meyers, and Ben Maddow (1959)

Secrets of the Reef, Lloyd Ritter, Robert Young, and Murray Lerner (1956)

The Silent World, Jacques-Yves Cousteau (1956)

Skid Row, Allan King (1957)

Skyscraper, Shirley Clarke (1958)

Song of the Rivers, Joris Ivens and Vladimir Pozner (1954)

Sponge Divers of Tarpon Springs, Lewis Jacobs (1951)

Steps of Age, Ben Maddow and Helen Levitt (1951)

Sunday in Peking, Chris Marker (1955)

Third Avenue El, Carson Davidson (1955)

Thursday's Children, Guy Brenton and Lindsay Anderson (1955)

Toby and the Tall Corn, Richard Leacock (1954)

Together, Lorenza Mazzetti and Denis Horne (1956)

Toute la mémoire du monde, Alain Resnais (1956)

"True Life Adventure" series, Walt Disney (1955)

The Undefeated, Paul Dickson (1950)

The Valiant Heart, George Stoney (1953)

"Victory at Sea" series, Henry Salomon and Isaac Kleinerman (1952–3)

Waters of Time, Basil Wright (1951)

We Are the Lambeth Boys, Karel Reisz (1959)

Weegee's New York, Weegee (Arthur Fellig) (1950)

World Without End, Paul Rotha and Basil Wright (1954)

PART FIVE / 1960–1970

In the Year of the Pig (1969),
directed by Emile de Antonio

Point of Order! (1964), directed by Daniel Talbot and Emile de Antonio

Documentary Becomes Engaged and Vérité
by Lewis Jacobs

*In the field of putting ideas on film, worship of the word "documen-
tary" needs to be reassessed. It is a hopeless corruption of a term that
has come to be identified with "pamphlet films" and dull narratives.*

THOROLD DICKINSON

Never were Americans so happy to see a decade come to an end.
A "slum of a decade" John Updike called it. The assassinations of
the Kennedys and Dr. King, racial violence in the cities, campus
explosions, pollution, drug abuse, crime, a loss of confidence in
national leadership, and above all the disgrace of the Vietnam war
and the final degradation of Mylai tore at the sinews of the country.
So much political and social turbulence rocked the nation that no
single event, however critical, dominated the period in the way the
Great Depression had overshadowed the 1930s or the hot and cold
wars had commanded the forties and fifties. The endless mixture of
eruptive conditions provided the documentary — particularly the
television documentary — with a wide spectrum of compelling topics and themes.

From *The Children Were Watching* (1960), which pinpointed
the historic confrontation on school integration, to *Woodstock*
(1970), which recorded one of the most extraordinary mobiliza-
tions in the country's history, documentary films did an extraordinary job of sorting out the confusions and fears of a beset society
and illuminating the new attitudes rising out of the chaos.

The first of the crises to be dealt with was the black struggle for
equality. Television films of sit-ins, sleep-ins, mass rallies, clashes
with police, and the crescendo of black demands for "freedom now!"
brought the fight for civil rights into the home of virtually every
American family. In *Crisis: Behind a Presidential Commitment*
(1963) Gregory Shuker placed cameras in the offices of the President and Attorney General to capture the tension of Governor
George Wallace's attempt to bar the entrance of black students to

the University of Alabama. *An Interview With Bruce Gordon* (1964) by Harold Becker recorded with sensitivity the views of a courageous young organizer of the Student Non-Violent Coordinating Committee during a drive to register black voters in the South. Arthur Barron's *My Childhood: Hubert Humphrey's South Dakota and James Baldwin's Harlem* (1964) drew a disquieting comparison between white and black America. Stuart Schulberg's *The Angry Voices of Watts* (1966) showed, in the devastation of the black community of Los Angeles, the utter frustration and anger of the rioters. William Jersey's *A Time for Burning* (1966) was a touching portrayal of a minister who was turned out by his parishioners for supporting civil rights causes. *Cicero March* (1968), by the Film Group of Chicago, captured the electricity of a march by blacks through the heart of a hostile white community. *Still a Brother* (1969) by William Greaves and William Branch, dealt with the choice facing the black middle class: whether to emulate white attitudes and values and thereby gain membership, if limited, in white society, or unite with ghetto and rural blacks to forge a new political force. *Tumult, Turmoil and Turbulence* (1969) spanned the short history of the civil rights movement from its non-violent beginning in Birmingham to the angry young fists of Black Power upraised at Cornell University. By the time Perry Wolff's *The Battle of East St. Louis* appeared in 1970 — the film showed black and white community leaders trying to arrive at solutions in a three-day "encounter" — there did not seem to be any segment of the country that needed to be persuaded of the desirability of reversing the process of black and white alienation.

At the same time there were a number of documentaries which undertook to explain the complex — and in some cases, hidden — events affecting the course of national leadership and international policy. Many of these documentaries were distinguished by boldness, resourcefulness, and incisiveness, and imparted to the American television public an intelligence and sophistication it had never known before.

The U-2 Affair (Albert Wasserman, 1960) vividly reconstructed the Eisenhower Administration's bungling of the U-2 incident, in which an American spy plane was shot down in the Soviet Union, and the resultant break-up of an important American-Soviet summit meeting. *Primary* (Richard Leacock and Albert Maysles, 1960) was an intimate and candid observation of the Wisconsin campaigns conducted by John F. Kennedy and Hubert Humphrey for the Democratic Presidential nomination. *Yanqui, no!* (Richard Leacock, Albert Maysles, and D. A. Pennebaker, 1960) was an analytical and revealing presentation of Latin American hostility to the United States and acceptance of Communist influences. *The Making of the President* (Mel Stuart, 1963), based on Theodore White's best seller, limned the highlights of the Kennedy-Nixon race for the Presidency, providing new insights into the personalities of both men as well as the uniquely American ritual of selecting a national leader. *Point of Order!* (Emile de Antonio and Daniel Talbot, 1963) was a compilation of the most memorable moments of television coverage of the Army-McCarthy hearings, giving an important perspective to this incredible episode in American history. *Cuba: Bay of Pigs* (Len Giovannitti, 1964) gathered the essential elements of the Bay of Pigs fiasco and examined the reasons for the failure of this enterprise. The same director's *Cuba: The Missile Crisis* (1964) captured the tension of the confrontation between the United States and Russia over the Soviet attempt to establish missile bases in Cuba.

The harrowing events surrounding the assassination of President Kennedy in 1962 led to three affecting documentaries. All were striking examples of the new use of archive material which the filmmakers had learned to utilize, with astute editing, to form cohesive images and conclusions from miscellaneous facts. The results were a new kind of personal journalism detailed with considerable pictorial skill and feeling. *Four Days in November* (Mel Stuart, 1964) traced the activities of Lee Harvey Oswald leading to the shooting, the arrangements for the President's security, and preparations for the luncheon at the Dallas Trade Mart that he never attended.

Years of Lightning, Day of Drums (Bruce Herschensohn, 1968) was an eloquent elegy for the murdered President and his New Frontier program. Scenes of the Peace Corps, the Alliance for Progress, the space program, the drive for racial equality, the fight for global freedom from want, and the slowing of the arms race were counterpointed with successive glimpses of the funeral cortege so that the effect became one of "great activity being embraced in disaster, triumph in tragedy." Produced by the United States Information Agency for distribution overseas, the picture so impressed officials abroad and in Washington that Congress passed a special resolution to allow its release in the United States.

The third film about Kennedy's assassination, *Rush to Judgment* (Emile de Antonio, 1967), was based on the controversial book by Mark Lane, who sought to refute the Warren Commission report on the circumstances of the shocking murder. The film, like the book, piled contention on contention, raising many disturbing questions about the possibility of a conspiracy.

Chicago: The Seasons Change (1969), made by a group of concerned filmmakers, documented one of the most explosive events in recent political history — the Democratic convention in Chicago in 1968. The film consolidated and put into sharp focus what millions of Americans had already seen on television (either with horror or delight, depending on one's view), the brutality of the Chicago police in dealing with the young demonstrators outside the convention hall and with those who came to witness what was going on, including convention delegates and newsmen.

Many films explored the American problem of poverty amid plenty. *War on Poverty* (1965) concentrated on a single neighborhood, telling its story through the impressions of two boys, one black, the other white. *The View From City Hall* (1968) studied the city of Boston as a place with "too many problems and too little time to solve them." *Challenge of Urban Renewal* (1966) and *Cities Have No Limits* (1968) depicted the problems created by the mass migrations from city to suburbs, leaving behind pockets of poverty and despair. *Smalltown U.S.A.* (1968) examined the rapidly increasing technology in American society and considered ways in which it could be used to keep small towns alive. *Incident in Roxbury* (1968), *A Piece of the Action* (1968), and *The Besieged Majority* (1970) treated poverty as a spreading disease ravaging the individual victim psychologically as well as physically, and producing debilitating effects on all of society. Especially effective in dealing with poverty in personal terms were *Manhattan Battleground* (William Jersey, 1964), *The Tenement* (Jay McMullen, 1967) and *Appalachia: Rich Land, Poor People* (Fred Willis, Richard Pierce, and Adam Giffard, 1969), each of which addressed itself to the experience of poverty by showing the intimate details of day-to-day living. *Hunger in America* (1968), produced and written by Martin Carr and Peter Davis for CBS Reports, visually detailed the widespread incidence of poverty. The film showed starving people in four sections of the country to illustrate the sad contradiction of an affluent nation in which millions live in deprivation.

The alienation of youth, which burst upon the American consciousness with full force in the sixties, was a major topic for filmmakers, but the scope and the ramifications of this revolution for the most part eluded the groping camera.

An early and fairly representative attempt to delve into this vast subject was *Drop-Out* (1963), which dealt with the increasing number of students who for a great many reasons, including a rejection of an archaic educational system, as well as traditional middle-class aspirations, chose to put their futures in jeopardy by leaving school. *Teen-Age Revolution* (1965) compared the life styles of the competitive adult world with the search by youth for a more satisfying sense of identification and a better rationale for living. *The New Morality* (1967) further explored the breakdown of traditional patterns of life among the young and their quest for an independent ethic far removed from the ken of their elders. Two other films which contributed some understanding of this reaching out for new values were *Sixteen in Webster Groves* (1966) and *High School* (1969), both of which exposed the unyielding pressures of the older generation to mold the new generation according to its own lights.

A film that recorded and explained with partisan zeal one of the most far-reaching developments in the youth revolution was *The Berkeley Rebels* (1965), which dealt with the historic demonstrations at the University of California at Berkeley for university reform and personal liberty. The film's ardor in supporting the Berkeley activists set the pattern for a flurry of similarly angry pictures depicting the rampant spread of what came to be known euphemistically as "campus unrest." More restrained was *Confrontation* (1969), which showed how a small incident arising from student demands at San Francisco State College suddenly erupted into a bitter conflict that spread throughout the city and the state.

If the polarization of the generations needed further definition, *Pull the House Down* (1970) provided it. Again the confrontation: on campus violence, sexual freedom, racism, drugs, Vietnam. The film summed up the arguments on both sides, and in the process showed that after a decade of hostility the split was wider than ever.

The pervasive problem of drug abuse, which afflicted families in every stratum of society, became a major subject for filmmakers in the late sixties. The objectives of their films were three-fold: to show how widespread the evil had become, to probe the reasons for its growth, and to show the effects on drug-users (and their families). *From Runaway to Hippie* (1969) examined the changed lives of young middle-class Americans who fled to a drug-oriented commune and gradually sank into the degenerate world of heroin. *Marijuana* (1969) looked at the "turned-on" generation through the blue haze of pot. *The Addicted* (1969) explored the confusing sociological and psychological conditions that drive youthful escapists to a realm of drug fantasy. *The Losers* (1970) was a blunt report on how drugs had destroyed the lives of a group of addicts ranging in age from 12 to 20. *The Trip Back* (1970) singled out a young college graduate of affluent background who was reduced to a life of prostitution and thievery to support her habit.

While these films showed youth as demeaning life, another group of films on the hippie-trippy rituals of the young showed a joyous outlook on living. These dealt with the phenomenon of rock music, that great uniting force first bestowed on the youth of the world by the Beatles, and which came to have its ultimate expression in such mammoth outdoor gatherings as those depicted by *Monterey Pop* (1967) by D. A. Pennebaker and *Woodstock* (1970) by Michael Wadleigh. The rock festivals of the sixties were extraordinary events — celebrations of the joy of rock, dancing, pot, peace, lovemaking, and, most of all, a transcendental togetherness that came to symbolize the classic microcosm of youth culture at its zenith. The films *Monterey Pop* and *Woodstock* are memorable because they captured all that, and as such are unique artifacts of an era that Max Lerner called "the too-much decade."

For all its excesses, American youth deserves everlasting credit for its passionate and courageous fight against the shame of the Vietnam war. It was the young — campaigning in Washington, in the streets, in the schools, in the homes, in jails, and even within the armed services — who forced a turnaround in the American attitude toward the war. Vietnam, the "living room war," became the best reported war in history, thanks, of course, to television. But the nightly news clips of death and destruction, by their frequency, served only to dull the sensitivity of most viewers. Even such unforgettable news films as Morley Safer's report of American troops setting fire to the homes of South Vietnamese farmers evoked little reaction.

Independent American filmmakers were slow to take issue with the Government's position. In part, it was because the White House and the Pentagon had done such a good job of beclouding the issues.

In part, it was fear of antagonizing these powerful forces. In part, it was fear of being assailed by the public as unpatriotic, of giving "aid and comfort to the enemy." As the Johnson Administration escalated the war, bumper stickers with the slogan "Support Our Boys in Vietnam" were everywhere and the peace demonstrations of the "flower children" often were broken up by fist-swinging patriots. One of the first critical films to appear was *Faces of Imperialism* (1967) by the former CBS correspondent David Schoenbrun, a brilliant and articulate newsman whose sense of outrage propelled him into a one-man campaign to end the war. His film, based on scholarly research but persuasive in its presentation, was a bitter condemnation of foreign incursions into Southeast Asia.

Time of the Locust (1967) by Peter Gessner employed combat footage from international sources juxtaposed with the statements of American officials to reveal the callousness of American policy. *In the Year of the Pig* (1969) by Emile de Antonio also used war footage from international sources, together with material from television companies, to expose contradictions in pronouncements by American military leaders, and to show, within a succinct historical framework, the cynicism of the military.

A number of filmmakers went into combat zones to show what the one- or two-minute news reports could not show — what it really means to live, day after day, with the fear of violent death. In two of these films, *The Anderson Platoon* (1967) by a former Life correspondent, Pierre Schoendorffer, and *A Face of War* (1968) by Eugene Jones, the camera accompanied an American platoon on a mission to destroy an enemy that is never visible. The grave reality of war in this strange, hostile country was the central concern of both films. There was no attempt to editorialize. The images were allowed to speak for themselves: the faces of the men as they fought, or trudged wearily along jungle paths, or sprawled exhausted on the grass to eat their rations, or suddenly died.

Another dimension to the tragedy of the Vietnam war was provided by *Inside North Vietnam* (1967). Made by Felix Greene, who made *China*, the film told the story of the war from the point of view of the adversary. Here, too, the core of the film was the effect of the conflict on individuals. People from all walks of life — including a farmer whose family had been killed in an air raid and a nurse whose hospital had been bombed out — recounted in personal terms the pain of war. Like the other two documentaries the film was not designed to argue the case for one ideology or the other, but to show the suffering that people inflict upon people.

The flood of events which gave urgency to documentary filmmaking in the sixties was accompanied by a sharp break in the mode of documentary expression itself. Until that time, the doctrine that had characterized the genre and shaped its development had largely materialized from Grierson's principle that documentary was "the dramatization of actuality." This criterion had unquestionably enabled the film of fact to achieve a genuinely independent form and it conspicuously motivated some of the best works in the genre and in the art of film itself.

Then early in the decade another kind of documentary began to emerge. It showed a revolutionary technique, a distinctive style, and a commitment to subject matter that ranged from an intimate form of journalism to a heightened form of theatricality. It was called *cinéma-vérité*, "truth film," so named by Jean Rouch, a French anthropologist and filmmaker, to describe the kind of film that recorded life directly, without rearrangement or staging of any kind.

The name *cinéma-vérité*, as well as its intention, was ostensibly derived from the theories of Dziga Vertov, the Soviet cameraman-director who in 1922 had defined his documentary credo as "kino-pravda," film truth. It denoted a type of documentary film that photographed reality without any preconceived notions — either of shooting or arranging it. Truth was to be achieved by a direct encounter with uncontrolled life where the camera — in a figurative sense — set out to discover the genuineness of a particular human scene.

Vertov's philosophy of documentary had little effect on his contemporaries. It was television, years later, that provided the impulse for the successful development of this kind of film. Years of effort to achieve a more elastic style of film journalism and to give the viewer a stronger sense of "being there," eventually led to a film approach that sought to present objective appraisals of events and personalities with immediacy, deeper insight, more speed, and at comparatively low cost. Out of such considerations, came the prerequisites, the opportunity, and the technique for *cinéma-vérité*.

Because *cinéma-vérité* took its shape and quality from the actual, spontaneous sequence of action and sound as they occurred at the moment of recording, new motion picture equipment had to be developed that would free the medium from the inconveniences of cumbersome apparatus and large technical crews. The conventional heavy, blimped camera and sound recording units were inflexible, costly, awkward, and totally unsuitable for the kind of movie that sought to capture the emotional truth of unstaged human situations quickly, candidly, and with a sense of immediacy or directness. The convention of "setting up" each shot for the camera and the sound recorder made it difficult, if not impossible, to film the way events take place in real life.

By the late fifties however, technological advances produced a lightweight, handheld reflex motion picture camera and compact, miniaturized tape recorders, both powered by small battery units that enabled synchronized pictures and dialogue to be recorded quickly, easily, and at low cost. What's more, the new equipment required only a crew of two — and, if necessary, could be handled by one person. The gain in mobility and flexibility allowed the film-maker for the first time to enter directly — but without intruding — into the very heart of the situation he was documenting. Instead of staging or directing the subject, the subject was allowed to lead the camera and shape its own coherence at the very time of shooting, with action following action naturally. The result was a strong feeling of immediacy and involvement that transmitted to an audience a keen sense of participation.

The first expression of the new documentary style in the United States was by a group of young filmmakers called the Drew Associates, made up of Richard Leacock, Robert Drew, D. A. Pennebaker, and Albert Maysles. Their first *vérité* film, which was made for television, was *Primary* (1960), a record of the Wisconsin campaigns of Kennedy and Humphrey. This was followed by a series of Time-Life productions, the "Living Camera," which included *Eddie Sachs* (1960), *Jane* (1962), *Petey and Johnny* (1962), *Crisis* (1963), and *The Chair* (1963). In this series the Drew group refined the technique of *cinéma-vérité* to give it a special ability to impart arresting observations, intense atmosphere, and a high degree of characterization, particularly of individuals under stress. Even though these documentaries dealt with real people in real situations, much of what was recorded — because of "significant happenings" — had the effect of compelling fiction.

The films of the Drew Associates gave an enormous impetus to the further development of *cinéma-vérité*. Prominent among the films utilizing the technique were Arthur Zegart's *The Battle of Newburgh* (1962) and *The Business of Gambling* (1963); Arthur Barron's and Don Horan's *My Childhood: Hubert Humphrey's South Dakota and James Baldwin's Harlem* (1964); Gene Marner's (with Arthur Barron) *Birth and Death* (1968); William Jersey's *Manhattan Battleground* (1963), *Prisoner At Large* (1963), and *A Time For Burning* (1966), and Frederick Wiseman's *The Titicut Follies* (1967), *Law and Order* (1969), *High School* (1969), and *Hospital* (1970). All were sharply individualized, deeply absorbing and unusually persuasive. In the best of them there was a purity of tone, a clarity of purpose, and a great depth of feeling that testified to the intensity and versatility of *cinéma-vérité*. Together with the Drew Associates, these filmmakers seemed responsive in their various ways to the new documentary vision and cohered, at least on the home screen, into something like a *vérité* movement.

After becoming a dominant trend of major television documentaries, *cinéma-vérité,* or "direct cinema" as it soon was to be called, began to appear on the screens of first-run motion picture theaters in large cities. There a more exciting use of the technique was made by feature-length documentaries. These aimed at establishing dramatic continuity, without plot or storyline, by recording the "reality" inherent in human personality and human relationships.

Five films that drew heavily on the values of *cinéma-vérité* were developed by the simple device of showing an individual in the normal conduct of his life. The main line of this cinematic thrust was laid down by Wolf Koenig's and Roman Kroitor's *Lonely Boy* (1961), which explored the absurdities that went into creating the public image of a teen-age idol, singer Paul Anka. This was followed by the Maysles brothers' *Showman* (1962), a portrait of the mercurial film mogul Joseph E. Levine which, however, was somewhat less incisive than the fictional characters he himself put on the screen. D. A. Pennebaker's *Don't Look Back* (1967) was a more skillfully etched picture of singer-composer Bob Dylan, revealing a withdrawn personality against the temptuous background of a successful concert tour through England.

Two other films, appearing within weeks of each other in 1969, were concerned with a side of American life far removed from the glamour and excitement of show business. The Maysles brothers' *Salesman* and David Hoffman's *King, Murray* both revealed, with rare intimacy, the lives of two pitchmen. The first was a lonely and forlorn door-to-door Bible salesman who plied his trade with a persistence and guile born of desperation. The second was a boisterous and crude, but successful, insurance agent — compulsively fast-talking, fast-moving, and on a never-ending ego trip. Both films induced strong viewer reaction: a mixture of pity and revulsion for the Bible salesman, and unmitigated revulsion for the latter.

In all five films, the intimacy and bare-boned honesty of *cinéma-vérité* provided some absorbing insights of character. At times the viewer had the sensation of spying through a keyhole at private and uninhibited acts. But overall what ultimately emerged — despite the disclosures of some fundamental truths about the human condition — was the realization that it was not enough for filmmakers to be committed to so inflexible and ingenuous a belief in the significance of surface details and to trust so implicitly in chance to gain an imaginative coherence.

Less constricted were the theatrical releases of a Canadian, Allan King, whose films, *Warrendale* (1968) and *A Married Couple* (1970), rose above the bric-a-brac of mere observation.

The power of *cinéma-vérité* to seize the immediate, the extemporaneous, the unexpected, and, with these unstructured elements, to build dramatic impact became especially clear in *Warrendale,* a grim study of a center for emotionally disturbed children. Nightmarishly enacted before the camera were the haunting fears, the convulsive outbursts, the bitter truths of mental illness, made all the more intense for the viewer because the victims were children. The grinding pain of the reality was so overwhelming that the Canadian Broadcasting Corporation, which had commissioned the film, refused to show it. (It was shown, eventually, in a small number of U.S. theaters.)

King's *A Married Couple* was a far more difficult film to make. It was concerned with a marriage in crisis — the conflicts and tensions of a young couple struggling to keep their marriage from falling apart. The husband and wife in the film were not actors, but a real couple, friends of the director. During the course of the shooting their marriage actually came close to dissolving, aptly providing theme and form for the movie.

Here, as in *Warrendale,* the filmmaker's strategy was not to intervene, not to direct, not to ask or require anything from the observed couple, but to "allow them to take any initiative they might wish to take." For months King and his crew worked at all hours of the day and night as silent observers, photographing and recording whatever they were doing and saying, but never communicating with them. King's purpose was merely to remove the walls from the home of a single married couple and thereby reveal a universal truth — the inexorability of conflict between two sensitive, independent souls locked into a relationship decreed by polite society. By and large the technique of *cinéma-vérité* served the director's commitment well, not only in isolating the normal tensions arising from a marriage but also in revealing the intimate personality characteristics of these two individuals and the small incidents that brought frustration and bitterness to their relationship. To this extent the searching eye of the camera made its points without artful inflation. Inherent in this technique, however, was a shortcoming. The effort to maintain a rising dramatic interest from insistently literal and mundane actions, without the ability to probe the nuances of these actions, diminished the final result.

In France, *cinéma-vérité* shifted away from the explorations of individuals under stress to a critical examination of the milieu in which people moved. Jean Rouch, an anthropologist, and Chris Marker, a poet and essayist, had each developed a quietly personal idiom in numerous shorts. Their first features in *cinéma-vérité* style, done independently, both dealt with the simple objective of finding out what Parisians were thinking and feeling about the human condition.

Rouch's *Chronicle of a Summer* (1961), made in collaboration with Edgar Morin, a sociologist, approached this objective by stopping random people on the street and asking if they were happy. Follow-up interviews of these people were conducted at weekly intervals, with the questions probing deeper and deeper into their personal problems and their views on world problems. Finally, the subjects of the interviews were shown on the film and given opportunity to express any further thoughts they might have. These comments were incorporated into the finished film. *Chronicle of a Summer* was talky and fragmented and almost without form, but its *cinéma-vérité* style gave it a freshness that made it arresting.

A *cinéma-vérité* documentary of even greater power and virtuosity was Chris Marker's *Le Joli Mai* (1963). Like Rouch's film, it involved a probing into the lives of random Parisians and the social forces imposed on them. But there the similarities between the two films ended. Marker's film was made during the month of May 1962 (two years after the Rouch film), a significant and transitional month in French history. It was the "first spring of peacetime" since 1939. It was the month of Salan's trial, the end of the Algerian war, the ending of the OAS demonstrations and the big railroad strike. It was a time still haunted by a troubled past, but with a future that held hope for tranquility and progress. This sense of movement was the core of *Le Joli Mai*'s vision and gave it an essential distinction.

In his earlier shorts, which dealt with travels to far-off lands, Marker had developed a poetic talent augmented by a far-ranging erudition and a sharp wit. These qualities were strikingly integrated in *Le Joli Mai*. He depicted not the tourist bureau's Paris, but the Paris of the "unfree" — a clothing salesman, a clerk, a house painter, a black student, a young couple wanting to get married, an Algerian worker. With a camera that explored every facet of their personality, the people were deftly interviewed to reveal their political confusions, their small ambitions, their capitulation to an oppressive city life. These images were counterpointed with those of the city itself — gloomy, forbidding, and yet the loveliest in the world — to add insights of social and psychological data to the searching persistence of the interrogation.

The second half of the film dealt with news events aimed as a comment on the vulnerability and lack of sophistication of the people interviewed in the first section. Here swift images of police clashes, demonstrators marching in mourning, the violent responses to the acquittal of Salan, the massive railroad and Renault strikes, night club revelry, and other newsreel-like images with social resonance, summarized like a fever chart the social system and the ideas of those who felt themselves "unfree" to question its power.

Le Joli Mai had an incredible quality of cohesiveness despite its diversified nuances, parentheses, thoughts, and qualifications. Metaphors and images flashed and sparkled and interwove a film of patterned expressiveness. Yet there was no stiffness or pedantry in its ordered, rhythmic vision. Its substance, its texture, its mingling of forms in a documentary totality and its scrupulous concern for style, made it the decade's most distinguished example of the flexibility, vitality, and art of *cinéma-vérité*.

The Question of Reality
by Satyajit Ray

This selection by the world-famous director of the "World of Apu" films, originally appeared in "Four Times Five," a 1969 publication of the Films Division of India's Ministry of Information and Broadcasting.

Grierson once defined the documentary as "the creative interpretation of reality." I have often wondered if this was not a little misleading; because the question that immediately arises from the definition is: What is reality? Surely it is not only what constitutes the tangible aspects of everyday existence. Subtle and complex human relationships, which many of the best fiction films deal with, are also as much a part of reality as those other aspects generally probed by documentary makers. Even fables and myths and fairy tales have their roots in reality. Krishna, Ravana, Aladdin, Cinderella, Jack the Giant Killer—all have their prototypes in real life. Therefore, in a sense, fables and myths are also creative interpretations of reality. In fact, all artists in all branches of non-abstract art are engaged in the same pursuit that Grierson has assigned exclusively to the makers of documentary films.

Potemkin is ostensibly about a naval mutiny that took place in Russia in 1905. In filming it, Eisenstein took wide liberties with recorded facts. Many of the most telling details in the film are invented. The massacre by the white cossacks didn't take place on the Odessa steps at all. So the setting of the most famous sequence in the film may be said to be fictional. Moreover, Eisenstein cast the film in the mould of the 5-act Greek drama; and yet, in shooting it he used the methods of the documentary.

Is *Potemkin* then fact or fiction? Or does it fall between two stools? I personally think that the film will never pass muster as a faithful account of a historical event, but as a creative interpretation of a naval mutiny, it will remain a valid and artistic statement.

When Flaherty went to the South Sea islands to make a documentary, he found that the native women had given up wearing grass skirts and had taken to cotton dresses. This clashed with his romantic preconception about the Tahitian women, and he promptly ordered grass skirts to be made for the women to wear in the film. The reality of *Moana*, therefore, is the subjective reality of Flaherty's preconception about Tahiti, and not of actual Tahitian life.

Due largely to TV, and more latterly to *cinéma-vérité* and other allied schools of filmmaking, the notion of preconception is on the way out. The thing to do now is to plunge straight into the heart of the subject. One of the common methods employed is the dogged pursuit of an individual (often a celebrity) with camera and microphone, recording his action and speech, both trite and significant. The footage is finally given some coherence by judicial selection and assemblage. The method raises obvious doubts. Leaving aside primitive people, and people in a traumatic state or a state of extreme intoxication, it is hard to imagine anybody being in a position to completely ignore the existence of instruments which hover around him, recording for posterity his words and deeds which are not primarily meant to be so recorded.

If he does it well, it proves he is a good actor. If not, he betrays a self-consciousness which gives the game away. And since acting of some sort is involved either way, the *vérité* aspect automatically comes under suspicion.

The Face to Face technique also presents problems. How can we ever be sure that an interviewee is making honest statements and not merely saying what he believes is the right thing to say? To me the really significant things that emerge from spot interviews are the details of people's behavior and speech under the scrutiny of the camera and the microphone.

Half the time I'm inclined to disbelieve what they are saying, but at all times I am fascinated by how they say it. The sharpest revelations of truth in the cinema come from details perceived through the eyes of artists. It is the sensitive artist's subjective approach to reality that ultimately matters, and this is true as much of documentaries as of fiction films.

Details can make both of them real, in the same way to the same degree, while lack of details can turn both into dead matter, in spite of all the surface verisimilitude that camera and microphone can impart. I like Sukhdev's *India '67* but not for its broad and percussive contrasts of poverty and affluence, beauty and squalor, modernity and primitivity—however well shot and cut they may be. I like it for its details—for the black beetle that crawls along the hot sand, for the street dog that pees on the parked bicycle, for the bead of perspiration that dangles on the nosetip of the begrimed musician.

The Fiction of Fact — and the Fact of Fiction
by Arthur Schlesinger, Jr.

*This selection is reprinted from the January 1964 issue of Show
magazine (New York), for which the historian turned film critic.*

One of the most questionable words in the vocabulary of film is
"documentary." It seems an honest, weatherbeaten word, conveying
the feeling that here, at last, there is no nonsense, no faking, only
the plain facts. Opposed to the documentary is the unlabeled and
dubious category of the fiction film, presumably given over to fantasy and falsehood.

Yet a moment's reflection suggests that the line between the
documentary and the fiction film is tenuous indeed. Both are artifacts; both are contrivances. Both are created by editing and selection. Both, wittingly or not, embody a viewpoint. The fact that one
eschews and the other employs professional actors becomes in the
end an economic detail. And the relation of any film to reality depends, not on the amateur standing of its elements, but on the artistic vision of those who must put the elements together.

I would be ashamed to utter these obvious thoughts except for
the continued impression that the word "documentary" implies a
superior degree of artistic purity. So we have this month a Swedish
documentary film, assembled by Tore Sjöberg, called *The Face of
War*. It purports to tell the story of the evolution in the twentieth century of man's capacity—and desire—to kill his fellow man. And it
pretends to tell this story in a frank, straightforward way, using old
newsreels and official films made by warring countries. Nothing is
staged, nothing re-enacted, nothing up anyone's sleeve. Yet the film
is as much a piece of argumentation and manipulation as any fiction
from Hollywood.

Inherently this had to be so. No one can compress the mass
murder of the twentieth century into two hours of film without criteria of selection; and selection is just another word for interpretation. Moreover, the American distributor has provided the film with
a spoken commentary to pound the argument home. The fact that
the argument is confused does not make the film any more "objective." The film's emotional premise is that all war is the unnecessary
consequence of human vanity and stupidity. World War I thus took

place because the Serbs killed an Austrian archduke and because "everybody loves a parade." This may be a defensible view of World War I, but it is hard to demonstrate that World War II was unnecessary and absurd, nor does the film try to do so. As a result, it is caught in a logical trap between its basic assumption that all wars are unnecessary and its tacit admission that some wars may have had their point.

A suspicious observer might detect a certain tendentiousness in its approach. The Soviet-Nazi pact, for example, goes unmentioned, as does the Soviet attack on Finland and the Communist participation in the Spanish Civil War. But the film is not Marxist; it is rather fuzzily pacifistic, as the insistent and jejune commentary makes abundantly clear. Its essential fallacy lies in its belief that war as a subject can be usefully separated from the issues which bring war about. The repetition, with heavy irony, of the "everybody loves a parade" line does not really supply a very profound explanation of the causes of war.

The pictures themselves are inescapably impressive and have been arranged with ingenuity and skill. There is little more fascinating than early newsreels. *The Face of War* has a wonderful selection —Maxim in bowler hat firing an early machinegun mounted on huge wheels, or the crowds swarming wildly across the streets of Petrograd during the Bolshevik Revolution. But, as the film approaches our own day, it begins to reach a point of diminishing return. The images of modern war are, in an awful sense, hackneyed. We have seen them too often—the bombs dropping from the plane, the tanks crashing their way through the woods, the submarine sighting a convoy. It is no good to say that one *should* still react; it is up to artist to renew the experience with freshness and intensity, and this Sjöberg fails to do. *The Face of War* concludes by doing what it seeks to condemn: it converts death into a statistic. Except for the Hiroshima footage at the very end, the last half of the film seems closer to stereotype than to felt experience.

The Most, the exciting Canadian film about Hugh M. Hefner, the publisher of Playboy, provides another example of the tendentiousness of the documentary. *The Most* pursues Mr. Hefner on his daily round, portraying him at work and at play, in moments of somber contemplation, of high-flown philosophizing, and of joyous exhilaration. Gordon Sheppard's direction and Donald Ginsberg's editing are brilliant, and Dudley Moore's score provides an appropriate and sardonic counterpoint. It is funny—and yet, though it is all in a sense "true," it has little to do with objective truth.

The fact that Mr. Hefner evidently collaborated with such enthusiasm in his own self-immolation does not alter the fact that the film is designed to make him look ridiculous—and succeeds savagely in doing so. The technique is simple and devastating: show a Playboy editor talking in his office about Hefner; then cut to the same man, a cigarette trickling out of the corner of his mouth, twisting at a Hefner party; then cut back to the office; and everything further the editor may say becomes ludicrous. Perhaps Hefner deserves this treatment. But if a team of documentary filmmakers had followed John the Baptist long enough, zeroed in when his guard was down, and cut the result with sarcasm as the main object, he could have been made to look pretty foolish, too.

Documentaries and Dollars

by Lou Hazam

This selection by Mr. Hazam, the well-known producer-writer of TV documentaries, appeared in the Winter 1963 issue of Television Quarterly.

The millennium of TV film documentaries has not yet arrived. Perhaps it never will. But the giant strides that television has recently made in this field promise, in the years immediately ahead, a steady growth in the number of documentary programs which will not only increase public understanding, but make a significant contribution to the art of filmmaking as well.

Much has been made of Mr. Newton Minow's contribution to a renewed emphasis upon documentary. (Mr. Minow at the time of this writing was chairman of the Federal Communications Commission.) We, too, agree that it has been great. But long before he appeared on the scene the networks were aware of the need to present more, and better, documentaries. At my own network (and I do not discount the remarkable achievements at other networks) *The Way of the Cross* was completed before the famous Minow speech, and *Vincent Van Gogh: A Self-Portrait* was begun and well underway before he launched his assault. Yet one must still agree that he is probably the documentarian's best friend—simply by dint of waiting off-stage.

But while Mr. Minow may be a force in assuring the continued presentation of documentaries, he can do little about their quality. The two factors, it seems to us, that are most responsible for the steadily maturing art of TV documentary are sufficient money to make them, and sponsors willing to buy them.

It is ridiculous to assume that on one day almost no one knew how to fashion a worthwhile documentary, and on the next almost everyone did. All of us had marched quite a way along the road to learning about documentaries before the medium encouraged us to do what we knew we could do. But without a doubt, money alone spelled a good deal of the difference between *knowing how* and *being able* to do the job.

Who would have believed, only a few years ago, that we would ever be given $100,000 to produce a television documentary? Yet in this season alone four of our NBC projects are budgeted at over this figure. You can do many things with a hundred thousand that you cannot do with twenty, and we are getting this money today because network officials have finally come to recognize that, with few exceptions, any true quality in production requires it.

And not only the networks have come upon this realization. Not so long ago, even a prayer couldn't unearth a sponsor of a TV documentary. It was believed that the audience for such programs was infinitesimal—so small as not to be worthy of serious attention. Today, on every network, few major documentaries take to the air without sponsorship. Sponsors have discovered that the audience is far more significant than they had imagined, not only in numbers but in composition. This has been a tremendous boon to documentarians. For while it is true more often than not that the networks fail to recover their full production costs from these sales, they nevertheless recoup some part of production costs and generally get their full price for the time sale—just as they do with "Wagon Train."

What specific improvements in the documentary art has all of this permitted? First, with so much at stake, we are given real encouragement by our employers. In the "old days" we were merely suffered, but now we are given more time to prepare a program. Money can pay for the needed time.

We are now able to range the world with our cameras, and are thus no longer forced to depend on what we can find in film libraries. In addition, correspondents—able, albeit expensive creatures—are often sent with us as observers-on-the-spot for news documentaries. This is a marked departure from simply stepping into a studio a few days before show time to "recite" a script against film which correspondents had no part in making.

The new budgets have enabled us to afford the services of imaginative cameramen, knowledgeable directors, and excellent writers. Many times, previously, we were sent out to make film documentaries with live-program directors who knew little of filmmaking techniques, and with news-cameramen who had previously shot little more than two-minute news sequences of fires, accidents, or sound-on-film statements from Congressmen emerging from hearings in Washington.

We are now able to hire researchers—recognized experts in their fields—to study a subject before we pursue it, and to inform and advise us. And, happily, we can often survey locations before we actually arrive at them.

We are now permitted to shoot more than just minimum film requirements, and select from this wealth of film the particularly good footage we need to fashion the best show. This permits us to enjoy that wonderful tool—"choice."

We can now send that once lowly, abused, and suspected person, the script-writer, out into the field, where he can "see" for himself, "sense" his story, and help create it on the spot. This enables him to endow his scripts with much more believability. Finally, the increases in budgets have enabled us to shoot in color if we wish.

But perhaps nowhere is the new aspect of the TV film documentary more clearly evident than in the knowledgeable use of filmmaking techniques. Now sufficiently supported by budget, more than anything else on the technical side they are serving to transform the once-plodding documentary—primitive in treatment and bereft of artistry—into an absorbing slice of life.

Rarely, for example, does today's TV documentary commit the unpardonable sin of talking its audience to death. Whole sequences are visually planned to speak for themselves—telling the story through a moving assortment of related shots, each planned to succeed the other in such a way that words are not needed at all. Gone forever are the scenes of white oxen in India pulling a plow while the narrator (voice over—as if hastening to serve up his conglomeration of facts before the picture gives out) runs the entire gamut of statistics on Indian agriculture, presenting facts which have little or no relationship to what is being witnessed on the screen. Instead, today's filmmakers shoot specific material which covers each important point being made by the narrator—i.e., the types of agriculture being practiced, the workers in the field, their home life, the economic result of their efforts, and so on.

Filmmaking techniques are maturing as rapidly in the editing room as in the field. Whatever estimates we make of the date when a film will be ready for airing will allow generously for editing time. This permits the most careful selection and use of each frame of footage, giving us time to try a variety of options in approach to an individual sequence before deciding upon the best one.

At one time, TV film editors were often regarded as technicians whose job required little artistry. Now the editor—at least among the knowing—is given a voice in the final decision on each sequence, and he often contributes the basic idea that takes the work beyond the mere "stringing together" of film which advances the story. In

The Way of the Cross, editor Connie Gochis—nominated for an Emmy for his work last season—created the sequence of the convulsed world, that followed upon the crucifixion of Jesus, with film "run-outs" from the end of each reel—footage that the cameraman and director never, in their wildest imaginings, might have considered to be useful.

This brings us to the abstract use of film—something seen quite often in one-reel art films, but rarely on TV. Not only in *The Way of the Cross,* but in *Vincent Van Gogh: A Self-Portrait* (for his insane spells) and in *Shakespeare: Soul of an Age* (for the witches in "Macbeth") we ventured into this area, particularly to treat ideas that could not be handled by a normal, straightforward use of camera. Today, our cameramen are instructed and encouraged to give us footage of this type when they feel it is called for and can be useful to us in the editing room. This freedom has resulted in such creative innovations as Scott Berner filming Miami at night with an exciting made-in-the-camera super-imposition for *U.S. #1,* and Guy Blanchard creating the "Macbeth" witches out of water bubbles and light reflection. In short, we are no longer fearful of such film.

Two other points are worth mentioning—both reflecting the dollar's contribution to documentary's new look.

First, music. With increased budgets we now have the wherewithal to pay a composer for a hand-tailored, original musical score. This is of singular importance, since music is that essential ingredient which serves to combine all the diverse units of a program and weld them into a single entity. It establishes mood, creates effects, accents important points, and carries the viewer from one scene to the next in the proper spirit. Formerly, music was regarded simply as "background" and was selected from those records or tapes for which clearance was available.

Today, however, those seeking to make films of stature enjoy much greater latitude in music use. The music is constantly improving in such documentaries, contributing considerably more than just "background." Since the composer is forced to write to exact time—10 seconds here, 12 seconds there, up 3 seconds, segue to a new theme and under narration for one minute and twenty-eight seconds, etc.—his is an especially difficult creative enterprise. But many composers have learned to do it and do it well, despite the handicaps we have imposed upon them. In addition, producers and editors have learned to cut entire film sequences to music— often fitting the picture to the score, rather than the reverse, and thereby sometimes securing an added effectiveness that would never come from simply dropping in music after all else is fixed and immutable.

And the dollars have led to a second important innovation in the TV documentary—its stars, men of performing ability who can command a public in their own right. Given money, we are now able to hire their talents to help us, thereby escaping the need to use announcers, or newsmen narrating film that has nothing to do with news. Thus, Lee J. Cobb gave us a memorable Vincent Van Gogh, and his performance was matched by an equally facile Martin Gabel, who narrated the program. Van Heflin accompanied us along highway *U.S. #1,* and his on-the-scene voiced-sentiments might, on other lips, have created far less impact. James Mason guided us 4,000 miles up the Nile; Sir Ralph Richardson presented our Shakespeare show, with Sir Michael Redgrave voicing the excerpts from the plays. Without Sir Michael, or a performer of equal stature, and forced to rely upon the questionable abilities once assigned to us, our program on Shakespeare literally would have been impossible.

There is nothing new about stars on TV, but there is something decidedly new about stars on documentaries. Normally, of course, the public expects the star always to be seen on camera, but our star usually is not seen—simply heard. Yet we have had no complaints. And aside from the high talent they bring to bear in our behalf, they often draw audiences to our documentaries because of their name-value alone—attracting many people who would not ordinarily watch such fare. They "dress up" the new documentary, and give it a totally different flavor from some of the undistinguished presentations of the past.

These, then, are some of the reasons why the TV film documentary is maturing, and some examples of how it has matured.

Do we continue to have problems? Of course. Few enterprises in TV are conducted in an atmosphere of sweet peace. Creative people, as a consequence of the arrangement of their genes, are often emotional people—impatient with rules and rebellious by nature. Administrative people, of necessity, are a generally rules-abiding people—conformists by nature. Maintaining the bridge between both is sometimes a difficult and trying job for the producer—himself invariably a hybrid. The conflict between the desire to produce a work of artistic distinction and the more understandable, and acceptable, need to produce a commercial success endures, but is slowly breaking down in face of repeated evidence that both can be accomplished in one and the same show.

Finally, the production schedule in documentaries—as with similar schedules throughout TV—is rarely considered inviolate. Normal and unforeseen business developments will repeatedly confound it, and much energy is spent in fighting to preserve the essential time needed for a proper job.

To these one might add many other trials and tribulations. We are plagued by such questions as "Why does it take so long to write script?" (Often we shoot from a treatment and no script at all, for lack of time.) Or "Why don't you go for a finished fiilm the first time around, instead of proceeding through such slow and laborious stages?" (There's a phrase for you—"the first time around!") Or "Is all that editing-overtime really necessary?" The list is endless.

Despite all this, every network continues to press forward with documentaries—producing and presenting the kind of factual shows which at one time not long ago were only fond dreams. At the same time the old saw about documentaries never being able to draw "the kind of audience" a plot-construction type of show draws is being put to bed. In our own experience, for example, our *Nile* program, we were told in hallowed tones by those who fill their day with such scripture, drew a "30-market multi-network Nielsen Rating" 33% share of the audience, outrating such formula fare as "The Untouchables," "Naked City," "Combat," and "Hawaiian Eye."

But perhaps the most surprising testament to the documentary's new status was evidenced in the 1961 Emmy Awards. Three documentaries—those Cinderellas of the "yore" of television—competed with such programs as "The Judy Garland Show" and "Victoria Regina" for the top prize "Best Show of the Year." They were *Walk in My Shoes* (ABC), *Biography of a Bookie Joint* (CBS), and *Vincent Van Gogh: A Self-Portrait* (NBC)—one from each of the major networks. No, none of them won. But the fact that they were nominated indicates that the documentary, like the automobile, is here to stay—thanks to the combination of the money made available by enlightened networks, intelligent sponsors, an eager new public, and a friendly Mr. Minow. "Smile heaven upon this fair conjunction. . . ."

Historic Hearings: From TV to Screen
by Daniel Talbot

This selection on the TV documentary Point of Order!,
*reprinted from The New York Times of January 12, 1964,
was written by the co-producer of the film. Mr. Talbot is the
author of a film anthology and a New York film exhibitor.*

The question has come up on many occasions: Why a film on the
Army-McCarthy Senate hearings now? Hasn't the atmosphere
changed since 1954 when the hearings took place, and, if so, why
resurrect that spectral age that crippled the minds of so many
Americans?

For a few years now we have been reading about the swift rise
in America of new radical-Right movements and figures. But, as
yet, no public figure has assumed the kind of power that Senator
McCarthy was able to wield in his day. So, why bring it up again
now?

In deciding to make *Point of Order!* it was our belief that the
television kinescopes of the hearings constituted one of the most
important political documents of our time. They are the key piece
of journalistic evidence in the drama of Right and Left politics that
we have been experiencing intensely these last ten years and that
appears to become even more intense with the emergence of the
radical Right.

How would we present this reorganized recapitulation of a
classic political struggle? We decided to keep the hero of the hearings: the TV cameras themselves. Even though these hearings were
watched daily by everybody, nobody, except for a handful, was in
a position to see every second on television, with the result that ten
years later we are all missing a scene here, a statement there. By
organizing the material of the hearings once more, cutting a wide
swath through 188 hours and by presenting everything critical that
happened, even though compressed, we felt that we could relive
authentically the life and meaning of that still important political
drama.

With the tenth anniversary of the hearings upon us, we have
already entered a new stage of American politics—to coin a word,
polimunications—the use of TV to project in depth personalities for
high offices. McCarthy was undoubtedly the first great star in this

new kind of mass political drama. With the coming election, this new form of political science will be as crucial a lever as it was in the preceding Presidential campaign. Here, in essence, is the point of not only the hearings but of all subsequent political airings over the tube: Show business has moved in on the technique of electing men to office.

The fact is, when we began our film we were extremely interested in the sheer theatricality of the hearings, which we configurated with those fascinating spring months of 1954, when more than twenty million Americans took many hours off every day from work and play to watch the action on television.

So now we have a movie called *Point of Order!*

"Point of Order!" "Point of Order!" "Mr. Chairman!" "Point of Order!" Those booming words have rung through the halls of our memory like some prophetic incantation! Our movie runs 97 minutes. The hearings ran 188 hours. Given such a rummage sale, our concern was not with presenting a minute-by-minute kaleidoscope of what happened. Rather, we undertook a characterological position toward our material. And, second, we wanted to make a "good show."

The project began three years ago. After several months of researching existing material on the hearings, testing footage for satisfactory 35mm blowup and concluding our arrangements for its acquisition, Emile de Antonio, my co-producer, and I began screening 16mm kinescopes in my apartment.

Our backgrounds varied. De Antonio, formerly a longshoreman, college philosophy teacher, barge captain, and prominent behind-the-scenes adviser to many famous American painters, had entered films by distributing the short subject, *Pull My Daisy*. Afterward, he produced a brilliant short called *Sunday*. My actual experience in filmmaking was nil, to the extent that I had never even seen a moviola prior to the making of our film. My background was strictly that of a viewer.

So we began screening at the house day and night for three months. When we were down to 12 hours, we thought we might book this stopgap film into local theaters (in effect, converting each theater into a local TV set) and charge $1 an hour or $5 for viewing this 12-hour film in its entirety. But we were worried that we would not be able to retain the full flavor of the hearings. Finally, when we had gotten down to three hours, the most important part of the pruning process was upon us: to arrive at a final cut in such a way that it would have sequential consistency, the historical feel of the hearings, a story sense, a point of view, and, hopefully, a sense of urgency.

It was at this point that we bogged down for a few months. And we also ran out of money. We decided that one of us would have to take over and make the final cut on a shoestring. It fell to de Antonio. Six months later he finished it in *his* apartment. We couldn't have been happier with the results. We were proud of not just the look of the film, but also its relevance to our scene today.

Chris Marker's *Le Joli Mai*
by Michael Kustow

*This selection is from Sight and Sound (London),
Spring 1964. Mr. Kustow is a British journalist.*

Chris Marker is a poet, a metaphysical poet in the strict sense of Dr. Johnson's definition: he yokes together the most heterogeneous ideas. Raw actuality and the most polished literary arabesques; a socialism infused with Popular Front fervor and a Left Bank aestheticism which sometimes verges on tweeness. Dr. Johnson complained about the violence with which disparates were yoked together by the Metaphysicals; we have made a similar criticism when we have complained in the past about the overplayfulness in some of Marker's work. But with *Le Joli Mai* he has made a film as comprehensive and lucid as a Donne poem; and, like the best of Donne, the film's audacities and conceits are welded into one by the freedom of its creator's personality.

"Pour faire du cinéma, il suffit de filmer des gens libres," says Godard. Marker's film is about free people in Paris in May 1962, "the first spring of peacetime." The Evian agreements had wound up the Algerian war in 1961: the last cries of France's long-drawn-out colonial agony echoed into *le joli mai*. But the country had come out of the dark tunnel, and new hopes were in the air. It was the month in which the final ritual obsequies, absurd and tragic—the last indignant demonstrations, the obligatory civic martyrs, the scandalous acquittal of Salan—had to be played out. After the deluge, the future was waiting; and Marker launched into his first full-length film to capture the grimaces of the past and the beckoning of things to come.

Le Joli Mai opens with a presentation of what is and always shall be: the city itself, Paris perceived in a panorama of rooftop landscapes, tranquil telephotos of distant crawling traffic, and Simone Signoret speaking a rich, tender eulogy by Giraudoux. Dull would he be of sight who could pass by such choice Olympian images. But Marker tweaks us out of this detachment into the first of his interviews—with a streetcorner clothing salesman whose nervous machinegun answers and obsession with "getting money in the till" set the rhythm of a whole set of characters who are driven by the city, whose very mannerisms, the way they use their hands, where their eyes go, betray their compulsive adapatation to its life.

These are the unfree people: the slum-dwellers in Aubervilliers (we see old people washing in the street while a commentator quotes an advertisement for luxury flats with Carrara marble facias); the two fifteen-year-old apprentice stockbrokers already aping the opinions of their elders; crabbed chauvinists outside the Bourse; the well-dressed caterpillars of the literary set releasing ceremonial doves from the roof of a posh apartment to celebrate a poetry prize; an inventor consumed with vanity; an uproarious lower-middle-class wedding party where all the guests are at least twenty years older than the married couple, and a great grainy close-up shows us the bride wincing at all the forced fun. *La mort saisit le vif.*

But Marker gives *le vif* its due. His interviewers deftly force the most pompous pundit to reveal his insufficiencies. And what the interviewers can't achieve, Marker looks after. The sequence outside the Bourse is shot with the utmost insolence, the camera wandering off into the crowd which has gathered to watch the interview, picking out a man who looks like Bernard Berenson and snatching an individual with cigar and dark glasses who's muttering, "They shouldn't be allowed to inerview minors." "Stop," says Marker, and sets up a new sequence (complete with clapper-board) in which the grumbler can give his point of view. Later, while the inventor is pontificating about Will and Success, the camera latches on to a daddy-long-legs crawling across his shirt, and once more Marker has used his aliveness to the instant moment to make a comment.

And the poet in Marker sets against this parade of stereotypes moments of liberation—the overjoyed mother who has just been given [public housing] showing it to her children for the first time; the woman in the slum who has stuck plastic flowers into her garden: "I put them in the garden until the others come up." The first part of the film ends with a soldier and his girl on a bridge, holding hands, scarcely daring to speak, their eyes lowered and their words hesitant, he incredibly young-looking, she like someone out of a thirties Carné film. "We believe in eternal happiness," says the soldier. But we know he must go to Algeria tomorrow, and can only see them as vulnerable, defenseless against the great events of the time.

Part Two thrusts us into the thick of these public events, and we begin to see why the interviews of Part One have harped so much on questions of political apathy and solidarity. A series of sharp Brechtian flashes show us *le plastiquage,* a police charge on February 9 which crushed eight people to death in the Métro, the half-million mourners at their funeral, the triumph of Salan, a railwaymen's strike, a strike at Renault's. In this part of the film Marker achieves a kind of anthropological quality, cutting newsreel-like shots of public events against two extraordinary dance sequences, which present the Madison and the twist as danced in Paris nightclubs. Here Michel Legrand's music, discordant as Thelonious Monk, pungently alienates the dancing, making us watch it like the rites of some strange tribe. This provides a poetic moment of summary, like the stills sequence in *Cuba, si!,* which asks: "What was the rest of the world talking about at this time? About people, countries, fabulous animals, about Algeria, France, America, space, time . . ." with Gagarin's face illustrating "space" and Eichmann's "time."

After such a summary the longer interviews with truly free people—"people free to question, to refuse, to undertake"—are all the more striking. Marker shows us two consulting engineers who voice one of the film's main themes: "Our dreams are too small for what already exists." We meet a wonderfully confident and humorous student from Dahomey who tells us with a great big smile on his face what a Negro in Paris feels like. Only his hands, which the camera watches clenched and striking the table, show the depth of feeling beneath the charm. The hands of the worker-priest who became a Communist militant, however, are open and accepting. Most disturbing of all is the Algerian worker who has stubbornly struggled through to his freedom against racism and brutality. The effort shows on him; he has only an icy, solitary freedom.

Marker draws back to sum up. He gives us a resting-point in the form of a speeded-up traffic sequence which is perhaps the one thing in the film that is old-style metropolis *Angst,* but he rises to a superb lyrical epilogue, centered on Fresnes Prison. Here Marker reveals that the whole film has been an attempt to see Paris as if through the eyes of a newly-released prisoner. All Marker's preoccupations —the future, the cosmos, a shared happiness, a shared suffering, death, art—are stated here, against *Hiroshima*-type tracking shots through dawn streets. We can now see the core of feeling that enabled Marker to order all the actuality he compiled. For he has made what he set out to make: a call to freedom.

Four Days in November
by John P. Hoggatt

*This trade review, which appeared in the weekly Variety
(New York), on October 7, 1964, was written in
Hollywood by a staff member of Daily Variety.*

With *Four Days in November,* David L. Wolper has produced a broad account of events of Nov. 22–25, 1963, that is solemn, sometimes majestic tribute to late President Kennedy.

Expertly pieced together from newsreel clips, footage by amateurs, some stockshots, and few scenes re-created for Wolper cameras, the documentary should hold great appeal for public, even though United Artists release tells little that's new.

Most striking plus value is suspense build-up, engendered by dramatic cutting back and forth between seemingly disparate scenes, which foreknowledge of events doesn't lessen. A minus rests in fact part of story could be depressing and painful for some, as when John Jr. salutes father's casket. More could be trimmed from 2-hour film, and occasionally script written by Theodore Strauss for narrator Richard Basehart—who described funeral as "some final act of purification"—gets sticky. Generally, it's restrained and factual.

Certain aspects of case highlighted in recent Warren Report aren't touched, particularly charges of poor coordination and rivalry of FBI and Secret Service. This data, made public long before report, logically could have been included, and spots existed for it in coverage of events leading up to fatal Nov. 22. No hint is given in this film that Dallas police were less than efficient, nor is mention made of Lee Harvey Oswald's trip to Mexico seeking Cuban visa or his earlier attempt to kill General Edward Walker. In view of Warren Report putting stamp of authenticity on these facts, they could be added before film is released.

Otherwise, producer-director Mel Stuart and film editor William T. Cartwright have created dramatic portrayal of recent history. Mood is set at opening as honor guard fires solemn 50-gun salute at state funeral. Then come words of John Kennedy, some hopeful, others prophetic ("this is not an easy job . . .").

Background of JFK's trip to Texas is told while film shuttles from politics to scenes of tranquil nation. Next comes step-by-step account of President's progress through Texas, along with contrasting scenes of Dallas newspaper maps of his route through city and close-up of Dallas Police Chief Curry, mindful of recent assaults on Adlai Stevenson, telling city "nothing must occur that is disrespectful to the President."

Effective device of camera panning through empty rooms of Oswald's boardinghouse and wife's home creates feeling of coming doom. Kennedy's happy speech in Fort Worth is shown, then pleasant ride past friendly crowds lining Dallas streets. Frequent shots of clocks ticking away toward 12:30 are interspersed with footage of procession.

Then in rapid succession come rifle shots, breakneck rush to hospital, pictures of growing crowds, and death announcement.

Remaining events of the four days are told in same fashion of suspense build-up and climax, including tracking down of Oswald, flight of body to Washington, succession to power of new President, Jack Ruby's slaying of Oswald, and finally the fitting, impressive state funeral. Through it all are sensitive shots of public reaction, U. S. and abroad, including a few tearful quotes from man-in-street interviews.

Footage was so well assembled that transitions from pro to amateur camerawork, from actual scenes to re-creations, were unnoticeable. Elmer Bernstein's score helped through rough spots.

Focus on Al Maysles
by Charles Reynolds

This article appeared in Popular Photography (New York), May 1964. Mr. Reynolds covers motion-picture news for the magazine.

Al Maysles does not have enough chairs in his Greenwich Village apartment for all the people he invites to a screening. So some sit on the floor, some stand, and several people lean against the side walls. His apartment is plain, painted white, with a small balcony used as a sleeping loft at one end. Under the balcony is the screen.

Actors, potential investors, museum directors, film distributors, magazine editors, television producers—all have gathered to see something revolutionary in motion pictures. Then the lights go out and a new Maysles film, *Showman*, starts on the screen. For the next 53 minutes the audience will live with top movie distributor-promoter Joe Levine, seeing and reacting to the real events of several months. They will see him as he negotiates for the release of his films; as he travels to Cannes to present the Oscar to Sophia Loren (an honor she has won for her performance in the Levine-distributed film, *Two Women*); as he speaks at a reunion of boyhood friends from the West End of Boston; as he argues (with David Susskind) about the art of the movies on a radio show; and in general as he wheels and deals his way through daily life surrounded by movie stars, fellow tycoons, yes-men and others involved in the unpredictable, glamorous, and high-pressure world of the movie mogul.

After the screening, the reactions will be many and varied. Some will see Joe Levine as a man having warmth that they would never have suspected; others will see the film as an uncompromising satirical portrait of a ruthless businessman; still others will be annoyed by the apparent formlessness of the film and will miss a dramatic structure which builds to a definite climax; a few will feel that they have had a revelation of personality and a glimpse at a new approach to filmmaking—one that has only begun to realize its potential.

Albert Maysles (pronounced MAY-suls), the maker of this controversial film, is a shaggy, soft-spoken 36-year-old ex-college instructor from Boston. The first minutes of conversation with him are most revealing. Secrets most others would hide, Maysles reveals if you just ask the right question. With him a "secret" is not a secret but a universal truth which he has uncovered, and he feels all are entitled to this information. He has learned much from others and others will learn from him—this is the way his world revolves. There is an intensity about him one finds in the talented few in photography. Searching for a comparison, one has to think of Robert Flaherty. Both have these traits in common: gentleness, self-confidence, and a unique dedication to and love for filmmaking. In talking about his kind of film, Maysles is both a powerful teacher and a missionary. One leaves him convinced that he knows what he's doing, he's right in doing it, and if one can help Maysles to do it, then one should.

Maysles's passion for recording life "as it actually happens" is equalled only by his sensitivity to the people and situations he films. If we accept John Grierson's much-quoted definition that documentary film is "the creative treatment of actuality," then we must place the work of Maysles solidly in the documentary tradition. It is, however, documentary with a difference. It is life observed by the camera rather than, as in the case of most documentaries, life re-created for it. To understand how this is achieved we must look at Maysles in action.

A Maysles documentary starts not with a plot but with the idea that a person or situation would be interesting to capture on film. If permission is granted to make the film, Al Maysles and his brother-and-partner David begin observing and shooting the subject. A specially built, blimped sound camera rests on Al's shoulders while David handles the sound which is synchronously recorded on a Nagra tape recorder. Unobtrusively, David aims a highly directional mike; sometimes one of the subjects may wear a second wireless mike under his clothing. The balance between the two mikes is then controlled by David during the recording process.

The situation is followed and anything which seems significant is filmed and recorded. Their rule is never to tamper, never to impose on what is before the camera, but to watch and wait and react freely, approaching the scene spontaneously without preconceived ideas. The movie camera is used in much the same manner as a 35mm photojournalist uses his miniature camera, and the success of the footage depends entirely on the spot judgment of the cameraman, his rapport with the subject and his sensitivity to the nuances of a situation as it naturally develops. The Maysles brothers work together as a closely knit team, one signaling the other as he senses that something significant is about to happen. The success of their approach depends on their ability to become part of the scene and be taken for granted so that the subject does not consciously "act" for the camera or modify his natural behavior.

The problem of remaining inconspicuous with a large camera balanced on one man's shoulder and with another man carrying a tape recorder and microphone (as well as the receiving equipment for a wireless mike) would seem to be formidable, if not insurmountable. The Maysles brothers have solved it neatly. As Al Maysles explains it:

"The problem of having people notice the camera is not as big as you might think. If you are overly concerned about the presence of the camera, the people you are filming will be concerned about it, too. The camera stays on my shoulder all the time and sometimes I am shooting with it and sometimes I am not. Since the camera is silent and it remains in the same position all day long, they can't tell. If they were to think about the camera all the time, they'd get very tired. It gets to be like part of the furniture in the room."

Al Maysles describes *Showman* as "a film about a man involved in something that is important to him." It is this involvement which also gives the film its true-to-life feeling. Joseph Levine is simply too involved in his day-to-day activities to be very concerned with whether or not someone is filming him. Thus we see, and interpret in our own terms, the real man as he lives his life.

Al Maysles has always been interested in two things, cameras and people. The first of these interests led to a lifelong hobby of photography and the second to his study of psychology in college and his job teaching psychology at Boston University. At age nine, his interest had been spurred by the purchase of a 35-cent Univex camera at a local hardware store, and before long he built his own enlarger from plywood and pipe and was avidly printing pictures. At the ripe old age of thirteen Maysles decided to give up photography until he could afford a Leica. By 1955 Maysles had gotten his Leica and was planning a trip to Russia. Although he had never handled a movie camera, he had the idea that he would like to make a 16mm movie on mental hospitals while he was in the Soviet Union. Before leaving the country he made a trip from Boston to New York and promptly wangled his way into an interview with a sympathetic CBS executive. CBS loaned him a 16mm Keystone camera with a 25mm fixed-focus lens and offered to pay him $1 a foot for any footage they could use. When he returned from Russia, they bought 20 feet of his footage and paid him $20 for it. The rest of the footage he made into a short film, and sold it to the drug firm of Smith, Kline and French for $2,500. Later the film was shown by the Canadian Broadcasting Company and on the NBC *Today* show. Al Maysles's career as a filmmaker was launched.

After making another film with his brother David (this time on *The Youth of Poland*), Al joined the firm of Drew Associates to make documentaries for television. It was while working for Drew, as one of the filmmakers of the documentary *Primary*, that he first got his hands on portable synch-sound equipment. Richard Leacock, the other cameraman on the production, had been developing a handheld camera that could be synchronized with a tape recorder without the use of any interconnecting cables. It was the design of this camera that gave Maysles the basic ideas for his own camera that he uses today.

After working as filmmaker on several films for Drew, Al Maysles decided in 1961 to join forces once again with his brother David (who had been assistant to the producer on features such as *Bus Stop* and *The Prince and the Showgirl*) and form their own company, Maysles Films, Inc. In addition to *Showman*, the Maysleses have made documentaries for television and a film celebrating the fiftieth anniversary of I.B.M.

What is revolutionary about the Maysles's films? First, of course, there is the approach. Documentary filmmakers have always aspired toward the ideal of the camera as an impartial and unobtrusive observer capturing the sight and sound of real life. Robert Flaherty made a tentative start in some scenes of *Louisiana Story*, but heavy and cumbersome sound equipment bogged him down. Fons Ianelli was an early pioneer in handheld synch-sound documentaries, with *The Young Fighter* and other films shown on television's *Omnibus*. Ianelli's system used a mechanical interlock between camera and recorder, but before long other filmmakers such as Morris Engel and Richard Leacock (who had been Flaherty's cameraman on *Louisiana Story*) were developing synch equipment in which the lightweight camera and tape recorder could be entirely separate from one another. Maysles's improvements on this camera and sound idea are three:

1. The Maysles camera balances correctly. Its weight is 30 pounds, but by positioning the magazines in the rear the camera is balanced when it rests on the shoulder and can be carried for extended periods of time—much longer than improperly balanced cameras of a fraction the weight. "Movie camera manufacturers are very concerned with camera engineering, but they are not concerned enough with human engineering," Maysles says.

2. You can see over the camera when you are not shooting. "When a regular camera is in front of you, a great part of your vision is blocked off," he says. "For me it's very important that I give all my attention to what's in front of the camera rather than on the camera itself. By positioning the viewing tube of the Angenieux zoom lens on my camera above the camera itself, the camera is always out of my field of view. In addition, all the controls are completely visible to the cameraman by simply glancing down."

3. All elements of the camera are part of the camera body. There are no battery packs hanging over the shoulder or any other accessories separate from the camera itself. Even the incident-light meter (a Spectra with pivoting light-collector) is fastened to the front of the camera.

The camera is run by a synchronous motor powered by a battery pack. If such a motor were connected to a standard powerline (supplying 110-volt, 60-cycle, AC power) it would run at a standard synchronous speed. Since the batteries give only 12 to 15 volts, a transformer is used to boost the voltage to 110. An inverter changes the DC delivered by the battery to AC. All that remains is to convert the battery power to 60 cycles. This is accomplished by the use of a tuningfork which vibrates at 60 cycles, the signal of which is amplified and controls the motor speed. This speed control is *very* accurate (Bulova's Accutron watch works by the same principle).

The tape recorder (which is not connected to the camera in any way) also contains a 60-cycle tuning fork. It does not, however, control the speed of the recorder's motor, for, even if this were very accurate, the ¼-in. tape could stretch, thus losing synch. Instead the signal is recorded on the edge of the tape itself, supplying a pulse which accurately controls the tape speed when rerecording is done on sprocketed 16mm magnetic tape. Thus, absolutely accurate synchronization of sound to film is obtained.

In spite of the fact that their major film, *Showman,* has not received general release (Levine has only agreed to a limited television release for the film and TV has not yet bought it), the Maysles brothers have established themselves as important figures in the vanguard of a new approach to documentary film. Recently Al Maysles acted as cameraman on one part of a four-part feature (tentatively titled *The Quarters of Paris*) being made in France. The short 16mm film was directed by Jean-Luc Godard (director of the New Wave hit, *Breathless*). The collaboration was such a success that Maysles and Godard are planning to make a feature film (in color) next year in the United States. Maysles has worked with Godard on a dramatic film using a plot and actors because he admires him immensely, but his greatest ambition is to use the "spontaneous camera" for the making of feature-length documentaries. "We did the film with Godard because he's so damned good, but our primary interest is still to make films out of life as it happens," he says.

To achieve this goal, Maysles is continuing to improve the design of his camera to make it still more portable and easy to handle. He is now completing a model which will cut the weight down from 30 to 14 pounds, including a 1,200-ft. magazine instead of the 400-ft. one the camera now uses. He is confident that he can reduce that weight (magazine included) to 10 pounds in the near future.

Ever planning future projects, Al and David Maysles have committed themselves to furthering a new type of filmic expression—an approach to film which almost perfectly embodies the venerable credo of Sir Francis Bacon that: "The contemplation of things as they are, without error or confusion, without substitution or imposture, is in itself a nobler thing than a whole harvest of invention."

One Man's Truth: An Interview With Richard Leacock by James Blue

This interview originally appeared in the Spring 1965 issue of Film Comment (New York). Mr. Blue is a documentary filmmaker.

LEACOCK: When I become intrigued by theater or by film or even by education, it is when I am not being *told* something, and I start to find out for myself. This is when it gets exciting for me. When I have *a basis for speculation*. The moment I sense that I'm being *told* the answer, I tend to start rejecting it. When I really start to dig a play or film is when I start to find something out—the way one can from actual experiences. One can start to *find things out*. One can start to put things together in one's own head and make one's own logic, draw one's own conclusions and find one's own morality from what one is experiencing. This is where it starts to work for me.

BLUE: Al and David Maysles would agree, I think, that the spectator should be given the liberty to make up his own mind about what he sees. Is there a common ground in your work?

LEACOCK: It's a pity, I've been meaning to talk to Al Maysles. Al is sort of making a religion or a virtue of merely looking. Just looking at everything. Looking everywhere. Some place in an article I used a limerick. Have you heard my favorite limerick?

> There once was a brainy baboon,
> Who always breathed down a bassoon.
> He said, "It appears
> That in billions of years
> I shall certainly hit on a tune."

There is the great danger of "Free Cinema" or whatever the hell you want to call it. You know: "My, this is the way it happened. Well, it actually happened this way! Well, this is the way it *happened!*" So what? What I want to know is: *Is it interesting?* Is there the basis here for finding something out?

What is it we filmmakers are doing, then? The closest I can come to an accurate definition is that the finished film—photographed and edited by the same filmmaker—is an aspect of the filmmaker's perception of what happened. This is assuming that he does no directing. No interference. In a funny sort of way, our films *are* the audience. A recorded audience. The films are a means of sharing *my* audience experience. Which is very different from being a playwright. We say we are filmmakers, but in a funny sort of way *we are the audience*. We do not have the burden of a director.

BLUE: In *Happy Mother's Day* you show us what you understand to be a social and economic dilemma: quintuplets are born into a modest-income family, which already has five other children. The family must give up its privacy to the intrusion of commercial exploitation in order to pay for the new babies. You say that you object to being *told something* as an audience, but are you not telling us what you want—by selecting what you want us to see?

LEACOCK: I would say that from that film you can draw a very wide spectrum of conclusions. But surely you've selected. Everything you do, you are selecting. But, you see, so does the physicist. When he describes the crystal to you, he doesn't tell you that it is pretty or ugly. That's personal opinion. It's irrelevant. Nor does he describe every aspect of a crystal. . . . He couldn't describe every aspect of the crystal; he doesn't *know* every aspect of the crystal. He'd have to give you the crystal. He describes those aspects that he *judges* to be significant and interesting. He is objective in the sense that he didn't cook it up. He found something out. He didn't create it.

It's no less objective to be selective. Objectivity has to do with, "Am I causing this to happen or is it happening irrespective of my being there?" That's one thing. Now selection is something else. The physicist is a very objective fellow, but *he is very selective*. He's much more selective than we are. He tells you *precisely* and *only* what he wants you to know. All the rest is irrelevant. Now if you want to go and nose around in it you can.

BLUE: You seek to be objective, then, in the sense that the phenomena you choose to pass on to us are not of your own making. But how can you be sure that they are not? The presence of the camera may alter the phenomena.

LEACOCK: Although we have reduced as much as we can the impact of the filming process on situations we go into, obviously we are affecting them. When you make an electrical measurement of a circuit, you do it with a voltmeter. Every physicist—and I used to be one—knows this. So you design your voltmeter so that very little goes through it. And in a very sensitive situation you need very much less going through it. Inevitably, you do change the situation.

But you know just how much you have changed it, and you argue your way out of the paper bag. You know. So we know this much is going *there,* so we discount *this.* Et cetera. Now, if there are a thousand people in a banquet hall and a newspaper man walks in, automatically it changes it. Not very much. You walk in with a camera . . . it changes it a little bit more, but not very much. Even with our minimal equipment, if we walk in on Mrs. Fisher, the mother of the quintuplets, alone when she is doing nothing, we are the only interesting thing in the room, so we change it enormously. But if we walk in on Mrs. Fisher when she's trying to get the kids off to school and she's mad as a hornet at them because they're late or something—then we change it very little. *And so it's a constantly changing thing of which one has to be aware.* The only way that I can summarize is [the way] that we try to film: we are really only successful in finding out anything when we are filming somebody who is more concerned with what he is doing than with the fact that we are filming him.

The relationship of the filmmaker to his subject is what I call a "gray" relationship. He must have *respect* for the person he's shooting, but he must not attempt to influence. Sometimes, in dealing with a celebrity, the filmmaker may fail to win the subject's respect. The celebrity may treat the filmmaker like an officeboy, to be let in or kept out. This is bad, because the person you're filming should not be making the selections. This is terribly important if you are going to succeed.

It was very difficult for us to gain the respect of the Fishers. Ironically, again we had a dilemma. The only way we could gain the respect of the Fishers was to stay away from them. Which was suicidal. It was nuts! But we had to do it. By "bugging" them, as everybody else was bugging them, we were driving them crazy. We were a part of the very thing that we were filming. We, too, were exploiting them! We got into a very complicated issue.

All the sightseers and newsmen wanted to take pictures at the place where Mr. Fisher used to work. He had taken a leave of absence and was no longer working there. So he said, "I guess I'll go down to work." He was trying to be helpful. These poor guys didn't seem to have anything to shoot, and Fisher was genuinely sorry for them. So he said to me, "Why don't we go down to the place where I work?" We went down, and we got out of the car, and he said, "Now don't you want me to go in?" And I said, "I don't want you to do anything." He said, "Well, don't you want me to go in and shake hands with the boss, and say hello to the boys?" I said "No!" I said, "Do *you* want to shake hands with the boys?" He said "No!" So I said, "Well, *don't.* Let's go home!" You see, once he does *that,* he will do something else that pleases me. I'm not interested in his pleasing me. I don't care how unhappy I am, *I don't want him to please me.* I want him to do what he wants to do. And once I start asking him to do things, I'm dead.

I think of myself as having a very rigid discipline. It's like writing a sonnet. The minute you break those rules you have something else. You don't have a sonnet. You might have something better, I don't know. It may work for a while, but you begin to get distortions.

So we left the Fishers alone. The film really isn't close to them. We were with them when a couple of charming things happened— like the birth of the kittens. That just happened. That's the most real scene in the whole picture. It had nothing to do with us. The kids found the kittens in the barn. They yelled at the others to come, and we just happened to be there. And it's the warmest, most charming scene.

BLUE: How do you know that you have enough material to make the film you want?

LEACOCK: With the quints' film, it was finished as far as I was concerned when we made the last shot of the film in the rain. That was it. I knew that this was the end of the film. (Note: The film ends with a parade, in honor of Mrs. Fisher, which is rained out.)

For the first couple of days after we got there we looked around. We realized the invasion of privacy. The realization of the dilemma came later. After that we had a clear idea of the film that we wanted to make, which I know was a half-hour film. But The Saturday Evening Post, which commissioned the film, said that I had to make an hour film. I called them up and said, "Look, there is not an hour film here." But we had to. So we got all sorts of irrelevant material. We interviewed nurses and got all sorts of stuff to pad it out. We made it into an hour and The Saturday Evening Post wasn't happy with it. So we bought it from them, and it took us about one evening simply to delete the padding, put it together, and it's the film as it stands today. Now, had we not been making the film for The Saturday Evening Post, we probably would have filmed more material making the dilemma of the Fisher family even more explicit, and it would have come out as really quite an unpleasant operation.

BLUE: We are right in the middle of the moral aspects of this kind of cinema. You are showing to us those aspects of what occurred that you consider relevant to the significance of the event. Would you allow yourself to arrange material out of sequence in order to support your sense of what is "true"?

LEACOCK: You avoid it like the plague. At least, I do. There is one shot in the quints' film that is brought in to fill out a sequence from another sequence. I'd just as soon we hadn't done it. It's not important. It's simply a close-up of Mrs. Fisher looking. But the basic, moral problem to me—the really difficult one that you're talking about—is the editing of the film, the honesty of the editing. And all you can do is sense whether it's there or not.

BLUE: Let's take the banquet scene. A girl is singing as prettily as she knows how, and we are getting a tremendously acid feeling from it. The mayor then makes a speech that seems incredibly ludicrous.

LEACOCK: Those are the shots of that moment. The mayor's speech in that scene is there *in toto,* without a single cut, because I knew that, if I edited that speech by cutting in reaction shots and things, no one would believe that that was his speech. It's not a moral, it's a practical, problem. Because I knew that your credence would have been stretched, I left it in one shot. Deliberately.

There are other moral problems that concern me even more. What about the whole question of invasion of privacy? I'm absolutely convinced that these new techniques can result in the most awful plethora of voyeurism, of peeping-tomism, of every kind of error. Just as the invention of the printing press and of mass communication media has resulted in the most God-awful collection of crap, pornography, junk, horseshit, and everything else that goes under the name of the publishing business, so the same thing has happened to the film industry. That's the price we pay. You can't have laws about moral questions, unfortunately. The closest I can get to a rule is my personal working rule: I have yet to make a film that I could not show to the people concerned and filmed and not get—it may be *grudging* approval—but their approval. That's not enough, either.

BLUE: Did the city council of Aberdeen, South Dakota, approve of *Happy Mother's Day?*

LEACOCK: No objection. Mrs. Fisher, they've all seen it. They don't think it's funny. The mayor sat up all night writing that speech. They all applauded afterwards. You heard it. It's fine. The lady who sang the song might be upset. She was upset to sing the bloody thing. The lady who talks to Mrs. Fisher about whether she should hold a bunch of mums in her arm or something—it's what she said. That's the way she thinks. That's the way she thinks you should act!

BLUE: No one in the film felt that he had been treated with ridicule?

LEACOCK: I don't think so. You get into a further thing: The Daily News, when they publish a front-page picture of a woman weeping over her child's dead body, you know they pay her, she agrees to it. It's okay. You can pay people off, and they'll agree to let you do it. But I think it's immoral—to sell a newspaper on some woman's agony. It's both immoral and not interesting.

But there are times when I'll break these rules. If I'm going after some guy who is socially immoral I'll break the rules. At which point they have the perfect right. For instance, anybody films me without my permission, I feel I have the right to knock their teeth out. Hidden cameras and things. I loathe hidden cameras. I don't believe in spying on people. But if I were doing a film on a bunch of goons, or on irresponsible people, or on a Dr. Goebbels or an incipient Hitler or a drug peddler, I might well hide some things. And if he finds out, I guess he has the right to knock *my* teeth in. That would be my tough luck.

Sometimes it's illuminating to see a person in a staggering situation. Look at that picture up there on the wall. It's from The Daily News. See those three people: the man and the woman and the woman standing behind her. That's taken at the moment that the lady in the middle learned that she had been sentenced to death. That is an incredible picture. She's listening to the verdict right there. A terrifying shot. It's a newspaper picture. I'd film that, too, if I could. These are all genuine moral questions, and morality is a tricky business.

Now, why are we filmmakers doing this? To me, it's to find out some important aspect of our society by watching our society, by *watching how things really happen* as opposed to the social image that people hold about the way things are *supposed* to happen. And by seeing discrepancies, by revealing the *things that are different from what is expected,* I think that people can find out something very important about themselves.

A hundred years ago the average person, who couldn't read or write, knew about the world only from direct experience. And as the means of communication increased—especially with the advent of film and now the tremendous thing that television is—we invented a set of clichés. We think we *know* things, but actually these are distorted or completely wrong or have the vital thought taken out of them. I have a deep feeling, for example, that I know what happens in a law court. Now, this is absurd, because I've never been in a law court. And my so-called deep feelings about what happens in a law court actually comes from movies that I've seen, that in turn were very likely made by people who had never been in a law court, either. And what we are getting is *the formation of self-perpetuated cultural myths,* which can get more and more inaccurate. I can give you other examples. Pearl Harbor Day. Tremendous banner headlines: *WAR.* When it came I was sure—I had a clear image—it was rather goofy, admittedly—I had visions that within a week there would be troops marching down the street, weeping girlfriends, I almost imagined that there would be an operatic tenor singing "Over There!" But no such thing. Nothing happened like that that I could tell.

Another thing was the coming to power of the Nazis. In Hollywood movies it's like this: one afternoon Hitler comes to power and that very night Storm Troopers run up the stairs and screaming Jews and labor people are dragged down into a big Mercedes-Benz. Baloney! I was in Germany in 1936 and 1937. You know it was just a slow, creeping, strange thing, terribly hard to put your finger on.

This relates to what education should be. I don't mean classrooms and blackboards and things. I don't terribly like that kind of education—I'm not very good at it. But coming to *know* ourselves, our own society, and other peoples' societies.

There are other problems: How is a national point of view changed? I don't think most white Americans have the faintest idea what discrimination is, what it's like to be born black and to be condemned to a role in life because of this accident of birth from the day one is born. People think that discrimination is being refused admittance to a restroom. But that's only one end of it. It's far more subtle and profound than this. Now, I haven't the foggiest idea how you do it in terms of this kind of filming, but I believe it is possible. You could begin to illuminate to the white people what is involved with the Negro and what's involved with them, too. I don't think that you can do it nearly as well by lecturing, by writing. *You have to see it to believe it.* This kind of filming has to be done by Negroes. It can't be done by whites. When I intrude into a private Negro home in the South, I just *know* that all the conversation changes. The distortion is enormous. All of a sudden you get "front-parlor-white-talk." And all the human, all the marvelous things just cease.

TV is the area where logically this should blossom. But everything about network television, as it exists today with its audience requirements, militates against honest reporting. You've got to "grab them by the jugular vein," as the phrase goes. By TV logic, the trouble with the quints' film is that it doesn't *sell* anything—it doesn't sell milk, it doesn't sell drugs, it doesn't sell motherhood. To qualify for TV, it's got to fascinate thirty million people (to me a million is more than I can conceive of—I know about a hundred. I really know about thirty). So it becomes terribly easy in TV to use the same techniques to reinforce preconceived notions of what happens to audiences.

In the case of the quints' film, because of a legal wrangle with Drew and things, we had to give ABC two prints of every single thing we shot synch-sound. And they edited a half-hour film that went on the air from identical footage to ours. And you cannot imagine two more different films. Now, the ABC film is all perfectly "true." It's just uninteresting. They are not distorting, except by omission. They simply were not aware of what was going on. They didn't see it in the material. It just became a mish-mash about sweet little children lying in cradles and girls singing songs and nurses telling you in interviews how the babies were born and all that sort of stuff. All of which was "true" and perfectly fine. It just missed what I found significant.

You can get into awful trouble when you have commercial television saying, *not* "give us something *interesting,*" but "give us something *exciting.*" In *The Chair*—for which, with Drew, I shot the lawyer scenes—many of the most interesting things that we got were omitted in editing, because they did not fit the conception required of the film: "Will he or won't he?" Will Paul Crump be saved from execution? For instance, the young lawyer was terribly pissed off when Louis Nizer came in on the case. And said so.

"Who's this s.o.b. coming out from New York?" And he was terribly concerned with the racetrack all the way through it. And sometimes you wondered, "How the hell is this guy ever going to get out?" He was never going to get the bloody brief written. But the scenes of walking down the corridor and things—might as well be frank— were shot a month after the whole incident was over, in order to conform to the "will he or won't he?" thing.

I'm not expecting twenty million people to be "grabbed" by what we are doing. Our films are a process of discovery. It has to relate to science. It relates to education. Now, of course, good drama should, too. This is the dilemma that Broadway has. It's not enough for a play to interest a small audience. It's got to be a total success or a total disaster. You know, great big intellectuals like Walter Kerr come and lower the boom on the bloody thing. This is becoming more and more the thing.

We've got to do something. There's got to be some sort of revolution. Like the small compact car. There's got to be some way where we can be satisfied by small audiences, with less gigantic sums, with more communication. We know the audience exists. We've had screening after screening and have packed the room with people who were fascinated by the quints' film. But we've got to find some way to *organize* an audience that we know exists. Television has put itself out of the field, so to speak. We could give it to theaters, but the short film has been condemned by the film industry even before it was tried. One of the problems is that this always gets mixed up with what is traditionally known as "culture." What happened to *Omnibus* is typical. You know: not badly produced Greek plays, modern dance, and the string quartet. Loses people in droves. I don't know how you get around it.

Our kind of filming should not be judged yet. What it can do. Where it can go. People can judge the particular film, but the *genre* of filming is so infantile at the moment; and we are all suffering under so many preconceptions as to form, style, methods of work, and everything else, because all our thinking has come basically from traditional journalism and traditional films and theater. I have a feeling, for instance, that Bob Drew tends to see these films in the form of the classical theatrical film.

BLUE: You have revolted against the structure of traditional drama. What elements do you think might contribute to an authentic structure for this kind of film?

LEACOCK: To me structure has always been a problem. The thing that fascinates me about Shakespeare's plays is that they use—by and large—very corny structures.

BLUE: Are you not talking about *plot?*

LEACOCK: But that *is* structure. And the fantastic thing about Shakespeare is that the important thing in the play has nothing to do with the structure or plot. The structure I'm talking about is what gets the audience all of a sudden to have the feeling that whatever it is has come to an end and it's time to go home. I'm very aware of structure, and I think that my own films—those that are totally my own, like *Toby*—have a very definite structure. There are key, trigger moments in *Toby* that were designed into it as structural moments. [*Toby* is about one of the last remaining touring tent shows.] All this time you've got a lot of putting up of tents, and suddenly I say that I want to move my audience from town into another phase. Toby looks at his watch, walks across the street, the soundtrack has some crazy old tune in double-time, and all of a sudden the thing changes pace. And this does something to you. *Happy Mother's Day* has a very definite structure. It starts out with the babies all over, the phenomenon, all this is sort of introductory, and then it starts to build and it builds way up to the end. With pace and everything else. The council meeting, at first, is the lowest point of activity, then it starts to pick up. Chronological order seems to be best. It's the basis on which you are working. And the closer you can get to *real* time, somehow, the better the thing works.

BLUE: Would you refuse to place anything out of sequence?

LEACOCK: No. The kitten sequence in the quints' film. It doesn't matter when that happens. There was no real chronology to the film except that the babies were born at the beginning, were a month old at the end, and there was a parade at the end.

BLUE: And the sequence where the family drives in circles in their old car around a photographer who takes their picture?

LEACOCK: That was the first thing we shot in the film.

BLUE: Would you ever allow yourself to recreate or provoke a scene in any way?

LEACOCK: Yes. But I prefer not to. This is how far I'd go: In the quints' film I couldn't get into any situation where a direct discussion of the subject at hand took place. So I asked someone to invite a group of people to their home and hash it out, to have a discussion. It was informal. It's the scene that is in the film. It's the one where the guy says, "I think we are talking out of two sides of our mouth." Once that discussion got going it had little or nothing to do with me. *They* were discussing. But I did ask the guy to invite the people to his home. It had happened like that all over town, but I wasn't there.

BLUE: In one scene, Mrs. Fisher is being offered a fur coat as a gift by a chic department store. She tries it on, but it is obvious that she is ill at ease. She doesn't seem to want this kind of life. This scene is revealing and important to the film. You have little else as telling as this scene. If your camera jammed, would you have felt justified in restaging it?

LEACOCK: Couldn't do it. It wouldn't work. For then I would have to tell everybody what to do. It would lose all. And, what's more, it would reveal that I want certain things of her.

At one moment I was in the radio station, and the guy was talking about the quints and the secretary suddenly stuck her head in the door and said, "Senator So-and-so is on the line from Washington." And he reacted and something happened, I don't know, I ran out of film or something. And I asked afterwards if the secretary couldn't stick her head in and say it. And we cracked up laughing. The difference was so gigantic. It was the same girl. Five minutes later you ask her to do it and it was absolutely grotesque. And when we ran the rushes here we all cracked up every time we looked at it. It was meaningless.

BLUE: You don't think you can stage a scene to achieve the results you want?

LEACOCK: Sure, you can. You hire actors. But then you are right back in the other department. Now if George Stoney, who made *All My Babies,* insists that he can do it, well, fine! I haven't seen a film where I'm convinced. He says he can do it better. I think you sense that his films are operating under other laws. He insists that it is better that way. Fine. I don't agree with him. I think it is perfectly obvious when they are staged. You know it's impossible for this to be real right away. The camera keeps leaping around the room in places where it can't possibly be.

I think that we are going to become more and more aware of a whole set of accepted grammar of filmmaking: the cutting, what the camera can and can't do. Grammar is changing at a mad speed! When I see somebody run out of a house, jump into a car, close the door, start up, and the next shot is taken through the windshield, today I say, "Bullshit! It's impossible! You can't do that!" But I have accepted this all my life. We are developing a new grammar. Grammar's important.

In the quints' film, two little kids run into the middle of the street, and they look down the street to see if they can see the band coming, because they can hear it already. And then they get scared and they run back. And this *is* the moment! It goes on. A drum-majorette—a tiny girl. The shooting there is . . . it has some miraculous quality of *being there!* It was purely intuitive shooting and somehow it has this sense of . . . you know, one has always seen this scene done in the regular movies. It has a sense of excitement. But one has *never* seen it for real before. I've seen it faked a million times. There's a difference.

BLUE: To you what makes one scene appear "authentic" and the other faked?

LEACOCK: Part of it is the *flow of single shots.* I find it terribly disturbing in fake real films when the camera jumps around. The same for the "greasiness." *Hud* was acclaimed a masterpiece of the American cinema. But the "greasiness" of that photography! Oh! those god-damned *pan* shots! The camera is like a man with a brace on his neck. "Bzzz-zup! Bzzz-zup!" Like this. Absolutely smooth. Gliding. It infuriates me. I think it destroys itself. They are destroying their own illusions.

BLUE: You feel that *Hud* was astride two streams: pretending to be real but imposing a theatrical grammar?

LEACOCK: Yes. I only object to the breaking of the rules of a "non-privileged camera" where the film is implicitly saying that "this is the way it is." As soon as your film ceases to say that, then your camera can do anything it damn pleases. *Hud,* in contrast, is supposed to be a "realistic" film.

BLUE: But what if the fictional film, in its attempt to be "realistic," adopts your techniques in an effort to appear more authentic: Shirley Clarke's *The Cool World* or Godard's sketch, shot by Al Maysles, for *Les Quartiers?* Will that satisfy you?

LEACOCK: That frightens me! I'll go out on a big limb here. The funny thing about the Greek theater is that they did not only *not* try to make things look real, they leaned over backwards in the opposite direction. They wanted it absolutely explicit that this man is not Creon. He is an actor. His name is Lembrobolis. You all know him. He lives in your village. We'll have drinks together afterwards. Now we're going to put a mask on him. And he's going to speak in a very strange artificial language, in verse. And you know perfectly well that Creon never went around talking in verse, and we don't want any confusion about this, so we are going to make it absolutely formal. We are now going to perform a *play*. Which has a great deal to do with reality, but *not* on this silly superficial level.

Now, as stagecraft developed, you could have a thunderstorm, then a shipwreck, and by the time you hit Ibsen, you had the hell-bent drive toward, "This is actually the way people are . . . this is how they really speak . . . this is how their drawingroom looks." Then you get into Chekhov and what happened? You got a crazy business! Then, a reaction *away* from realism in the theater, paralleling the advent of film, which is even *more* realistic. Everybody assumed that in this film medium *certainly* you had to be realistic. Everything looked so real. Meanwhile, the theater of this time—Brecht, Toller, *et al.*—had a violent reaction in the opposite direction. Finally, you got the dregs of the realists with Arthur Miller and others.

A realistic play is absurd today. I saw an Ibsen play performed in London recently. It was spooky! So, finally you've got theater going in the right direction. Now, film by and large is still persuaded that you should be realistic. You get films like *The Sporting Life* and it's confusing: it's terribly "realistic," then all of a sudden they have symbolic things—spiders on the wall and all that jazz—that don't fit in with realistic stuff at all. You have this funny clashing.

Then you've got what we are doing, which has suddenly arisen, which is totally different because this *really* has to do with reality.

But at the same time in film you have early beginnings in another direction—Eisenstein, who was never interested in realism in this sense; much earlier, the Germans in *Caligari;* and the closest to us: Resnais, who is hell-bent away from realism. This is a new area that nobody has really tackled. It presents terribly difficult problems because—it's true—the film is so inherently realistic.

You see, our work has nothing whatsoever to do with theater or drama as we've known it. The other uses of film—the theatrical uses—are going to go in the direction that theater is going: away from realism. All the guys who got more and more "realistic" have just come to a dead end. In a funny sort of way, my hunch is that what we are doing is the most important thing that film can do.

BLUE: But isn't "realism" merely a style to be used like expressionism?

LEACOCK: My own feeling is that this is "fraud." I don't like film used as fraud. I don't like to be hoodwinked. I don't want to play games. When I go to a musical, it's fine. *West Side Story*. I loved that. I know that Puerto Ricans don't dance and sing in the streets any more than anyone else does. It's an opera. It's a piece of theater. Wonderful. Absolutely wonderful. But when I go to "The Connection"—the play, not the film—and they tell me that they are *not* putting on a play—and I know bloody well they are putting on a play—what sort of nonsense is this!—I find it very, very aggravating. One of the actors comes up and tells you that he wants to cadge ten dollars off you because he wants to make a connection—aw, bullshit! I know he's doing it every night. I'm not an idiot. I don't want to be treated like an idiot! If I'm at a play, let's have a play! If we are going to look at reality, let's look at reality! And if the author has got something to say—if he wants to give me a lecture—then, for Chrissakes, have the honesty and self-respect to come out and tell me what he has on his mind! I love it that way! Keep it clean! Keep it straight!

Canada Carries On

by Rohama Lee

Miss Lee, former journalist and scriptwriter, is editor and publisher of Film News, a major publication in the audiovisual field.

Today there is a rising tide of filmmaking in Canada, a "new wave," especially among independent young filmmakers, many of them French-Canadians recently come into the field and bringing to it a special flavor. Not including the young people making their first film or two, there are about one hundred established production companies in Canada now, though some are one-man shops. This was not the situation in the fifties or even the early sixties, when production was almost exclusively that of the National Film Board of Canada plus a few other isolated sources, notably Crawley Films Limited, on its way to becoming what it is now, one of the largest (if not the largest) consistent producer of sponsored documentaries on the North American continent.

Now, however, the Canadian Broadcasting Corporation (CBC) itself has become extremely active in the documentary field and won many awards on both its English and French networks. When television came to Canada in the early fifties it was expected that live TV would prevail. Film was used only as an adjunct to studio productions for the most part. Soon, however (as early as September 1952), the CBC began to produce its own TV-oriented programs. This provided an expanding opportunity for development of production in Canada by such Canadians as Allan King (*Warrendale* and *The Married Couple*), whose *Skid Row,* made for CBC's Vancouver station (in 1957), had good exposure and was well acclaimed, although it is no longer in distribution except as a historical document.

There is production now in every one of the CBC-TV centers across the country—predominantly out of Toronto in English, and out of Montreal in French. CBC programs are seen on the television screens of many countries. CBC is also very decidedly going more and more into the nontheatrical field. For Europe the center of distribution is London, for the East it is Tokyo. Recently, through an arrangement with an affiliated distribution company, a selection of CBC's most suitable TV documentaries are being made available to nontheatrical audiences in the United States. Among these are

Galapagos, a series about these islands; *Wild Africa,* two related films on that continent's wild life; and *Shaibu*—Russian for hockey —which centers around the curiously important place this game has achieved, from both sociological and sports viewpoints, in the USSR.

The CBC is thus the largest producer of motion pictures in Canada, but has yet to become as well known outside of Canada as the National Film Board with its long-established documentary product.

The situation of the Film Board may be likened to that of an artist with a patron, a producer with an "angel." Money has been allocated to it by Parliament every year since 1939, without strings attached other than that the Board fulfill its function. This primarily is "to produce and distribute films designed to interpret Canada to Canadians and to other nations"; and "to engage in research in film activity and make available the results thereof to persons engaged in the production of films." It started its life in an old mill in Ottawa and spread out to a scramble of buildings. In 1954 it was moved into one of the most modern and best-equipped studios on the continent, in a suburb of Montreal. The National Film Board of Canada was created in 1939 by an act of Parliament drafted, at the government's request, by John Grierson, who had established the documentary movement in Britain before playing the same role in Canada.

As the NFBC's first Film Commissioner (1939–45) and its prime organizer, Grierson recruited documentary filmmakers from Britain and the United States to teach Canadian novices. It was through Grierson's plan for the Film Board that distribution offices were established in most of the major cities of Canada to stimulate the use of film and assist groups and organizations. The result has been a climate of acceptance of film that, to an amazing extent, has woven it into the very web and woof of Canadian life. From a country with no film tradition before World War II, Canada turned into a leading nation in the production and use of the information film. The NFBC is now a world phenomenon, imitated though not equaled in other countries. Canada has developed from pupil to teacher.

Many of the independent producers in Canada have NFBC (as well as CBC) background. The NFBC has also been a training ground for young filmmakers who have come to it from other countries. Because its production is not solely dependent on commercial return, as in the case of the private filmmaker, the NFBC has pioneered, and still pioneers, fields of specialized interest—as with the four films of the "Mental Mechanisms" series, directed by Robert Anderson, 1947–50, and the "Accidents Don't Happen" series, four films for the Department of Labor in 1946–47, scripted, directed, and edited by Donald Mulholland. Both of these series are still in vigorous circulation. This is the case also with the half-dozen films more recently shot in many cities of the world and based on "The City in History" by Lewis Mumford (*The City: Heaven and Hell; Cars or People?; The City as Man's Home;* etc.).

About one-third of NFBC's production is for government departments (Labor, Health and Welfare, Travel, etc.). The other two-thirds is split, in no particular proportion, between films for schools, made in collaboration with official educational bodies, and what has come to be variously designated as "enrichment films" or "film as art" (of which the works of Norman McLaren are an outstanding example). Whatever their genre, Canadian films draw their inspiration from a unique geographical background and the cultural heritage of many peoples.

All NFBC films are produced in English and French, both of which are official languages. The dominant Anglo-Saxons and French are interspersed with settlements of Ukrainians, Poles, Icelanders, and (more recently) Italians. The contributions of the Eskimo are also an important part of Canada's mosaic, as portrayed in *Eskimo Arts and Crafts, Eskimo Summer, The Eskimo in Life and Legend,* and *Eskimo Artist Kenojuak.* Made in 1950, the classic *How to Build an Igloo* is still a favorite with both in-school and adult audiences. The contribution of the Indian—represented in such films as *The Annanacks, Eskimo or Indian, Circle in the Sun,* and many others—is now extending into the field of film itself as this troubled people begins to use the camera on its own to tell its story in such striking reportage "Challenge for Change" documentaries as *You Are on Indian Land* (1969).

The goal has been to present didactic material in fresh and provocative forms and, toward this, the NFBC has been a pacesetter. Experimentation is encouraged, "style" and individuality are manifest in an outpouring of prizewinners by both English and French production units, working separately and together. Excellence is particularly evidenced in the area of character delineation or, if you will, the personality profile against an information background. The NFBC aims to express "in simple graphic terms" its "concern with man's humanity and his vision." It is difficult to pick the best from so large an assemblage of interesting films, taking personal taste into account also. For this writer, at this moment, the following come most readily to mind as outstanding NFBC documentaries:

Paul Tomkowicz, Street-Railway Switchman (9 mins., b/w, 1953)—From the "Faces of Canada" series, this is directed by Roman Kroitor, with scenario by Kroitor and Stanley Jackson, and sensitive photography by Lorne Batchelor. Described as "an item in a series devised to give new directors practical film-making experience," this intimate study of an elderly Polish-Canadian uses verbal material provided by him. Tomkowicz talks quietly about his work, his coming retirement, his attitude toward life. The atmosphere in the falling snow is low-key but powerful, in keeping with the controlled inner and outer strength of the big man who represents a fundamental dignity that is all-too-rarely recognized. Director-scenarist Kroitor and Tom Daly cooperated in an exemplary job of editing.

Lonely Boy (27 mins., b/w, 1961)—There is a particular shot of Paul Anka on stage in the focus of a spotlight, reminiscent of a cross between the rays of the Star of Bethlehem as pictured on Christmas cards and the light beam of an inquisitorial investigation. It tells the whole story of *Lonely Boy* who, actually and symbolically, is that phenomenon of these days: the teen-age performing idol who fills some sort of baffling need in modern youth. Here is a candid look, from both sides of the footlights, at Paul Anka himself (who supplies much of the commentary) and his screaming, swooning, writhing female adorers. Wolf Koenig and Roman Kroitor's direction, plus John Spotton and Guy Côté's editing, splice it all neatly together into a portrait that is intimately Anka, and also a graphic representation of the "loneliness" of the young in this generation.

Ladies and Gentlemen . . . Mr. Leonard Cohen (41 mins., b/w, 1965)—The status of this Canadian poet can be argued by literary critics, but that does not detract from this superb film study of a man who is also a poet; who is charming and full of humor, though nervous and self-conscious; cosmopolitan and "emancipated," yet also defensive about his Jewish background. It is the way that non-Jewish writer-director Donald Brittain has presented Cohen's attitude toward his origin that is extraordinary for its understanding of a complex emotion and its manifestations. The simple purpose of the film, tastefully and superlatively achieved, is to reveal as much as it can about a creative human being and his way of life. For the most part it shows him on a return trip to Canada from Greece where he chooses to live. He reads his poetry and speaks in a series of platform appearances; spends an evening with a few close friends; and, in the closing sequence, reacts to several scenes of this film as it is shown to him in a projection room.

Wrestling (29 mins., b/w, 1961)—This is the best possible introduction to the work of an NFBC French crew co-directed by Michel Brault, Marcel Carrière, Claude Fournier, and Claude Jutras, with Jacques Bobet as executive producer. Perhaps its outstanding feature is its skillful editing. But the visual had to be there to be so cleverly edited, and it is—in a tongue-in-cheek candid-camera report, against an ironic background of classical music, of a bout at the Montreal Forum where the star wrestlers play to the house. The film includes some of Montreal's backstreet wrestling parlors where tyros are drilled, but its chief interest (for sophisticated cinephiles particularly) lies in its razor-sharp, offguard portraits of the crowd as such, and the individuals singled out for close-up treatment. In the U.S., *Wrestling* won an Honorable Mention from the 13th Flaherty Film Award judges.

The Documentary Film and the Negro
by William J. Sloan

This study, by a staff member of The New York
Public Library, appeared in The Journal of the
Society of Cinematologists, 1964-65.

[Definition of terms: The term documentary is used in its broadest sense to refer to films that possess truth and project reality, and are intended primarily for nontheatrical use. Integration refers to the integration of the American Negro into American society as a whole, with emphasis on the areas of education, voting rights, housing, and employment.]

This study is concerned with the conscious efforts of films to promote better race relations between Negro and white in the United States. In its strictest sense the integration film did not become an established genre until after May of 1954, when the Supreme Court handed down its decision effecting integration in the schools. We can, however, examine the forerunner of the integration film.

In the mid-nineteen-thirties, the nonfiction film became an important means of communication. At that time in theatrical movies the Negro continued to be a stereotyped comic figure as he had been for the preceding quarter of a century. While the movies did not reflect informed opinion, they did, like the other popular media, undoubtedly mirror popular attitudes. Inadvertently the same attitudes were carried over into the documentary. One of the rare occasions when a Negro was the central figure of a film was in a *March of Time* production of 1935 where John Lomax interviewed the Negro folksinger Leadbelly and recorded his songs for the Library of Congress folksong collection. Quite unintentionally the patronizing attitude of the white interviewer is revealed. But even more fascinating is the Negro living up to the "Uncle Tom" image expected of him. Obviously this film was at least partially scripted, but even so it gives us an insight into one side of Negro-white relationships in the 1930s.

In the pre-World War II period there are a few productions that dealt with problems of the Negro. Perhaps the most outstanding of these was *One Tenth of a Nation* (1940), directed by Henwar Rodakiewicz, that showed the need for better schooling for the

Southern Negro. During World War II the Federal government realized that every citizen must be urged to support the war effort to the utmost. To this end it was essential that the racial tensions be minimized and that the contribution of the Negro be recognized and encouraged. Therefore it undertook the production of a number of films on the Negro—as a soldier, sailor, farmer, jazz musician, and college student. *The Negro Soldier* (1944), produced by Frank Capra for the Office of War Information, achieved the most popular success and had wide theatrical showings. The idea that Negro and white had a common goal in fighting the enemies of democracy inevitably promoted ideals of integration. Later on, the government withdrew these films from public circulation at a time when they could have become a forceful tool for the fostering of good race relations after the war.

The early postwar period saw for a while at least an idealistic reaffirmation of basic democratic principles. One result was a spate of films on the general theme of brotherhood. A few dealt specifically with the Negro. The Anti-Defamation League and Julien Bryan's International Film Foundation were leaders in this field. On the whole, however, the films of the period tended to oversimplify the very complicated issues of prejudice and race relations, so that today they seem old-fashioned and naïve. It might be noted, too, that the documentary film in general at this time was at a low point and tied to outworn formulas.

In this same period, standing somewhat apart from the brotherhood-race-relations film, were several films directed by George Stoney. They were unique in that they were made for a Negro audience to provide health education—and were sponsored by Southern state governments. In most instances, the participants in the films were Negroes. Of these, the two that have received the most acclaim are *All My Babies* (1953) and *Palmour Street* (1950), both sponsored by the State Health Department of Georgia. They were not primarily integration films, but because they were honest and sincere and treated the Negro with dignity—in fact ignored the presence of skin color—they created a new image of the Negro.

However, the landmark affecting integration was the Supreme Court school decision of May 1954. Although it took some time before filmmakers picked up the challenge, when they did so, they now had specific goals to promote and to document in the integration struggle, such as integrated schools, voter registration, housing, and job opportunities. The Supreme Court decision had hardly been handed down when Edward R. Murrow went with his cameramen into the South to get white and colored reaction to it as part of his "See It Now" series, *Segregation in the Schools* (1954), for CBS-TV. He followed this approach later with a compelling picture of race problems in *Clinton and the Law* (1957), shot in Clinton, Tennessee. It raised television journalism to a high level.

Outside of television production, one of the most effective documentaries made in the years immediately following the Supreme Court decision was *A City Decides* (1957), made by Charles Guggenheim for the Fund for the Republic. As with most integration films made during these years, it was aimed primarily at preparing the white community for integration. In this instance, it was school integration in St. Louis. The film was noteworthy in that it revealed, at least briefly, the fears of Negro parents in having their children attend school with white children. Production standards were high, but, typical of documentaries of the period, it used careful staging of non-actors with voice-over narration. All sound was dubbed in the sound studio. By 1965 the techniques seem frightfully dated. Another style of film used often in the mid-fifties and continuing somewhat abated into the present was the dramatic form—documentary in purpose and in the sense that some roles were played by non-actors and shooting was done on location. *All the Way Home* (1958) has been one of the most successful of these. A highly polished production (it should not be confused with the feature film of the same title), it was directed by Lee Bobker, with a fine script by Muriel Rukeyser. It examines the reaction in an all-white neighborhood when a homeowner decides to sell his house to a Negro. Indicative of our changing social patterns, it is used far more today by suburban groups than when it was made six years ago. The dramatic form has also been a popular format with unions and churches when they have sponsored films to promote racial understanding. Examples are the feature length *Burden of Truth* (1957), a United Steel Workers film, and *No Man Is an Island* (1959), originally produced for the religious television program "Look Up and Live."

The dawning of the new decade of the nineteen-sixties brought a new development in the documentary film. The *cinéma-vérité* or direct cinema style became part of the lexicon of documentary filmmakers. It was characterized by the use of lightweight portable cameras and tape recorders with directional microphones. The documentary now, in the hands of some filmmakers, became a document in the purest sense, in that it recorded visually and aurally the actual event. With what would seem like hardly a pause for thought the makers of integration films embraced the new style. The resulting films displayed a wide range of quality. However, they treated the Negro not as a cipher involving principles of justice and injustice, but as a human being, for the first time since the films of George Stoney of the early fifties.

The commercial television networks in the early sixties led the way. In 1960 CBS-TV produced *Sit-in,* stylistically a transition film between the techniques of the "See It Now" series and the new freer approaches. This was followed in 1961 by *Walk in My Shoes,* directed for ABC-TV by Nicholas Webster. One of the most impressive films yet made concerning integration, it shows in its fifty-four-minute span a cross-section of what constitutes the Negro community in the United States. Lagging slightly behind commercial television, the educational network, National Educational Television, in 1964 made two noteworthy productions. One was *The Run From Race,* on the subject of housing by George Stoney; the other was *Confronted,* which candidly recorded actual situations where white and Negro were in conflict. The latter is one of purest examples of *cinéma-vérité.* The Federal government has again become concerned about the position of the Negro to the point of sponsoring film production. Especially, it is concerned with the image of America abroad. The United States Information Agency has sponsored James Blue's *The March* (1964), which perhaps more than any other film captures the crusading spirit behind the civil-rights movement. It recently commissioned Charles Guggenheim, who made the previously mentioned *A City Decides,* to make *Nine From Little Rock* (1965), about the nine Negro pupils who ended segregation in Central High in. Little Rock in 1957. Unfortunately, USIA films cannot be shown in this country.

One of the most startling developments in integration films has been the influx of young, independent filmmakers. They suddenly emerged in 1963–1964, and began turning out a flood of low-budget films. Technically their films are often flawed, less in the photography than the recording of the candid dialogue. But in the total commitment to the cause of integration they are unsurpassed. Two productions can serve to illustrate the type of worthy independent films being made. In *Interview With Bruce Gordon* (1964), produced by Harold Becker, a Negro civil-rights worker talks candidly about himself and Negro rights, and at the same time reveals himself completely to the viewer. The entire film is shot in close-up of the speaker's face. *The Streets of Greenwood* (1964), directed by a team of filmmakers, records the integration struggle in Greenwood, Mississippi. Although it uses *cinéma-vérité* techniques, it also uses voice-over narration and is more structured than most films of this type. Like the Bruce Gordon film, by not attempting too much, it says a great deal about integration.

To sum up, the integration film has grown in a decade, from a few isolated productions, to become a significant part of documentary film production. As the full integration of the Negro into American society has become one of the central issues in American life, inevitably films more and more are reflecting this concern and are promoting integration. And new technological advances are making it possible for filmmakers to record and interpret the issues of integration with ever-increasing effectiveness.

A Chronicle of the Human Experience: *Dead Birds*
by Robert Gardner

This first-hand account is an altered version of an article
by Mr. Gardner in the Fall 1969 issue of Film Library
Quarterly (New York). It is to be included in a forthcoming
book by Mr. Gardner and Dr. Karl Heider.

The idea of making a major ethnographic film in the highlands of West Irian took shape shortly after the Film Study Center of the Peabody Museum at Harvard produced *The Hunters,* a seventy-minute film photographed during several expeditions to the Kalahari Desert. With a film on a primitive hunting society finished, it seemed appropriate to start thinking of one about an agricultural group. Making such a film would mean that two of the three basic ecological adaptations of human society would have been documented. Material I have gathered on three pastoral groups in Ethiopia during 1968 will be released as full-length films in 1971. With their appearance the third pattern, pastoralism, will be represented.

During most of 1960 I was in contact with Dr. Victor J. DeBruyn, head of the Native Affairs Office in what was then Netherlands New Guinea. We had several long and informative discussions during his visits to America on United Nations business. These resulted in a proposal by his government that the Film Study Center undertake ethnographic film research in the Baliem valley, high in the Central New Guinea highlands. From the beginning I decided that the New Guinea work would be done by professionals trained and experienced in both film and anthropology. The goals were to produce at the end of three years a major film, a scientific monograph, a general book, a book of still photographs, and a comprehensive series of sound recordings, all of which has now been completed.

This plan demanded a varied team. I found at Harvard, at the end of his professional training as an anthropologist, Karl Heider. It was his responsibility to do the major ethnographic research and writing. Peter Matthiessen, a writer of fiction as well as nonfiction, agreed to write an account from an ecological standpoint for general readership. The Netherlands Government loaned us a Dutch sociologist, Jan Broekhuyse, whose government service in New

Guinea included research among a highland group not too distant culturally and linguistically from those with whom we eventually lived. Eliot Elisofon, a professional photographer and colleague at the Peabody Museum, came for a few weeks of fruitful still photography. The main still photographic responsibility fell on Michael Rockefeller, a recent graduate of Harvard College who came for six months to the highland and then drowned in a tragic accident at sea off the southern coast of New Guinea while collecting sculpture for the Museum of Primitive Art. Michael also spent much of his time in the highlands as an assistant recording sound.

The expedition located in March 1961 on the north-easterly slope of the Baliem valley wall. In February, during a preliminary search, Jan Broekhuyse and I came upon a group of hamlets which Heider since has very appropriately labelled the Dugum Dani Neighborhood. This place was selected for a variety of reasons, both anthropological and cinematographic. I was looking above all for as indigenously pure a society as possible. This meant finding a group sufficiently remote from governmental and missionary activities to have escaped the kinds of influence which lead to significant social or technological change. It was well known to New Guinea highlands experts that the Dani were a thriving group of agriculturalists using a stone technology and practicing ritual warfare between sib-based confederacies. By 1961, after several years of missionary and government pacification, large parts of the 300-square-mile valley had been persuaded to stop fighting and were rapidly acquiring at least the outward trappings of a new technology and religion. In the Dugum Neighborhood, on the other hand, the only signs of acculturation were a few steel axes and some bits of red cloth introduced through neighboring mission stations which, though only a few miles distant, were otherwise blocked by intervening tribal war frontiers.

Fortunately our initial contact was immensely successful. First, Jan Broekhuyse and I were accompanied by a native of the valley who came from a village near the main government post and who had elected to serve as a native constable when approached by recruiters two or three years before. This man was a relaxed, bright, and humorous individual to whom, since he spoke Malay, we could explain our purpose in detail. Once he understood that we wanted no more than to observe and as far as possible participate in traditional Dani life, he was both willing and able to communicate convincingly our intentions to the people we met in the Dugum Neighborhood.

Second, I had brought some very fine specimens of *Cymbium Diadema* (the Bailer shell) which I had been told would better than anything else serve as tokens of our gratitude. When, on first meeting with the Dugum Dani, our interpreter had explained our purpose and we had shown the shell, there was no doubt that the majority of Dani present were at once relieved and intrigued. Any concern they may have had regarding our motives was largely dispelled by a fluent and complete explanation in their own language. Since we had wealth in the form of shells, it was clear that our presence would work to their own advantage.

We gave them shells and, later, salt, steel axes and knives. Sometimes we bartered small cowrie and snail shells when people carried supplies from our boat mooring on the Aikhe, a tributary of the Baliem that came out of the escarpment near the Dugum Neighborhood, or when we wanted their vegetables to eat and artifacts for the museum. We also made gifts to the people with whom we spent the most time, and we brought large shells to funerals according to custom. Although we never became part of the Dani exchange system, we tried to use it tactfully to facilitate our way in their world. It is fair to say that, from the afternoon of our first contact until the last member left nearly 26 months later, our relations with the Dugum Dani were virtually ideal. I worried a little during the time between our first contact and our return almost a month later. A visit by an expedition of our size and complexity could be considerably more threatening than the rather casual first encounter. However, neither our numbers nor our baggage did more than provoke a seemingly boundless curiosity, and our serious work began the moment we established a small camp between two clusters of Dani villages.

As far as my film effort was concerned, one essential advantage lay in the fact that the Dugum Dani did not know what a camera was. I decided to protect this innocence by keeping all photographs and magazines hidden. I had heard of missionaries in the valley disturbing other groups of Dani by showing them pictures of people who had since died. Several of them nearly lost their life trying in this way to be friendly. My concern was somewhat different. I wanted above all to photograph authentic Dani behavior. I had had experience with Bushmen in the Kalahari who had become sufficiently self-conscious and camera-wise that they were performing as much as they were simply being themselves. We explained to the Dani that our cameras, both still and cinema, were used by us to see them more clearly. Often I asked them to look through the finder of a Nikon or an Arriflex to show them how it made people or things bigger and more visible. I don't think the cameras were ever in themselves a threat to the Dani. They were accepted as being no more or less puzzling than our clothes, typewriters, or tooth-brushes. This was true as well of the tape recorders, which, how-ever, we demonstrated more freely as time went by, by playing back songs and other sounds to everyone's great delight.

The immense number of problems confronting anyone wanting to make an ethnographic film can be sorted into three main cate-gories: conceptual, technical, and procedural. Conceptual problems start the moment one attempts to define an ethnographic film. I sus-pect that for many people an ethnographic film is a kind of pictorial monograph dealing with one or more aspects of a primitive society. The word ethnographic has a vaguely scientific ring to it and this reassures those who are obsessed with the thought that film is dis-reputable. The assumption is that an ethnographic film has, some-how, a better chance at being a responsible documentary. From the standpoint of content, I think it is probably true that ethno-graphic filmmakers have a greater concern for facts and the meaning of facts than commercial documentarists. But, it is not enough for the ethnographic filmmaker to say that he is interested in making a factual film and then proceed to neglect all canons of cinema. I have sat through hours of murky and meaningless ethnographic film because the principal virtue of photography, to amplify visually, had been completely overlooked. In the vain attempt to proceed objectively and show everything, too many ethnographic films end up in almost continuous long shots showing nothing. An ethno-graphic film like all others must have a form which can derive only from the appropriate and imaginative use of the medium. Every filmmaker must decide what he wants his film to do and say, and he must also, of course, know how to say it. This is a matter of tech-nique and procedure.

From the technical point of view a great deal could be written. Too many aspiring ethnographic filmmakers train on the job, having read the instruction manual for the camera they just bought on the flight taking them to the field. Film cameras are frequently regarded as another slightly more complex implement for taking fieldnotes. Film is a language whose proper and profitable use depends on an acquaintance with its own idiom. Fundamentally, it is descriptive. A camera with a choice of lenses that permit a variety of magnifications can isolate and describe almost any visual phenomenon with enormous clarity and fidelity. It would be impossible, for example, to describe firemaking in words with anything approaching the interest and parsimony of expression available in motion pictures. What film cannot do is, in the midst of showing how a fire is made, to say, "It is taboo for boys to make fire this way." It would in fact take an enormous number of film shots, if they were not to be acted like a charade, in order to get across the idea which can be stated here in ten simple words.

By this I do not wish to imply that film's usefulness to ethnography or anthropology stops with material culture and technology. There is another, perhaps higher but certainly very different, faculty of this medium, and that is its power to evoke. Filming the example already mentioned—of a man making a fire by sawing a piece of wood with a bamboo thong—can not only explain the technique involved but, depending on the time of day or night, the place in which it happens, whether or not the man is alone, etc., etc., can suggest a mood or feeling which is also very much a part of the real environment. Such evocation is accomplished in film with the same conviction that characterizes its descriptive potentialities. Film, because it is a medium in time, is a way to unfold something. It can be about how fire is made by one warrior or it can be about an entire neighborhood of Dani living a complex existence capable of evoking an immense range of meanings and moods. These moods and meanings, which may emerge through nothing more than the expression on a particular face at a particular time, are gathered in by the senses of an audience and then often evoke a succession of additional emotions and intellectual responses.

Under procedure I include all the activity and decisions which determine the length, the point of view, and the complexity of a film's final form. Procedure, in short, has everything to do with style. In New Guinea I knew that I wanted to make a long film on a major theme. I had decided to spend an initial period of weeks or even months making choices regarding which major aspects of Dani life I would select. It was also during this time that I met and eventually came to know the individuals who became the major figures in *Dead Birds*. I had known, long before reaching New Guinea, that I would probably use individuals to convey the facts and the moods of a larger social group. During my first visit to the Dugum Neighborhood I was struck by the vitality of Dani ideas and behavior regarding violence and death. A significant proportion of their time and energy went into activities related to elaborate and dangerous warfare between neighboring groups. Along the frontier separating the Dugum Dani from their adversaries, stretched a line of watchtowers manned during daylight hours in defense against deadly raids and ambushes. The probability of violence was continuous, and everyone lived by rules designed to avert its intended consequence of death. Children did not wander from their villages, women did not go to unwatched gardens, and men went armed at all times.

It was obvious that much of Dani life was animated by their commitment to a system of controlled hostility. There was really no doubt concerning the choice of themes if my task was to portray the essential quality of Dani life. Very early I made the decision to focus my work on those institutions and activities in Dani society which explained their involvement with violence.

It meant, among other things, that most of my time was spent observing and filming in the men's world. It was almost impossible to concern myself with women except when their lives touched on their husbands' or children's. Actually Dani women maintain a rather formidable and exclusive female company. Had I chosen agriculture as the dominant topic for a film, there would have been considerable difficulty entering that domain, since women do most of the productive work. In deciding to focus on the topic of violence I was well aware that much of Dani existence would elude me. On the other hand, I was convinced that the topic I had chosen was of such central importance to the whole nature and significance of the Dani world that by treating it exhaustively I had my best chance to illuminate the culture as a whole.

My plan was very simple. I would choose a man and a boy whose experiences of half a year could be pieced together to provide an understanding of Dani reality. I could not film every moment of their existence for six months, nor did I wish to. What I could and did do was to follow them closely and film those events which I thought added insight to the problem of living a Dani life. *Dead Birds* is not an exact chronicle of all events in the Dugum

Neighborhood from February to September 1961. There are compressions of time which exclude vast portions of actuality. There are events made parallel in time which occurred sequentially. But there is no scene or event which did not come about spontaneously and genuinely. It is all real human experience recorded selectively and deliberately by instruments I like to think were designed for precisely those purposes. Finally, it should be remembered that film is enormously expensive in time, energy, and money, and that great amounts of all three resources have been ludicrously squandered. It is also a medium which many people feel confident can be used to rescue for future generations what ours is rapidly changing all over the world. It is for those concerned to decide whether, in the time that remains, vital and meaningful chronicles of the experience of vast segments of mankind will be lost or saved.

Chronicle of a Summer — Ten Years After

by Ellen Freyer

This reappraisal of a ranking documentary a decade after it was made is published here for the first time. The author is a filmmaker and free-lance film critic.

I have just seen *Chronicle of a Summer,* ten years after it was made. Although I'd heard about this film as one of the first and best *cinéma-vérité* documentaries made in France, I could never find it shown anywhere until this summer, when it ran for one day only at the New Yorker Theater.

Chronicle of a Summer is a feature film made by two anthropologist-filmmakers, Jean Rouch and Edgar Morin. It is an attempt to discover how several people in Paris feel about their lives in the summer of 1960. Rouch had been using 16mm film in Africa. He used portable cameras and portable tape-recorders to be as direct and as free as possible from cultural bias. On one of his return trips to Paris, Rouch got together with Morin and decided to use the same techniques to study "this strange tribe living in Paris."

In the film, we meet many people, and several of these are followed in their daily lives and encounters—Marceline, a German refugee, Marilou, an Italian woman working in Paris, Landry, a Black African student, and Angelo, a Renault factoryworker. Rouch and Morin participate throughout the film, astutely conducting interviews, stimulating dinner-party conversations, and provoking encounters. The participants' reactions upon seeing themselves in the first cut was so interesting that they decided to shoot their reactions to the final cut, and this is included toward the end of the film. At the very end, Rouch and Morin, walking through the halls of the Musée de l'Homme, discuss their reactions to this experiment in *cinéma-vérité*. Rouch, influenced by the 1959 Florence Festival of Ethnographical Films, and by Lionel Rogosin's *On the Bowery,* had felt that a new *cinéma-vérité* was possible: "I'm speaking here of the documentary and not the fiction film. There is a truth that the fiction film cannot capture and that is the authenticity of the real, the lived. Even the great Soviet films and the Italian neorealists did not quite capture reality live, as it were."

I cannot understand why this film has received so little attention or appreciation among American filmmakers or filmgoers. It is, first of all, a unique and moving film. It also has historic and stylistic significance. To anyone familiar with Godard's work, it is immediately apparent that this film, rather than Brecht, is the source of Godard's distinctive stylistic devices, such as direct interviewing with the Nagra in full view. Godard has adapted the techniques of *Chronicle of a Summer* to a fiction setting. Rouch himself suggested this as the possible future of *cinéma-vérité* in an interview he gave after the completion of *Chronicle of a Summer*. The film is also noteworthy because it raises questions which I think are particularly pertinent to documentary filmmakers today. How does one probe spiritual and emotional reality through nonfiction techniques? How does one capture the sense of immediacy made possible with *vérité* and not have the film become trivial, gross, or boring? How does one create structure without plot? without melodrama? without waiting for a crisis or even re-creating one? How does one have development without it necessarily being linear or narrative?

Perhaps *Chronicle of a Summer* has been disregarded because at its first appearance in this country it was not particularly well received. At the 1963 Flaherty Film Seminar, it was presented along with the American *vérité* productions, *The Chair* by Richard Leacock, and *Showman* by the Maysles brothers. In an article in Film Comment discussing the seminar, Austin Lamont criticized *Chronicle of a Summer* for being less powerful than the American films because it seemed "to have been manipulated arbitrarily both in shooting and editing." Yet, I would say that it is this very manipulation which makes the film still work today and achieve poetry as well as fact, artistic form as well as realistic content.

It was through the skillful and varied editing that a subject which neither was inherently dramatic like that of *The Chair,* nor had for its star a strong personality, as did *Showman* which was about Joseph E. Levine, managed to draw and keep my attention. When I sat down to watch the film in July 1970, I had no particular interest in what the people in Paris were thinking or feeling about their lives in July 1960. Yet, I found myself getting involved in the people and the particular political context of their lives, which, though connected with the Algerian war and riots in the Congo, seemed strangely relevant to contemporary America. I found myself also involved with Rouch and Morin in their passion for film as a means of probing levels of cultural and psychological understanding, and exploring the differences between the roles we play, the roles we think we play, and the roles others see us as playing. *Chronicle of a Summer* becomes a documentary about the inability to separate documentary from fiction.

Marcel Brault, now of the Canadian Film Board, and Raoul Coutard, famous as Godard's cameraman, were obviously not afraid of "manipulation," for the photography is carefully selected, composed, and varied with regard to composition, texture, light and dark, and movement. In the tense interview with Marilou, the camera is close and still, while in the outdoor activities it moves and floats with the subject. This adds significantly to the film, increasing the sense of place and environment, and varying the moods. A good example is the particularly beautiful and expressive sequence with Marceline at Les Halles. The shot begins with a close-up of Marceline talking to herself. As the voice continues, the camera pulls back slowly, taking in the fantastic structure with its strong patterns of light and dark. As Marceline gets smaller and smaller the enveloping space expresses with increasing poetry her loneliness and isolation in her own memories.

The soundtrack is also "manipulated" for expressive purposes. Synch sound is used effectively in direct interviews, but the filmmakers were not afraid of silence. In the interview with Marilou, the camera stays on her when she stops talking, letting her hands and face speak in a touching and painful way. The use of music is restrained and appropriate, as in the apartment of the bohemian couple who have an unusual musicbox. Street sounds and natural noises are used in the sequence where we follow Angelo, the factory-worker, through his daily routine. While none of this is high-key or dramatic, neither is it overly talky, superfluous or redundant, but is varied effectively to bring out the subject and mood of the sequence.

In fact, the film can almost serve as a primer for a young filmmaker on how effectively to use and edit all the devices available in making a *vérité* documentary. It is a particularly good example because, while the filmmakers adopted the 16mm technology of TV and achieved the intimacy and immediacy which is possible with that equipment, they were not afraid to assert their sense of creative film form. Perhaps equally as important and intimately related, they regarded the documentary not as a report, but as a trip in which they admit to being among the travelers. Rouch felt that if a work is to express a truth *beyond* scientific accuracy, it must reflect the emotional reality of a participant as well as the objectivity of an outsider. I think this is a crucial point which accounts for the success of what could have been a very dull and stolid film. It is my feeling that even *cinéma-vérité* must have a subjective commitment on the part of the filmmaker if it is to rise above the level of reportage and become a meaningful and artistic film experience.

By appearing throughout the film, by seeking the active collaboration of the other participants, by overtly arranging and obviously handling the form of the film, Rouch and Morin are distinctly different from the mainstream of American *vérité* filmmakers. As James Blue has pointed out so well in his series of article-interviews in Film Comment, most of the well-known Americans, such as Drew, Leacock, Pennebaker, and the Maysleses, fear such involvement and interaction and believe that it would somehow contaminate the "truth" believed to exist independently somewhere out there. Every effort is made in shooting and editing to have the filmmaker as invisible as possible and to assure the spectator that what he is seeing is in no way tampered with. It's "the real thing." For them, truth lies with the subject, not with the filmmaker. The camera is a recording device, a peephole. According to David Maysles, "Things as they come in real life are much more exciting than anything you could invent or stage. We observe and shoot things as they happen. The excitement comes from seeing something revealed before our own eyes." Revelation, as James Blue points out so brilliantly, has replaced creation. Creation means manipulation, and for Americans that is a dirty word. This approach is still dominant as evidenced in the most recent issue of Filmmakers Newsletter, where Richard Leacock discusses the problems involved in filming a Merce Cunningham dance. He concludes his piece with the following: "Sandy was a dripping heap of sweated exhaustion, as was I. And I suspect that he learned again that *filming, when it really counts, is instant revelation* if, I repeat, IF you can capture some worthwhile aspect of what you experience."

Related to this is the underlying belief in the kind of effect the camera has on an individual. Rouch and Morin felt that rather than inhibiting someone, the camera acts to free them. A person who has the pretext of just "acting for the film" can reveal his deepest feelings more easily. This frees the filmmaker to participate actively in the situation, even to provoke situations, without feelings of guilt. Sometimes the person responds and sometimes they do not. The camera is not a passive recording device but an active tool for discovery.

A successful example of provocation in *Chronicle of a Summer* occurs at an afternoon picnic. Landry, the African student, is asked if he knows the meaning of the numbers that are tattooed on Marceline's arm. He doesn't, and jokes about them being her phone number! This shocking lack of knowledge and political isolation, in addition to being a telling and dramatic moment, prompted Rouch to film a sequence in which Marceline tells about her experiences in the concentration camps. Place de la Concorde was selected as the background, because German soldiers were usually there. "But when we got to the Place de la Concorde there were no more German soldiers. Nothing. So I said, 'It makes no difference, Marceline, you hang the tape recorder over your shoulder and take the necktie microphone, and you just go for a walk around the Place de la Concorde . . .' And she came out with this monologue, which I think is extraordinary, where she just talks to herself—no one could hear her. And when I stopped the scene, Marceline said 'I haven't finished yet.' Then by chance we came upon Les Halles. All of a sudden she began to talk—not of the camp—but of her return! Why? Because Les Halles resembles a railroad station. And by association of ideas, she immediately began to talk of her return, when her family came to meet her but her father wasn't there. All of a sudden an encounter [took] place between two unusual things that normally are not related, and a structure was created because of this meeting." What excited Rouch was "not to film life as it is—but life as it is provoked!"

The camera gave Marceline the pretext she needed to reveal feelings she could not face otherwise. Afterwards she denied them by saying she was play-acting. But Rouch and Morin, who knew her personally for many years and had heard her talk about her experiences before, claim this was the first time she spoke completely openly and honestly and said things she had never mentioned in all the years they had known her. For her, and for Marilou, the film experience came to be a great personal catharsis. "Perhaps," suggests Rouch, "fiction is the only way that we can truly face ourselves." The interviews with Marilou, a 27-year-old Italian woman living in Paris and working as a secretary at the Cahiers du Cinéma, are highly charged with all the intimacy and intensity of a psychoanalytic session. After discovering what powerful effects the camera could have, Rouch and Morin began to have second thoughts about using it! What was their role, their responsibility in this type of situation, with its unexpected and extreme intimacies? To what extent is this justified as a film experience, and when does it become personal psychodrama? Rouch gets cold feet and suggests that perhaps *cinéma-vérité* is a technique to add reality, not to uncover it. Perhaps only actors should be used, so that their personal life would not (ostensibly) be affected by the experience! "A western shot in this technique would be fascinating."

While such a western undoubtedly could be fascinating, and in fact *cinéma-vérité* is now often used to "add reality," should one fear the kind of intense personal and emotional encounter we have with Marilou and Marceline? Personally, I felt they were two of the most powerful moments in the film. The fear in confronting someone's deeply personal and even neurotic feelings is perhaps the fear of admitting that they exist at all. Such encounters are a moral threat, it seems to me, to the person who in the name of objectivity insists on separating himself from the subject. Could not the technique of psychodrama be a useful method for the *vérité* director to affect a deeper experience from the viewer? A documentary whose aim is to change social conditions confronts us with the social realities. Shouldn't a documentary attempting to change emotional and cultural conditions confront us with the emotional realities?

It is interesting to notice how this particular type of *vérité* "documentary of the soul" has continued in *Titicut Follies, Warrendale, Portrait of Jason, Chelsea Girls, Queen, Groupies,* and *Trash.* In all cases, the subjects can be viewed as outsiders living in a separate world from that of the viewer or the filmmaker. There is "them" and there is "us." The brilliance of a film like *Warrendale* is that the filmmaker obviously does not feel this way, and is committed to the children as human beings rather than as freaks for his camera. "The film is not really about disturbed children," said King. "It's about anger, rage, and grief in everybody, particularly focused around the experience of loss and death." It seems to me no accident that King abandoned even the pretext of the "disturbed" when he made his next film about that middle-class institution, *A Married Couple.*

"We have tried, Morin and I, to find a new form of humanism," said Rouch. "Jean and I were in agreement on one point. That it was necessary to make a film with total authenticity, true as a documentary but having the content of a fiction film, the inner life of the people." While Morin calls this inner life the content of a fiction film, I would agree with him after seeing *Chronicle of a Summer* that it must also be the content of a documentary if it is to do more than satisfy the consumer needs of a society by filling its audience with observations, facts, news. This is only possible when the film-maker risks identifying with the subject and admits his own subjectivity and involvement. By pretending that he is detached and invisible, the *vérité* filmmaker deceives himself and perpetrates the myth that he is presenting an objective, nonpersonal reality. The problem of making a documentary which is neither falsely detached nor sentimentally romanticized, but emotionally committed and aesthetically relevant, is a difficult one. Ultimately it is answered by the individual artist's unique solution in his own work. In *Chronicle of a Summer* Rouch and Morin used the device of showing themselves making the film: this prevents the viewer from "fictionalizing" and then dismissing the subject. This device also raised the question of the boundaries between life and art, or, in this case between documentary and fiction. While this has been done in the theater, I have not seen it before in a documentary film. The interaction between art as object and life as object has been a major preoccupation in the visual arts for the past decade and is undoubtedly a major reason for the film's influence on Godard in his attempts to bring film aesthetically up to date. The problem has been dealt with in this country, but from a fiction point of view, in the films of Jim McBride (*David Holzman's Diary, My Girlfriend's Wedding*) and Stanton Kaye (*Georg, Brandy*).

"Truth and Beauty have two poles," said Godard, "documentary and fiction. You can start with either one." I think the reason why *Chronicle of a Summer* still works today, and is an important film, is that Rouch and Morin made a *cinéma-vérité* documentary which tries to include the truth of "fiction."

Rossif's *To Die in Madrid*
by Judith Crist

*This review appeared in the September 27, 1965, issue of the
New York Herald Tribune. Mrs. Crist has collected her work in
"The Private Eye, the Cowboy, and the Very Naked Girl"
(Holt Rinehart & Winston, New York, 1968).*

To Die in Madrid, an 85-minute documentary film, is the story of
the Spanish Civil War. It is concerned not primarily with the political complexities but with the human significance of the conflict
nearly 30 years ago that marked a new era not only for Spain but
also for the world and its warfare. There nationalism and the
Church took a stand against social reform; there the portentous
confrontation between Hitler's crack Condor Legion and the vol-
unteers of the International Brigades took place; above all, for the
first time civilians became military targets and fought and died,
while politicians palavered and the world watched.

The camera eyes of the world were also on Spain and it is from
the contemporary newsreels as well as timeless photographs that this
film recreates a time and a tragedy in both terrifying and lyrical
terms—in the gentle horror of Lorca's death, the quiet nobility of
Unamuno's declaration, the throbbing fervor of La Pasionaria's
words, the agonized stillness of a child's corpse, the antlike scurry-
ing of civilians at a bomber's approach, the classic drama of the
Alcazar.

Madeleine Chapsal's text, brilliantly translated by Helen Scott,
is brought to dramatic life by the voices of John Gielgud, Irene
Worth, William Hutt, and George Gonneau, and underlined by
Maurice Jarre's score.

One does not use the word "masterpiece" lightly. But, both as an
historic film record and a human document, *To Die in Madrid*
stands as a masterpiece.

A Time for Burning: An Interpretation
by Frederick Goldman

This article was written especially for this anthology.
Mr. Goldman, a film educator, is the author of a secondary
school textbook on motion pictures.

One difference between art and non-art, Tolstoy wrote, is that a work of art is capable of many interpretations, many levels of meaning. Hence some viewers, focused on a single-level experience, can shrug off *A Time for Burning:* the ostensible "story"—woven about a good Christian's effort in 1966 to initiate a dialogue with neighboring Negroes—is admittedly dated because the civil-rights movement has moved far beyond the point when such a simple "brotherhood gesture" can be considered meaningful. But more thoughtful individuals recognize that the film's significance goes deeper than this bare plot outline. Willing to explore beyond the trees into the forest, they penetrate the story-surface of the film; they probe its philosophic ramifications, the conclusions and significance to be deduced therefrom; they evaluate the means employed by the film-makers to illustrate a very tangled issue.

As in any work of art, explication requires effort, thought, and repeated viewing. The basic story is deceptively simple: with Negroes now living only three blocks from Augustana Lutheran Church, its young minister, L. William Youngdahl, urges his congregation to organize exchange of home-visits with members of two neighboring Negro churches (one of which is also Lutheran). Only 10 couples on "each side" are to be involved. He points out: "This is the smallest step we know of—dialogue, understanding." The minister is gentle, but persistent. He pushes his program through the Social Ministry Committee, but it gets stalled by resistance in Council meetings. Meanwhile, rumors have been spreading, an opposition faction has formed, some parishioners have started to boycott services, and dissension threatens to split the congregation.

The thrust for a positive forward movement bogs down. Mounting resistance forces Youngdahl to resign; nobody is quite sure *who* engineers the coup, or how strong the group. We hear one Council member say: "The power structure forced him to resign." The "well-meaning" leaders, who have been "discussing the problem" and temporizing, can only express shock and bewilderment, as they dimly perceive the tragedy in which they have acted as unwitting accomplices. One asks: "100 years of preaching—where has it gone?"

The simple plot is laced with sinew. Prejudice and resentments are so ingrained among adults of *both* races that dealing with them logically lies outside the syntax of rational discourse. In fact, the *only* people in the film who seem able to think and act simply, intelligently, and constructively, are the young—both black and white. Perhaps that is the ultimate message of the film.

Human voices dominate the soundtrack: monologues, dialogues, and diatribes. Normally, this crutch will identify a poor documentary, and reveal the filmmaker's poverty of imagination. In *A Time for Burning* the omnipresence of the voices and the endless discussions are indispensable to a full exploration of the problem —and act as catalyst in the revelation.

Resisting the proposal for exchanging home-visits with ten black couples, the whites throw up a smokescreen of arguments. *The church will lose members. The action is too precipitate; the congregation will need further "education" before undertaking such a "radical" measure. The action is too specific; the congregation should be led gradually, with a more "general" approach first. If we lose 100 members, we would destroy what we built up in 100 years. "We've done nothing in this area for 100 years, so why start now?" The teen-agers in the white and black churches are already visiting each other, which has upset white parents. "I just can't be in the same room with them." The neighborhood will deteriorate and property values will decline* (these arguments are voiced by white *ministers*). *The children already have adequate contacts with blacks in school—some even swim in the same pools. Artificial "forcing" of integration is not healthy; first we should extend a "ministry" to them (as to handicapped persons). Our church might become integrated. The Negroes are antagonistic, proof that the time is not good. "There are so many areas we could be working in —why pick this one?" We're not ready in November and December is too busy. It's a tough decision; let's put it off. The "prophetic mission of our ministry" does not require the move, as "it is not dishonest to refrain from telling the truth." Etc., etc., etc.*

Sensible rebuttals by two white women cut through the thickets of oblique, obfuscatory resistance language. But the men don't listen. Otherwise, only the white youngsters seem to comprehend the simplicity, the essential *rightness* of the invitation to talk with their coreligionists. But the elders don't listen. One tells a black youth: "You're upsetting our people because of your presence!"

On their side, the blacks range from gentle skepticism to angry accusations. They posit the fundamental moral imperative that a Christian congregation and a Christian minister *must* face the issue of race schism, prejudice, and persecution. Yet they have a better understanding of the political realities—in fact, warn Youngdahl of his danger. They correctly define the nature of prejudice, recognizing its existence even among minority groups within the white community. They analyze and easily dispel the myths of neighborhood deterioration and erosion of property values. They contrast the demand that they shed blood in Korea, Laos, and Vietnam "in white men's wars" with deprivation of their constitutional rights in the U. S. South. "If we should fight, we should fight the white man right here."

All this is the stuff of speeches, pamphlets, and editorials. Withal, the filmic *handling* of the material makes it fresh and true and achingly real.

Character insights and development, in-group and out-group attitudes—and unpredictable, dramatic confrontations—are exposed with swift, lean economy, in a series of shots and scenes which are simple, natural, almost humdrum in their non-virtuosity. *Cinéma-vérité* is achieved effortlessly; one can only wonder *how* producer-director William C. Jersey managed to persuade people to strip their psyches bare under the lights and the unblinking eye of the camera. The *presence* of film technicians inevitably affects the participants, yet not one false note can be discerned. A limited number of photographed scenes with lip-synchronized and tape-recorded voices have been cut and intercut so artfully that they build mounting tension until the crisis is reached.

Yet, there isn't a moment of didactic exposition. What we learn, we learn from the deeds and words of those involved: white adults are, in the main, too ensnarled in emotional and subconscious attitudes to see the issue morally or rationally; the challenge to their sincerity as Christians is almost completely ignored. Only one Board member even tries to grapple with the ethical question. His enlightenment comes too late to save the honor of his church, or protect the pastor.

We learn that the blacks were angry, but were then still willing to talk. They had already grown skeptical of the white man's sincerity, but they weren't yet black militants. Their spokesman is a barber, Ernest Chambers, in whose shop adult Negroes argue with passion, but not hate. The camera scans the walls plastered with newspaper and magazine clippings of lynchings, murders, persecution. It focuses, ever so briefly, upon an adolescent and a younger boy in the barber's chairs, absorbing their education silently. In other scenes, youths in the neighboring Negro church explore the problem calmly, exhibiting remarkable sympathy and understanding. Clear-eyed, they identify the hypocrisy: how can the white church call itself Christian, how can its shepherd call himself a minister, if this moral issue is evaded? The answer comes softly from a black teen-ager: "The church is not a showplace for saints; it is a hospital for sinners."

One feels the sad sense of *déjà-vu,* listening now to outdated arguments. Less than five years ago, the goal of simply initiating a dialogue was still potentially constructive. The positions hadn't yet hardened. Martin Luther King, Jr., was alive and providing both moral and practical leadership in building bridges between the races. The Panthers hadn't yet emerged. Paramilitary training within the black community hadn't yet become an organized program. Race-obsession and race-hate hadn't yet taken hold. The film records that fateful time when "brotherhood" was not yet an epithet of contempt. We witness one of those critical moments in history when, in Stefan Zweig's metaphor, the "tide of fortune" could have gone another way; but in Shakespeare's epitaph, "for want of a nail, a kingdom was lost . . ." We hear a black *minister* calmly conclude: "We're at the point now where demonstrations don't work any more. We have only one choice—race riots."

The film exhibits Aristotelian unity of time, place, action. The story begins with a brilliant four-scene sequence through which Youngdahl voices the need for redress of centuries of neglect and oppression of Negroes by the white church, concluding with: "By what we say, by how we act, we teach; we witness." The perfunctory response by a woman's club officer is: "Thank you, pastor. We Christians have to be up and doing." The story ends with a similar multiple-scene sequence of white worshipers taking Holy Communion, intercut with shots of black worshipers also kneeling for the same ceremony—in separate churches.

La commedia è finita. Or is it? When Youngdahl's voice is heard announcing his decision to resign, we are in the dark, empty church; a small door in the background is open (to the pastor's study), and light shines forth. Thus, producer-director Jersey reminds us that a battle has been lost, but there is still the war to fight; we hear Youngdahl's declaration of faith and determination to carry on. The film could well have ended with that eloquent, visual metaphor. Instead, a song swells on the soundtrack—emotionally stirring and inspirational, but gratuitous and anticlimactic.

Except for this slip—or concession to the television medium's supposed need for "entertainment values" and "broad popular appeal"—Jersey's touch is unerring. His rhythm and emotional temperature are even. Nobody is painted as a villain. Even Bill Youngdahl does not emerge as a hero; he is but a reasonable man of conscience who attempts to achieve a moral and spiritual objective by using calm and moral arguments; his patience is portrayed repeatedly, but is inadequate to the resistance.

The picture is studded with perceptive visual and aural comments. Omaha's mayor appeals to the white power structure for support in the integration movement—on patriotic (and political) grounds, as so many of their young Negroes are now returning from Vietnam. His eloquence becomes hollow as we realize he is reading a prepared speech. "If the church will not become involved, then I fear for our future." On the wall behind him, a gilt-framed, white Jesus looks over the scene, impassively. During another scene, a Board member's voice is heard, soliloquizing his perplexity ("How many years must I prepare myself; what am I waiting for?"); on the screen, his family around the dinnertable bow heads and thank God for His bounty.

As the battle lines are drawn, a marvelous sound-montage of all the contesting voices carries us through several scenes, including Youngdahl playing "regular fellow" in a handball game with members of his Board's power structure, then making pastoral calls in the hospital, and then saying goodbye to worshipers, after services. During these three scenes, reprised arguments and rebuttals accelerate into confused babble. In the handball scene, the minister slams the sphere repeatedly; it is a four-wall court, so the ball keeps bouncing back, a brilliant visual metaphor for his frustration.

L. William Youngdahl's personality is low-key and thoughtful. As the protagonist, he is cool and almost dispassionate—far from Ibsen's Doctor Thomas Stockman in "An Enemy of the People," raging against the ignorance and stupidity of his neighbors and erstwhile friends. We can't credit William Jersey for setting the emotional tone of his "lead" and "supporting players"—but we should recognize his taste in manipulating camera, sound, editing selectivity, and transitions so that the film as a whole maintains the tempo and quality of the "actors" and their "performances."

This is the final judgment of a work of art: skill in using the materials and tools in such a way that the whole is of a piece, a unity so subtly achieved that no single component dominates, but all reinforce and enhance each other in the total statement.

We might presume to add one postscript to Tolstoy's definition of art, in its application to the complex, chimerical chemistry of cinema. Just as we marvel at the subtlety of Rembrandt's chiaroscuro, the tonal balance in a Corot portrait, the faceted elegance of a Bach suite, we must applaud William Jersey and his collaborators for their sensitive orchestration of form and content—so successful we are almost never aware of technique when it is employed. Only later, in reflection, do we realize that the film is not only a "documentary," but an experience which transcends time, place, and events, into the universality of art. Its power and our appreciation grow with each rescreening.

Special appreciation should go to the Lutheran Film Associates, a church-affiliated group which had the vision to sponsor *A Time for Burning* during the trial and agony of one of its constituents— and the courage to confess *mea culpa*. During his ordeal, Youngdahl is calm: "I don't feel threatened, I have a strange feeling of peace," he reassures those who are concerned about his danger. Of such stuff are martyrs made. This viewer is less at peace: I do feel threatened, and sense that *A Time for Burning* is more a jeremiad than a documentary.

Documentary — Where's the Wonder?
by Daniel Klugherz

This study of the documentary in television appeared
originally in Television Quarterly (New York), Summer
1967. The author is a television documentarian.

Documentary film has had an uneven history on television. At the outset, in the late 40s, documentary was relegated to a subordinate role, appearing in the form of "classics" that were really more at home on a theater screen. In the 50s, documentary began to be an integral part of programing: American documentary, which had always lacked a consistent sponsor, had at last found one in television. The early 60s was a period of discovery during which *cinéma-vérité* infused new life into the documentary form and opened a wide range of subjects to more authentic representation. But the 60s has also burdened documentary with an unending demand for program material. New subjects are becoming harder to find and *cinéma-vérité,* so fresh a few years ago, seems already overused. Today the documentary seems to be drying up, both in style and in content—in danger of becoming as formulated as the network situation comedy.

Symptomatic of the current predicament is a growing tendency to confine the documentary to one form—the Report. The Report, so the announcement goes, is "produced under the supervision and control" of the news department. This type of documentary is essentially a straightforward journalistic statement. It depends heavily upon a network correspondent, his interviews with experts, the recitation of facts and figures, and, finally, a summary of the pros and cons with, perhaps, some answers.

The Report may be an effective means of conveying an idea through narration with pictures to illustrate. What the Report does not do is exploit the art of film as a means of heightening experience.

The most impressive film on the Vietnam war, the one which has had the strongest impact, drew upon the classical documentary technique. *Mills of the Gods,* produced by Beryl Fox for the Canadian Broadcasting Corporation, used montage, weaving images and sounds into impressions; underscored mood with music; and moved from sequence to sequence intuitively, searching for and finding its own dramatic shape. Even the observation and analysis by the late Bernard Fall did not disturb the emotional texture of the work, which aimed at showing how the war affected the civilian and the soldier. The film was subtly critical of American policy but transcended its bias by virtue of its intense personal observation. Because it was artistic, it was also powerful; one received a sharper sense of the war than from any other film report thus far. The program went behind the headlines and the expert's analysis, to give an interpretation that stirred curiosity and created wonder long after the program was over.

Tucked away within the network news departments, competing with hard news, the documentary is being given too few opportunities to explore its potential. Occasionally the creative documentarian has been allowed to play in a limited area—to produce light essays. But for the most part a newsminded attitude has dictated that documentary be pretty straight reporting.

If documentary is to be regarded as a form of news for the convenience of television organization, it is important to stress a fundamental difference between the news and documentary approach. The correspondent may cover a story in depth, but he is primarily interested in gathering facts. The documentarian, after understanding the facts, spends time—hangs around, not quite knowing what specifics may turn up. He looks for the expressive personality, the situation that catches the spirit of what he is after. As far as possible, he keeps his story from being too well-defined too early, allowing the aspects that seem true to gather up and announce their validity as film. He thinks in the language of film, finding what transmits well in picture and sound, imagining what might cut together effectively. As he observes, he considers style and content simultaneously—possible uses of voices or music, dramatic pacing and build-up. These techniques need not reduce but enhance the image of reality in documentaries. They help the audience to sense the atmosphere of a foreign city more truly and dramatically than the correspondent who stands before the camera, with a view of the city behind him, and tells the audience what it ought to know.

Admittedly it is more difficult to use film style than it used to be; we spot all too quickly the self-conscious filmic touch in this era of hard-news reporting. However, occasional documentaries do come along and prove how effective a freer style can be.

In the CBS program, *The Italians,* produced by Perry Wolff, there were several excellent sequences developed through montage: nine ways in which Italians say no; the parading that goes on in a small town because Italians, at least in this characterization, are devoted to show and, when the opportunity comes, to spectacle. A priceless sequence was arrived at through careful development: we had seen Italian youths dancing to rock-and-roll music and we had heard some baroque music to help emphasize an important facet of the Italian character and history. The rock-and-roll dancers came on again, but this time the filmmaker artfully substituted a baroque selection, commenting, "They are dancing to music they don't even hear." The counterpoint, the strange bobbing about of the young dancers to the lofty ancient music, combined two eras in a highly expressive use of the medium.

The Italians was a rarity, a stylistic *tour de force*. It was presented under news-department auspices, obviously barely making the grade as headline material. Today the dictates of hot news on television restrict the documentary scope to Important Subjects. The choice is limited—Vietnam, civil rights, drug addiction, air and water pollution, sexual mores, old age, and perhaps a few others on a convenient but unimaginative list. Even educational television, while exploring new styles on "NET Journal," has hesitated about trying "small" subjects, looking intently, along with commercial networks, for issue-loaded material. With this programming demand, the documentary on both commercial and noncommercial television faces early exhaustion.

Working on a smaller canvas is one possible answer to the problem of subject matter. *Storm Signal,* produced by Jim Lipscomb, told of a husband's drug addiction and how it gradually took hold on his wife. The personalized account gave one a deeper, more vivid impression of addiction than a survey of expert opinions combined with several case histories. And there is no reason why there cannot be more experimentation of the small subject that does not seem fraught with social significance. Some years ago, *Ed and Frank,* a documentary by Dennis Mitchell of England, chose simply to portray two Americans, an artist and a salesman. By cutting back and forth between their very different lives, the types were characterized more sharply. Such seeming insignificance may not look very exciting in the listings of evening programs, but it may be the source for documentaries that entertain as well as broaden our understanding of the current, unreported, scene.

Another answer that might make any of the large subjects seem as unique and fresh as *Mills of the Gods* is to encourage the work of artist-reporters. The documentary was defined by John Grierson, father of the documentary movement in England, as "the creative interpretation of actuality." Today, the creative aspect is missing. Audiences are getting fairness and flatness; curiosity, passion, and insight, expressed by a film artist—these hallmarks of documentary —are being forgotten.

Still another possibility, the personal vision of the filmmaker, may be a salvation for the documentary. Compare the work of Robert Flaherty, a half-century ago, with the depersonalized travelogues of his time. The Fitzpatrick machinery ground out standard short subjects, aglow with descriptions of the exotic, but not with the sense of it. Superficial impressions kept the audience at a distance, as on a quick tour. Flaherty, on the other hand, is highly subjective in his accounts of Eskimos, Samoans, and Aran Islanders. One doesn't have to agree with Flaherty's romantic outlook to appreciate his lively, human response and observation. Today the details in *Nanook of the North* are still vivid—the building of the igloo, the family sleeping together, the dogs outside being covered by snow—and one still reacts to the good humor and warmth of the people, whom Flaherty knew so well and was therefore able to portray so memorably. Flaherty's films have stature as documents not because they pretend to be objective but, rather, because they reveal an artist's interaction with what he saw. The singleness of his viewpoint allows the audience to see more directly and to appreciate, as in any artist's work, a deeper truth.

Another tenet of early documentary—that the commonplace can be made as interesting as the exotic—is presently worth recalling. Under Grierson, British documentary in the 30s undertook to portray the familiar in new terms. W. H. Auden's verse accompanied a film that celebrated the routine of postal delivery in *Night Mail*. Grierson's *Drifters,* a rhythmic study of fishermen, fish, a trawler, and the sea, brought audiences closer to lives that had not seemed worth their notice. Just as Flaherty reminds us of the value of a subjective approach, English documentary suggests the poetic possibilities of the medium and the challenge of subjects that are not in the headlines.

While some of the traditional documentary film values might serve as guides for today, television has evolved its own special needs and demands. The mass audience doesn't care much for the purely poetic or impressionistic film. Pictorial long shots, instead of producing the stunning effect, may turn up looking like spaghetti on the home screen. The creative possibilities are shifting. With the picture image less sharp, the soundtrack has greater impact. And the old, standard movie close-up—from shoulders to above the head—has now moved in closer to study the face from chin to forehead.

What the medium of television has discovered is visual variety in the human face. One of the earliest instances of how remarkably interesting two faces per half-hour could be was Mike Wallace's "Close-Up," a live interview program. Wallace's style was more needling than it might need have been but, as oddities and ordinary people answered questions about themselves, the tight close-up gave the audience fascinating glimpses of the inner personality.

The interview has become key material in television documentary. Cameramen now expend a huge proportion of total footage on interviews or conversations. But, even here, documentary style can be manifested. Who is selected for the interview, how the situation is set up and, most important, how the dialogue is permitted to flow—identify the director's style and disclose his point of view.

We require that an interviewer be unobtrusive but, as in traditional documentary, we need his taste and feeling to help us get involved. In an Intertel production for NET, *Germany and Its Shadow,* Producer Arthur Zegart sought to reach the sensitive nerve endings of Germans today—those who wanted to forget the past and those willing to remember. His questions were troubled, uncertain, and sometimes blunt; he was on his own determined search, and not in the "objective" style of the professional interviewer. The Germans reacted to Zegart, and the result was not a report so much as a personally-discovered answer to questions that trouble all of us. In *Mills of the Gods,* the manner of interviewing yielded a highly effective sequence made up of comments by our GIs in Vietnam; their talk about why they felt they were there was nervous and uncertain, with a poignant immediacy for the viewer. The timing was important, the interviews being conducted directly after the GIs disembarked. The intent of the interviewer was, clearly, to find the overtones—not what was said. The grim fact touching the GIs—and, for a moment, the audience, too—was that war was now close by and words no longer seemed important.

Conveying a sense of actuality is an art, but a decade or so ago an innovation in technique brought to the home screen a new actuality, stronger than filmmakers had ever been able to create before. The roving hand-held camera with portable sound equipment, which has given rise to the *cinéma-vérité* movement, caught completely unstaged talk and expressions on film. The first results, programs like *Yanqui, no!* and *Primary,* radically changed our standards of authenticity. No longer would the director have to tell people to act naturally within an unnaturally lit-up area limited by the fixed positions of camera and microphone. Now *cinéma-vérité* allowed them to pursue normal routines while the camera accurately reflected their unselfconscious selves. In its early days *cinéma-vérité* was uncomfortably shaky, dark or out of focus, but technique has improved. Today the staged look has been virtually eliminated from documentary.

This new wave in documentary has yielded some fascinating films, but too often has relied upon the magic of pure technique. The technique was trained on subjects with strong emotional content: the rivalry of two high-school football teams and the big game climax; a story about a criminal's plight in a death-house; others ranging from the tension surrounding the integration of New Orleans public schools to that facing a racing driver before a key race of his career. During the enthusiastic beginnings of the *cinéma-vérité* movement, the major creative task seemed to be to find the highly charged atmosphere—to go where the action was. Great stress was placed upon the objectivity of the filmmaker, who carefully avoided using many of the devices to which documentary directors often turn in order to highlight or strengthen an effect. (For example, a more traditional director will sometimes find an excuse to have an action repeated, or he might set up a confrontation between two people who would not ordinarily meet; and he might go further to suggest the character of the dialogue that would be natural and expected.) The *cinéma-vérité* filmmaker rejected any of the traditional devices as artificial; he looked for the right moment, as it happened, to press the camera release, feeling a strong obligation to suppress himself.

Having to rely on strong subjects, *cinéma-vérité* has had trouble finding a supply of right ones. And the drive to be objective, which has deadened hour-long reports of headline subjects, had led *cinéma-vérité* into the same blind alley—where the subject is all and interpretation is nothing.

Cinéma-vérité has been, and can be, used creatively—as a means, not as an end in itself. The highly successful *A Time for Burning* illustrates how a special slant, a way of seeing events and people, can enter into the making of a film utilizing the technique. In this story about a Lutheran pastor's small step toward integrating his church, one feels that many of the situations were thoughtfully arranged: the pastor's visit to the outspoken Negro barber; a member of the church board talking things over with his wife; the Negro youths gathered together for comment. Throughout, a filmmaker's point of view seems to have guided the filming and final design of the program.

A broad category of documentary films, dealing with ideas and issues, has depended heavily upon the method of *cinéma-vérité* to perk up content and thus help solve a central and almost insoluble problem—how to take essentially literary ideas and translate them into a visual language for television. Can a viable film be made about such abstract ideas as individualism, democracy, communism, alienation, nationalism—material which will inevitably be a future province for television documentary? An answer to the problem, rarely successful, has been the straight talk-show in which attempts are made to illustrate pictorially—as if remembering that the program is not a seminar but a film. Too often documentaries have been expected to come to grips with an idea with the straightforward logic of a magazine article—to explore a number of facets, to include all the salient features, and to reach a logical conclusion.

But film has its own language. The editorial movement is from image to image, from sound to sound—a series of psychological rather than logical connections. The idea is explored through a series of experiences which the audience can share. These experiences, or sequences, form the basic structure of a documentary. They take time. (There is room for just about three effective sequences in a half-hour show.) Ideas that would be important in a written piece often do not register and must be subordinated to the visual experience. A recent NET film, *The Difference Between Us,* compared education in England and the U.S. The film compared a secondary school in England—strict, old-fashioned, interested mainly in its bright boys—with a free-swinging, too-permissive high school in the States. Going back and forth to compare the two school systems and, at the same time, evaluating the strengths and weaknesses of each, was perhaps too much for the film to bear. Another film, *To Live Till You Die,* compared the lives of an old person in Sweden and another in Italy and was more successful because there were fewer ideas to deal with. In these and other cases, documentarians are searching for styles that extend the range of the filmic essay.

How ideas come alive on television, instead of being merely stated, is a problem of style to which television critics give relatively little attention. A critical review of a television documentary is usually a report on content with little attention to film technique except for occasional references to pictorial beauty or "impressionistic" treatment. Two films on the same subject, one handled with imagination and skill, the other a straight report, are likely to receive quite the same kind of critical treatment. The reviewer finds it easier to confront the ideas than the style of the documentary.

Today, with public television on the horizon, we are still deep in the routines and styles set by commercial television. For the coming era we need to encourage the creativity of artist-reporters, skilled in selecting and interpreting what may rouse our curiosity, make us wonder, move us, make us act.

Recently, television documentary has concentrated on the definitive statement. Now the opportunity must be made for the imaginative statement. We must give the documentary form the widest choice of subject and the freest expression.

Sorriest Spectacle: *The Titicut Follies*
by Richard Schickel

*Originally published in Life, this review is reprinted from "Film
67/68: An Anthology by the National Society of Film Critics"
(Simon & Schuster, New York, 1968). Mr. Schickel, Life's film
reviewer, is author of "The Disney Version" and "Movies:
The History of an Art and an Institution."*

The Titicut Follies is a documentary film that tells you more than you
could possibly want to know—but no less than you should know—
about life behind the walls of one of those institutions where we
file and forget the criminally insane—in this instance the prison-
hospital maintained for them by the state of Massachusetts at
Bridgewater. It is a movie which avoids nothing as it relentlessly
pursues the horrible truth of a horrible situation and, in the process,
reveals once again the seemingly infinite capacity of man to visit
inhumanity on his fellow man.

It has been regarded by critics, the public, and the Massachusetts
attorney general's office (which has been seeking in sundry ways
to prevent its exhibition) as an exposé, and certainly it is that. We
are assured by the film's producer-director, Frederick Wiseman,
that the issues raised in it extend far beyond the boundaries of the
Bay State, that, indeed, Bridgewater is, compared to snakepits
elsewhere, a rather decent place. If so, we can be glad Mr. Wiseman
took his cameras only to this one, for what he reveals of existence
there is as harrowing as any normal viewer can stand.

The Bridgewater atmosphere is one of aimless hopelessness
punctuated by outbursts of unthinking, almost ritualized violence.
A psychiatrist turns an interview into a sadistic assault on such
shreds of sanity as his inmate-victim may still retain; or, with
malicious cheerfulness, he force-feeds an old man—already near
death—while we wonder whether the ash from the doctor's care-
lessly dangling cigarette is really going to fall into the glop being
funneled into the convulsively shuddering throat, or the guards
will vary their routine by tormenting—with words and a slap—a
naked inhabitant of the violent ward who has soiled his cell in the
night.

A society's treatment of the least of its citizens is perhaps the
best measure of its humanity, its civilization; the repulsive reality

revealed in *The Titicut Follies* sickens, shames, and forces one to contemplate our capacity for callousness. No one seeing this film can believe anything except that reform of the conditions it reports is urgent business, both as a matter of simple decency and as a symbolic act of concern for all who are desperately downtrodden.

Yet there is a dimension to the film that transcends the reformist. That, of course, is the aesthetic. Because it was shot with a hand-held camera, edited with deliberate lack of slickness, and eschews even a voice-over narration to neatly tie things together, cue our responses, and lend it an air of conscious artistry, this dimension has been overlooked. But it is present, not so much in the merely adequate structure—which involves cutting back and forth between a variety show put on by the inmates (the "Titicut Follies" of the title) and the daily life of the place—but in sequences quite casually thrown at us within the larger scheme.

Examples: An inmate delivering an interminable, rational-sounding theory of history and politics which is, of course, totally mad; another inmate tonelessly singing to no one "The Ballad of the Green Berets," the lengthy lyrics of which for some reason he has perfectly memorized; a paranoid at first making perfect sense as he argues the case for his release until, driven desperate by the seeming incomprehension of his listeners, he presses too hard and begins unconsciously to reveal the depth of his illness.

The result in these instances is a shock of partial recognition, a sudden realization that insanity is a matter of degree and that these people are uncomfortably like us, their behavior only a comparatively slight exaggeration of that state we call normal.

A similar identification is felt with the good folks of prison society—the rough-hewn but kindly head guard; the volunteer worker who somehow manages to organize a game of pin-the-tail-on-the-donkey without self-consciousness or patronization; the simple-hearted nurse who finds her reward in a thank-you letter from a released inmate. The ordinary human decency of these people is extraordinarily touching in this context. It is what we like to think we would offer if we were the sort who lit candles instead of occasionally cursing the darkness, and it is both poignant and maddening to realize that such goodness is enough, that the dismal atmosphere created by the state must inevitably snuff out the little lights they—or we in their situation—manage to fan into flame.

A couple of years ago there was a great twittering over "Marat/

Sade," an artful theatrical representation of life in an eighteenth-century French madhouse. Much was made of playwright Peter Weiss's cleverness in turning the asylum into a microcosm in which we could observe all the world's insanity. It seemed to me that the work's self-consciousness diminished its force. It was too easy to take—safely removed from us in time and place, always careful at dangerous moments to remind us of its artificiality, of the fact that these were just a lot of actors miming craziness and not to worry.

There are no such easy outs for us in *The Titicut Follies*. When we enter its microcosm we cannot forget that its "actors" are there to stay, trapped forever in their own desperate inventions. The knowledge that they cannot wipe off their make-up, hang up their costumes, and stroll over to Sardi's for a drink is what gives the film a power more forceful than any artifice can grant. When a work achieves that kind of power it must be regarded as art, however artlessly, or even crudely, it generates it.

Allan King's *Warrendale*
by Stanley Kauffmann

Originally published in the New Republic, this review is reprinted from "Film 68/69: An Anthology by the National Society of Film Critics" (Simon & Schuster, New York, 1969). Mr. Kauffmann, film critic for the magazine, is author of "A World on Film" and the more recently published "Figures of Light."

Warrendale is so moving, so fascinating and fine, that I hesitate to say what it's about. The moment I mention the subject, the reader will perhaps think that the film is noble and worthwhile but that he is willing to take its worth for granted and spare himself. This would be self-cheating—not of information or duty, but of humanity and, in a paradoxical way, of joy. *Warrendale* is a documentary about emotionally disturbed children. It is not a study, it is not propaganda. It is an *experience,* passionate and compassionate.

The title is the (former) name of a center in Ontario for disturbed children, not brain-damaged or mentally defective children. In 1966 a Canadian filmmaker named Allan King was commissioned by the Canadian Broadcasting Corporation to make a film about the place. He spent a month getting acquainted with the children in House Two. Then he brought in his cameraman William Brayne and his soundman Russel Heise for about two weeks of similar visits. Then they shot film for five weeks in and around the house. Out of forty hours of footage, this hundred-minute film was edited by Peter Moseley. Hurrah—just plain, simple hurrah—for all of them.

Most feature films are made by men who first create or help create or somehow acquire fictional scripts and then guide actors and other artists to the fulfillment of the fiction. With a film like *Warrendale,* nothing can be created except—a huge exception—the confidence of the subjects. The filmmakers have to know really who their subjects are, and the subjects have to believe it. In short, the prime requirement is not film talent as such, though these men have enough, but empathy, communion, credibility. The most brilliant filmmaker alive would have been powerless to make *Warrendale* without the confidence of those children (and the adult staff). That confidence, in King and his colleagues, shines from the screen —principally by virtue of the film's very existence.

It starts with the counselor of the house, a young woman named Terry, waking the children one morning and having a tussle with a teen-age girl who refuses to get up, who pulls the blankets over her head and fights Terry. My reaction the first time I saw this film (I've seen it twice) was that the girl was perfectly right: who *would* want to get up when there was a camera grinding away in the bedroom? And I began to warm up all my prejudices against the intrusiveness of much *cinéma-vérité*. But it didn't take long to see that my feeling was quite misplaced, that the girl's reaction was (one might say) natural—she didn't want to get up just as naturally as if she and Terry had been alone. This is proved by the spontaneity of all the other actions in the picture, including many by that girl. The camera quite obviously became just another occupant of the house. At one point, one of the boys, blithely playing Red Light with some of the other children in the street outside, confides to the camera that he can see his friends' steps with his back turned because of the reflections in the lens.

The basic Warrendale technique is "holding": when a child has an emotional seizure, an outsize tantrum, one of the attendants— sometimes two or three—pins his arms and legs and lets him rip. Complete freedom of feeling is the essence, with restraint to keep the child from hurting himself and to provide a sense of physical contact, the *caring* of somebody else. We see this method used frequently with these volatile children. But, crucially, a foreword tells us that this is *not a documentary about a technique,* it is a personal, selective record of an experience. I have no idea whether the "holding" technique is good or bad therapy. I do know that King's film about the place where it was used brought me close, in a naked and tribal way, to five or six emotionally disturbed children. It revealed not only the personalities but the worth of these children. There's a boy named Tony, about ten, splay-toothed and curly-haired, whose every second expression is "Fuck off," repeated in a pathetic defensive litany. When he's struggling in the counselor's arms during one of his tantrums, swearing furiously, I could only think, because of what I knew about him, even because of what he was doing at the moment and why he was doing it, "That's a *wonderful* kid. That's a terrific human being." King had led that boy on to film before then, had shown him playing and blushing and teasing and talking; now, because Tony was *present,* his tantrum seemed one of his ways to express an exceptional sensitivity.

The film merely presents some events in the life of the house. The central point is the sudden death of the relatively young Negro cook, a woman evidently dear to everyone. The chief counselor decides to announce it to all the children at once, and the resulting scene is heartbreaking—but not in a bedlam horror sense. Before the meeting one of the counselors asks the chief how they can explain the death to the kids when they don't understand it themselves. What we see with the children is this bafflement and fright *in extremis*. All the children feel various kinds of guilt for the cook's death. This, enormously amplified in them, is something that all of us feel at sudden death, particularly of the young: not directly responsible, as the children feel, but haunted by the sense that we ought to have been able to do *something*.

This experience is a model of the whole film. These children act out, in exaggerated and baroque ways, many feelings that other children, other people, feel and suppress or understand objectively and can control. These children have little objectivity or control, and they just let go: guilt about having been unloved in their homes, as if they had earned neglect, as if they were undeserving of this place and its care; fear to love because of the fear of loss of the beloved; unbridled anger at the teeming mysteries of just one ordinary modern day's existence. Society has not (or not yet) given them the means to control their fears and to invent answers as it has given to many adults and to the clergyman who presides over the cook's funeral.

Any film that is an impromptu record is likely to have roughnesses and omissions. For instance, it's clear that King was caught slightly short because the cook died early in the filming and he had only a little footage of her. (Understandably, he shifts her death to a point near the end of the film; strict chronology was not important, and the film would have run downhill if he had followed it.) Some of the sound could be clearer, some of the sequences fuller. A few of the children are left virtually unnoticed, like a pretty teen-age girl, flirtatiously dressed, who sits in the background chewing gum and reading magazines while other children are threshing about in counselors' arms.

But much more bothersome are two extrinsic facts. The first is that the Canadian Broadcasting Corporation, having commissioned this film, refused to show it because it contains—often—the words "fuck" and "bullshit." I hope that at least some members of the

CBC felt that this decision was a fucking disgrace. Would it have been impossible to show this utterly humane, basically ennobling film late at night, even if it meant canceling for one evening some acid-in-the-face private-eye thriller with scrubbed language?

Second is the fact that Warrendale has now changed hands and methods, largely (I'm told) because of controversy over this film. I'm as incompetent to comment on the political questions as the therapeutic. I do know that, watching this film and knowing that at least some of the children have been moved and are being treated differently, I felt that something warm and organic and nourishing had been hurt.

Last year we saw a documentary called *Titicut Follies,* made in a Massachusetts institution for the criminally insane, a picture that no doubt originated in a genuine impulse to expose oppressive conditions but that, I thought, began to get some gawking kicks out of showing them. I mention that picture only to assure those who saw it or who wouldn't see it that *Warrendale* has not the slightest resemblance to it. It is not an exposé, it is not a chamber of horrors. It is a *union* with some children who become very precious to us before the one hundred minutes are up. Partly this is because they are in themselves interesting and they are allowed—induced—to be *there;* partly it's because they seem to be us, under a distorting magnifying-glass. Jean Renoir has called Allan King "a great artist"— not a bad compliment from a man who is a pretty fair artist himself. Inarguably, King has evoked those children's inner selves so powerfully on the screen that he has snared us up there, too.

466

A Variety of Hells

by John Simon

This review is reprinted from The New Leader (New York) of April 28, 1969, for which the author is film critic. He is also drama critic for The Hudson Review and author of "Acid Test" (1963), "Private Screenings" (1967), and "Movies Into Film" (1971).

The Maysles brothers' new documentary, *Salesman,* follows four Catholic Bible salesmen as they push the Good Book from door to door, attend sales conferences, get pep talks and threats from their sales manager, exchange satisfied or dissatisfied accounts of the day's activities in their motel bedrooms, immerse themselves in TV or the swimming pool, sleep and set out again to badger and bamboozle and, sometimes, sell. Already much discussion has been stirred up by the film: Is it an invasion of the privacy of those unhappy people whose living rooms and kitchens are assaulted by worse than salesmen—*cinéma-vérité* cameras? Is it unfair to the poor, decent fellows who happen to be selling Bibles instead of Fuller brushes, and are therefore pilloried as Pharisees? Is it possible to capture the truth of these encounters and lives when cameras and tape recorders are present, or do distortions grow like tumors? Does the editing of the film disingenuously introduce editorial comment where none is admitted to be?

All these questions, I think, have their relevance, but beg the most important questions. How does the filmmaker, in a situation like this, avoid having a pronounced view on the subject, and how, having such a view, can he still appear impartial? And if he succeeds in *looking* impartial, how can he avoid being either wishy-washy or a hypocrite? It seems inconceivable to me that he could simply say: "This just happens; it's just there."

Poor people are beleaguered by conniving men who tell them, truthfully, that they got their names through the local church. Their Catholicism is appealed to, questioned, played upon. Often they commit themselves to buying one of those hideous, expensive, gilt-edged Du Pont fabricoid plastic-and-nylon-bound Bibles that look like a cross between American Heritage and the Reader's Digest; usually they have to pay on the installment plan, although, besides a few slick reproductions of famous Biblical paintings, it offers nothing that these folks' old Bibles don't provide just as well.

The neuroses and even psychoses that the salesmen and their dog, the camera, uncover are sometimes alarming; but the placid benightedness in other houses is scarcely more comforting. The way religion is bandied about, merchandised, paid unctuous lip service to, makes the notorious dance around the Golden Calf seem, by comparison, the Spring Frolic at Miss Porter's School. I believe any righteous man, whether devout Catholic or atheist, would have to be disgusted by this.

Nevertheless, it is possible to argue, I imagine, that even this horrible method spreads the word of God and serves a purpose. In that case, the film would have to be more committed to what it shows, just as in the opposite case it would have to be much more severe. But why, someone will ask, can't the film remain neutral? Why can't it present its data as a journalistic report does on poverty, a war, or a riot—without taking sides, but not, presumably, without private opinions? The answer is that a 90-minute film involves much more planning, organizing, arranging, selecting, editing—contains much more patterning and good or bad artifice—than any straight, direct newspaper account. It therefore imposes on us the need to judge it as a construct, a work of art, and forthwith a new set of aesthetic and moral expectations must be reckoned with.

Both from watching the film and from hearing the Maysleses talk about it, a certain moral ambiguity, a slipperiness based as much on fuzzy thinking as on wanting to have it both ways, comes to light. The film tries to be at once tough and sentimental, mocking and sympathetic, all of which is epitomized, perhaps inadvertently, in its advertisement. This shows Jesus Christ, complete with halo, carrying two salesman's suitcases. What is the symbology of this ad: Has Jesus become Willy Loman, or has Willy assumed the role of Christ? Are we debunking religion or apotheosizing that quintessential American, the salesman? Or are we laughing at both Savior and Salesman? The issues involved are too grave to permit the Maysles brothers to get away with statements about how they really "like" these salesmen while the advertising copy they release suggests an exposé of dark doings.

And now the other criticisms become meaningful. Wilfrid Sheed has rightly objected that the film does not show how the Church is involved with this activity. Nat Hentoff, while professing boundless admiration for the filmmakers, expressed his conviction that the salesmen are shown here at their worst, that their essential humanity is sacrificed for dramatic effect. I myself am inclined to believe that they are even less sympathetic than the film shows or could show— *vide* E. E. Cummings: "a salesman is an it that stinks . . . / whether it's in lonjewray/ or shrouds is immaterial it stinks/ a salesman is an it that stinks to please." If the salesmen were shown not only on the road but also at home, I suspect that sorer truths would be revealed.

Still, almost despite itself, the film does achieve some impressively depressing revelations. There are the Sales Manager and his wife, two figures so crude and complacent and, in his case, menacing, as to sum up in themselves the sociopolitical nightmare we live in. There is the Theological Consultant for the Bible company who, at a testimonial dinner, makes a speech that is worthy of the pen of Günter Grass. There are the salesmen themselves who, with the exception of the film's quasi-hero (who has since switched to the more secular selling of roofing and siding), show no qualms about the oily or jocular, butch or sanctimonious chicanery they practice. And, above all, there are the victims, the people. Their witlessness, especially when trying to be witty; their boredom and boringness; their oafishness and pathos; their callousness and hauntedness; the perhaps inevitable degradation of ignorance they live in, which is nevertheless an accusation and a challenge.

Andrew Sarris has criticized the film (like Hentoff, from a liberal standpoint) for generating an easy sense of superiority in the viewer. This is a correct indictment, considering how superficial and unearned is the superiority of the average middle-class moviegoer. But, at the same time, it avoids the issue: that anyone with genuine aspirations to independent thought, aesthetic sensibility, the life of the spirit must feel profoundly shocked and revolted by the lives of these his fellow men, with or without benefit of Bible salesmen.

The Maysleses have gone out with their equipment to capture something quaintly unwholesome yet typical; or something typically human and thus, supposedly, forgivable; or something—anything —that presented itself to their mechanically reinforced sensibilities. Instead, they have come back with something Swiftian, scandalous, frightening, and heartbreaking. They have stumbled on to something much bigger than they realize: a condemnation—however fragmented, fortuitous, and even inept—of the human condition, of man himself; but also of a society plagued by superstition, idiot competitiveness, and stultifying materialism.

History Right in the Face
by Joseph Morgenstern

*This selection appeared originally in
Newsweek, November 10, 1969.*

In a new documentary on Vietnam, *In the Year of the Pig,* we hear
of a conversation that took place between a journalist-historian, the
late Bernard Fall, and Pham Van Dong, the Premier of North
Vietnam. The more help the United States might give the Saigon
government, Pham insisted, the less popular the government would
become, and then it would need even more help, which would make
it even less popular. Wasn't that, asked Fall, a vicious circle? No,
Pham replied; a downward spiral. This is a harrowing film, particularly now that the United States is going through a revolution
of falling expectations about hopes for a Vietnam victory. It is also,
however, an enormously valuable film, for it goes back more than
a decade and lets us see and hear for ourselves how leaders led us
to believe that the downward spiral was a forward march.

In the Year of the Pig lays no claim to impartiality. It seeks to
portray the United States role in Vietnam as that of a demented
giant. Producer-director Emile de Antonio, whose previous films
include a fine documentary on Sen. Joseph McCarthy, *Point of
Order,* and a poor documentary on President Kennedy's assassination, *Rush to Judgment,* marshals as much evidence as he can find,
and a good bit of propaganda, too, to convince us that we have no
business being in Vietnam and no chance of getting out until we
understand what we're doing there.

The director is sloppy about identifying speakers, or re-identify-
ing them when their voices recur offscreen. He relies overmuch on
North Vietnamese propaganda films; are *all* women beautiful north
of the 17th parallel? He breaks up engrossing narratives, such as
that of Harry Ashmore, by intercutting them with equally engrossing observations, such as those of Yale professor Paul Mus. He
allows Steve Addiss's otherwise forceful score to descend into easy
musical mockery of "La Marseillaise" and "The Battle Hymn of the
Republic."

I wish these flaws didn't exist, but I'm thankful that the film
exists, and I will forget slowly, if at all, its juxtapositions of thinking

men, unthinking men, and raving maniacs in American Life. "I wouldn't trade one dead American for 50 dead Chinamen," says Gen. Mark Clark. "We must be willing to continue our bombing until we have destroyed every work of man in North Vietnam, if this is what it takes to win the war," says Curtis LeMay. "They looked determined and reverent at the same time," George S. Patton III says of the soldiers he saw at a memorial service in Vietnam, "but still they're a bloody good bunch of killers."

It serves us our recent history right smack in the face, like a napalm pie. A certain amount of it is familiar enough to duck or discount. We've seen bombs fall, people die, and babies cry on TV. On TV, however, recent history means that which happened yesterday. *In the Year of the Pig* has a better memory than that. It goes back for a few remarkable scenes to the 30s when Saigon was a far, placid Paris in which gentlemen sipped their Pernods at sidewalk cafés while the waiters kept starving pedicab drivers from their sight. It goes back to the 40s, when Ho Chi Minh was a jungle wraith overhung by Gauloise clouds. And it goes back to the 50s and early 60s, to the early American blunderers, blitherers, bamboozlers, escalaters, deceivers, and self-deceivers who told us why we were in Vietnam and how we were going to get out with our honor and credibility intact.

How can recent history seem so ancient? (The fall of Dienbienphu, Bao Dai in Cannes, the curl of John Foster Dulles's lips.) How can rhetoric we once listened to—sat still and listened to, however skeptically—now drive us up the wall, the prison wall of the terrible present? (Secretary of Defense Wilson assuring us in 1954 that we were sending only equipment and technicians, but no troops, Dulles explaining his domino theory, President Eisenhower fawning over Ngo Dinh Diem, Gerald Ford proclaiming the Vietnamese "economic miracle," Dean Rusk standing pat.) Is it simply that events have discredited our prophets? Or do we loathe our past with a particular passion because the present refuses to dawn?

King's *A Married Couple*

by Ron Blumer

This review appeared in Take One (Montreal), December 30, 1969. Mr. Blumer is a Canadian filmmaker and critic.

"Life is a comedy to those who think; a tragedy to those who feel." Horace Walpole's adage is also applicable to Allan King's new film, *A Married Couple*. The movie is a frequently painful, often funny, embarrassingly intimate portrait of a couple whose marriage is breaking up. Although it is not a staged film, it is photographed in color with the same clarity and sensitivity of a studio job; though not a fictional film, it is often more dramatic than anything that could have come from a screenwriter's pen. Allan King, who with *Warrendale* had shown himself to be one of Canada's most talented filmmakers, has done it again, and this time with a movie that is so interesting in so many ways that one hardly knows where to begin talking about it.

In order to produce this film, the director and crew actually moved in with the husband and wife and lived with them for three months. When they went to bed, the camera was there and running; when they got up in the morning, it was also ready and waiting. Using newly developed, very portable 16mm cameras and specialized sound equipment, the film team stood relatively removed from the action and recorded what ensued. To overcome the inevitable self-consciousness, King ran the camera empty for the first three weeks so that the all-seeing eyes and the all-hearing ears would recede into the wallpaper.

Obviously, the presence of the cameras could not be completely ignored, but the personalities of the actors in this life-drama inevitably began to show through. To those who would doubt that such a thing is possible, I would recommend that they go see the movie. Time and time again, one finds oneself wincing and looking away from the screen because what is coming from it is obviously too real.

In many ways this is a very funny film; the tragedy comes with the sudden awareness that this is not a stage performance, but two very real people suffering from very common problems. The laughter that rings throughout the auditorium is often the nervous laughter produced by the situation hitting a little too close to the nerve of reality as we experience it. We are brought into this couple's lives in the most intimate ways imaginable. We meet their kid, and their dog, we see their home and their surroundings.

Later on in the film, when you see them in bed together, you realize that they are really in bed together; when you see them fighting, you know that they are really fighting, and all the horror flows from the screen unsoftened by the detachment of fiction.

The technique in *cinéma-vérité* is to shoot literally miles of film and select from this mass of images and sound 90 minutes that will contain the quintessence of the situation within some overall cinematic structure. It is this art of selecting and shaping which so few directors of this school have completely mastered. Don Pennebaker (*Monterey Pop, Don't Look Back,* etc.), in a recent talk in Montreal, presented himself as a sort of direct transmitter of reality using his art to place us in situations that would otherwise be inaccessible to us. Unfortunately, the loose construction and sloppy ramblings of most of his films reflect only too well these limited theories put into practice.

Allan King's work in this style is at the other end of the spectrum. *A Married Couple* is nothing short of a polished jewel in terms of how it was put together. What was finally selected is relevant, powerful, and to the point. The film, as a whole, is as tight as any pre-scripted work, with all the nuances, all the dialogue, and all the other subtleties found in the best conventional cinema.

Within this tight structure, cinema's little-explored ability to transmit whole chunks of reality is thrown in as an extra bonus. The square screen puts a frame around the situation so that we can step outside of ourselves and see the mechanisms of behavior in action.

Marriage, as seen from my side of the veil, has always appeared to me a very peculiar convention, notwithstanding its obvious popularity. The wife in this film says to a friend at one point, "The world is filled with so many people; why do I have to have only one of them?" The practice of isolating two human beings and having them interact for the rest of their lives is one peculiar to our constipated society.

The couple in this film have been together for eight years and their patterns of behavior with respect to each other have long been pre-programmed. Ideally, the two should be interacting as a unit; in fact, as with many marriages, the interaction is a destructive one.

Like the slow drip of a faucet it is the little things which assume epic proportions, and everything from feeding the dog to cleaning the house is potentially explosive.

The couple selected for this microscopic viewing is not a particularly typical one. The husband is a witty ad copy [writer] and the wife is quite intelligent or at least well-educated. The objects with which their world is cluttered, the modern furniture, the Beatle records, and the late foreign model car are all typical of the well-off hip couples. . . . The mental attitudes, their ideas of freedom, of women's rights versus male supremacy are equally familiar scenery.

Unlike other social documentaries, the problems all come from within, and the basic rottenness of their relationship turns everything they touch sour. We sit and witness two people clinging to each other and at the same time destroying each other. This is not a very pretty film, but not because things are so continually dreadful, but because everything is so real and so common.

Anyone contemplating marriage, indeed any man born of woman, should see this film. Although unrelentingly specific, this movie leads one to re-think the entire concept of marriage. When it works it can be the most beautiful thing in the world—when it's bad, it's awful.

474

Three Documentaries
by Molly Haskell

This selection originally appeared in the January 29, 1970 issue of The Village Voice (New York).

In "One-Dimensional Man," Herbert Marcuse describes the de-eroticization of the human environment—the elimination of a huge field of eroticized activity and experience through technology and urbanization, and the replacement of transcendent erotic (creative and procreative) drives with localized libidinous gratification. Rollo May describes the same ascendancy of sex over eroticism, but in psychoanalytical rather than sociological terms.

For striking examples of After and Before, of a de-eroticized hell and a lost paradise, see *Johnny Cash,* a documentary about the country-and-western singer, and Allan King's *A Married Couple.* In King's film, an educated, middle-class, vaguely liberated, and moderately aware couple argue about money and their marriage, walk around in the nude, eat dinner in their underwear, pick their teeth, say fuck, make love, go skinny-dipping with their son. It is a depressing exhibition and the most de-eroticized environment this side of a New York cocktail party.

In *Johnny Cash,* the weather-beaten, western-hero singer and his ageless wife—a kind of Alice-Pat Quinn type, only real country —imbue the simplest acts of radiant, eroticized joy, and take their nourishment, through the twin roots of love and loss, directly from nature. They bus across-country to engagements, and between times are back with family and friends, close to the land. Cash pulls playfully and sensually at a donkey's ear; they tease the old people; take a bus to Memphis; kiss behind a magazine; go by the sharecropper's cottage where they used to live; she brushes dandruff off his shoulder while he is in the middle of a song; they sing at an Indian reservation and a state penitentiary—a gathering of rapt, innocent-looking faces in mystical rapport. At one point, Cash and Bob Dylan are at a taping session. There is more than a table between them—Dylan trying to look back to where none of us can return, not the effete Easterner or the deracinated Westerner, not Dylan, not even the hippie communes (neo-pioneers, grafted to the soil). In the beginning of the film, Johnny Cash says the reason country music is sad is because it's about loss. Most of his songs are about direct loss—death, flood, the surrender of a friendly filling station to a superhighway. How much greater is our loss, being indirect, that in listening to Johnny Cash we cannot feel sorrow and catharsis, but only nostalgia.

Johnny Cash is not a great or even comprehensive documentary. Robert Elfstrom's camera is too obtrusive, swooping and soaring unnecessarily; and Cash has none of the exhibitionist in him. He remains ambiguous: outgoing and private, wry and sincere, secretive as a laconic country singer should be. But sometimes the less it tries to tell us, the better a documentary is, and *Johnny Cash* is all the richer for its opacity.

A Married Couple, on the other hand, reveals everything and nothing. Antoinette and Billy Edwards open their pockets inside out, and nothing falls on the floor. Allan King, as anyone who has seen *Warrendale* can testify, is a genius at knowing where to put his camera and when to put film in it. His friends the Edwardses have not only opened their doors and souls to him, but seem to have been catalyzed by the camera into forcing their marriage to a showdown.

The fact that they would allow the film to be made—that they have so little of themselves to keep from each other, and therefore little between them to keep from the world—tells more about them than all their raw harangues. As they argue, it is obvious that their problems have nothing to do with money or furniture or even marriage, that their bids for power arise from their own insubstantial egos, from a shaky sense of self.

If Antoinette and Billy Edwards want to place themselves on record, fine, but I refuse to sit in as character judge, or make the missing connections between character and condition. The film is suspended between psychology and sociology and, like so many documentaries, tries to promote selected gleaning into self-evident generalizations. We may respond urgently and personally to the children at Warrendale, but we are not entitled to condemn their unseen and unknown parents for withholding the love they may never have had to give. If a documentary film asks us to evaluate it as a statement and a vision, it is assuming the prerogatives, without properties, of art. Art uses metaphor and imagination to join the worlds of reality and fantasy, the particular and the general, to illuminate, to offer a picture signed by the artist and in some way complete. In *A Married Woman* (which he even tried to name *The*

Married Woman), Godard's most detached and sociological film, he at least presented a self-contained, artistic, non-objective truth, and took moral responsibility for it.

Since any judgment of documentary is likely to be a projection of the critic, we can only tread gingerly and try to acknowledge our own predispositions. *Other Voices* is a study, through five of his patients, of the special confrontation techniques developed by Dr. Albert Honig at his clinic-home for psychotics in Pennsylvania. It is an awkwardly filmed, dangerously incomplete, but fascinating glimpse of schizophrenia, mainly because of three mad, disturbingly poetic male patients.

Honig's technique is physical and verbal assault on his patients, to jar them into direct responses while providing the emotional stability of a family situation. Even with more information, it would be impossible to measure the effectiveness of his approach, since most of the patients have been written off as hopeless before they arrived. Since one can see neither overall progress nor the alternative loneliness, instead of our being cheered by each faltering step toward reality, it is the case of psychotic fantasy which exercises strong emotional fascination.

Of the five patients, two are barely articulate, and David Sawyer (producer-director) and Robert Elfstrom (co-director and photographer) sensibly stay mostly with the other three, who turn out to be "naturals" as they stunningly act out excerpts of their psychoses. Peter, a handsome Harvard graduate (background: drugs and mental breakdown), enters like gentle reason itself and gradually retreats into fear and isolation; 32-year-old Bill gives a vivid idiosyncratic account of arguments with his brother (actually dead) whose voice comes over the radio; and the 14-year-old Mark longs to follow his father who died when he was seven and is convinced he will be reincarnated as a dog free of human pain. During the course of the film (and his treatment), he loses weight and changes perceptibly, but he is more than half in love with easeful death, and the shocking knowledge comes to us near the end of the film that he has taken his life. Paradoxically but understandably, his suicide came when life had begun to offer an alternative to death. But, as Honig points out, the forces of health are often more frightening than those of death. Somehow, I cannot take a tragic view of Mark's decision not to undertake the struggle toward reality.

Documenting America
by David Denby

*This selection is reprinted from the March 1970
issue of the Atlantic Monthly.*

In the last three years a young law professor and urban planner from
Boston named Frederick Wiseman has made feature-length documentaries about four of the central institutions of our society; a
state asylum for the criminally insane *(Titicut Follies),* a city
police force *(Law and Order),* a large urban public high school
(High School), and now, a public hospital in New York—the title,
as you may have guessed, *Hospital.* The conspicuous plainness of
the titles is consistent with the overall tone, which even by documentary standards is austere. Wiseman's films have no music, no
subtitles, narration, or explanation of any kind, and the shooting
style, apart from some unnecessary spotting of mouths and nervously tapping fingers, is mostly a level stare. Compared with such
recent empty-headed exercises as "minimal cinema" (the films of
Jean-Marie Straub) or "the basic recording function of the medium"
(Warhol), this austerity of style is remarkable for the richness of
human experience it allows us to encounter. There's nothing minimal or basic about Wiseman's sensibility; the outward blankness is
reminiscent of Hemingway, Orwell, and the Depression photographers.

Hospital was shown on NET on February 2, and watching it
was not an easy experience. Seen without the usual glamour and
pornography, the human body in a state of disintegration undergoes
a tragedy which is mainly squalid, and the incoherence and plain
terror of the sufferers won't allow us to sustain any such nonsense
as "the nobility of suffering" or "the dignity of pain." Wiseman
situated himself in the receiving area of the hospital, and many of
the patients are studied in their initial encounter with a hospital
doctor (in some cases it seems like the first encounter with any doctor in years). In a public hospital most of the patients are poor, and
people [who don't have any] money have a different notion of health
care than people who do; they don't see a doctor until troubles
accumulate and reach a crisis. As we watch, we realize that for
many the hospital is still a place where you go to die or suffer

miserably, and we hear doctors repeatedly saying, "You'll be all right . . . all right," just to reduce their patients' fear.

These middle-class doctors come off rather well. I don't mean to suggest that there's anything especially noble in their treating patients who don't pay them directly, and we may take it for granted they will fight tenaciously for their patients' lives; but it's heartening to see them also fighting with all the authority and wit they can muster for the patients' human rights within the city hospital and welfare systems. Each patient is treated with considerable attention to his particular life situation (not just his symptoms), a procedure which appears both humane and, psychologically, an essential part of the treatment. Finally, this aspect of taking personal interest in the patients—which extends to the nurses, orderlies, and New York cops, nasally angelic and gentle—becomes very moving to watch. If bourgeois individualism accounts for the difference between what we see here and what we've read about doctor-patient relationships in early nineteenth-century hospitals, then for once we might offer a modest tribute to middle-class values. (That those values also account for the inadequacies of our public health and welfare systems is momentarily beside the point.) Looking at some of these young doctors, we wonder how they can face this chaos and misery every day. How long does it take before they become insensitive to their patients or set up offices in Westchester and private hospitals? We see one older man, a psychiatrist, who's still at it, and he's become tougher and smarter. In an interview with a young black homosexual, he advises the boy not to tell the welfare people he's been hustling to support himself, if he expects to get any money. It may be cynical, but we can't help admiring such an open solidarity with the patient against the system.

Since Wiseman hasn't hesitated to expose authority working brutally or obtusely in his earlier films, we can believe he didn't see any of the same thing here. I won't easily forget a certain psychiatrist in *Titicut Follies,* humiliating a new inmate with vulgar questions and force-feeding a dying older one while his cigarette ash hung over the open funnel. Or the "Dean of Discipline" in *High School,* living his fantasy of the tough/wise drill sergeant, making a student who feels he's innocent take his punishment with the line: "We're out to establish that you can be a man and that you can take orders." The earlier films were about the corruption of authority, its degeneration into petty tyranny and ego-boosting; the people who

ran the institutions he filmed may not have had much status themselves, but they were invested with the sanctions of law and society's
approval, and they knew how to make their charges feel small. In
a harsh way, the films were funny. They were full of helpless prisoners, but with few exceptions the prison guards were so ugly that
there was an exhilaration in watching to see precisely how they
would disgrace themselves next. In *Hospital* we are in a different
world, and the image we are likely to remember is that of the
young doctor angrily rapping his hand on the table because he
can't provide an elderly patient with all the services he requires. If
the movie suggests obliquely that our national health-care system
is a mess, it shows a particular institution within the system doing
its job rather well.

Only at the very end do we get a characteristically sardonic
touch, a religious service for a bedraggled group of patients in which
a priest drones a mechanical sermon, quotes Bishop Sheen ("Thank
God for God"), and passes around a collection basket (where could
the Church find any more unfortunate than the people in the
room?). As the man goes on about "realizing our insufficiency before God, our nothingness before Him," and tells the patients they
must be less *selfish,* we may conclude that religious consolation looks
pretty dreary next to the passionate scientific humanism of the doctors. It's a quiet echo of the devastating final scene of *High School,*
when, after watching students being browbeaten by petty regulations and stupefied by miserable dull teaching for ninety minutes,
we see the principal read a letter to the faculty from a former student, a boy "who might have been a nobody." Now he's stationed
on an aircraft carrier off Vietnam, about to land behind the DMZ,
and he writes: "Please don't say anything to Mrs. C. She would
only worry over me. I am not worth it. I am only a body doing a
job." After finishing the letter, the principal smiles through her
tears and concludes that "we are very successful at Northeast High
School." They are a success because the boy has adopted the "right"
attitudes about his school and his society, and it hardly matters to
them that he has lost all sense of himself along the way; the meaning
they have given his life is their meaning, not his, and they aren't
aware that the difference is crucial. Wiseman's films are political
in the largest sense: they're about power relations in our society
and the way we are affected by the institutions that we pass through.
Although he clearly stands on the left he isn't narrowly ideological;

the bias seems not so much partisan as radically humanist and libertarian.

Despite the decency and hopefulness we see in *Hospital,* someone may legitimately ask, Must we look at the blasted and the dying —the alcoholics, the addicts, the coronaries? The tendency of all of Wiseman's films is to establish an elite audience of the tough-minded and the strong-stomached; here, I think, many who might qualify will shudder and turn away, and I'm not sure I blame them. But by bringing disaster down to individual scale in *Hospital,* Wiseman has offered us an unusual choice: we may turn away if we like, but if we keep our eyes on the screen, it's impossible not to become involved with these people and caught up by their stories.

We don't have those emotions simply because he goes further than other filmmakers, although he does do that. The results grow out of a good deal of arduous work, as I learned when I talked with Wiseman in the offices of the urban-planning company he set up with Donald Schon in 1966. First, he arranges his own financing, so that he's not tied down to a sponsor who wants to look good or a foundation that's afraid of rocking the boat. After getting permission to make the film in a certain institution, he enters the scene with a cameraman (William Brayne, who shot *Hospital,* also did *Law and Order*) and portable 16mm equipment and just hangs around for a while watching things happen; when the institution grows accustomed to the strangers and loses its camera-shyness, they begin to shoot—central relationships, trivial moments, and inadvertences, thousands and thousands of feet, until Wiseman feels he has enough. The editing takes months of close work. Wiseman practices what is known in the textbooks as continuity editing: that is, he tries to sustain within each sequence the illusion of real time and the unity of real space, no matter how much the footage has been cut down from its original length. (The final cut usually contains around one twenty-fifth of the entire footage.) When he is done, he has lots of little "stories," and rather than group them in solid blocks to illustrate "points" as in most documentaries, he arranges them fairly subtly for contrast, balance, and thematic complexity.

Obviously, the possibilities for distortion and simplification in editing are endless, but Wiseman is unique for the complexity and ambivalence he leaves in. In *Law and Order,* there is a scene in which the cops rough up and arrest a new prostitute in town; as the sequence develops it becomes obvious from their tone that they're only frightening her, letting her know she has certain obligations regarding them if she wants to continue working. Everyone knows this complicity goes on, but who else has captured it on film? Also in *Law and Order,* we see a white cop arresting a black teen-ager who has been stealing things and banging up cars in a black neighborhood; the cop is having a good time because the neighborhood is assisting him to get rid of a boy who has become a menace, and as the boy gets more desperate, shouting at a black man who is helping out ("silly-ass nigger") and threatening to kill everyone, we feel pretty bitter about that cop; but later we hear him tell another policeman that the boy may be released, and he's *afraid*— what happens to our easy attitudes now?

Scenes like these could never fit into a standard network documentary, with its point-A, point-B structure and its narrator to balance things out and assure you that although the world may be difficult, your ever-vigilant news staff is staying right on top of things. The narrator's function in those films is often as much psychological as it is informational; his presence implies a balanced, judicious authority which the viewer can trust, relieving him at the same time of the difficulty of forming his own relation to the material (if all the difficulties haven't already been edited out). Wiseman never uses narration or interviews with experts or public opinion polls or anything that lessens the burden of our response.

When Wiseman screened *High School* for an audience of students and parents in a Boston suburb, some of the students stood up afterwards and denounced their own school on the grounds that it was exactly like the one in the film: coercive, petty, dull, unconcerned with the world outside. But then the parents said, "What are you talking about? That looks like a good school to us; it teaches respect for authority, the value of hard work, a realistic attitude toward college . . ." Other filmmakers might see this incident as evidence of failure, an inability to make one's point of view clear, but Wiseman does not. He intended *High School* as a study of middle-class ideology, in which the teachers and the school's operating values (as opposed to its announced values) acted as surrogates for the parents and their values, and the kids got pounded into shape. The response showed how correctly he perceived the school; the kids watching the film may have seen their position clearly for the first time.

Intransigent men like Wiseman often run into trouble with

authorities and the press. After exposing the horrors of the Bridge-water facility in *Titicut Follies,* he was widely denounced in the Massachusetts Statehouse as an enemy of the people, and the law-suits piled up. The later films have had an easier time, but as long as Wiseman keeps his camera pointed toward the center of our society and not toward hippie communes and rock festivals, his work will be the cause of anger and contention.

The Present State of the Documentary
by James Arnold

This study, by a member of the faculty of Marquette University, appeared in Films 1968, annual publication of The National Catholic Office for Motion Pictures (New York).

Despite the authentic claims of film as an art, the fundamental power of the medium, as Siegfried Kracauer and André Bazin recognized, is its ability to take you there, some place where you might not ordinarily go, or even want to go, to witness something that "really happened." This kind of trip has always been a basic aim of the documentary filmmaker, and developments in movie-making technology have deepened the possibilities to a degree that is both exquisite and alarming. With only slight losses in ultimate quality, cameras and sound equipment have become portable (one man or woman can carry them anywhere), virtually foolproof (a well-coordinated layman can learn their intricacies creditably in a few hours), and unobtrusive (subjects, already conditioned to a camera-filled world, hardly notice them).

Filmmakers now have the physical capacity to observe and record every aspect of human life under the most difficult and confining conditions, with little fear of disturbing the "truth" of reality by the presence of their crew, lights, ponderous equipment, etc. (There may always be reasonable doubt about the camera-consciousness of subjects, especially if they are professionals used to being "on"; e.g., how really candid were the sequences on CBS's "60 Minutes" of Nixon and Humphrey in their hotelrooms watching themselves win the nominations?) At the same time, a permissive society has slowly broadened the legal and moral limits of documentary subject matter; the relaxation of old codes and taboos has had its impact on nonfiction as well as fiction films. Blessed with this double push toward freedom, most documentarists have been busy probing their new limits, lugging their new portable gear into previously unexplored territories. Their style (capturing reality without prejudging or altering its shape) is called *cinéma-vérité* and now dominates the whole field of the documentary; their subject matter has tended to be somewhat more bizarre and a great deal more personal.

This development has its sobering aspects. After all, the dream of the documentarist, who would watch and record through his lens all that is meaningful and significant in human life, is not so vastly different from the dream of the Peeping Tom. The difference is in the definition of what is meaningful and significant. The power to get and then show "almost anything" on film carries with it heavy responsibility, and a surprising amount of time at gatherings of film professionals (such as the annual Robert Flaherty seminars) is devoted to ethical questions. The impulses of conscience are strong, but so are the impulses of reporter, explorer, and showman which bring a man into the documentary profession in the first place.

Freedom in documentary also has its practical limits. There is a major built-in inhibition in the nature of the market, which is chiefly distribution through television, schools, and libraries. Even the most liberal of these outlets (and National Educational Television and its Public Broadcast Laboratory have undoubtedly spurred the most adventuresome documentaries) maintain restrictions on content and even on style. The only alternative market is in theaters, where documentaries have never had great success without some special mass appeal (the sex and sadism of the *Mondo*-type films, the names of Dylan and Baez to carry a *vérité* film like *Don't Look Back*). The avant-garde documentarists, anxious for more freedom, are looking increasingly to theatrical distribution, a fact that is likely to push them toward more sensational subjects. An instructive example is the case of Allan King's *Warrendale*. Originally intended for Canadian television, it was never shown, perhaps partly because of its four-letter words, but chiefly because of its severe *vérité* style, which never allows a clear explanation of what is going on. Now it is being shown in theaters, where its honesty and lack of sensationalism will be a commercial handicap. (The history of *One Step Away,* rejected by NET-PBL as "too strong," is similar.) So the documentarist has freedom to "do" but considerably less freedom to "sell," and the latter is often crucial in raising money for his project in the initial stages.

On top of all this there is a continuing intramural struggle between more traditional filmmakers (chiefly those working for and in the news departments of the networks), who want to absorb *vérité* techniques into the structure of the standard objective film report, and the new generation, who want to abandon "old-fashioned" and "restrictive" preconceptions and do all the fresh, exciting, and unpredictable things that *vérité* allows them to do. In

McLuhanesque terms, the conflict is between those who see the documentary as a "hot" or structured package, with verbal interpretation of the visual realities, and those who see the documentary as "cool," unstructured, ambiguous, an image of reality that emotionally involves the viewer and forces him to his own subjective conclusions.

The argument has several roots. One is perhaps philosophical: does the filmmaker simply record reality, and let the structure of that reality control his editing and selection of shots? Or is he an interpretive expert or artist, who imposes his own reactions and vision, and shapes his film to produce a specific emotional or intellectual effect? Another root is simply the ancient dispute between the journalist, who hopes to remain detached from the event and somehow explain it, and the filmmaker showman, who is more interested in shaking up his audience and making it undergo an emotional experience.

The most interesting films of 1968 were decidedly in the "cool" category: *Warrendale,* an exploration of a new technique in the treatment of disturbed children; Frederick Wiseman's legally troubled *Titicut Follies,* an exposé of conditions in a mental hospital; Arthur Barron's *Birth and Death,* dealing with the arrival of a young couple's first child and the lingering demise of a cancer patient; David Neuman and Ed Pincus's *One Step Away,* which follows the troubles of a hippie couple in San Francisco; and Allan Grant's *What Color Is the Wind?,* an account of the daily life of a blind four-year-old boy. All of these were *vérité* films, with little or no narration and little structure beyond what was provided by the events themselves. (Indeed, a viewer is well into both *Warrendale* and *Titicut* before he even suspects where he is.)

Perhaps the best examples of the many traditional or "hot" documentaries were Martin Carr's *Hunger in America* (CBS) and Morton Silverstein's *What Harvest for the Reaper?* (NET), an examination of the problems of farm migrants much in the *Harvest of Shame* tradition. Both films rely on narrative and take strong editorial stands, but also include many *vérité* passages.

In the old documentaries, the filmmaker discovered things and told you about them, much as the traditional artist does; in the new documentary, as in the new art, the viewer is presented with complexity and makes his own discoveries. The difference was amusingly exemplified at the 1968 Flaherty seminar, with the screening of young Jim McBride's *David Holzman's Diary*. This fictional feature which combines *vérité* with the styles of Warhol and Godard, purports to be a personal documentary in which the filmmaker hero describes and films a whole week in his hectic life. When the film is over, the closing credits reveal it is fiction. The Flaherty audience of experts had been fooled and was now outraged. The insights they believed they had been discovering in "cool" fashion for themselves in Holzman's real life had actually been discovered by director McBride, who then served it up to them in a traditional "hot" fiction film.

Regardless of differences in approach, documentarists tend to measure achievement by their success in getting "new" or "impossible" footage. The films that excited them most in 1968 broke new ground because of both *vérité* equipment and their daring entry into previously uncovered subjects. The amazing thing about *Warrendale* is that King was able to get inside a small cottage and film intimate moments of affection and violence without noticeably falsifying them, an effect made possible only by months of rapport-building, hanging about and finally becoming "invisible" to children and staff. In *Titicut,* the triumph was mainly in getting all those incredible unstaged shots of inhumanity in a mental hospital. In Robin Spry's *Flowers on a One-way Street*, it was capturing on film the tragicomedy of a big city government (Toronto) hung up on its own procedural red tape, a matter (for Spry) largely of patience and good luck. In Lewis Freedman's *Interview With Ingmar Bergman,* only the rare footage of an English-language interview with the enigmatic Swede saved what was otherwise a muffed opportunity for enlightenment, and in Brian Moser's *End of a Revolution* there were the fascinating shots of Guevara and Debray in Bolivia, the hard-nosed comments by the Green Beret sergeant, and the unforgettable glimpse of the U.S. Ambassador playing croquet amid the intrigue.

By its nature *vérité* involves shattering some taboos, e.g., the vulgar language incidental to *Warrendale, Titicut,* and *Don't Look Back,* the nudity in *Titicut,* the drug use and lovemaking in *One Step Away.* But documentarists now also feel free, like many novelists, to detail the lives of marginal groups and social outcasts whose activities may be shocking and offensive to the general public. This may be done responsibly or exploitatively. Among many 1968 documentaries in this general taboo-breaking category were those dealing with drug users (Sheldon Rochlin's *Head*), hippies (Jack O'Connell's *Revolution*), a male prostitute (Shirley Clarke's *Portrait of Jason*), and a transvestite beauty contest (Frank Simon's *The Queen*). Filmmakers were also absorbed by the subject of birth and the mechanics of sex, with films ranging in quality from the amateurish *Miracle of Love* to Lennart Nillsson's awesome *Beginning of Life* (with its color close-ups of the foetus in various stages of development); actual childbirth was shown not only in *Birth and Death* but also in *Helga*, ABC's *How Life Begins* (a survey of reproduction in all species), and Eugene Jones's Vietnam documentary, *A Face of War*.

Long-range, however, the most mischievous documentary steps were via *vérité* into the private lives of ordinary people: the dehumanizing patient-objects of *Titicut*, the shallow men of the Duluth Lions Club in Arthur Barron's *Great American Novel*, the comical middle-class "soldiers" of the Pope's army in Canada's prizewinning *Avec tambours et trompettes*, the Wallace-admiring family in Elizabeth Farmer's *Hear Us, O Lord*. In these and many other similar films, one has the uncomfortable feeling that people, once persuaded to sign a legal release, are used as a source of sophisticated entertainment. In Lord Snowden's *Don't Count the Candles* real old people are used to demonstrate the misery of old age in a youth-oriented world. In *Birth and Death* we are obviously voyeurs at sacred private moments, and in *One Step Away* we are in a private bedroom watching a real husband make love to a real "other woman" while his wife looks on.

Some, perhaps all, of these films have social relevance and an aspect of legitimate public interest, but the line between useful knowledge and mere curiosity is inevitably fuzzy. Filmmakers fret over such problems, but usually avoid solving them. Thus Shirley Clarke confessed being "monstrous" to Jason in order to have him bare his soul on film, and worried about the film's effect on his life. But the resulting footage is truly harrowing and unique, and Miss Clarke could not resist either distributing it or touring the college circuit with it in person. Documentarists are disturbed also by older ethical problems, such as whether a camerman first photographs a "victim" or gives him first-aid and spoils the picture. At the Flaherty seminar, some were highly critical of Silverstein (*What Harvest for the Reaper?*) for simply following with his camera while a crew chief recruited black laborers he intended to exploit.

There have also been interesting experiments in cross-breeding documentary and fiction. Already mentioned is *David Holzman's Diary,* in which an utterly convincing *vérité* and "home movie" style, as well as large numbers of "real" people, are used to tell a fictional story. *The Great American Novel* was a unique attempt to gain modern documentation for the insights of two old novels ("Babbitt," "The Grapes of Wrath"), and John Lord's *Four Days to Omaha* (NBC "Experiment in Television") unsuccessfully tried to blend fiction with interviews of real Englishmen recalling the days before the Normandy invasion. Still another approach is that of French journalist Danielle Hunebelle, who uses real people to act out make-believe situations. Her *Negroes Next Door* has whites in St. Louis improvising their impulsive reactions to the hypothesis that a black family is moving into their neighborhood. Some documentarists are also not above prodding reality a bit: e.g., in *No Vietnamese Ever Called Me Nigger,* David Loeb Weiss used an aggressive and pretty blonde interviewer in Harlem deliberately to arouse hostile responses to on-the-street questions about whether blacks were being fairly treated by the draft.

If these were the problems at the frontiers of documentary-making at the end of 1968, there are also brief observations necessary to describe the state of the genre in its more controversial forms back "in the mainstream":

¶ Perhaps never has there been so much impressive (and largely unappreciated) work in the areas of wildlife and nature study which are always popular and seldom controversial: e.g., the brilliant ABC-Wolper Cousteau series, *Search in the Deep,* and the CBS-Wolper "National Geographic" series, especially Jeffrey Myrow's beautiful film on the national parks.

¶ The film approach to the problems of race and cities was too often simply a collection of interviews with experts and endless confrontations and panel discussions. There was too little pictorial documentation. The best films on this subject were probably the *vérité Hear Us, O Lord* (NET-PBL), with its insight into backlash; William Greaves's more conventional but enlightening *Still a Brother* (NET), an examination of the black middle class; some of the expert compilation films in CBS' "Of Black America" summer series; and *Color Me Black,* Richard McCutchen's study (for NET) of student unrest at middle-class Howard University.

¶ The responsible but dreary network series on urban problems were, with few exceptions, outdone in film expertise by several poetic explorations of cities in terms of their music and culture: e.g., Ed Spiegel's *Music of Chicago* for NBC's "Telephone Hour" series, which went *vérité* and was altogether a milestone in the history of musical documentary; *West Pole,* Ralph Gleason's survey of the new adult Pop culture in San Francisco; and Marc Brugnoni's sensitive *New York Night*. Urban renewal, perhaps the dreariest of city subjects, received fresh treatment in Manfred Kirchheimer's wordless yet profound *Claws,* the ultimate in "cool" documentaries which unfortunately has been shown so far only at the Flaherty seminar.

¶ Religion has received little distinguished attention from documentarists, but in 1968 there were Stuart Schulberg's *New American Catholic* and its memorable use of the four-way split screen to record varying reactions to progressive movements in the Church, and Palmer Williams's hard-hitting but wordy *Business of Religion* (CBS). Best films in this category were probably Peter Adair's *Holy Ghost People,* a *vérité* study of Appalachian snake-handlers, and the highly praised, highly visual *Beggar at the Gates,* WBZ-TV examination of the problems of modern churches in turmoil.

¶ Memorable compilation films included Jack Kaufman's three-hour version (for ABC-Wolper) of William L. Shirer's *Rise and Fall of the Third Reich,* the showing on NET of Paul Rotha's 1961 *Life of Adolf Hitler,* Harry Chapin's intelligent and cinema history-oriented boxing film, *The Legendary Champions,* and [*Point of Order*], Emile de Antonio's kinescope record of the traumatic Army-McCarthy hearings of 1954.

¶ The special ability of film, aided by the close-up and most recently by *vérité,* to capture and reveal a personality, encourages an annual rush of portrait documentaries. The most interesting during 1968 were Thomas Teichman's pure *vérité* study of jazz bassist-composer Charles Mingus, Warren Forma's inspiring and highly visual sketch of Gordon Parks, and Dick Fontaine's extraordinary profile (for NET) of the complexity of Norman Mailer.

¶ The most novel and courageous sports documentary of the year was John Sharnik's little-heralded *The Football Scholars* (CBS), which forthrightly detailed colleges' exploitation of high-school football stars.

¶ If there were a prize for controversy, it would have to go to the opposing film reports on the violence surrounding the Democratic Convention in Chicago, *What Trees Do They Plant?* and *The*

Seasons Change. These films, using the same events to come to opposite conclusions, amply demonstrate that "film truth" is a slippery
thing. There was also CBS' *Hunger in America,* a brave network
effort which may have made mistakes (picturing an infant victim
of premature birth as dying of malnutrition) but achieved the kind
of reformist impact dear to the hearts of social documentarists of
all ages and philosophies.

¶ Despite all the footage on Vietnam, there were only two outstanding war documentaries, Eugene Jones's *A Face of War* and
Peter Watkins's *Culloden.* Watkins' bloody reconstruction (shown
on NET) devastated the British "victory" and Bonnie Prince
Charles Stuart with the ruthless hindsight of 200 years. It also
showed that the documentary of "reconstructed history" is far from
dead. Unfortunately, *A Face of War* did not receive the attention it
deserved. A review of the film follows.

A Face of War (Commonwealth United), Eugene S. Jones's sadly
overlooked documentary represents one of the best cinematic treatments of the Vietnam conflict. In this regard, it measures up to the
achievement of *The Anderson Platoon* several years ago.

Although the documentary gives the impression of unstudied
episodes from a search-and-kill operation conducted by Mike Company, of the 3rd Battalion, 7th Marine Regiment, it is actually a
carefully structured piece of work. As must be the case in true documentary, however, the ordering of footage is designed to allow reality to speak with its own voice, rather than to establish a point or
argue a position. An example of this type of structure, which is true
to the engagement described, is the pacing of the narrative development (told entirely in images, with no voice-over narration). The
cautious stillness of the initial search gives way to a brief, violent
battle as the company is ambushed. A field Mass gives a period of
reflection (the sermon is on life and death) before the briefing that
leads to a helicopter drop, pursuit of a sniper, and another respite
as villagers are given medical care, and a child is delivered by a
Marine medic. A shattering explosion jars us out of the quiet, as a
truck hits a mine and mangled bodies writhe in pain, while anxious
voices summon the helicopters, "Get those choppers in . . . these
guys are hurtin'." Heavy equipment evacuates the peasants and destroys the village, as the Company moves out across a rice paddy
on its continuing mission.

The contrasts, like a pulse of the operation, give the viewer a chance to reflect on the events, and to make his own judgment concerning what has happened. There is enough waste of human life, enough misery of terrified Vietnamese peasants to confirm a pacifist's conviction that the war is senseless; there is enough quiet heroism and genuine concern for the people of the land by the Marines to justify a defense of U.S. policy in that country. The film, however, is not a blandly neutral document, but a powerfully moving portrait of humanity, soldier and civilian, foreigner and native, in a brutal war. The Viet Cong are never seen except as bodies frozen in the cruel contortions of death . . . they are as invisible to us as they are frustratingly invisible to the Marines. At times we are invited to take the Marine's point of view: the camera pokes through elephant grass, peers across rice paddies, searches the skies for life-saving choppers. At other times, we see what the peasants see: burning villages, giant machines that roar through a peaceful compound, burning and destroying.

The film shows considerable restraint in failing to exploit what might potentially be emotional blockbusters: the peasants' suffering, the amiability of the Marines, the vindictive reaction to ambushes and mine explosions. But more than this, the ironic paradox of beauty amid destruction becomes almost a style in the film: flares dropping "through" a tangle of barbed wire in beautiful abstract patterns; the sacramental ritual of sipping coffee in silhouette at evening; the lovely land that has absorbed so much blood and so many explosions over the past twenty years. Perhaps the strongest feature of the film is its exploration, not of "a" face of war, but of the human faces of soldier and peasant, the former growing from apparent adolescence to manhood by the cruel means the twentieth century has devised; the latter reflecting the wrinkled countenance of an older culture being invaded by that century. Ultimately, the value of the film lies in our ability to see our own face in it.

Woodstock: One for the Money
by Stephen MacDonald

*This report on the most commercially successful documentary of
the year was published in The Wall Street Journal, March 27, 1970.*

Toward the end of *Woodstock,* a farmer named Max Yagur climbs
on the performers' platform to be introduced to the audience, which
stretches to the horizon and at that moment constitutes the second
largest city in New York. The land on which the audience sits,
stands, and lies belongs to Mr. Yagur, and he tells the kids ("I call
you kids because I have children older than you myself") how
pleased he was that, despite the shortage of food, water, shelter,
toilets, and police, there had been no violence. "You have proved
something to the world," he shouts, and he flashes the peace sign.

What the Woodstock weekend proved is not agreed upon as
unanimously as the applauding crowd might have hoped. Even
before the ugly events a few months later, when a man was stabbed
to death and several others, including performers, were beaten at a
"festival" in California, Woodstock had polarized the nation.

But *Woodstock,* the movie, is an icon to Woodstock, the festival.
Its purpose is to celebate the ritual gathering of the young—not
to examine it, to persuade its detractors, or to intrude on its fantasies. And celebrate it does. Michael Wadleigh, who directed and
controlled the entire creative process, divided his crew into two
teams, one to photograph the performances and the other to document the "scene." In the three-hour version released yesterday by
Warner Bros., more than half is given to the performances. (The
movie has 13 individuals or groups. Far more performed at the
festival, but movie contracts couldn't be arranged.)

Considering how few options are available in photographing
more-or-less stationary stage action, Mr. Wadleigh has been remarkably inventive. He uses close-ups of rhythmic faces, hands,
feet, and torsos, sometimes splitting the screen to show more than
one performer at a time, or more than one aspect of a single performer. The multi-channel soundtrack is superb, and it is likely
that many who were at Woodstock will see and hear the musicians
for the first time when they go to the movie. Rock music has never
been better photographed.

But the music wasn't what made Woodstock memorable or controversial, and unfortunately the documentary footage doesn't add up to more than scattered mementoes—fun for people who were there and want to relive it, essential for people who didn't go but wish they had, but not much of a revelation for those who would like to understand Woodstock.

Several vignettes give an idea of the happy atmosphere that surrounded the place. The young people camping, dancing, sliding in the mud, doing exercises in a group—yes, even skinny-dipping and passing pot around—have an innocence and lightheartedness about them that comes across very appealingly. One or two scenes also show the childlike despair of some who wanted to leave the festival site and couldn't because of the traffic.

Rain played an important part in the weekend, and one long scene shows how the staff and audience reacted when a black storm appeared in the distance, moving toward the site. An announcer tried to prepare the crowd and keep it calm, while other staffers covered amplifiers and other electronic equipment. When the torrent hit, most people huddled under blankets and ponchos. One girl danced about blithely, smiling at the sky.

The interviews are more disturbing. The young people chosen were, for the most part, wholly inarticulate. The producers were generous with praise of their own generosity, and too many people were content to congratulate themselves or to predict the dawn of a new civilization based on love and grass. None of the interviewers pressed very hard.

Several townspeople were interviewed, and although some thought the festival was fine, some did not. But the film treats all of them—even those who contributed food—in a faintly mocking way, as if they were quaint old squares.

One thing Woodstock proved is that young people are commercially exploitable, that, ironic as it may seem, a great deal of money can be made cultivating people who identify with the notion that affluence is the curse of our civilization. Not that Woodstock was a commercial success. Poor planning, especially a failure to match the facilities to the crowd, or vice versa, wrecked the commercial aspects. For the backers, therefore, this film and a subsequent record and tape album are an important attempt to recover a lost investment. In that sense, *Woodstock* should be even more successful than Woodstock.

Toward New Goals in Documentary
by Arthur Barron

This selection originally appeared in Film Library Journal (New York), Winter 1968-69. The author is a producer of television documentaries.

Every Tuesday night from 10 to 11 P.M., the CBS television network presents a series of broadcasts called "The CBS News Hour." This program is the direct descendant of "See It Now" and "CBS Reports," the remarkable documentary series of the late 50s and 60s produced by the team of Ed Murrow and Fred Friendly, who gave us *Harvest of Shame, The Population Explosion, McCarthy and His Critics,* and many other documentary films of distinction. Like its predecessors, the Tuesday night news hour presents weekly documentary films which bear on the pressing issues of today. It is an hour of welcome reality in an otherwise dreary schedule of fantasy and escape.

CBS is proud of this weekly news hour. It should be. It is the only regularly scheduled prime-time documentary series on the air today. The network spends an average of $100,000 for each of these films, and a producer is permitted to work on them as long as necessary to do them justice. My last project for CBS, for example, a documentary evocation of three great American novels, "Babbitt," "The Grapes of Wrath," and "Moby Dick," which was presented in two separate one-hour programs, occupied me for well over a year. Moreover, the "News Hour" attracts large audiences, an average of some seven-and-a-half million viewers each Tuesday night, and as many as fifteen-and-a-half million viewers for films of such widespread interest as *The Warren Report.*

Some of these films are quite worthy, either because of their inventiveness, as in *The Italians,* a film based on the Barzini book, or because of their candor, as in *Morley Safer's Vietnam,* or their beauty, as in *Gauguin in Tahiti,* or their cinematic power, as in *The Anderson Platoon.* (They are rarely ever notable for their boldness, I might add in passing. No matter how newsworthy, certain subjects never seem to get done. To my knowledge, network television has never presented a film on the FBI, or the military-industrial complex, or on Congressional ethics, or on any number of other sacred cows.

But the timidity of television and its role as pillar of the Establishment is another subject for another time.)

Instead, consider the list of programs which did actually make it on the air last season on the Tuesday night "News Hour." There were 48 films in all. Eleven of which, the largest single category, dealt with Vietnam: *The Letters of Ho Chi Minh, Air War in the North,* etc. Six of the films dealt with other foreign affairs issues: *How Israel Won the War, Inside Red China,* etc. Eight of the films dealt with domestic social problems other than race: *Air Pollution, The College Admissions Crisis,* etc. Four films dealt with race: *The Tenement, Can We Prevent Tomorrow's Riots?* Six films dealt with politics: *Young Mr. Eisenhower, What Happened to Alf Landon?,* etc. Two films, *Inside Pop* and *Gauguin in Tahiti,* dealt with art. Four films persisted in following the test format with diminishing returns. We had *The National Drivers' Test, The National Science Test, The National Current Events Test,* and *The National Sports and Physical Fitness Test.* It's an unrewarding format, but if they ever decide to do a *National Sex Test,* I'd like to produce it myself. Finally, there were seven films on various subjects: *Scotland, Mind Research,* etc.

Something that strikes me immediately about this list is that virtually all the films represent only one documentary tradition, the reportage tradition of journalism. If you examine this list, you will find that, almost without exception, they are news documentaries. And this emphasis on news, on reportage is not exclusive to CBS; it is true of all the commercial networks as well as the educational network, NET. It is true of the new Public Broadcast Laboratory. It is true of the local independent stations around the country.

You have all seen such films, some are better than others, but they all share the same characteristics. They are all about war, peace, crime—the great issues. They are all topical. They are filled with facts, peopled with experts and authorities. They are word-logic pictures; play the soundtrack without the picture and you will still understand the point of the film. Indeed, the pictures are often there merely to illustrate the words, often spoken by a stentorian and authoritative narrator. Sometimes controversy is offered (controversy often surrounds them when they are aired), but the controversy is balanced. If Mario Savio speaks, then Clark Kerr must speak, too. Kerr is in my film *The Berkeley Rebels* because CBS put him there. If I were to make a film with Anne Frank, presumably Hilter would have to have equal time. Objectivity also characterizes the news documentary, not merely in the sense of "fair," but cinematically objective. One is quite aware, in watching these films, that the film-maker, in this case CBS, is not inside the film, but outside, observing and recording the events, not living them. In these films, CBS is presenting a forum for the presentation of ideas, always ready to evaluate, instruct, interpret, always keeping its cool, not grooving with the film, but being objective, somehow above it all.

And, finally, all of these documentaries have a common purpose; to inform and instruct. It is a purpose which sees film as politically useful and is based in political theory, i.e., the Jeffersonian idea of the marketplace of ideas and the role of an informed electorate; that democracy is doomed unless the public is informed. "In the ICBM age," Fred Friendly, former president of CBS News and now communications guru to McGeorge Bundy of the Ford Foundation, thunders, "what you don't know can kill you; our job is to see that you know." Thus, film as knowledge; knowledge as the cement of society. Then there's Lenin's notion that film is the most powerful weapon in the hands of the masses. Film creating revolutionary consciousness. Film ripping the veil from the face of fantasy and exposing the pus-filled sores. Film as an instrument of class struggle.

The belief that the documentary's chief function is in energizing, motivating, and informing the masses by rendering the complex issues of the day understandable and meaningful is the theory underlying the new documentary. If anyone wanted to, he could trace its history with a progression of names and titles: Lumière, Grierson and the British School, Pudovkin and Eisenstein, *The March of Time,* Pathé News, the Office of War Information, "See It Now," "CBS Reports," "NBC White Paper," "NET Journal," ABC's recent four-hour special on Africa—onwards and upwards!

But there is another great and different tradition in documentary film. The fact that it is so neglected in television is strange, since its first great exponent, its first supreme originator was an American. I mean, of course, Robert Flaherty. I mean his unforgettable characters: *Nanook,* the *Man of Aran,* the Cajun boy in *Louisiana Story.* I mean the tradition of human revelation, the personal documentary.

In Flaherty's work, we see the distinguishing characteristics of this kind of documentary. Not great issues, but human events in human scale: a man trying to catch a seal in order to eat. Not topicality, but timelessness: the eternal struggle of Man against Nature.

Not fact and information, but emotion, drama: a boy shaking in fright at his first view of an oil derrick. Not expertise and authority, but ordinary, real, human beings swept up in the currents of life. Not rationality, but tears, rage, tenderness. Not the reporter, but the poet.

In Flaherty's work, as in all personal documentary, i.e., in the films of Flaherty's successors today: Pennebaker, Leacock, the Maysleses, Jersey, Pincus, a similar pattern is followed. A person whom we get to know and care about is confronted with a problem with which he can identify personally. He surmounts the problem, or he fails to surmount it, but we live through it with him. The problem is not irrelevant to the great issues of our time. The issue is there, but it is not the starting-point; the human being is the starting-point. The social issue is the backdrop against which the human drama unfolds. In *A Time for Burning,* the remarkable film by Bill Jersey for the Lutheran Film Associates, race relations provides a backdrop, but we are really involved with the minister of a Lutheran Church in Omaha, Reverend Youngdahl. He wants to take a very small step forward and have his parishioners, on a voluntary basis, exchange home-visits with the members of Omaha's Black Lutheran Church. He is caught between the militants in the Negro community, who scorn the step as too timid, and the elders of his own church, who see the step as too bold. Reverend Youngdahl, ground between these two poles, is forced to resign. But the film grips like a good novel. The plot sweeps us along. Man's inhumanity to man is revealed. *A Time for Burning* was offered to CBS, but it was turned down. Where, on the list of last season's "News Hour" films, is a personal documentary? Where is the film about a young man who flees to Canada to repudiate the draft? Where on the list is a film about a man whose marriage is breaking up? Where is a film about a middle-aged man, mortgaged to the hilt and laid off from his job at the ad agency? Where is the film about the lonely woman searching for a man through an endless procession of singles weekends at ski resorts? Where is the story of a man dying from lung cancer? Where is the story of a factory worker scraping the money together to marry off his daughter in a style which will please his social-climbing wife? These films are not on the list, not one of them. They are not even in the planning stage. "Hickey, they've taken the life out of the booze," the derelict sighs in Eugene O'Neill's "The

Iceman Cometh." I tell you they've taken the life out of the film. Why? Why have they done it? It's something to wonder about.

Part of the problem is that the people in charge of news at the networks, the presidents and vice-presidents, come out of the tradition of reportage. Many worked for newspapers or magazines or radio before television. They're word people. They went through World War II, many of them working on films like "Why We Fight" or *The M-1 Rifle* or *Your Office of Price Administration*. They are newsmen. They pride themselves on being reporters. They are in their fifties and not hip to the new film. This is important. For example, the kinds of equipment that make it possible to get inside your subjects, to follow them quickly with a minimum of interference and direction, to reveal their essence are relatively new. It is fast film, the shoulder brace and the hand-held camera, the quiet 16mm Eclair, the Nagra, the radio mike. All this, but especially the film sensibilities that accompany it are also fairly new. Call it *cinéma-vérité*, personal cinema, underground film—the network establishment hasn't caught up with it yet. They're still amortizing a lot of bulky 35mm equipment and fairly ancient old-wave cameramen, well entrenched and impervious to change. The union hangup is part of this. Try making a personal film with the kind of crew the new work contracts call for, 6, 8, 12 men! *A Time for Burning* was made with two. The FCC, I suppose, is another reason why personal films aren't made. There it is in black and white. To keep your license to broadcast, the FCC regulations say you must inform the public on the vital issues of the day. And this is a considerable factor.

Network politics is a factor, too. There is bad blood in every network between the programing department (the people who provide the entertainment) and the news department. There is competition for money and air time, and since the program people make money, and those in news lose it, the programers usually win the fights. For example, instead of running a news program on the Foreign Relations Committee, the CBS programing department put on a re-run of "I Love Lucy." Besides wanting us on the air as little as possible, programing wants us to stick to our own thing, which is news information. Vietnam? O.K. A film about a broken marriage? Why, that's not news. Our soap operas take care of that. And so the news department is careful to stick to journalism. That's why film-makers, who want to make personal documentaries, films that inform, but inform the heart, must look elsewhere.

But beyond all of this, there seems to me to be a deeper under-lying reason why the personal documentary is notable chiefly for its absence. I think that reason is that we live in an uptight society. I think we are afraid of honest emotion. I think we dig all those facts and figures because they're so very remote. We can be detached. I think we're afraid in this America of tenderness, afraid of anger, afraid of laying our guts on the table. I think we feel we have to keep the lid on very tight because if we don't our kids are going to turn on, our blacks are going to kill, our poor are going to bust right into our living rooms and slash up all that nice Naugahyde with machetes, our bank accounts are going to go down the drain, and the whole mess is going to come unglued. I think all that fear exists, and we'd rather keep it nice and cerebral.

As for me, I'd like a little less information and a lot more feeling. I think we know enough facts; what we don't know is how to feel, to identify with others. I think the goal of the filmmaker should be to help make us more feeling, more human. We should try more to be novelists and poets of film, rather than such damn good reporters. I want to make people weep and cry. I want to approach documen-tary with all the skill and sensibility that Fellini and Bergman and Godard bring to fiction films.

But, at the networks, it's business as usual. They're working on next year's list of films at CBS: a film on the legal profession, on Japan, on the affluent Negro, on tax-exempt foundations, and so on and so on.

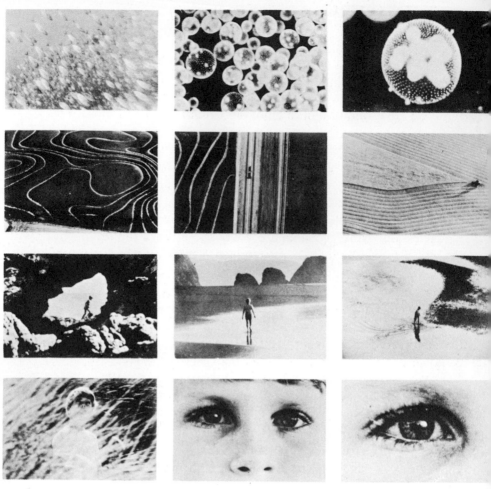

The Searching Eye (1964), Saul Bass

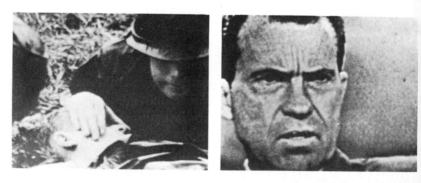

Kinestasis 60 (1970), Charles Braverman

Johnny Cash (1969),
directed by Arthur **Barron**

Terminus (1961), directed
by **John Schlesinger**

The Olive Trees of Justice (1961),
directed by James Blue

French Lunch (1968), directed by Nell Cox

Shooting *Black Journal* (1969), William Greaves, director

Crisis: Behind a Presidential Commitment (1963), Gregory Shuker

Lonely Boy (1961), Wolf Koenig and Roman Kroitor

Chronicle of a Summer (1961), directed by **Jean Rouch and Edgar Morin**

Tokyo Olympiad (1964), directed by Ken Ichikawa

The Moods of Surfing (1968), Jim Freeman and Greg MacGillivary

Civil Rights Movement: The South (1966), NBC

(Shooting)
Sixteen in Webster Groves (1966), directed by Arthur Barron

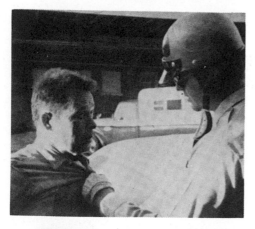

Law and Order (1969), directed by Frederick Wiseman

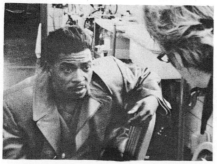

Hospital (1970), directed by Frederick Wiseman

Dead Birds (1963),
directed by Robert Gardner

Warrendale (1968),
directed by Allan King

The Chelsea Girls (1966),
directed by Andy Warhol

Monterey Pop (1967),
directed by D. A. Pennebaker
and Richard Leacock

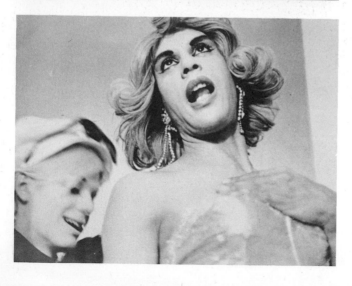

The Queen (1968),
directed by Frank Simon

Woodstock

Years of Lightning, Day of Drums (1966),
directed by Bruce Herschensohn

(Shooting) *Salesman* (1966),
directed by
Albert and David Maysles

A Selection of Documentaries of the Period

Abel Gance: Yesterday and Tomorrow, Nelly Kaplan (1962)

The Adolescents, Michel Brault, Hiroshi Teshigahara, Jean Rouch, and Gian Vittorio Baldi (1964)

Africa, Eliot Elisofon (1967)

The American Woman in the Twentieth Century, William Cartwright and Bob Fresco (1963)

And Now, Miguel, Joseph Krumgold (1966)

The Anderson Platoon, Pierre Schoendorffer (1967)

Angola: Journey to a War, Robert Young (1961)

The Angry Voices of Watts, Stuart Schulberg (1966)

Appalachia: Rich Land, Poor People, Richard Pierce, Jack Willis, and Adam Giffard (1969)

A Valparaiso, Joris Ivens (1963)

Banks and the Poor, Mort Silverstein (1970)

The Battle of East St. Louis, Peter Wolff (1970)

The Battle of Newburgh, Arthur Zegart (1962)

The Beatles, Albert Maysles (1962)

The Berkeley Rebels, Arthur Barron (1965)

Biography of a Bookie Joint, Jay McMullen (1961)

Birth and Death, Arthur Barron and Eugene Marner (1968)

Blind Gary Davis, Harold Becker (1963)

Blood on the Balcony, Pasquale Prumas (1963)

The Burma Surgeon Today, Wade Bingham (1961)

The Business of Gambling, Arthur Zegart (1963)

The Business of Health: Medicine, Money and Politics, Stephen Fleischman (1961)

The Chair, Gregory Shuker, Richard Leacock, and D. A. Pennebaker (1963)

The Chelsea Girls, Andy Warhol (1966)

Chicago: The Seasons Change, Film Group of Chicago (1969)

The Children Were Watching, Richard Leacock (1960)

China!, Felix Greene (1965)

A Choice of Destinies, William Greaves (1970)

Chronicle of a Summer, Jean Rouch and Edgar Morin (1961)

Cicero March, Film Group of Chicago (1968)

Crisis: Behind a Presidential Commitment, Richard Leacock and D. A. Pennebaker (1963)

Cuba: Bay of Pigs, Len Giovannitti (1964)

Cuba, si!, Chris Marker (1961)

Cuba: The Missile Crisis, Len Giovannitti (1964)

Dead Birds, Robert Gardner (1963)

The Death of Stalin, Len Giovannitti (1963)

Diaries, Notes & Sketches, Jonas Mekas (1964–9)

Don't Look Back, D. A. Pennebaker and Richard Leacock (1965)

The Dream of Wild Horses, Denys Colomb de Daunant (1960)

Dylan Thomas' A Child's Christmas in Wales, Marvin Lichtner (1961)

Easter Island, Arnold Eagle (1969)

The Eleanor Roosevelt Story, Sidney Glazier (1968)

The Endless Summer, Bruce Brown (1968)

Escape to Freedom, Marshall Flaum (1963)

A Face of War, Eugene Jones (1968)

Faces of Imperialism, David Schoenbrun (1967)

Far From Vietnam, Alain Resnais, Jean-Luc Godard, Joris Ivens, Agnès Varda, Claude Lelouch, Chris Marker, and William Klein (1967)

Fidel, Saul Landau (1969)

Fire Rescue, John G. Fuller (1962)

Flavio, Gordon Parks (1964)

La Fleur de l'âge, see: *The Adolescents*

Football, Richard Leacock (1961)

Forty Million Shoes, Douglas Leiterman (1961)

Four Days in November, Mel Stuart (1964)

Free Fall, Arthur Lipsett (1965)

French Lunch, Nell Cox (1968)

Frontiers of News, Willard Van Dyke (1964)

Goal, Abidine Dino and Ross Devenish (1966)

Good Times, Wonderful Times, Lionel Rogosin (1965)

The Grand Olympics, Romolo Marcellini (1961)

The Great American Novel, Arthur Barron (1968)

Greece: The Golden Age, Lou Hazam (1963)

Happy Mother's Day, Richard Leacock (1964)

Harvest of Shame, David Lowe (1960)

Head Start in Mississippi, Adam Gifford (1968)

Here at the Water's Edge, Leo Hurwitz (1961)

High School, Frederick Wiseman (1969)

High Wire: The Great Wallendas, George Freeland (1964)

Hiroshima–Nagasaki—August 1945, Erik Barnouw (1970)

Hospital, Frederick Wiseman (1970)

I Am Pablo Neruda, Harold Mantell (1967)

In the Year of the Pig, Emile de Antonio (1969)

Indian Summer, Jules Schwerin (1960)

Inside North Vietnam, Felix Greene (1967)

An Interview With Bruce Gordon, Harold Becker (1964)

Jane, Richard Leacock (1962)

Johnny Cash, Arthur Barron (1970)

Le Joli Mai, Chris Marker (1962)

Journey to Chinale, William Baldwin and Ernest Nukanen (1968)

Junkyard by the Sea, Warren Wallace and Edmund Bert Gerrard (1960)

Kenya, Richard Leacock (1961)

King, Murray, David Hoffman (1969)

A King's Story, Harry Booth (1967)

The Koumiko Mystery, Chris Marker (1965)

Ladies and Gentlemen . . . Mr. Leonard Cohen, Donald Brittain (1965)

Language of Faces, John Korty (1961)

Law and Order, Frederick Wiseman (1969)

Letter from Colombia, James Blue (1964)

Life of Adolf Hitler, Paul Rotha (1961)

Lonely Boy, Wolf Koenig and Roman Kroitor (1961)

Love ("Ai"), Takahiko Ismura (1963)

The Making of the President, 1960, Mel Stuart and Theodore H. White (1963)

Malcolm X: Struggle for Freedom, Lebert Bethune (1967)

Man in Our Image, Marc Norelli (1968)

Manhattan Battleground, William Jersey (1963)

The March, James Blue (1964)

A Married Couple, Allan King (1970)

Meet Comrade Student, Nicholas Webster (1962)

Mein Kampf, Erwin Leiser (1961)

The Miners' Lament, William Weston (1963)

Mingus, Thomas Reichman (1960)

Mondo Cane, Gualtiero Jacopetti (1962)

Mondo Pazzo, Gualtiero Jacopetti (1965)

Monterey Pop, Richard Leacock and D. A. Pennebaker (1967)

Morley Safer's Vietnam (1967)

The Most, Richard Ballentine and Gordon Sheppard (1963)

My Childhood: Hubert Humphrey's South Dakota and James Baldwin's Harlem, Don Horan (1964)

Nehru, Richard Leacock (1962)

New Frontier, Richard Leacock (1961)

New York in the Twenties, Burton Benjamin (1961)

No Vietnamese Ever Called Me Nigger, David Loeb Weiss (1969)

The Olive Trees of Justice, James Blue (1962)

On the Road to Button Bay, Robert L. Drew (1962)

One More River, Douglas Leiterman (1963)

Orient Express, Thomas Priestley (1964)

Other Voices, David H. Sawyer (1970)

Our Trip to Africa, see: *Unsere Afrikareise*

Paris in the Twenties, Burton Benjamin (1960)

Picture of a Cuban, Stanley H. Bloom (1962)

A Place to Stand, Christopher Chauman (1967)

The Plots Against Hitler, Burton Benjamin (1963)

Point of Order!, Emile de Antonio and Daniel Talbot (1964)

Polar Life, Graeme Ferguson (1967)

Pop Buell, Hoosier Farmer in Laos, Willard Van Dyke (1965)

Portrait of Jason, Shirley Clarke (1967)

Postscript to Empire, Michael Alexander (1961)

Primary, Richard Leacock, Robert Drew, D. A. Pennebaker, and Albert Maysles (1960)

Prisoner at Large, William Jersey (1963)

The Queen, Frank Simon (1968)

Railway With a Heart of Gold, Carson Davidson (1965)

The Real West, Donald B. Hyatt (1961)

Rice, Willard Van Dyke (1964)

The Rise of Labor, Don Horan (1963)

The Run from Race, George Stoney (1964)

Rush to Judgment, Emile de Antonio and Mark Lane (1967)

Sailing, Hattum Hoving (1963)

Salesman, Albert and David Maysles (1969)

School at Rincon Santo, James Blue (1963)

Seawards the Great Ships, Hillary Harris (1960)

Settlement and Conflict, Michel Brault (1967)

Shakespeare: Soul of an Age, Guy Blanchard (1962)

Showman, Albert and David Maysles (1962)

Sighet, Sighet, Harold Becker (1967)

Sixteen in Webster Groves, Arthur Barron (1966)

The Sixties, Charles Braverman (1970)

Skater Dater, Noel Black (1966)

The Sky Above—the Mud Below, Pierre-Dominique Gaisseau (1962)

So That Men Are Free, Willard Van Dyke (1962)

Speaking of Angola, Stefano de Stefani (1970)

Still a Brother, William Greaves (1969)

Stravinsky, Richard Leacock (1966)

Strip, Peter Davis (1967)

Sunday in the Park, Dan Drassin (1961)

Superfluous People, Warren Wallace and Edmund Bert Gerard (1962)

Tagore, Satyajit Ray (1961)

Taming the Mekong River, Willard Van Dyke (1965)

Teenage Revolution, Kent MacKenzie (1965)

The Tenement, Jay McMullen (1967)

That War in Korea, Donald B. Hyatt (1963)

The Three-Way Street, Robert Cirace (1962)

A Time for Burning, William C. Jersey (1966)

Time of the Locust, Peter Gessner (1967)

The Titicut Follies, Frederick Wiseman and John Marshall (1967)

To Be a Man, Murray Lerner (1966)

To Be Alive!, Francis Thompson and Alexander Hammid (1964)

To Die in Madrid, Frédéric Rossif (1962)

Tokyo Olympiad, Kon Ichikawa (1964)

Trial—City and County of Denver vs. Lauren R. Watson, Denis Sanders (1970)

Troublemakers, Robert Machover and Norman Fruchter (1966)

The U-2 Affair, Albert Wasserman (1960)

Universe, Roman Kroitor and Colin Low (1960)

Unsere Afrikareise, Peter Kubelka (1966)

Vali, Sheldon Rochlin (1967)

A Vanishing Breed: Portrait of a Country Editor, Sam Rosenberg (1963)

The Vatican, John Secondari

Verdict for Tomorrow, Leo Hurwitz (1961)

Vincent Van Gogh: A Self-Portrait, Ray Garner (1961)

Walk in My Shoes, Nicholas Webster (1961)

The War Game, Peter Watkins (1966)

Warrendale, Allan King (1968)

We Are Young, Francis Thompson and Alexander Hammid (1967)

Wednesday's Child, Ralph McGraw (1963)

What Harvest for the Reaper? Mort Silverstein (1967)

Wholly Communion, Peter Whitehead (1966)

Women of the World, Gualtiero Jacopetti (1963)

Woodstock, Michael Wadleigh (1970)

The World of Billy Graham, Eugene S. Jones (1961)

The World of Carl Sandburg, Kirk Browning (1966)

The World of Jacqueline Kennedy, Eugene S. Jones (1962)

World Without Sun, Jacques-Yves Cousteau (1964)

Wrestling, Michel Brault, Marcel Carrière, Claude Fournier, and Claude Jutras (1961)

Yanqui, no!, Richard Leacock, Albert Maysles, and D. A. Pennebaker (1960)

Years of Lightning, Day of Drums, Bruce Herschensohn (1966)

A Selected Bibliography

ALPERT, HOLLIS. *The Dreams and the Dreamers*. New York: The Macmillan Company, 1962.

ARMES, ROY. *French Cinema since 1946*. 2 vols. Cranbury, N. J.: A. S. Barnes, 1966.

The Arts Enquiry. *The Factual Film*. London: Oxford University Press, 1947.

Association of Documentary Film Producers. *Living Films: A Catalog of Documentary Films and Their Makers*. New York 1940.

BADDELEY, W. HUGH. *The Techniques of Documentary Film Production*. New York: Hastings House, 1963.

BARNOUW, ERIK. *A History of Broadcasting in the United States*. Vol. II (1933–1953), *The Golden Web;* vol. III (1953–1970), *The Image Empire*. New York: Oxford University Press, 1968 and 1970.

BARNOUW, ERIK, and KRISHNASWAMY, SUBRAMANYAM. *The Indian Film*. New York and London: Columbia University Press, 1963.

BENOIT-LÉVY, JEAN, *The Art of the Motion Picture*. New York: Arno Press, 1970 (reprint of Coward-McCann edition of 1946).

BINING, ARTHUR CECIL. *The Rise of American Economic Life*. Third Edition. New York: Charles Scribner's Sons, 1958.

BLUEM, A. WILLIAM. *Documentary in American Television*. New York: Hastings House, 1965.

British Film Institute. *Monthly Film Bulletin*. London: 1933–1971.

BROOKS, JOHN. *The Great Leap*. New York: Harper and Row, 1966.

CALDER-MARSHALL, ARTHUR. The *Innocent Eye: The Life of Robert J. Flaherty*. New York: Harcourt, Brace and World, 1966 (also, Baltimore: Penguin paperback, 1970).

COLE, BARRY G., ed. *Television: Selections from TV Guide Magazine*. New York: The Free Press, 1970.

FLAHERTY, FRANCES HUBBARD. *The Odyssey of a Film-Maker*. Urbana, Ill.: University of Illinois Press, 1960.

FREIDEL, FRANK. *America in the Twentieth Century*. New York: Alfred A. Knopf, 1960.

GRIFFITH, RICHARD. *The World of Robert Flaherty*. New York: Duell, Sloan and Pearce, 1953.

HARDY, FORSYTH, ed. *Grierson on Documentary*. New rev. ed. Berkeley and Los Angeles: University of California Press, 1966.

HAZARD, PATRICK D., ed. *TV as Art*. Chicago: National Council of Teachers of English, 1966.

HUGHES, ROBERT, ed. *Film: Book 2*. New York: Grove Press, 1962.

IVENS, JORIS. *Apprentice to Films*. New York: Harcourt, Brace, 1946.

————.*The Camera and I*. New York: International Publishers, 1970.

JARVIE, I. C. *Movies and Society*. New York: Basic Books, 1970.

KENNEY, WILLIAM. *The Crucial Years, 1940–1945*. New York: Macfadden Books, 1962.

KIRK, JOHN G., ed. *America Now.* New York: Atheneum, 1968.

KNIGHT, ARTHUR. *The Liveliest Art.* New York: Macmillan, 1957 (also NAL–Mentor paperback, 1959).

KRACAUER, SIEGFRIED. *From Caligari to Hitler.* Princeton, N.J.: Princeton University Press, 1947.

————.*Theory of Film.* New York: Oxford University Press, 1960.

KYROU, ADO. *Luis Buñuel: An Introduction.* Translated by Adrienne Foulke. New York: Simon and Schuster, 1963.

LAWSON, JOHN HOWARD. *Film: The Creative Process.* New York: Hill and Wang, 1964.

LEONARD, HAROLD, ed. *The Film Index: A Bibliography.* Vol. I: *The Film as Art.* New York: Arno Press, 1970 (reprint of H. W. Wilson 1941 edition).

LEYDA, JAY. *Films Beget Films.* New York: Hill and Wang, 1964.

————. *Kino: A History of the Russian and Soviet Film.* New York: Macmillan, 1960.

LINDGREN, ERNEST. *The Film as Art.* New York: Macmillan, 1963.

LINK, ARTHUR S. *American Epoch.* New York: Alfred A. Knopf, 1960.

Editors of Look. *Movielot to Beachhead.* New York: Doubleday, Doran, and Company, Inc., April 1945.

LORENTZ, PARE. *The River: A Scenario.* New York: Stackpole and Sons, 1938.

LUCCOCK, HALFORD. *American Mirror.* New York: Macmillan, 1940.

MACCANN, RICHARD DYER, ed. *Film: A Montage of Theories.* New York: E. P. Dutton Paperback, 1966.

MANVELL, ROGER. *The Film and the Public.* Baltimore: Penguin Books Paperback, 1955.

————, ed. *Experiment in the Film.* London: Grey Walls Press, 1948.

MONTAGU, IVOR. *Film World.* Baltimore: Penguin Books Paperback, 1964.

READ, HERBERT. *Icon and Idea.* Cambridge, Mass.: Harvard University Press, 1955.

ROSENBERG, BERNARD, and WHITE, DAVID MANNING, eds. *Mass Culture: The Popular Arts in America.* Glencoe, Ill.: Free Press, 1957.

ROTHA, PAUL. *Documentary Film.* London: Faber and Faber, 1952.

————. *Television in the Making.* London: Focal Press, 1956.

SCHLESINGER, ARTHUR, JR. *Violence: America in the Sixties.* New York: New American Library, 1968.

SCHUSTACK, EDWARD H. *The Documentary Film.* New York: Film and Sprocket Society of City College of New York, 1938.

SELDES, GILBERT. *The Public Arts.* New York: Simon and Schuster, 1956.

SNYDER, ROBERT L. *Pare Lorentz and the Documentary Film.* Norman, Okla.: University of Oklahoma Press, 1968.

SPOTTISWOODE, RAYMOND. *A Grammar of the Film.* Berkeley and Los Angeles: University of California Press, 1950 (new edition of 1935 Faber and Faber edition, London).

STARR, CECILE, ed. *Ideas on Film.* New York: Funk and Wagnalls, 1951.

SWALLOW, NORMAN. *Factual Television.* New York: Hastings House, 1966.

THOMPSON, DENYS, ed. *Discrimination and Popular Culture.* Baltimore: Penguin Books Paperback, 1964.

THOMSON, DAVID. *Movie Man.* New York: Stein and Day, 1967.

WHITE, DAVID MANNING, and AVERSON, RICHARD, eds. *Sight, Sound, and Society.* Boston: Beacon Press, 1968.

Principal Distributors of Documentary Films

ACI Films
35 West 45th Street
New York, N. Y. 10036

American Documentary Films
379 Bay Street
San Francisco, Calif. 94133

Audio/Brandon
34 MacQuesten Parkway South
Mt. Vernon, N.Y. 10550

Avco-Embassy Films
1301 Avenue of the Americas
New York, N.Y. 10019

CBS Education and Publishing Group
383 Madison Avenue
New York, N.Y. 10017

CCM Films, Inc.
866 Third Avenue
New York, N.Y. 10022

Contemporary Films/McGraw-Hill
330 West 42nd Street
New York, N.Y. 10036

Encyclopedia Britannica
Educational Corporation
425 N. Michigan Avenue
Chicago, Ill. 60611

Film Images/Radim Films, Inc.
17 West 60th Street
New York, N.Y. 10023

Film-Makers' Cooperative
175 Lexington Avenue
New York, N.Y. 10016

Films, Inc.
1144 Wilmette Avenue
Wilmette, Ill. 60091

Graphic Curriculum, Inc.
P.O. Box 565
New York, N.Y. 10021

International Film Bureau
332 S. Michigan Avenue
Chicago, Ill. 60604

Janus Film Library
24 West 58th Street
New York, N.Y. 10019

Museum of Modern Art Film Library
11 West 53rd Street
New York, N.Y. 10019

National Audio-Visual Center
National Archives and Records Service
Washington, D.C. 20409

The National Information Center
for Education Media
University Park
Los Angeles, Calif. 90007

NBC Educational Enterprises
Room 1040, 30 Rockefeller Plaza
New York, N.Y. 10020

NET Film Service
Indiana University AV Center
Bloomington, Ind. 47401

Pyramid Films
Box 1048
Santa Monica, Calif. 90406

Sterling Educational Films
241 East 34th Street
New York, N.Y. 10016

Texture Films
1600 Broadway
New York, N.Y. 10036

Time-Life Films
43 West 16th Street
New York, N.Y. 10011

Twyman Films, Inc.
329 Salem Avenue
Dayton, Ohio 45401

Universal Education and Visual Arts
221 Park Avenue South
New York, N.Y. 10003

Universal Sixteen
630 Ninth Avenue
New York, N.Y. 10036

Walter Reade 16
241 East 34th Street
New York, N.Y. 10016

Acknowledgments

I wish to thank the following authors, representatives, and publishers for their courtesy in granting me permission to reprint the selections included in this anthology:

Lindsay Anderson, "Some Aspects of the Work of Humphrey Jennings," reprinted by permission of the author. Dr. James Arnold, "The Present State of the Documentary," © 1969 by The National Catholic Office for Motion Pictures, from Films, 1968. Arthur Barron, "Toward New Goals in Documentary," by permission of the author. Iris Barry, *"A Diary for Timothy,"* reprinted from Film News, November 1945, by permission of Film News. Ben Belitt, "The Camera Reconnoiters," reprinted from The Nation, November 20, 1937, with permission of the publisher. Burton Benjamin, "The Documentary Heritage," reprinted from Television Quarterly, February 1962, with permission of the author. Oswell Blakeston, "Two Vertov Films," reprinted from Close Up, August 1929, by permission of the author. James Blue, "One Man's Truth: An Interview with Richard Leacock," reprinted by permission of the author. Ron Blumer, "King's *A Married Couple,*" reprinted from Take One, December 30, 1969, with permission of the author. Julien Bryan, "War Is, Was, and Always Will Be, Hell," reprinted from U. S. Camera, March 1940, with permission of the author. Noel Burch, "Four French Documentaries," © 1959 by The Regents of the University of California, reprinted from Film Quarterly, Vol. XIII, No. 1, pp. 56-61, by permission of The Regents. Jay Chapman, "Two Aspects of the City: Cavalcanti and Ruttmann," by permission of the author. Harold Clurman, "Flaherty's *Louisiana Story,*" reprinted from Tomorrow magazine, October 1948, with permission of the author. Judith Crist, "Rossif's *To Die in Madrid,*" reprinted from the New York Herald Tribune, September 27, 1965, with permission of the author. David Denby, "Documenting America," copyright © 1970, by The Atlantic Monthly Company, Boston, Mass., reprinted with permission. Martin S. Dworkin, *"The Lonely Night:* Dramatic Power," reprinted by permission of the author. Robert T. Elson, "De Rochemont's *The March of Time,*" reprinted from "Time Inc., The Intimate History of a Publishing Enterprise, 1923-1941," Atheneum, New York, 1968 with permission of Time Inc. Harrison Engle, "Thirty Years of Social Inquiry," by permission of the author. William K. Everson, *"The Triumph of the Will,"* reprinted from Infinity magazine, September 1964, by permission of the author and publisher. Manny Farber, "One for the Ages: *Desert Victory,"* reprinted by permission of The New Republic, © 1945, Harrison-Blaine of New Jersey. Mary Losey Field, "Joris Ivens's *Power and the Land,*" reprinted from Direction magazine, November 1940, with permission of the author. Ellen Freyer, *"Chronicle of a Summer —* Ten Years After," printed here by permission of the author. Robert G. Gardner, "A Chronicle of the Human Experience: *Dead Birds,*" reprinted from The Library Quarterly, Fall 1969, with permission of the author. Evelyn Gerstein, "English Documentary Films," reprinted from New Theatre magazine, January 1936, with permission of the author. Robert Gessner, "Movies About Us," reprinted by permission of the author. Frederick Goldman, *"A Time for Burning:* An Interpretation," printed here by permission of the author. Richard Griffith, *"Film and Reality:* The Background," reprinted by permission of Amos Vogel; *"Grass* and *Chang,"* from "The Silent Film: Part I," copyright 1949, The Museum of Modern Art, New York, and reprinted by permission of the author. H. Forsyth Hardy, "British

Documentaries in the War," reprinted from "20 Years of British Films," Falcon Press, 1947, with permission of the author. Molly Haskell, "Three Documentaries," reprinted by permission of The Village Voice, copyrighted by The Village Voice, Inc., 1970, and by the author. Lou Hazam, "Documentaries and Dollars," reprinted from Television Quarterly by permission of the author. Morris Helprin, "The Making of *Que viva Mexico!*," reprinted from Experimental Cinema, No. 4, 1934, by permission of the editors of Experimental Cinema. Elizabeth Henderson, translation of "Symposium on Soviet Documentary," by permission of the author. John P. Hoggatt, *"Four Days in November,"* by permission of Variety. Leo T. Hurwitz, "The Revolutionary Film—Next Step," reprinted from New Theatre, May 1934, with permission of the author. Joris Ivens, "The Making of *Rain*," reprinted from "The Camera and I" by permission of International Publishers, Inc., copyright © 1969. Stanley Kauffmann, "Allan King's *Warrendale*," reprinted from "Film 68/69," and the more recently published "Figures of Light," Harper & Row, 1971, by permission of the author and publisher. Boris Kaufman, "Jean Vigo's *A propos de Nice*," reprinted by permission of the author. Herbert Kline, "Films Without Make-Believe," reprinted by permission of the author. Daniel Klugherz, "Documentary—Where's the Wonder?," reprinted from Television Quarterly, Summer 1967, by permission of the author. Arthur Knight, "Sweden's Arne Sucksdorff," reprinted by permission of the author. Siegfried Kracauer, "Cross-Section Films," reprinted from "Caligari to Hitler," Princeton University Press, 1947, with permission by Mrs. L. Kracauer. Michael Kustow, "Chris Marker's *Le Joli Mai*," reprinted from Sight and Sound, Spring 1964, with permission of the publisher. Rohama Lee, "Canada Carries On," reprinted by permission of the author and Film News. Agustin Aragon Leiva, "Eisenstein's Film on Mexico," reprinted from Experimental Cinema, No. 4, 1934, by permission of the editors. Pare Lorentz, *"The Ramparts We Watch,"* by permission of McCall's. Richard Dyer MacCann, "World War II: Armed Forces Documentary," by permission of the author. Stephen MacDonald, *"Woodstock:* One for the Money," reprinted from The Wall Street Journal, March 27, 1970, by permission of the author. Marya Mannes, "The Hot Documentary," reprinted by permission of Harold Ober Associates Incorporated, copyright © 1935 by The Reporter Magazine Company. Sidney Meyers and Jay Leyda, "Joris Ivens: Artist in Documentary," reprinted from The Magazine of Art, July 1938, with permission of Edna O. Meyers and Jay Leyda. Sidney Meyers, "An Event: *The Wave*," reprinted from New Theatre, November 1936, with permission of Edna O. Meyers. Warren Miller, "Progress in Documentary," courtesy of American Dialog and Joseph North. Joseph Morgenstern, "History Right in the Face," © November 10, 1969 by Newsweek Inc., with permission of the publisher. Harry Alan Potamkin, "Grierson's *Drifters*," by permission of Mrs. Elizabeth Goldman. Satyajit Ray, "The Question of Reality," reprinted from "Four Times Five," published by the Films Division, Ministry of Information & Broadcasting, Government of India. Charles Reynolds, "Focus on Al Maysles," reprinted from Popular Photography, May 1964, with permission of the author and publisher. Walter Rosenblum, *"The Quiet One:* A Milestone," reprinted from Photo-Notes, Spring 1949, with permission of the author. Richard Schickel, "Sorriest Spectacle: *The Titicut Follies*," from Life Magazine, December 1, 1967, copyright © 1968 by Richard Schickel, reprinted by permission of the Sterling Lord Agency. Arthur Schlesinger, Jr., "The Fiction of Fact—and the Fact of Fiction," reprinted from Show magazine, January 1964, by permission of the author and publisher. Gilbert Seldes, "Pare Lorentz's *The River*," by permission of the author. Marie Seton, *"Three Songs About Lenin,"* Film Art, Winter 1934; "Basil Wright's *Song of Ceylon*," Film Art, Autumn 1935, with permission of the author. John Simon, "A Variety of Hells," reprinted with permission from The New Leader, April 28, 1969, copyright The American Labor Conference on International Affairs, Inc. William J. Sloan, "The Documentary Film and the Negro," by permission of the author. Cecile Starr, "Through the Psychiatric Looking Glass," reprinted by permission of the author. Theodore Strauss, "The Giant Shinnies Down the Beanstalk," Thomas M. Pryor, "Films and Truth Campaign," Bosley Crowther, *"The Silent World,"* © 1941/51/56 by The New York Times Company, reprinted by permission. Mark Sufrin, "Filming Skid Row," by permission of the author. Norman Swallow, "The Current Affairs Documentary," reprinted from "Factual Television," Focal Press, 1966, by permission of the publisher. Daniel Talbot, "Historic Hearings: From TV to Screen," reprinted by permission of the author. Time review, "An Angry Film: *The Native Land,"* reprinted by permission from Time, The Weekly Newsmagazine, copyright Time Inc., 1942. Parker Tyler, "Leni Riefenstahl's *Olympia,"* reprinted from "Classics of the Foreign Film," Citadel, New York, 1962, with permission of the author; "Documentary Technique in Film Fiction," reprinted from American Quarterly, Summer 1949, with permission of the author. Dai Vaughan, "The Man with the Movie Camera," reprinted by permission of the author. Herman G. Weinberg, "Marco Polo, Modern Style," reprinted by permission of the author. William Whitebait, "Rouquier's *Farrebique,"* reprinted from the New Statesman, October 5, 1946, with permission of the author. John H. Winge, "Some New American Documentaries: In Defense of Liberty," reprinted from Sight and Sound, Spring 1939, with permission of the publisher. Archer Winsten, "Lionel Rogosin's *Come Back, Africa,"* "Underside of a City: *The Savage Eye,"* and *"The City* Goes to the Fair," by permission of the author. Basil Wright, *"Land Without Bread* and *Spanish Earth,"* by permission of the author.

Photos courtesy of Frederick Wiseman; Leacock, Pennebaker; British Film Institute; Film News; Harold Becker; Film Comment; Paul Rotha; Frontier Films; Paul Strand; Film and Foto League; New York University Film Library; U.S. Farm Security Administration; Willard Van Dyke; U.S. Department of Agriculture; Museum of Modern Art Film Library; Rural Electrification Administration; Julien Bryan; and the Lewis Jacobs Collection.

L.J.

Index of Names and Titles

By Lewis Jacobs

The Documentary Tradition
The Movies as Medium
The Emergence of Film Art
Introduction to the Art of Movies
The Rise of the American Film